Makers of the
Twentieth-Century Novel

MAKERS
TWENTIETH-
NOVEL

LEWISBURG
BUCKNELL UNIVERSITY PRESS
LONDON: ASSOCIATED UNIVERSITY PRESSES

OF THE
CENTURY

Edited by

HARRY R. GARVIN

© 1977 by Associated University Presses, Inc.

Associated University Presses, Inc.
Cranbury, New Jersey 08512

Associated University Presses
Magdalen House
136–148 Tooley Street
London SE1 2TT, England

Library of Congress Cataloging in Publication Data
Main entry under title:

Makers of the twentieth-century novel.

     Includes bibliographical references.
     1. Fiction—20th century—History and criticism—Addresses, essays, lectures.
I. Garvin, Harry Raphael, 1917–
PN3503.M25   809.3'3   74-4975
ISBN   0-8387-1522-2

PRINTED IN THE UNITED STATES OF AMERICA

29/3/90

Contents

Preface

Preface

The essays for this collection were selected because of their intrinsic critical vitality, significance, and special interest at present. With very rare exceptions, I avoided choosing an essay for which *Bucknell Review* had already given an author and publisher permission to reprint. A number of the essays were accepted by the editors of *Bucknell Review* but have not been published. All the essays are copyrighted by *Bucknell Review* exclusively.

To increase the vitality and current significance of an article that had already been published in *Bucknell Review,* I offered the author an opportunity to revise and comment on his essay in the light of the most recent criticism and scholarship. The reader of this collection should find the authors' responses to be of critical and human interest. A critic rarely is offered a peremptory opportunity to confront his published essay.

In the collection the emphasis is on the early masters: Joyce, Virginia Woolf, Conrad, D. H. Lawrence, Proust, Gide, Malraux, Mann, Kafka, James, Faulkner, Fitzgerald, Nabokov. For post-World War II novelists, the essays interpret writers who are offering new directions to the European and American novel: Robbe-Grillet, Nathalie Sarraute, Bellow, Hawkes, Barth. For the collection I have written an introductory essay exploring a few of the inner differences and similarities between the American and European novels of our century.

To enhance the usefulness of this book, I preferred in many cases to select an essay emphasizing a heterodox critical position, or dealing with either a less-known work or an unusual aspect of the maker.

H. R. G.

American and European Makers of the Twentieth-Century Novel

HARRY R. GARVIN
Bucknell University

Four elements can help distinguish the American novel from the European: the "nonintellectuality" of the American novel; the absence in America of a *major* tradition of the novel of manners; a basically "romantic" rather than "classical" approach to the novel and life in the United States; and a special and creative use by Americans of symbolic and stylistic techniques. Here I shall discuss mainly the first two distinguishing elements, borrowing like a landlord from my earlier essays on related issues. Because I consider these four elements distinctive and not unique, the generalizations below are intended to be tolerant rather than dogmatic.

I

The United States, unlike Europe, has not developed an important tradition of the novel of ideas (*roman à thèse, roman d'analyse, roman où l'on discute*); American novelists in our century are clearly less "intellectual" than European novelists. My point requires a few stipulations concerning two major kinds of novels of ideas: the philosophic novel and the "treatise" novel. I prefer the term *treatise* to thesis novel because the connotations of *treatise* make my distinction clearer if not more persuasive. Both the philosophic and the treatise novels are concerned with ideas directly related to some philosophical position, to some readily recognized doctrine about politics, art, religion, or psychology. Some examples are Dostoevski's *The Possessed* and *The Brothers Karamazov*, Mann's *Der Zauberberg* and *Doktor Faustus*, Joyce's *Portrait of the Artist as a Young Man*, Gide's *Les Faux-Monnayeurs*, Huxley's *Brave New World*, Camus's *La Peste*, and, to move back in time, *Candide, Rasselas*, and the novels of Thomas

---

This is the first publication of the essay.

Love Peacock. Obviously, a philosophic novel may, for other purposes, be considered also under other novelistic terms or genres.

In a treatise novel, the author has a strong tendency to fit his situations and characters to his doctrine, to permit his plot and characters to be caught within the imperatives of his intellectual thesis. A philosophic novel, by contrast, is not Procrustean; the characters and occasions escape the rigidity of a thesis, though touching the doctrine at crucial points. A philosophic novel reveals some of the metaphysical emanations from a doctrine, tries to discover some of the secrets within an idea, secrets hidden from the formal doctrine, rather than to explore it as an intellectual problem. A treatise novel is more concerned with formulations (intellectual and psychological), with "closed envelopes" and didactic ends, as in forgotten proletarian novels. A treatise novel is often a tale to adorn a moral; the author contrives situations and characters to exemplify preconceived, peremptory theses; he has a tendency to hammer his characters and themes flat. The literary fate of treatise novels is a footnote. A philosophic novel incarnates ideas, makes use of open analyses, and seeks to realize some of the inexhaustible ambiguities of the human heart confronting fundamental issues, often at the expense of formal clarity of doctrine.

For example, Camus's L'Étranger (1942) deepens and goes beyond his doctrine of the Absurd in Le Mythe de Sisyphe (1942) and escapes the rigid parts of this thesis. Indeed, long before Camus himself became conscious of his intellectual dissatisfaction with Le Mythe de Sisyphe, he had in L'Étranger intuitively moved away from his doctrine in Le Mythe de Sisyphe and toward his later thesis in "Remarque sur la révolte" (1945) and in L'Homme révolté (1951), where he developed his thesis on rebellion and revolution fully. And Sartre's novels, with the exception of La Nausée, are mainly treatise novels that rarely seem to go beyond and beneath his philosophy of existentialism and phenomenology. It is the European novelist rather than the American who is tempted by abstract ideas and by doctrinal theses, by the seductive chance to become a monarch of the intellect while in the very citadel of art.

The American novelist of this century, with rare exceptions like Saul Bellow and John Barth, is barely tempted. One of the characteristics of our culture is that in the United States there is a notorious tradition of anti-intellectualism, even though for some time now American philosophers, sociologists, literary critics, and poets have been at least as ingeniously intellectual as their European colleagues. But American novelists, especially in our century, do not use large, philosophical ideas as such, and indeed deliberately avoid revealing openly in their novels that they have read any philosophy or history or even literature. Widely read novelists like Hemingway, Steinbeck, and Faulkner kept their learning and reading out of their novels. From the point of view of open intellectuality, compare the novels of Hemingway with those of Malraux and Camus (except L'Étranger), of Steinbeck and Faulkner with those of Gide and Sartre, of Dos Passos and Dreiser with those of Mann. What is more, Faulkner and Hemingway, unlike most European novelists, were not professional literary critics or political and philosophical essayists. American novelists are not considered members of an intellectual elite, have no political power, are never culture-heroes. Compare the European novelists, particularly the French.

Unlike the distinctive American novelists, the European novelists of our century have had a clear tendency to give their novels an intellectual scope that includes philosophy, theology, religion, psychology, and science. Such European novelists have put on the novel some new burdens, the heavy intellectual burdens of our century. And the best European novelists have not written treatise novels because they make artistic use of highly intellectualized ideas in order to carry these new burdens. In general, the American novelists are probably as conscious of and as concerned with these burdens, but their strategy and their literary techniques are different. The American deals with the fundamental problems far more *indirectly* than the European; he relies much less on intellectual analysis and much more on the indirection of symbols. I wish here merely to suggest, without providing arguments, that American novelists have successfully used these indirect approaches to ideas because they have developed new techniques with symbols, words, style.

Much is lost as well as gained by such symbolic indirections. Intellectualized ideas have enlarged the art as well as the scope of novels by Thomas Mann, Proust, Joyce, Conrad, D. H. Lawrence, and Malraux. One should distinguish sharply between an author's "closed analysis" and an "open analysis" in the novel. When in a novel one of these European makers analyzes a character or a situation, he does not wish to *enclose* the meanings and to limit our understanding to the analysis only, but rather to beckon us into appreciation of ineffable feelings going beyond the analysis. It is therefore a limitation in the American novelists in the earlier decades of this century not to have found the artistic means of investing their novels with intellectualized ideas (the explicitly developed ideas of Faulkner, Dreiser, Dos Passos, Richard Wright being among the least important elements in their novels). But one should discern here an American strategy—a strategy involving artistic self-discipline, a determination not to incorporate large ideas until they have been refined in the crucible of art, until they have been made to undergo a sea change. Then the American novelist can be deep without seeming to be intellectual. Only recently has there been, particularly in Bellow and Barth and perhaps in Mailer, Malamud, and Roth, a clear tendency to deal with ideas directly—a tendency that I find welcome and perhaps prophetic.

II

Even in novels of manners, which lend themselves readily to direct social and philosophic reflection, the American novelist, compared with the European, moved more to the indirections and nuances of symbols than to intellectual commentary. When T. S. Eliot said that Henry James "had a mind so fine that no idea could violate it," he did not mean that James has little intellect and few ideas but that James's ideas underwent a sea change before they appeared in his novels. In his literary handling of ideas, James, our greatest novelist of manners, is in the American grain.

Most contemporary critics do not consider the novel of manners itself in the American grain. Some of them have strict views about what the American novel has been and should be, as if the house of American fiction can have no more room for the novel of manners. I agree with them that, unlike Europe, the United States has not excelled in the novel of manners, has not made it the center of its novelistic tradition, but I do not at all share the common depreciation of the novel of manners in the United States as a genteel aberration, a misbegotten child out of place in the New World.

The term *novel of manners* has been used loosely, vaguely. James W. Tuttleton's *The Novel of Manners in America* (1972) should help clarify the term as well as its major issues even when his strong defenses of the American achievements are not persuasive. Having developed my own views on the novel of manners before Tuttleton's book was published, I have in this essay taken the liberty of dealing with the book by implication only. My use of the term is frankly more restrictive, and my notions on the historical background and on the achievements and future of this kind of American novel are often substantially different from his.

Let me begin by naming some European and American novelists who in my view most clearly point up the meaning of the term. Among the English and French I would unhesitatingly cite Fanny Burney, Jane Austen, Thackeray, Trollope, Meredith, Arnold Bennett, Galsworthy, Balzac, Proust. American novelists would include Howells, James, Edith Wharton, Ellen Glasgow, Fitzgerald, Marquand, O'Hara, Cozzens, Auchincloss, Cheever, Updike.

The deliberate omission of Smollett, Dickens, even Richardson and Fielding, as well as Dreiser and Sinclair Lewis, Dos Passos and Farrell does not mean that a case cannot be made for their inclusion, even by my own criteria; each has special characteristics that keep me from including him, but in this essay I shall not confront the issues that would thereby need to be raised. Furthermore, neither are Faulkner, Hemingway, Carson McCullers, Flannery O'Connor, Bellow and Malamud, Ellison and Baldwin novelists of manners; the reason is not that their works raise issues that transcend the question of manners but that their attitudes toward society and man are uncharacteristic of the novelists of manners as described below.

For the novelist of manners, society is the dominant force in the lives of his characters, the solid power confronting them. The characters define themselves and realize themselves in relation mainly to society and its values rather than to a private world of their own making. The novel thereby is directly concerned with the customs, habits, and conventions of a specific place and time, is concerned with a class or classes in movement, and with what Lionel Trilling refers to as the buzz and hum of implications. (I should note here that I thoroughly disagree with Trilling on some fundamental issues surrounding the novel of manners and particularly the American novel.) Society in a novel of manners is presented as reasonably stable and as capable of fostering genuine values in the most worthy characters.

The perspective of such a novelist crucially distinguishes him from other kinds of novelists. He assumes the *persona* of an insider in society rather than an outsider or stranger. As an insider he is a critic, even a harsh critic, of the excesses of society and of the individuals in it when they oppose social values that are reasonable, commonsensical, or new and profound. The novelist characteristically takes the position of a sensitive member of the *haute bourgeoisie* who finds himself between the extremes; he takes the position of a critic who often sees society and men and women in terms of comedy, irony, satire. He characteristically wants to look at many sides of a character or an issue. He is deeply alive to the "surfaces" of the visible, actual world and wants to see how he may penetrate a surface and sound the depths at the same time. Nor is he an obvious propagandist or a brilliant subjectivist hovering near the unconscious, near underground feelings and thoughts. And he is likely to be something of a conservative in regard to human nature and even to political and social issues. In a special sense, therefore, he often assumes—

consciously or unconsciously, intentionally or not—some of the masks of the conservative neoclassical comic and satiric authors of the seventeenth and eighteenth centuries. The romantic temper in any of its extremes is absent from his work even when present in his life. In his work he cannot be an anarchist or a nihilist or a misanthrope, though he may espouse various degrees of misogyny. Thackeray and Meredith, and even the harsher Balzac and Flaubert (in *Madame Bovary*) did not wish to destroy the societies they exposed or to force man to despise his society completely in order to achieve his own salvation.

Put into historical and psychological context, the neoclassical, conservative, and bourgeois attitudes suggested above take on an added meaning. I shall mention only two matters. First, the realistic novel not only had one of its powerful origins in bourgeois needs but persisted in its rather conservative attitudes whenever the novel of manners or the historical romance dominated. The contrast between early British nineteenth-century novelists and poets is persuasive. Conservatives like Jane Austen and Sir Walter Scott in their novels were defending proper values in past and passing society, while most of the Romantic poets were developing revolutionary approaches to society, to man and nature, to the levels of unconsciousness as the sources of the creative imagination and of the knowledge of self and the world. In the Romantic Period, revolutionary bards and conservative novelists often moved in opposite directions, pushing the novel and poetry toward their future tensions and crises of the later nineteenth century.

Second, nineteenth-century novelists of manners recognized that the novel of sensibility and the Gothic novel were their natural antagonists; both of these genres are in the romantic mode. Jane Austen reduced romantical and weeping sensibility to prostration before the altar of sense, and in *Northanger Abbey* ridicules the Gothic novel, which was the first important novelistic reaction against the realistic bourgeois novel. To be sure, there are some strains of sentimentality in some novelists of manners (Thackeray, for example) and strains of romantical sensibility in some others (as in Meredith), but these are minor paradoxes and do not disturb the main argument here. I shall point out later that the twentieth century saw the end of the long domination of the novel of manners even in Europe. Now I wish to fortify my notion that not even in the nineteenth century did America develop a major tradition in the novel of manners.

Almost without exception the great and minor European novelists of the last century wrote novels of manners; however, in the last two centuries only one major American writer, Henry James, has been a novelist of manners. In fairness, I should mention here my bias, which today is common enough: that Hawthorne, Melville, James, Hemingway, and Faulkner mark the Great Tradition of the American novel. The best American novelists of manners mentioned earlier in the essay belong to the second or third order of achievement. (I consider Dreiser, Lewis, Farrell, and Dos Passos "social" novelists; they basically did not have and did not want the perspectives of the novelist of manners as described above.)

The famous complaints of Cooper, Hawthorne, James, and Edith Wharton that the United States lacked social texture, lacked a polished society with classes and customs touched with implication, were more rhetorical than accurate. Their defensive overstatements were intended to justify what these authors really wanted to write: not realistic novels of manners in the European mode but purely American "romances," or romances with a definite social base, or a different kind of novel of manners. James, for example, wanted to write mainly novels of manners about Americans in Europe rather than at home, novels with subtle touches of romance arising from his own delicate American passion for extremes. William Dean Howells (1837–1920) in his nineteenth-century novels of manners finally proved beyond doubt that for almost any writer American society had become complex enough socially to make possible a realistic novel of manners. Indeed, I think that the social *materials* for such a novel were actually available in a number of American cities long before they were exploited by writers like Howells and James. After all, Henry James himself in 1881 wrote a realistic novel of manners, *Washington Square,* concerning New York society of about 1830.

As I have observed, the novel of manners is marked by reason and reasonableness, by a worldly and objective view of the individual and society. But the characteristic American romanticism has from the beginning kept pulling the novelist, even James, from the realistic, objective center toward the dark peripheries. By contrast with the French, British, and Italian traditions, our American culture has never experienced *deeply* a neoclassical period in literature and the arts. The major American insights of the American novelists have nearly always been not into society or even into the individual in relation to society but rather into the individual soul with its darkness and subjectivism. The major American insights are not into the moral problems arising from the realistic relationships among classes and individuals; our best novelists move more readily into the metaphysical problems of the isolated individual in relation to himself, to nature, to death, to disbelief, to God. This metaphysical absorption is dominant even in Faulkner, despite his large concern with social materials. Faulkner is not a novelist of manners because he does not have the perspectives of such a novelist, because he is much more directly interested in the ontological dimension than in the realistic surface. And it is significant that Hemingway, who everyone agrees is characteristically American, did not write a single novel with an American social setting.

Some distinctions may be necessary here. For I do not deny that Americans and their novelists are interested in society and classes or that Europeans are interested in the ontological estate of individuals. Notorious is the American concern with status, class, money, success. But Americans are not deeply intrigued by classes (which have been and are much more fluid in America than in Europe) or by manners (which continue to be more uniform in the United States). Our first reaction to ritual is suspicion; our first reaction to social elaboration is a smile or a laugh. Americans do not even have an expression similar to *bella figura.* Americans seem to be more acutely absorbed in the inner life of an individual, and our novelists even more so. A protagonist in an American novel rarely defines himself primarily in terms of society; there is a tradition here that readily applauds anyone who bypasses or escapes from society. The initiation of Huck Finn, Nick Adams, Ike McCaslin, and Eugene Gant is not into society but away from it; their final self-knowledge is only tangentially related to social issues. Class, status, money, manners, society stick in our minds but not in our imaginations. Compare the traditional German *Bildungsroman* (*Entwicklungsroman*), in which protagonists, ever since the eighteenth century, are finally initiated into society; only since World War II does the protagonist (but only in West Germany, not East Germany) end up outside society.

Among the masters of the American novel, only Henry James is an exception to the above generalizations, but only partly so. Like most European novelists, James had a high ideal of class and talent, of pride and privilege and responsibility, and he knew the lure and pull of society even upon Americans. But he also knew that Americans, compared with Europeans, do not take naturally to society. Indeed, James's Americans seem to be eternal pilgrims in search of what society and class cannot ultimately give them. For James, society at best is only a valuable testing ground for the inner American drama: [the poignant search of the individual for private identity in any society, her or his subjective struggle with innocence and ignorance and evil and with the complex fate of being an American.] Howells probably knew more details about American society than James did, but he lacked James's sense of tragedy. Like the European novelist of manners, James had the conviction that manners make the inner man and are true indicators of his moral estate, that manners can be the outward signs of inner grace or disgrace. These convictions suggest the European side of Henry James and perhaps of many complex Americans; his distinctively American side is in his conception of the passionate American pilgrims and in his creative narrative techniques, particularly his kind of symbolism. Thus, though James is the only great American novelist who writes about manners, he does so in a peculiarly American way. More than any American novelist of manners, Henry James has the imagination of disaster, an imagination that turns him toward the centers of American sensibility.

James's achievement should convince us that even in an American novelist there is nothing inherently superficial in a close attention to manners and surfaces, nothing inherently inferior in the novel of manners as such. The probing of surface to uncover depths is a traditional and noble task, and tragic intensities lie just beneath as well as far beneath these surfaces. There is nothing inherently profound or new in searching for meaning and meaninglessness by entering at once into the depths. Surrealism is after all only one way to reveal the subliminal and unconscious depths within painters and others. Like all innovators, the first literary explorers of depths leave trodden paths for others to descry and follow. And cults soon arise: of alienation and post-alienation, or radical innocence and radical guilt, of wastelanders and post-wastelanders. The most radical techniques and fiery insights turn into literary conventions. The unexplored depths and surfaces remain infinite, for novelists and others to explore.

It is fashionable now to continue to be condescending toward the novel of manners—especially among critics and novelists (Mailer, e.g.) who are primarily interested in experimental techniques (e.g., Joyce, Stein, Woolf, and Hawkes, Nabokov, Barth, Vonnegut), or in the anti-novel and meta-novel and the essay-as-art novel (Podhoretz), or in radical political and social issues. To be sure, our best novelists have not been strongly attracted to manners and surfaces, and novelists other than James who have been, are clearly not giants in imagination. The conviction—as represented by Richard Chase, Lionel Trilling, Leslie Fiedler, and Marius Bewley—that an absorption in manners goes and will go against the American grain is probably accurate enough. In the fifties, sixties, and now the seventies, things stranger than manners have lured the imagination of our best and most characteristic novelists. But this fact need not be an inevitable prophecy about the novel in America.

III

Why, then, did European novelists wait until the twentieth century to break away from their major tradition of the conservative novel of manners? (German novelists, in whom the romantic mode clearly dominated the neoclassical, never did develop a strong tradition of the realistic novel of manners.) Indeed, in recent years French writers have been among the most exciting experimentalists in language and style, subject matter and genre: Robbe-Grillet, Nathalie Sarraute, Butor, Bataille, Leiris, Michaux, Ionescu, Beckett. Of course the master innovators in language and style in our century wrote in English (Stein, Joyce, Woolf, Faulkner, Dos Passos); and I cannot resist pointing out that Gertrude Stein in *Tender Buttons* (1914) and in subsequent innovative works like *Four Saints in Three Acts* (1929) and *Four in America* (completed in 1933) long ago anticipated Robbe-Grillet and other phenomenological new novelists in France when they cut away the accretions of meaning from words.

I shall indicate here only the direction my fuller explanation of the shift away from manners would take. First, during the Romantic movements in nineteenth-century Europe, the major rebellions of the individual against society were expressed in poetry rather than in the more conservative novel. The disturbing Gothic novel of the late eighteenth and early nineteenth century was an aberration from the main tradition of the realistic bourgeois novel, and no major European novelists wrote predominantly Gothic novels. Indeed, the romantic, Gothic impulses of European novelists have long been tempered by the realism in the novel of manners and by the strong classical traditions in Mediterranean Europe.

Second, many European novelists in our century began—for the first time in the history of the European novel—to share strongly what may be called the American sensibility, a special inner sensibility that began to emerge in colonial times and became manifest in our time. Independently or not, European novelists had to develop a similar sensibility in order to respond profoundly to the new spiritual crises of the estranged man of the twentieth century. Our century has often been characterized in terms of isolation, skepticism, discontinuity, anxiety, violence, a passion for extremes, alienation, and rebellion. Increasingly in our century, the innovating artist thinks he should search within himself and society for the new shades in the inner sensibility of the immediate moment, should try to discover the variation of feeling in the smallest possible temporal spiral within a decade. And even if such a novelist might have preferred the perspectives of a novelist of manners, the main subject of his work could hardly have been a stable society and nuances in manners. He may sometimes reveal a poignant yearning, as Bellow does, for example, for the fine values possible to a passionate individual in a welcoming and deserving society. But no serious novelist can help responding to the cataclysms of our century.

In essays on the American sensibility and identity I have elsewhere argued that the qualities of alienation and rebellion characterizing our century have *always* been near the center of the American spirit and have been revealed, at least in our novels and poetry, with increasing clarity since the second half of the nineteenth century. In the twentieth century the major American writers have been expressing not only the dark inner image of the wandering American but also the spirit of our age as a whole. It should not be surprising, therefore, to discover that the traditional novel of manners lost its hold on the imagination of European novelists when they were startled by the new inner forces in our century and by the work of American writers. The twentieth century may not finally turn out to be the American Century, but so far it has been the century of American sensibility.

Baudelaire, Stephen Dedalus, and Shem the Penman

J. MITCHELL MORSE

Temple University

COMMENT BY THE AUTHOR

Since writing this article I have read more, thought more, lived more; my view of Joyce and of Baudelaire has accordingly changed; I think it is now less in accord with conventional romantic notions and more in accord with the evidence of the texts; I therefore believe that Stephen Dedalus and Shem the Penman are not representations of the ideal artist Joyce wished to become, but portraits of Joyce as a young man struggling to make himself an artist.

As I have indicated in later articles, the struggle involves many mistakes and is often ludicrous, because both characters are deluded by the romantic notion that artists are necessarily unsocial and often anti-social, neurotic, insane, or criminal. They therefore play that romantic role; they are both, therefore, less artists than bohemians. It is a corny and essentially servile catering to condescension.

On this point Henri Mürger's preface to his amusing novel Scènes de la vie de Bohème *is instructive. It deals with the lives of a poet, a painter, and a composer who most of the time do anything rather than write, paint, compose; who have no technique, no ideas, no artistic purpose; who are no more artists than an astrologer is a scientist.*

Joyce did not conceive himself in such terms. Baudelaire did not conceive himself in such terms. And if neither was a public official like Chaucer or Milton or Goethe, or a widely popular writer like Shakespeare or Dickens or Balzac, or a busy hospital administrator like Rabelais, or a busy physician like William Carlos Williams, or a busy corporation lawyer like Wallace Stevens, they were both very busy writers: serious artists who spent most of their time writing rather

First published: 7, no. 3 (1958):187–98. Slightly revised for this book.

*than sitting in cafés or organizing costume balls, and who had more influence
on literature than on the neighborhood bohemianism. I believe that the portraits
of Stephen and of Shem are largely ironic, and especially that Joyce intended
Stephen's ecstasies on Dollymount Strand and in his diary to be read with a
smile as adolescent gush.*

Stephen Dedalus and Shem the Penman obviously have many features in common
with Joyce, and many of the things they do are things Joyce did. But they represent
him less as he was than as he wished to be or thought he might become; they are
not really self-portraits but representations of the ideal in whose image Joyce
tried to create himself: the free, disinterested, uncommitted artist who could serve
as the conscience of his race.

Stephen Hero was a self-portrait; I suggest that Joyce threw it into the fire
not because he was discouraged by the publishers' delays (after all, he did not
throw *Dubliners* into the fire) but because he had developed a larger purpose
for which he saw it would not do. *A Portrait of the Artist as a Young Man,* though
it contains autobiographical elements, seems to be less a self-portrait—at whatever
distance in time—than the partial realization of a project Baudelaire had proposed
for himself but had never got around to: *"Portrait de l'artiste, en général"* (MC,
XV).[1]

Baudelaire himself, as man and artist, supplied many elements for the portrait
Joyce drew—or rather the three portraits showing the evolution of the artist in
general: a boyish Stephen full of terrible and beautiful dreams, a somewhat older
Stephen bitterly confronting the reality of outward experience, and finally Shem,
mad, visionary, completely asocial, wrong in his own or in any generation, and yet
eternally right in that his work endures. There are also, of course, elements from
a variety of other sources: from such poets, for example, as Cyrano de Bergerac,
Heine, Morgenstern, Poe, and Swift, and from such fictional characters as Roger
Chillingworth (who like Shem has "the wrong shoulder higher than the right")
and Rameau's nephew (who like Shem is "all ears" but has "a deaf heart"—"I have
spent my life with good musicians and bad people," he says, "whence my ear has
become very sharp and my heart quite deaf").[2] Investigation of such analogues
may help us to answer the questions, Who is Stephen? and Who is Shem? It may
also throw an indirect light on the more difficult question, Who is Joyce?

Consider the elements drawn from Baudelaire.

When the poet is born, at the beginning of *Les Fleurs du mal,* his mother cries
to Heaven that this is too great a punishment for the passing pleasure of conception
—she would rather have borne a knot of vipers than such a monster. The whole
world hates him; even his wife, despising him, tries to tempt him into damnation.
But the poet is serene and is not mocked, for his kingdom is not of this world.

Such is the ideal. The reality is somewhat different, for such holy self-confidence

---

1. MC is the abbreviation for *Mon Coeur mis à nu;* and F is the abbreviation for *Fusées.*
Roman numbers are those in Baudelaire's *Journaux intimes,* ed. Jacques Crepet and Georges
Blin (Paris: Corti, 1949). Numbers in parentheses following titles of Joyce's works refer to
pages in the Modern Library editions of *Ulysses* (New York, 1946) and *A Portrait of the
Artist as a Young Man* (New York, n.d.), and to pages in *Finnegans Wake* (New York: Viking,
1939) and *Stephen Hero,* 22nd ed. (New York, 1955).

2. Denis Diderot, *Rameau's Nephew,* trans. Jacques Barzun (New York: Bobbs-Merrill,
1956), p. 73. Cf. *Finnegans Wake,* p. 169.

is not easy. To be convinced of the objective validity of one's personal vision is easy enough, is the merest naiveté, especially if one sees the world from the same angle as everyone else; to be convinced of the objective validity of one's personal vision even though realizing that it is unique is also easy—this is fanaticism; but to be convinced of the objective validity of one's personal vision *because* it is unique, to have therefore no desire to share it with anyone else, and yet to wish to express it perfectly in all its uniqueness and incommunicability—this is to be mad; nevertheless, if through skill one can convey to others not one's personal vision but a conviction of its uniqueness and importance, then one is an artist. The perfection of this ideal no man ever attains, of course; the last infirmity of the noble mind is the desire to communicate with others.

Baudelaire had moments of clairvoyant perception remarkably like those which Joyce in *Stephen Hero* called epiphanies: moments in which a vulgar gesture, a phrase or intonation, a clock, a store window, or any "stray image of the street" becomes "a sudden spiritual manifestation" (pp. 210–11). In *Ulysses* Stephen says that a shout in the street is God; as early as his youthful essay "Ibsen's New Drama," Joyce had said, "At some chance expression, the mind is tortured with some question, and in a flash long reaches of life are opened up in a vista."[3] "There are moments," said Baudelaire, "when time and space are more profound, and the feeling of existence is immensely augmented. . . . In certain almost supernatural states of soul, the depth of life is fully revealed in the spectacle before our eyes, however ordinary it may be. It becomes the symbol of the depth of life" (F, XI). Man, he said in the poem "Correspondances" (which Joyce knew by heart),[4] walks through forests of symbols—perfumes, colors, sounds—

> *Comme de longs échos qui de loin se confondent*
> *Dans une ténébreuse et profonde unité.*

Baudelaire's own chief purpose was to reveal such symbolic correspondences and to communicate their almost supernatural significance: "To glorify the cult of images (my great, my unique, my primitive passion)."

Realizing that such a mission could hardly be valued by the conventional world of letters and that he would find it more profitable to conform to some accepted literary mode, he mockingly proposed to do so: "To produce a *poncif*," he wrote in his journal, "that is genius. I must produce a *poncif*." In his notes on the Salon of 1846 he defined *poncif* as everything that is banal, vulgar, and lifeless: "When a singer puts his hand on his heart, it ordinarily means, 'I will love her forever!' If he clenches his fists and stares at the prompter or at the boards, that signifies, 'He shall die, the traitor!'—Such is *poncif*."[5] But of course to write such stuff was impossible for Baudelaire, who regarded any accommodation to the tastes, values, or feelings of others, even for love, as prostitution. Perhaps even more than art, fidelity was his great passion. Fidelity to what? To himself, through all waverings, lapses, vagaries, uncertainties, and inconsistencies. Such extreme

---

3. James A. Joyce, *Ibsen's New Drama* [From *The Fortnightly Review,* London, April 1900] (London: Ulysses Book Shop, 1930), p. 36.

4. William York Tindall, *James Joyce: His Way of Interpreting the Modern World* (New York: Scribner, 1950), p. 109. In *Finnegans Wake* Shaun calls Shem "my shemblable! My freer!" (p. 489).

5. Baudelaire, *Curiosités esthétiques* (Paris, n.d.), p. 157.

egocentricity sometimes involved him in despicable behavior. "Fidelity," he wrote to Madame Sabatier, assuring her of his devotion, "fidelity is one of the signs of genius."[6] But that was ambiguous and deceptive, for on the morning after she yielded to him he told her he had a horror of passion, lest the loved image dominate his life. That, he said, would be ignominious.[7] All he had really wanted was the same sort of one-night affair that Dedalus wants to have with Emma Clery in *Stephen Hero.* Stephen tells the outraged Emma, "There is no such thing as love in the world," and in the *Portrait* he denies any understanding of what the word *love* means. This parallels and perhaps echoes the statement of the Stranger in the first of Baudelaire's *Poèmes en prose,* who when asked if he does not love his friends replies, "You use a word whose meaning so far is unknown to me." He is speaking of the word *friend,* but in the context he also means *love.* Baudelaire's attitude represented an extreme reaction against one of the social effects of the French Revolution: the replacement of hereditary class relationships by what Karl Marx called the cash nexus, and in consequence an increasingly obvious commercialization of social relationships. The cash nexus is of course no more impersonal than the class nexus or the lack of nexus; it may even be less impersonal. To Baudelaire's taste, however, it was unreal and invalid; it lacked essential truth; it was a low, dishonest way of life. He felt that all human relationships, however intimate, would soon be commercialized, and that all but commercial motives would be devalued and tend to disappear. He was perhaps the first to make the now familiar anti-democratic charge that society was becoming "Americanized"; the world would perish, he predicted, of opportunism and of the desire to sell oneself—"*par l'avilissement des coeurs.*"

The Joycean artist of course does not share Baudelaire's reactionary or romantic yearning for a pre-capitalist society; neither is he so pessimistic as to believe that the commercial life will obliterate all other ways of living. Nevertheless, he shares Baudelaire's distaste for the economic man. "There is no reason why life should lose all grace and nobility," says Stephen Hero, "even though Columbus discovered America." For him as for Baudelaire, the gracious and noble life must be won internally; he has no faith in social reformers. In the *Portrait* the good but stupid McCann, who submits to clerical censorship of his magazine, says, "Dedalus, you're an anti-social being, wrapped up in yourself. I'm not. I'm a democrat: and I'll work and act for social liberty and equality among all classes and sexes in the United States of the Europe of the future." That was a kind of Americanization more innocent but hardly more interesting to the artist's intelligence.

Baudelaire's motives were of course less disinterested than Joyce's; nevertheless, he had a similar distaste for politics: "I have no convictions, as the people of my century understand the term, for I have no ambition. In me there is no basis for any conviction. There is a certain laziness or rather a certain softness among decent people. Only brigands are convinced—of what?—that they must succeed. And they do succeed. Why should I succeed, since I don't even want to try? One can found glorious empires on crime, and noble religions on imposture. Nevertheless, I have certain convictions, in a higher sense which cannot be understood by the people of my time" (MC, VII). He took a sort of adolescent pride in the neuroticism of this attitude. Because he dreaded being "lost in that vile world, elbowed

---

6. *Baudelaire par lui-même,* ed. Pascal Pia (Paris: Editions du Seuil, 1954), p. 56.
7. *Ibid.,* p. 58.

by the crowds," he treasured like a miser his own tastes and even his eccentricities as safeguards against prostitution: "I have cultivated my hysteria with joy and terror." Such self-cultivation precluded even love, whose self-surrender he feared; for him even art, being a way of communicating one's feelings, one's insights, one's self, to others, was a form of prostitution, albeit one that permitted a degree of self-possession: "Invincible taste for prostitution in the heart of man, whence is born his horror of solitude. He wants to be *two*. The man of genius wants to be *one,* and to prostitute himself in a particular way. It is that horror of solitude, the need to forget the *I* in contact with alien flesh, that man nobly calls the *need* to love" (MC, XXXVI).

In some people, however, the taste for prostitution is opposed by a taste for themselves, for their own excellence or aspiration toward excellence: "To be a great man and a saint *for oneself*—that is the only thing that matters." Stephen Hero also seeks "a *bonum arduum*," to "live a free and noble life" through "silence, exile and cunning." On two occasions Baudelaire said there were only three great men: "the priest, the warrior, the poet. To know, to kill, and to create." "The poet, the priest and the soldier, the man who sings, the man who blesses, the man who sacrifices others and himself." But there was a fourth, more compatible with the ideal of complete self-dedication, and this was the man Baudelaire himself strove to be: the man of taste and elegance, whom he called, in English and with a capital D, the Dandy. Walter Pater is an example; Bernard Berenson is another; we think also of Plotinus, John of Salisbury, Marsiglio Ficino, Sir Thomas More, and Confucius—the man with a care for dignity and propriety and grace, to be achieved through "prayer, good grooming, and work"—the man who strives to be always at his best, inwardly and outwardly. For Baudelaire, ideally, this achievement required leisure and money, since it should involve good eating and good cigars and so on; but such things, though highly desirable, were not essential. The main thing was the disposition and the unintermitted effort: "The Dandy must ceaselessly aspire to be sublime; he must live and sleep before a mirror" (MC, III).

It is not a matter of being fashionable, or even of leading fashion. In the process of dissipating his fortune Baudelaire had clothes made to his own design, of the richest materials and by the best tailors, but without any regard to what was fashionable, and certainly without any desire to be imitated. Similarly with regard to his inward life, the Dandy is not concerned with being either conventional or unconventional (since the man who must say No is as much a slave to convention as the one who must say Yes); he is concerned simply with expressing himself. Baudelaire praises the "correct audacity" of Théodore de Banville, *"cet air de maîtrise et ce beau nonchaloir."*[8] In the *Portrait* Stephen says, "I will try to express myself in some mode of life or art as freely as I can and as wholly as I can"; and when he adds that the only arms he will permit himself are "silence, exile and cunning," he expresses a taste for economy and restraint and a disdain for vulgar contention that are of the essence of intellectual Dandyism.

Baudelaire expressed his prejudice against women by saying, "Woman is the opposite of the Dandy. Therefore she must horrify us." The conception inevitably reminds us of Molly Bloom: "Woman is hungry and wants to eat; thirsty and wants to drink; in rut and wants to be bedded. Fine and worthy! Woman is

---

8. *Les Fleurs du mal* (Paris: Editions de Cluny, 1941), p. 175.

natural, which is to say abominable. Besides, she is always vulgar, which is to say the opposite of the Dandy." Like Anna Livia Plurabelle, she, "doesn't know how to separate her soul from her body.—A satirist would say that she has only a body." For this reason, said Baudelaire, "I have always been astonished that women are allowed to enter churches. What conversation can they have with God?" In *Stephen Hero* Joyce expresses similar doubts as to women's religious experience: "The general attitude of women towards religion puzzled and often maddened Stephen. His nature was incapable of achieving such an attitude of insincerity or stupidity."

Stephen is angry at Emma Clery because he feels that she has rejected his unconventional proposition not out of a "spirit of chastity" but out of "menial fear." This is a recurrent theme in all Joyce's work. Stephen Hero, echoing the church fathers, calls lust, ambition, and gluttony "servile" passions; he almost weeps at the "unredeemable servility" of three clerks playing billiards; in the *Portrait* Stephen is depressed by the statue of Thomas Moore with its "servile head" and repelled when his friend Davin responds to the verses he recites "by a dull stare of terror in the eyes, the terror of soul of a starving Irish village in which the curfew was still a nightly fear." The most disgusting thing about the characters in "Ivy Day in the Committee Room" is their servile opportunism; in *Ulysses* that is the attitude of Buck Mulligan toward the Englishman Haines; in *Finnegans Wake* Shaun goes to meet the conqueror of his country shouting "Itch dean"—I itch to serve, Chief. Baudelaire took a similar view of his own countrymen: "The Frenchman is a barnyard animal so tame that he doesn't dare to leap over any fence. See his tastes in art and literature."

What is the public taste he scorns? A taste for "the nice young girl of the publishers. The nice young girl of the editors-in-chief. The frightful nice young girl, monster, assassin of art. . . . In her is all the abjectness of the street-corner loafer and the college student." It reads almost like Joyce's denunciation of the Irish Literary Theatre, in which the nice young girls and proper young men of "the cultivated rabblement," tittering coyly when Mélisande lets down her hair, "are not sure but they are the trustees of every intellectual and poetic pleasure."[9] One of Baudelaire's unrealized projects was "A pretty picture to paint: the literary rabble." Joyce realized it brilliantly in the library scene of *Ulysses.*

An artist who thinks the public taste corrupted and declines to cater to it must of course stand alone. In the days of the patron and the limited audience the artist had other problems, but this one did not exist; in the nineteenth century, when the publishing industry was progressively adapting itself to the reading habits of a large public whose morality and taste were merely means of getting on in the world, a disinterested artist could hardly expect to be understood or approved of. Baudelaire, being a snob as well, took a perverse pride in not being appreciated. With more devotion to logic than to fact, he even disapproved of printing, which he called "a great obstacle to the development of the Beautiful." In his notes on the Salon of 1859 he also denounced photography, whose progress he said had greatly contributed to the impoverishment of French artistic genius.[10] So intense was his hatred of mechanical reproduction that he even looked askance at stenography.[11]

---

9. Herbert Gorman, *James Joyce* (New York: Rinehart, 1948), p. 72.
10. *Curiosités esthétiques,* p. 260.
11. *Ibid.,* p. 261.

Under such conditions he could be heard only as an enemy. That is precisely his conception of the artist's role: "The man of letters is the enemy of society." He must have "a Satanic turn of mind." He becomes defiant—"To be a useful citizen has always seemed to me a hideous thing"—and even vainglorious: "On the day when a young writer corrects his first proof, he is as proud as a student who has just got his first dose of the pox." Society reacts with at least equal scorn: "If a poet asked the state to grant him the right to keep several bourgeois in his stable we should be very much astonished, whereas if a bourgeois asked for roasted poet we should find it quite natural" (F, XI). In *Finnegans Wake* Shaun drinks a cup of poet soup and says, "That was a damn good cup of scald. You could trot a mouse on it" (pp. 455–56).

Under the pressure of such widespread disapproval the poet begins to doubt his own worth as a human being. Baudelaire notes in his journal, "Those who like me are contemned—I would even say contemptible if I cared to flatter respectable people" (F, XXVI).[12] Accordingly, he develops a distaste even for those who like him: "Many friends, many gloves—for fear of the itch." Disapproval, like a familiar drug, becomes a necessity for him: "When I shall have inspired universal disgust and horror, I shall have conquered solitude." This essentially childish need to be noticed is perhaps another necessary condition of greatness, or at least of eminence. The nineteenth century was acutely aware of it, expressing it in such diverse forms as Oscar Wilde's saying, "The only thing worse than being talked about is not being talked about," and P. T. Barnum's saying, "There's no such thing as bad publicity. I don't care what the papers say about me, as long as they mention my name." In his letters, Joyce correctly guessed that Shane Leslie's attack on *Ulysses* would help to sell it. The figure of Shem the Penman in *Finnegans Wake* is in this tradition. He conquers solitude by arousing disgust. Seen only through the unfriendly eyes of Shaun, he is "a sham and a low sham," "a dirty little blacking beetle," a "national apostate, who was cowardly gun and camera shy," "his cheeks and trousers changing color every time a gat croaked," "a bad fast man," "an antinomian," a "fraid born fraud," "covetous," "a dem scrounger," "a certain gay young nobleman whimpering to the name of Low Swine who always addresses women out of the one corner of his mouth, lives on loans and is furtivefree yours of age," "the supreme prig," "the prattlepate parnella," "the cull," "the accomplished washout," "the noxious pervert," on whose "perfect lowness" people looked "with the contemp of the contempibles," "the pleb," "this mental and moral defective," "always blaspheming," a "low waster," "this Calumnious Column of Cloaxity, this Bengalese Beacon of Biloxity, this Annamite Aper of Atroxity," "this semidemented zany," "the bumpersprinkler," etc., etc., etc. He was "toed out" of all decent houses and "ordered off the gorgeous premises in most cases on account of his smell which all cookmaids eminently objected to." They "turned him down and assisted nature by shoeing the source of annoyance out of the place altogether and taytotally on the heat of the moment, holding one another's gonk (for no one, hound or scrublady, not even the Turk, ungreekable in purscent of the armenable,[13] dared whiff the polecat at close range)" (pp. 170 ff.). In the solitude that results, Shem writes his book. Shaun of course does not understand it,

---

12. In *Finnegans Wake* Joyce calls those who try to master the Devil by giving him lessons "the Baddelaries partisans" (p. 4).

13. My son Jonathan points out that this echoes Oscar Wilde's description of a foxhunt as "the unspeakable in pursuit of the uneatable."

and Shem of course does not explain it to him. Like Shem and like Joyce, Baudelaire was content to let his work speak for itself: "Those who understand understand, and for those who can't or won't understand I see no point in piling up explanations.[14]

Nevertheless, if the artist is lucky he will not only conquer solitude but also influence others for their good. "The man of letters stirs up capitals and gives them a taste for intellectual gymnastics." Of course they try not to develop such a taste: "Nations don't have great men except despite themselves. Thus the great man is the conqueror of his whole nation." And again, "Nations have no great men but despite themselves—like families. They do everything they can to avoid having any. Therefore, the great man needs, in order to exist, a power of attack greater than the force of resistance developed by millions of individuals" (F, VII). Here surely is the Joycean great man, the fabulous "hawklike man" who by the power of his art would touch the conscience of "the most belated race in Europe."[15]

For Baudelaire too the greatest of all great men, the Dandy who disinterestedly seeks to be sublime, is an ideal most nearly realized by the artist. For the Baudelairean as well as for the Joycean artist solitude is a necessary condition: "The more man cultivates the arts, the less he bands together. He more and more consciously divorces the mind from the brute. Only brutes band together well, and sex is the lyricism of the people. To have sexual intercourse is to enter another, and the artist never comes out of himself" (MC, XXXIX). Baudelaire denies any spiritual value to the sacred prostitution of the pagans: it is the result merely of "nervous excitation." When Lynch, in the *Portrait,* tells Stephen that he once wrote his name in pencil on the backside of the Venus of Praxiteles, Stephen replies that that was the result not of aesthetic pleasure but of "a purely reflex action of the nerves" (p. 241).

But solitude, though a necessary condition, is not enough to produce an artist. For among the other conditions he must meet is one that appears to negate solitude: a taste for life. Baudelaire was conscious of the strain between the two necessities; Stephen Dedalus saw that, far from contradicting each other, they are inseparably joined, since life comes from within, from oneself, not from the presence of others. The others are merely the raw material from which the artist creates life, the Platonic matter on which he imposes form. He must know them, but he must not identify himself with them or become involved with them; he must inwardly withdraw. "From earliest childhood," Baudelaire wrote in his journal, "I have had in my heart two contradictory feelings, the horror of life and the ecstasy of life." And again, "The feeling of solitude, since my childhood. Notwithstanding my family—and especially among my friends—the feeling of a destiny forever solitary. Nevertheless, a very keen taste for life and for pleasure" (MC, XL). Stephen's analysis goes farther. For him there can be no life without solitude: life is born of solitude or not at all. In the *Portrait,* he finds, "His destiny was to be elusive of social or religious orders. . . . He was destined to learn his own wisdom apart from others or to learn the wisdom of others himself wandering among the snares of the world" (p. 188). "You're a terrible man, Stevie," his friend Davin tells him, "always alone." "I do not fear to be alone," he tells Cranly. In his ecstasy on the strand he is conscious of being "near to the wild heart of life"; he sings "wildly to the sea, crying to greet the advent of the life that had

14. *Baudelaire par lui-même,* pp. 7–8.
15. Gorman, p. 72.

cried to him"; in his diary, shortly before leaving Ireland, he writes, "Wild spring. Scudding clouds. O life!" And on the day before leaving he says, "I may learn in my own life and away from home and friends what the heart is and what it feels. . . . Welcome, O life! I go to encounter for the millionth time the reality of experience and to forge in the smithy of my soul the uncreated conscience of my race."

But any man who attempts to create the conscience of his race is liable to have trouble with the censors. When *Les Fleurs du mal* was condemned, Baudelaire said, "France has a horror of poetry, of true poetry," the kind of poetry he described as "profound, complex, bitter, and (in appearance) coldly diabolic." The public wanted only "sentiment, heart-throbs, and other feminine slop." He called the popular literary lecturer Émile Deschanel "a professor for young ladies."[16] That is Shaun's most engaging role in *Finnegans Wake*. Addressing the Leapyear Girls, he says, "I'd burn the books that grieve you," suggests that they might like "Mary Liddlelambe's flitsy tales, especially with the scentaminted sauce," advises them to read "pious fiction," "sifted science" and the lives of the saints, and recommends the perusal of "your *Weekly Standerd,* our verile organ." As for Shem's book, he says, "I am, pay Gay, in juxtaposition to say it is not a nice production. It is a pinch of scribble, not wortha bottle of cabbis. Overdrawn! Puffedly offal tosh! Besides its auctionable, all about crime and libel! . . . The fuellest filth ever fired since Charley Lucan's. Flummery is what I would call it if you were to ask me to put it what pronounced opinion I might possibly orally have about them bagses of trash" (pp. 419–20).

The philistine professor condemns the poet's work as trash for reasons that, it seems to me, have nothing to do with its quality. He would be just as ready to condemn real trash if it offended his notions of moral, social, political, or philosophical propriety—but of course real trash does not seriously concern itself with such matters, even though the author may think he is being serious. Being unable to distinguish good writing from bad, the professor for young ladies is guided by the established canon and the accepted styles; he thus admires a great deal of good work; he rejects only what he instinctively feels to be disturbing, to be a clear and present danger to conventional values. He will even accept new forms if their content does not grieve him. He accepted the imagists, for example. He rejects the good work of a new poet essentially because he feels it to be the expression of an unsympathetic personality. And there is no doubt that in the cases of Baudelaire and Joyce the personality was unsympathetic; Joyce was an extremely unsocial being, and Baudelaire—in all but his art—was contemptible. The rejection of them is due to the philistine's inability to distinguish between artistic values and social values.

Joyce was quite aware of this fact; Baudelaire apparently was not. As Sartre has pointed out, Baudelaire *chose* his sad career—living in dull idleness, consorting with prostitutes, seeking honors he sneered at, asking favors of people he reviled behind their backs, etc. Joyce, with more understanding of the philistine's point of view, with better humor, and looking down from a greater height of detachment on Baudelaire's personal failures and his own, drew a portrait of the artist in general that stands unequaled.

---

16. See *Baudelaire par lui-même,* pp. 129–30.

A Portrait of the Artist in *Finnegans Wake*

BERNARD BENSTOCK
University of Illinois

COMMENT BY THE AUTHOR

A lot of Liffey water has gone under O'Connell Bridge since the days of audacious Finnegans Wake *commentary in the late fifties, when a great deal was heard about "keys" to unlock mysteries and "central theses" on what it is all about. Many valuable tools have now been made available, a concordance and various lexicons, a second census (with a third in the offing), and studies of the text and the notebooks. Most important is the continual appearance since 1961 of* A Wake Newslitter, *edited by two of the most adroit Wakeans, Clive Hart and Fritz Senn, and since 1963 of the* James Joyce Quarterly. *Yet the basic difficulties with* Finnegans Wake *remain and the Wakeans have become less willing to speculate on overall ideas in the text.* Joyce's unusual self-involvement in Finnegans Wake is clearer than ever and readily discerned by almost all who read the book habitually, but the significance of that involvement seems murky to many. I still consider the presence of the artist in the work to be an identification of the antisocial writer with the common lot of humanity, but I would now add that an important touch of superstition is there as well: weaving oneself into the fabric is Joyce's figure in the carpet.*

In lieu of an overall meaning scholars have settled for explications of bits and pieces. Symbol-hunting and motif-hunting have been productive, as witness Clive Hart's "Index of Motifs" in his Structure *and Motif in* Finnegans Wake. *Under "Once upon a time" he finds nine echoes, although four of them fall short of the full "Once upon a time and a very good time it was." To the four of those that I had noted should be added a fifth: "once upon a spray what a queer and queasy*

First published: 9, no. 4 (1961): 257–71. Unrevised.

spree it was." Yet isolating motifs and symbols and foreign languages rarely brings us any closer to satisfactory explanation of the book, and often the successful accumulation of a large body of evidence finds itself its own reward. In investigating the ages of Shem and Earwicker I have since isolated 21 such references, ranging from 39 to 60, but almost all within the forties and fifties. Not always do they seem to be primarily ages, but are numbers that have primary meaning elsewhere and may be ages as well. Not often are they specifically attached to Shem or Earwicker, but since all characters eventually return to the basic five in the Wake, *this may not be a handicap. Only occasionally does a designation seem perfectly right, as in the instance Earwicker is listed as "most frifty," an allusion to Huck Finn's claim that his pap was "most fifty." Here the literary allusion serves as corroborative evidence, particularly because of Joyce's interest in that other "Finn" book.*

Some of the most valuable contributions in the past decade have been made by research into the manuscripts and notebooks, especially the work of David Hayman (A First Draft Version of Finnegans Wake), *Walton Litz* (The Art of James Joyce), *and Fred Higginson* (Anna Livia Plurabelle). *It becomes possible now to verify certain conjectures and watch others disintegrate under the microscope. My assumption that Judge Woolsey appears in the* Wake *as "woolies," regardless of the aptness in the text, must be scrapped: the passage was written before the judge delivered his monumental verdict on* Ulysses, *and as much as Joyce hoped to be prophetic in* Finnegans Wake, *it is not the scholar's function to substantiate prophecy. In fact, the new caution with regard to* Wake *criticism, although it does not prevent speculation, does limit the possibilities. No longer would I write a sentence that begins, "It is nonetheless obvious that Joyce is caricaturing himself in the* Wake," *even if it still seems perfectly obvious to me. Words of absolute authority like* obvious *are best deleted from any discussions of a work that is becoming less obvious as the exegeses accumulate.*

The extent to which James Joyce involves himself personally in the events of *Finnegans Wake* becomes important in the light of various accusations alluding to Joyce's withdrawal from society and his indifference to the plight of the artist in that society. The Stephen Dedalus who was of primary significance in *A Portrait of the Artist as a Young Man* as the young artist critical of his environment had become decidedly secondary in importance in *Ulysses* where the Leopold Bloom personification of the Joycean Everyman dominated the social landscape. Yet, as both Dedalus and Bloom contain aspects of Joyce's personality (an indication that the artist's insistence in *A Portrait* that he has been "refined out of existence" is an abstract metaphor for Joyce through which the "personal" artist reveals himself in relation to his environment), so also do Shem the Penman and H. C. Earwicker contain aspects of Joyce's personality. As such Shem and Earwicker are governed by the same laws of artistic reproduction that ordinarily control the autobiographic hero in the novel: that elements of degree and proportion temper the self-involvement of the author and produce something that is at once the artist as he sees himself and the artist as seen by the world which he sees. (Thomas Wolfe's contention, when charged with autobiographic involvement, that Lemuel Gulliver is the autobiographic creation of Jonathan Swift's mind, is a clear statement of that literary dictum.) When we see Shem, we see not Joyce, but a portrait of Joyce, a replica, a facsimile, and—most often—a caricature. In fact, Shem is best understandable as a caricature of the Stephen Dedalus we have already met, and is thus twice removed from reality. It is in this guise that Shem sees himself (or is seen by Shaun) as a character in someone's semi-autobiographic novel, and he laughs at the image of himself: "young Master Shemmy on his very first debouch at the very dawn of protohistory seeing himself such and such . . . asking, when is a man not a man?" (pp. 169–70).[1]

In burlesque fashion Joyce not only returns to his Stephen-hero stranded at the age of twenty-two at the end of *Ulysses,* but actually recapitulates the autobiographic events of the *Portrait* and its successor. The opening sentence of *A Portrait of the Artist,* "Once upon a time and a very good time it was there was a moocow," is echoed four times in *Finnegans Wake,* e.g., "Eins within a space and a wearywide space it wast ere wohned a Mookse" (p. 152).[2] This is more than a mere preoccupation with the universality of the fairy-tale opening, as J. S. Atherton maintains;[3] it is a conscious parody of that young man's novel about his young self, and the *Wake* goes on to restate the themes of *A Portrait* in comic form as a basis for the material on which the new work is built. It is characteristic of this reiteration of earlier material that Joyce magnifies the events of the first page of his *Portrait* into even larger proportions: Stephen as a baby wets his bed—"When you wet the bed, first it is warm then it gets cold"—and Jerry, the Shem-figure as a child, breaks the continuity of the dream by crying in the night—"A cry off" (p. 558)—and the anxious parents come to investigate. He has wet his bed in Stephen-fashion: "And he has pipettishly bespilled himself from his foundingpen as illspent from inkinghorn" (p. 563). This childish and involuntary act prefigures his career as a writer, and it is significant that Joyce's last work is not only in itself in cyclical form, but this bedwetting, occurring as it does toward the end of the night's sleep (and the flow of the river out to sea at morning), reverts to the opening of *A Portrait*—Joyce's autobiographic work also makes a complete cycle.

It is of course difficult to determine the dividing line between autobiographic fact and literary fiction, and Shem is often a composite of the biographer's Joyce and the author's Stephen. Two sections of the *Wake* in particular offer a mine of such information: Book I, chapter 7 (Shem the Penman) and Book II, chapter 1 (The Mime of Mick, Nick, and the Maggies). In tracing Stephen Dedalus through these pages we find that Shem like Stephen was sickly as a child: "one generally, for luvvomony hoped or at any rate suspected . . . that he would early turn out badly, develop hereditary pulmonary T.B." (p. 172); he is terrified by thunder: "Tumult, son of Thunder, self exiled in upon his ego a nightlong a shaking betwixtween white or reddr hawrors, noondayterrorised to skin and bone" (p. 184); and spends his time as a young man boasting to a companion during a stroll of his literary prowess:

[No one] ever nursed such a spoiled opinion of his monstrous marvellosity as did this mental and moral defective . . . Who was known to grognt rather than gunnard . . . while drinking heavily of spirits to that interlocutor . . . he used to pal around with . . . that he was avoopf (parn me!) aware of no other shaggspick, other Shakhisbeard . . . if reams stood to reason and his lankalivline

---

1. James Joyce, *Finnegans Wake* (New York: Viking, 1939). All parenthetical numbers refer to pages in this edition. Quotations include corrections made from Joyce's *errata.*

2. See p. 69, 1. 7; p. 453, 1. 20; p. 516, 1. 1.

3. *The Books at the Wake* (New York: Viking, 1959), p. 7.

lasted he would wipe alley english spooker, multaphoniaksically spuking, off the face of the erse. (Pp. 177–78)

Like Stephen, Shem declares his "non-serviam": "Do you hold yourself then for some god in the manger, Shehohem that you will neither serve not let serve, pray nor let pray?" (p. 188), and denounces the sacraments of the church (p. 227), swearing to pursue a program familiar to the reader of *A Portrait*—silence, exile, and cunning (p. 229). The family fortunes (like those of the Dedaluses) are in sad decline: "Ones propsperups treed, now stohong baroque" (p. 230), but young Shem, having penned his erotic-religious poem, muses over the possibility of failure as a poet:

who thought him a Fonar all, feastking of shellies by googling Lovvey, regally freytherem, eagelly plumed, and wasbut gumboil owrithy prods wretched some horsery megee plods coffin acid odarkery pluds dense floppens mugurdy. (P. 231)

Rather than a Shelley or a Lovelace, he might well become a poor journalistic doggerel-writer like such nineteenth-century Irish hacks as O'Reilly, McGee, O'Dogherty, or MacCarthy.[4] To avoid such pitfalls, Shem acknowledges his heritage from the Greeks and Hebrews—"that greekenhearted yude!" (p. 171)—and announces his exile from Ireland: "he would not throw himself in Liffey . . . he refused to saffrocake himself with a sod" (p. 172).

Even the grotesque caricature that opens the Shem chapter bears a resemblance to Joyce: "fortytwo hairs off his uncrown, eighteen to his mock lip, a trio of barbels from his megageg chin . . . all ears, an artificial tongue with a natural curl" (p. 169), suggesting Joyce's thinning hairline, sparse mustache (over his mocking lips), and slight chinbeard, his ear for language, and the style of his literary expression. He goes on to spoof (and explicate) that style in his explanation of Shem "unconsciously explaining, for inkstands, with a meticulosity bordering on the insane, the various meanings of all the different foreign parts of speech he misused" (p. 173). As a part of Shem's experiences is included his exile to Trieste, "his citadear of refuge" (p. 62), where he teaches at the "beurlads scoel" (p. 467), the "beerlitz" (p. 182), where he is "an Irish emigrant the wrong way out" (p. 190) and a cosmopolite, a "Europasianised Afferyank" (p. 191), having deserted the fine whiskey and good stout of Dublin to drink "some sort of rhubarbarous maundarin yellagreen funkleblue windigut diodying applejack squeezed from sour grapefruice" (p. 171). World War I finds him in Swiss exile (both from the war in Europe and the insurrection in his native land) with his drink and his pen:

on that surprisingly bludgeony Unity Sunday when the grand germogall allstar bout was harrily the rage between our weltingtoms extraordinary and our petty-thicks the marshalaisy and Irish eyes of welcome were smiling daggers down their backs, when the roth, vice and blause met the noyr blank and rogues and the grim white and cold bet the black fighting tans, categorically unimperatived by

---

4. Joseph Campbell and Henry Morton Robinson, *A Skeleton Key to* Finnegans Wake (New York: Harcourt, Brace, 1944), p. 148, n. 17, refers to them as "second-rate Irish-American journalist-poets," but Atherton (p. 104) stresses that they were "Irish minor poets" primarily.

the maxims, a rank funk getting the better of him, the scut in a bad fit of pyjamas fled like a leveret for his bare lives . . . kuskykorked himself up tight in his ink-battle house, badly the worse for boosegas, there to stay in afar for the life . . . he collapsed carefully under a bedtick from Schwitzer's . . . his cheeks and trousers changing colour every time a gat croaked. (Pp. 176–77)

The campaign of slander reputedly waged against him, the hints at his cultivated depravities, the broadsides, poems, and letters he wrote—Atherton notes that every early Joyce work is mentioned at least once in *Finnegans Wake*[5]—and difficulties concerning the publications of the earlier work are all part of Shem's background, directly derived from Joyce's own. Richard Ellmann's biography refers to Shaun's comments on the pirating of Shem's "unique hornbook" (p. 422);[6] many other such references can be noted, particularly the direct one about Samuel Roth, bow-dlerizer of *Ulysses,* in the passage on the Great War and the Easter Rebellion, where all wars become Joyce's personal war against the "roth, vice and blause": Roth, the Vice League, and the pale bluenoses. Even Judge Woolsey who finally ruled *Ulysses* acceptable in America is mentioned several pages later: "Was there ever heard of such lowdown blackguardism? Positively it woolies one to think over it" (p. 180).

But the highlight of the Shem chapter is the self-portrait of Joyce as the poet of the doomed world commenting on the destruction he has viewed in the world during his lifetime, a world's tribulations and his own, and even regret on the estrangement of the brothers—"O hell, here comes our funeral! O pest, I'll miss the post!" (p. 190). He addresses himself as a "sniffer of carrion, premature grave-digger, seeker of the nest of evil in the bosom of a good word" (p. 189), and although "blind," he sees the devastation wrought by the Easter Rebellion—"the dynamitisation of colleagues, the reducing of records to ashes, the levelling of all customs by blazes" (p. 189); he nonetheless involves himself in the affairs of the country which he felt he would "farsooner" (p. 171) desert, finding himself merrily fuming over his "new Irish stew" (p. 190). That stew may be interpreted as both the new Irish nation evolving from the ruins of rebellion and civil war—a nation that Joyce openly disavowed but apparently nursed a secret hope for—and his own literary *pot-au-feu,* again indicating that despite his misgivings and animosities Joyce closely associated his own fortunes with those of the Ireland that produced him.

There are many descriptions of Shem throughout *Finnegans Wake,* and with typically Joycean whimsey they contradict themselves with consistency. This is important if one assumes that autobiographically Joyce not only sees himself as the Shem-figure, the artist, the nonconformist, in the *Wake,* but also as the composite man, the synthesis of himself and his conformist brother with whom he forms the totality of the hero, Humphrey Chimpden Earwicker. Many references to age that have hitherto been overlooked occur throughout the book, both for Earwicker and Shem; and they invariably range between forty and the middle fifties—Joyce's age during the seventeen-year period in which he was composing his last work: Shem is "furtivefree yours of age" (p. 173) while Earwicker is "most frifty" (p. 25) and "a man of around fifty" (p. 506). A case might well be constructed in the light of Shem's age in the forties and Earwicker's in the fifties that Joyce, as he progressed during the writing of *Finnegans Wake,* might have come to realize

---

5. Atherton, pp. 106–10.

6. *James Joyce* (New York: Oxford University Press, 1959), p. 592.

the synthesis necessary in order to identify with Everyman; and it might therefore be significant that the final reference in the text to age occurs in Anna Livia's closing soliloquy, "fiftyseven" (p. 620), Joyce's age on the birthday-publication date of *Finnegans Wake.*

It is nonetheless obvious that Joyce is caricaturing himself in the *Wake,* even to the extent of harping upon his blindness and his famous black eyepatch: "a blind of black sailcloth over its wan phwinshogue . . . dejected into day and night with jesuit bark and bitter bite, calicohydrants of zolfer and scoppialamina by full and forty Queasisanos" (pp. 182–83); "the simian has no sentiment secretions but weep cataracts for all me, Pain the Shamman!" (p. 192). "I wisht I had better glances to peer to you" (p. 626), Anna Livia Plurabelle says, as she is flowing out to sea at the end of *Finnegans Wake,* strengthening the temptation to assert that Joyce's personal attempt to identify himself with the broadest expanse of humanity personified by Earwicker actually reaches its culmination in his final identification with the All-Woman who remains eternal.

But it is essentially Shem's preoccupation that Joyce is parodying in the *Wake;* Shem is writing a book—obviously *Finnegans Wake* itself—and it is in his many statements of purpose, descriptions of contents, and explanations of technique that Joyce proves himself to be writing a parody of a parody. *Finnegans Wake* is a "meandertale" (p. 18)—or "meanderthalltale" (p. 19)—in cyclical form, a "book of Doublends Jined" (p. 20) which is a

> continuous present tense integument slowly unfolded all marryvoising mood-moulded cyclewheeling history (thereby, he said, reflecting from his own individual personal life unlivable, transaccidentated through the slow fires of consciousness into a dividual chaos, perilous, potent, common to allflesh, human only, mortal) but with each word that would not pass away the squidself which he had squirtscreened from the crystalline world waned chagreenold and doriangrayer in its dudhud. (P. 186)

Here Joyce implies the use of the Viconian cyclical pattern of recurring history that he employs in *Finnegans Wake;* he is presenting the unfolding panorama of continuous history through his use of representative individuals who are characteristic of himself. His process is a conscious one—all the material he collects is fused through his consciousness: it is the material that constitutes his antagonists, man divided in chaos against himself. His domain is the realm of humankind; his technique is complicated by the smokescreen which, like the squid, he squirts over the clear water—the ink of his art that refuses to paint the story of man in terms of black and white, but insists upon realizing the various shadings, the dual character of Wilde's handsome Dorian and his distorted image, his real self.

This then is Shem, at once Joyce's self-portrait and self-caricature, a continuation of Stephen and a burlesque of him. At those instances when Shem is most like Joyce, his younger brother Shaun most resembles Joyce's brother, Stanislaus. Other prototypes for Shaun have been mentioned on occasion, including, as both Hugh Kenner and Richard Ellmann suggest,[7] Eamon De Valera, the successful Irish politician who was born the same year as Joyce; a reference to "Da Valorem's Dominical Brayers" (p. 342) is one of many linking De Valera to Shaun. Also,

---

7. Hugh Kenner, *Dublin's Joyce* (London: Chatto & Windus, 1955), pp. 357–59; Ellmann, p. 635.

since Shem is a continuation of Stephen, Shaun is a logical development of Malachi Mulligan (Oliver St. John Gogarty), the medical student who was taking his "varsatile examinations in the ologies" (p. 468). Together De Valera and Gogarty are present in the disintegration of Haun (Shaun the Ghost): "ere Molochy wars bring the devil era" (p. 473) to add a third level of meaning to the puns on the battles in heaven and in Ireland. But it is primarily Stanislaus who bears the brunt of Joyce's invective and emerges as the primary prototype for the bourgeois brother, as Joyce finds himself pitted against these three successful Irish nonartists, his professor brother, his doctor "friend," and his politician countryman. Only recent documentation begins to fill in the lacunae left by the "faithful" who formed Joyce's Paris circle, beginning with the publication in 1950 of Stanislaus Joyce's memoir—the two translations of which were individually titled *Recollections of James Joyce by His Brother* and "James Joyce: A Memoir"[8]—and reaching its culmination with Richard Ellmann's definitive biography in 1959. Both works present a portrait of the relationship between the brothers during their later years that makes the incidents in *Finnegans Wake* more meaningful. In the Fable of the Ondt and the Gracehoper, Joyce presents Shem as the carefree spendthrift and Shaun as the thrifty solid citizen, and although in his biography Ellmann sees Wyndham Lewis as the primary model for the Ondt,[9] his earlier article on the subject notes that

> James was extravagant in fancy and in finance, and the proceeds of Stanislaus's lessons often ended—after James, smiling and smoking a cigarette, had presented his latest need—in his brother's pocket. When James revamped in *Finnegans Wake* the fable of the dancing grasshopper and saving ant, he drew upon his experience with Stanislaus by letting the grasshopper carry the day.[10]

It should be noted that the Gracehoper has "jingled through a jungle of love and debts" (p. 416), while the Ondt, "a weltall fellow, raumybult and abelboodied, bynear saw altitudinous wee a schelling in kopfers" (p. 416)—the German words *raum* and *kopf* and the Austrian currency strongly suggest the prewar days in Trieste shared by James and Stanislaus Joyce.

No one who has ever read Stanislaus's admonitions to his brother concerning drinking and immorality, or has noted his impatience with the obscurities of *Ulysses* and *Finnegans Wake,* can fail to hear Stanislaus's voice issuing from the Ondt: "Grouscious me and scarab my sahul! What a bagateller it is! Libelulous! Inzanzarity! Pou! Pschla! Ptuh! What a zeit for the goths!" (p. 415) or hear him criticize Joyce's Paris coterie: "Let him be Artalone the Weeps with his parisites peeling off him I'll be Highfee the Crackasider. Flunkey Footle furloughed foul, writing off his phoney" (p. 418). But the Gracehoper forgives the Ondt's malice, as Joyce apparently forgave Stanislaus's when he sent him a copy of *Finnegans Wake*—which Stanislaus refused to accept. It is just this sort of moral unctuousness that must have precipitated the comment in the Night Lessons footnotes (written,

8. Stanislaus Joyce, *Recollections of James Joyce by His Brother*, trans. Ellsworth Mason (New York: James Joyce Society, 1950); "James Joyce: A Memoir," trans. Felix Giovanelli, *Hudson Review* 2 (Winter 1949): 485–514.

9. Ellmann, p. 608.

10. Ellmann, "The Grasshopper and the Ant—Notes on James Joyce and His Brother, Stanislaus," *The Reporter* 12 (Dec. 1956): 36.

not by Shem, as most commentators blithely assume, but by the far more impartial Issy): "The stanidsglass effect, you could sugerly swear buttermilt would not melt down his dripping ducks" (p. 277).

The controversy between John Henry Raleigh and Ellsworth Mason concerning the part played by Stanislaus as a model for Shaun can now be decided in Raleigh's favor in the light of Stanislaus's memoir and Ellmann's biography. Raleigh accurately perceived the "loving irony" of the guilty forgiving the innocent[11] in *Finnegans Wake,* where Joyce's flower girls sing the praises of their sun-god, Chuff (Shaun), in a long paean full of *double entendres* beginning: "Enchainted, dear sweet Stainusless, young confessor, dearer dearest" (p. 237). The biographical details from Stanislaus's life are minute in detail and carefully hidden, as Mason notes when he uncovers in this hymn of praise the significance of the mock-Egyptian phrase "Elleb Inam, Titep Notep" (p. 237), "which, spelled backwards as 'Belle mani, petit peton,' reflects the vanity about his hands and feet that Stanislaus actually had as a boy."[12] Such minutiae are neither accidental nor merely whims; Joyce is attempting to deal personally and privately as well as objectively with the real problems in his own life. His relationship with Stanislaus is important to him, and he deals with the brother conflict from apparent personal experience, working toward a synthesis that Stanislaus was unable to accept. It is significant that Joyce always allows Shem to apologize to Shaun (as after being beaten by Shaun during the Night Lessons): "I can't say if it's the weight you strike me to the quick or that red mass I was looking at but at the present momentum, potential as I am, I'm seeing rayingbogeys rings round me. Honours to you and may you be commended for our exhibitiveness!" (p. 304). Again in the "Ondt" fable it is the Gracehoper (Shem) who apologizes:

> I forgive you, grondt Ondt, said the Gracehoper, weeping,
> For their sukes of the sakes you are safe in whose keeping. (P. 418)

It is ironic, therefore, to note that Stanislaus refused to forgive (in refusing the proffered copy of the *Wake*), just as Joyce had predicted in the book when Shaun (as Prof. Jones), having been asked by Shem if he would help him save his soul, retorts, "No, blank ye! So you think I have impulsivism?" (p. 149). Remembering this gesture, we have only to read Stanislaus's account: "Joyce went to Paris, after which I saw him but rarely. I wrangled with him over *Finnegans Wake,* by correspondence and at different encounters in Paris, Salzburg, or Zurich."[13] He adds that when *"Finnegans Wake* was published, on the author's fifty-eighth [*sic*] birthday, my brother wrote to me offering a copy in homage. I refused it."[14] And his final comment on the subject reads: "There is little need to tell how much regret this refusal has since cost me—even less when the uselessness of all regret is considered."[15] It would be interesting, therefore, to know whether Prof. Joyce ever read a copy of the book he refused to accept, especially since his memoir

11. " 'My Brother's Keeper'—Stanislaus Joyce and 'Finnegans Wake,' " *Modern Language Notes* 68 (Feb. 1953): 108 *et passim.*

12. Ellsworth Mason, "Mr. Stanislaus Joyce and John Henry Raleigh," *Modern Language Notes* 70 (March 1955): 188, n. 3.

13. S. Joyce, "James Joyce: A Memoir," p. 512.

14. *Ibid.,* p. 514.

15. *Ibid.*

anticipates the theme of the antagonistic brothers in James Joyces's own Cain-Abel configuration: Stanislaus notes that in writing about James he runs the risk of "playing the part of Cain if I criticize and call a spade a spade."[16] James had already spared him that role by taking it for himself in the *Wake*.

It is the character of Shem, however, that most concerns us when investigating Joyce's actual participation in the portrait of the world that he saw around him; he viewed that world as torn between the antithetical aspects of the nature of contemporary man: his proper, moralistic brother and his amoral—if not immoral—artistic self. He attempts to move away from the introspective hero who began to wane in significance in *Ulysses* in order to concentrate on the nature of man around him, on the world in which he played an atypical but important role as the nonconforming artist. Joyce seeks to see beyond himself in portraying Shem, however; his Stephen was only a particular type of artist reacting to a particular environment; and no matter how typical that interaction may have been in his eyes, it had to be expanded to include every facet of the artist in every reaction to the hostile bourgeois. The contrast between Shaunness and Shemism is outstanding, of course; and many commentators have been alert to codify that contrast—particularly Campbell and Robinson in their *Skeleton Key* and J. Mitchell Morse in chapters 4 and 5 of *The Sympathetic Alien* (New York, 1959)—but one must note that Joyce seems to be singularly aware that any sort of even division of all attributes to either one type of man or the other is decidedly unreal. His purpose is to present these caricatures as two-dimensional facets of the nature of the single hero, of the Earwickerian Everyman who embodies both Shem and Shaun; whereas there is no single prototype for H. C. E., Shem and Shaun are based on nineteenth-century theatrical personages: Shaun is Dion Boucicault's Sean the Post, and Shem is an equally two-dimensional stage-Irishman, as John Peale Bishop notes:

> His name is a corruption of Jim the Penman, a forger in an old comedy that used to be played in Dublin, but under that name I think we shall find that Joyce has introduced himself into *Finnegans Wake,* just as in *The Portrait* [*sic*] and *Ulysses* he is brought in as Stephen Dedalus.[17]

Shem and Shaun exist in the *Wake* primarily as they are seen by their society, the bourgeois world accepting its hero in the guise of the stage Sean of *Arrah-na-Pogue* and its artistic villain as a harmless Richard Pigott, portrayed in the nineteenth century by Sir Charles Young's *Jim the Penman*. But behind the cardboard figure lurks the flesh-and-blood artist, the mature Joyce, conscious of his own excesses as "the artist as a young man," conscious of the world's view of the artist, but peering out at the world with a new artistic objectivity from behind the eye-slits of the painted face of the literary forger. Joyce is that forger in the dual sense of the word: as Stephen intended, he is forging "in the smithy of my soul the uncreated conscience of my race." Harry Levin views the figure of Joyce playing his part behind Shem's façade:

> From Shem to Seumas to James is an easy modulation for Joyce, and there can be no doubt that the autobiographical interest of the book is centered upon this

16. *Ibid.,* p. 485.
17. "Finnegans Wake," *Southern Review* 5 (Winter 1940): 445.

character, the black sheep of the family. In more than one passage Joyce seems to be announcing—in evasive jargon, to be sure—that he is Shem: "Immi ammi Semmi."[18]

The autobiographical aspects that Joyce chooses to include in the *Wake* are important: they reflect Joyce's attitude as an artist toward mankind and the world's attitude toward the artist; they are selected from the dual position of what Joyce thinks is important about his life and what the world chooses to highlight. As such Shem is at work on the same project:

> what do you think Vulgariano did but study with stolen fruit how cutely to copy all their various styles of signature so as one day to utter an epical forged cheque on the public for his own private profit. (P. 181)

Here is Shem, like Stephen, seeking the "signatures of all things" in order to write his epic while the world mistrusts his methods and motives—they see him creating a forgery while he sees himself forging with the hammer and anvil of his artistry. He predicts that his literary work will be obscure and difficult to comprehend but insists upon the inevitability and invincibility of communication among people (p. 232); he will tamper with language—"making a bolderdash for lubberty of speech" (p. 233)—even to the point of slaughtering language—"as raskly and as baskly as your cheesechalk cow cudd spanich" (p. 233) is Joyce's version of the French comment, *Il parle français comme une vache espagnole* (in itself containing the pun on *Basque-vache*)—but his literary jesting will be in earnest, for he will only be "letting on he'd jest be japers and his tail cooked up" (p. 233).

When any significant event in the author's life became magnified in importance to him, there was a good chance of its finding its way into *Finnegans Wake*. A pair of trousers twice played such a role: while in Rome, Herbert Gorman reports, Joyce worked in a bank:

> It was a sedentary occupation; Joyce sat down all day, and it was not long before the rapidly thinning seat of his solitary pair of trousers became one of his major problems in the Holy City. Towards the end of his first month (and it was an extremely hot August) he was gloomily announcing to his brother in Trieste: "There are two great patches on the seat of my trousers so that I cannot leave off my coat in the office and sit stewing for hours."[19]

And a second reference in Gorman's biography to trousers concerns a production of *The Importance of Being Earnest* in Zurich during the first World War,[20] but Gorman's "authorized" biography fails to mention that Joyce had cabled Prime Minister Lloyd George of England about the affair. Harry Levin notes that "when he cabled Lloyd George, who had other things on his mind during the first World War, *re* a pair of trousers and *The Importance of Being Earnest,* he was behaving like an aggrieved schoolboy unjustly pandied."[21] Perhaps Joyce realized that this was schoolboy behavior, for in the Night Lessons scene schoolboy Dolph notes in

18. *James Joyce* (Norfolk, Conn.: New Directions, 1941), pp. 161–62.
19. *James Joyce* (New York: Rinehart, 1948), p. 163.
20. *Ibid.*, p. 253, *passim.*
21. Levin, pp. 54–55.

the margin: *"How matches metroosers?"* (p. 280). And a reference to the earlier patched trouser seat in Rome is found during the Yawn inquest: "have you forgotten poor Alby Sobrinos, Geoff, you blighter, identifiable by the necessary white patch on his rear?" (p. 488).

As Joyce tells us, "he scrabbled and scratched and scriobbled and skrevened nameless shamelessness about everybody ever he met" (p. 182); the "official" biography of himself he refers to as *"the Martyrology of Gorman"* (p. 349). His mistress-wife, Nora Barnacle, is the "highbosomheaving Missmisstress Morna of the allsweetheartening bridemuredemeanour!" (p. 189) and he "barnacled up to the eyes when he repented after seven" (p. 423), which certainly seems to me to be a reference to Joyce's eventual marriage in 1931, some twenty-seven years after he and Nora had run off to the Continent together.

Biographer Gorman notes that "Mrs. McCormick was affronted when Joyce refused to be psychoanalyzed by Dr. Jung, a refusal, by the way, that he made flatly and angrily,"[22] thus losing Mrs. McCormick's patronage. And Joyce in *Finnegans Wake* adds his own explanation to this refusal;[23] the following dialogue takes place between the interrogators and the spook voice issuing from the exhausted body of Yawn:

> You have homosexual catheis of empathy between narcissism of the expert and steatopygic invertedness. Get yourself psychoanolised!
> —O, begor, I want no expert nursis symaphy from yours broons quadroons and I can psoakoonaloose myself any time I want (the fog follow you all!) without your interferences or any other pigeonstealer. (P. 522)

In the terminology of Joyce's psychology the initials of the father appearing here in *homosexual catheis of empathy* refer to the "Tiberiast duplex" (p. 123), the deposing of the father (H.C.E.-Tiberius) by the Christ-Shaun.[24] *Duplex* (dual Oedipus complex) and *narcissism* (certainly a characteristic of Shem as much as of Shaun) refer again to the split of the brothers, the ambivalence of love and hate that binds them and eventually synthesizes their differences. What Joyce refused from Jung personally he accepted from Jung's books professionally: the concept of the collective unconscious permeates *Finnegans Wake;* the history of the race lies dormant in the brain of Everyman-Earwicker and manifests itself in his epic dream. This is "the law of the Jungerl" (p. 268), and Joyce, like Jung, is one of the "grisly old Sykos who have done our unsmiling bit on 'alices, when they were yung and easily freudened" (p. 115); and Joyce, like his Alice-Iseult heroine, records:

> I will write down all your names in my gold pen and ink. Everyday, precious, while m'm'ry's leaves are falling deeply on my Jungfraud's Messongebook I will dream telepath posts dulcets on this isinglass stream (but don't tell him or I'll be the mort of him!). (P. 460)

Joyce seems to object to the malice of practicing psychoanalysis (*Sykos on 'alices*) but allows himself to psychoanalyze the entire race through the depiction of the

---

22. Gorman, p. 264.
23. See Atherton, pp. 38–39.
24. Campbell and Robinson, p. 15, n. 17.

sleeping mind of the individual. In his own guise Joyce comments on the Jung affair in a letter to Harriet Weaver dated 24 June 1921:

> A batch of people in Zurich persuaded themselves that I was gradually going mad and actually endeavoured to induce me to enter a sanatorium where a certain Doctor Jung (the Swiss Tweedledum who is not to be confused with the Viennese Tweedledee, Dr. Freud) amuses himself at the expense (in every sense of the word) of ladies and gentlemen who are troubled with bees in their bonnets.[25]

Despite the complex nature of the disassociated personalities in *Finnegans Wake,* of the opposite natures of the brothers uniting to form the *gestalt* of the father's personality, a dominant motif is sounded that identifies James Joyce with the essence of his text on contemporary man. That he drew upon his own experiences, his life, his family, his own personality, becomes readily apparent as we trip over numerous personal asides in *Finnegans Wake.* The death of Professor Stanislaus Joyce, whose *My Brother's Keeper* (New York, 1958) terminates short of including the important Trieste days in the lives of the Joyce brothers, now leaves only the written words of James and Stanislaus as a record of their relationship. Of the manuscripts from both camps *Finnegans Wake* stands as the most complete (if highly and fancifully fictionalized) statement of their mutual antagonism and affection, a vastly subjective transcript that the author signs with his own name and his pseudonym:

"Shem is as short for Shemus as Jem is joky for Jacob" (p. 169).

---

25. Stuart Gilbert, ed., *Letters of James Joyce* (New York: Viking, 1957), p. 166.

Unposted Letter: Joyce's Leopold Bloom

JOHN Z. BENNETT

In the Nausicaa episode of *Ulysses,* as Leopold Bloom rests upon his rock, already weary of his "very fatiguing day," he takes up a bit of stick and begins to write in the sand yet another of the book's innumerable "riddling sentences": "I AM A. . . ." But there is no more room, and the all-important "other word" is never added (p. 375).[1]

Bloom's critics of forty years, however, have supplied it indefatigably, and he has been made manifest in an astonishing variety of persons and attributes. He is Odysseus, or Christ (or a parody of Christ, or an unrealized Christ), or he is Adam, or the Flesh, or the Lion-as-Vegetable, or the Common Man in Isolation, or Everyman Afoot, and so on through transmutations as imaginative as those he suffers in Nighttown, until he becomes at last, inevitably, a mere robot.

Everyone understands that Joyce's artistic method—that of "manipulating what at first sight seems to be mere physical detail into dramatic symbolism"[2]— requires, invites, even dares such archetypal readings. But it may well be wondered whether, in such a plethora of solutions, it is not gratuitous to worry the puzzle further. Bloom himself rejects the effort and rubs away his letter to Gerty McDowell: "Hopeless thing, sand. Nothing grows in it. All fades" (p. 375). Furthermore, as R. M. Adams has remarked, there is a very real danger of vitiating criticism by "treating *Ulysses* as an enigma, not a novel."[3]

If the problem could be left at that, all would be well, no doubt. But the work *is* an enigma: even its most confident explicators have a curiously predictable tendency to begin in certitude and order only to end in frantic and fragmented pursuits of details through its interminable mazes. After all, merely as far as Bloom

First published: 14, no. 1 (1966): 1–3. Unrevised. Professor Bennett died in 1972.

1. All page references to *Ulysses* are to the Modern Library edition (New York, 1946).

2. Caroline Gordon, ed., *The House of Fiction* (New York: Scribner, 1950), p. 279.

3. *Surface and Symbol: The Consistency of James Joyce's* Ulysses (New York: Oxford University Press, 1962), p. 33.

himself is concerned, who *was* Phil Gilligan? And what was the quarrel about meadowland evaluations at Cuffes? And if at long last we have discovered where Moses was when the lights went out, still who is M'Intosh, that "once prosperous cit" who "loves a lady that is dead" (pp. 420, 327)? And *do* fish ever get seasick (p. 372)?

The number of such questions may eventually be raised to Bloom's own version of infinity, that is, to the 9th power of the 9th power of 9; but what is worse, such is Joyce's cunning, we cannot tell whether any problem is major or minor until all have been made relevant in the ultimate harmony of the book. We cannot, with Bloom, rub the sentence out.

The purpose of this study, therefore, is to confront yet once again the riddle of Leopold Bloom, generally as it is relevant to his "personal" role in the novel, and specifically as it is posed by his relationship to Molly, or, as it is stated in the inimitable style of Martha Clifford, whoever she is: "Are you not happy in your home you poor little naughty boy?" (p. 76).

It would seem that nothing could be more obvious than the answer to this question: dishonored, betrayed, a servant to the woman who treats him with scorn or indifference, Bloom is a very unhappy man in his home. His marriage is on the rocks, and indeed it has been for many years. What is not so apparent, however, especially in the symbolistic readings of Bloom, is why the marriage has foundered. On the contrary, such readings tend to obscure Bloom's identity as a "husband" in the novel, and particularly to obviate the literal and very real pain he suffers in being Poldy the Cuckold. Yet it is quite clear, for instance, that from the moment Bloom first sees Boylan's "bold hand" until he escapes into sleep, if indeed he does escape, the agony of his wife's latest infidelity is never dulled.

And to say that Bloom transcends these betrayals in the "equanimity" of knowing that adultery is no worse than a host of other sins creates more difficulties than it resolves. It is only in the dehumanized technic of Ithaca that such a judgment is possible; but then human problems also become entirely meaningless when they are so reduced to weights and measures. And furthermore, Bloom's equanimity looks very much like that same "inertia" which keeps him from deserting the house entirely (p. 713).[4]

In all justice, it may be argued, as many critics do argue, that the marriage of Leopold and Molly is not yet an absolute loss. There is still a kind of fondness between them. For Leopold, Molly in violet petticoats is still worth the horrendous and humiliating effort to get a modicum of sober sense out of Myles Crawford. And from Molly's point of view, it is pleasant to hear Poldy stumbling up the stairs with her breakfast; and, regarding his explanations of esoteric matters, if his efforts "leave us as wise as we were" (p. 729), "still he knows a lot of mixed up things" (p. 728).

But these values are ambiguous, ironically measuring, as well, Bloom's weakness and Molly's tyranny. There is little rapport, not to say faith between them. The meek Leopold is an incorrigible Don Juan, in thought if not always in deed: among the conquests in the bedroom of his brain are the lady at the Grosvenor, the girl in Eustace Street settling her garters, another running up the stairs at Greene's, as well as Lotty Clarke, Mrs. Miriam Dandrade, Bridie Kelley, Josie Powell "that was," Gerty McDowell, Mary Driscoll, Martha Clifford, and forty-four

---

4. For interesting "objections" to Joyce's science, see Adams, pp. 181 ff.

other applicants for the job of assisting a gentleman in the literary business of exchanging obscene letters.

And Molly it would seem (aside from her novels and her erotic reveries embracing thoughts of priests, Negroes, drunken sailors, violent assault by unknown men, and so on) has committed adultery with virtually every man Leopold knows and with a goodly number whom neither he nor Molly can even name.

Adams has questioned whether we are to take this estimate of Molly's lovers seriously. While granting the nymphomaniac tone of Molly's thoughts, he demonstrates that before Boylan it is quite possible that she had no adulterous relations with any of the "suitors," save possibly Bartell D'Arcy (p. 730).[5]

This opinion seems to be borne out by Bloom's own reactions to Boylan. It is true, for instance, that he thinks of various men in erotic relation to Molly—as Val Dillon, Lenehan, Father Farley, the gentleman with the opera glasses in the Gaiety Theatre, and others—but the irritation in these thoughts seems mild compared with his agony concerning Boylan's advent.

Furthermore, as opposed to the other affairs, the liaison with Boylan has a clear and definite history. Molly, apparently unknown to Leopold, has first seen Boylan in the D.B.C., where the communication of the "bold eye" together with a bit of foot eroticism was first effected (p. 729). But to Bloom's knowledge, and correctly, their first formal introduction occurred when "The full moon was the night we were Sunday fortnight . . . Walking down by the Tolka" (p. 165), that is, 29 May 1904,[6] the night May's band played Ponchielli's "Dance of the Hours" (pp. 69, 165, 368, 518, 725).

It was during the walk by the Tolka River that Boylan signaled the immemorial question upon Molly's hand and received her inevitable response. The date is very significant, for, as will be substantiated more fully, it was on this night of 29 May 1904, that Molly and Bloom last had sexual relations (p. 725).[7]

Yet the following morning Molly asks the fateful question about Boylan, and Bloom is overwhelmed: "No use humming then" (p. 69). The judgment implicit in Molly's behavior is obvious: Bloom is an inadequate lover. And the choice of the "usurper" is being announced. This fact is perfectly clear to Leopold, so much so that within the succeeding weeks he will send Milly away to Mullingar, a move that Molly understands for what it really means, and indeed actually approves of (p. 751).

The ascendancy of Boylan then becomes a constant and pervasive agony in Bloom's consciousness.[8] But whether Blazes is the literal-first or imaginative-latest in the series of Molly's infidelities, the marital betrayal, fact or fiction, is real to Leopold. And indeed perhaps its most sinister aspect is that it calls forth in him a profound pessimism, a sense of the "useless," the hopeless, a feeling of the unalterable futility of effort. Feelings of despair are dominant in Bloom's notions of Fate, Kismet, the circular stream of life: "Think you're escaping and run into

5. Adams, p. 37.

6. C. R. Cheney, ed., *Handbook of Dates for Students of English History* (London: Royal Historical Society, 1955), Table 13, p. 108.

7. This is a period of 18 days, evidently another example of Joyce's use of the "closed field," as hypothecated by Hugh Kenner in "Art in a Closed Field," *Virginia Quarterly Review* 38 (Autumn 1962): 604.

8. For further evidence of Boylan's intrusions, see pp. 61, 62, 63, 69, 74, 76, 91, 101, 122, 151, 152, 165, 170, 172, 180, 256, 260, 262, 268, 276, 363, 368, 375, 410, 518, 529, 550, 560, 561, 609, 626, 631, 634, 635, 638, 639, 717.

yourself" (p. 370), in the recurring thought that "all is lost," even becoming objectified in the watch that stops, "just when he and she" (p. 370).

Bloom's end is in its origins: love began as musical chairs and charades, or, as Molly says, "staring at one another for about 10 minutes as if we met somewhere" (p. 756). It ends in jangling quoits, met him pikehoses, and a literal Rip Van Winkle-Bloom. "Me," says Bloom, remembering with fervor and eloquence the great moment of the Howth Hill picnic, "and me now" (p. 173). The same memory leads to Molly's much considered "Yes"; but for Leopold it is only "Stuck, the flies buzzed" (p. 174).

Admittedly, this view of the Blooms' marital situation and of the primal importance of Molly's infidelity makes an assumption regarding Leopold's viability as a lover that has not been generally urged. Adams, for example, on the basis of the evidence (pp. 720–21) in *Ulysses,* agrees with the opinion that for ten years Molly "has been deprived of all sexual contact with her husband."[9] If this is so, then of course there is justification for Molly's treatment of Leopold.

The passage in question asserts of Leopold and Molly: "complete carnal intercourse, with ejaculation of semen within the natural female organ, having last taken place . . . 27 November 1893 . . . there remained a period of 10 years, 5 months and 18 days during which carnal intercourse had been incomplete, without ejaculation of semen within the natural female organ."[10] The important term in this commentary is *incomplete,* a term that does not imply continence, but on the contrary suggests rather some form of sexual congress brought to "unnatural" termination, or, in other words, a form of contraception, and specifically that form known as *coitus interruptus.*

Obviously such an interpretation assumes that Bloom is sexually potent, a power also not always granted him by his less generous critics, and not without reason. Bella-Bello Cohen, for instance, accuses him in these terms: "What else are you good for, an impotent thing like you?" (p. 528).

But surely Bloom's response to Gerty McDowell on Sandymount cancels this objection. And certainly Molly's evidence gives no support to the libel; for it is the speculation regarding *what* woman Leopold has been with, not whether he has been with one, that sets her entire monologue in motion: "Yes because he never did a thing like that before as ask to get his breakfast in bed with a couple of eggs . . . yes he came somewhere Im sure by his appetite anyway love its not or hed be off his feed thinking of her so either it was one of those night women . . . or else if its not that its some little bitch or other he got in with somewhere or picked up on the sly" (pp. 723–24).

Facile as Molly is at proving both sides of an argument with the same bit of evidence, the assumption of Bloom's potency is not controverted by her ambiguous response to his evident "appetite." Furthermore, in the process of "syllogizing" she reveals a significant fact: "Yes because he couldn't possibly do without it that long so he must do it somewhere and the last time he came on my bottom *when was it the night Boylan gave my hand a great squeeze going along by the Tolka* (p. 725, italics mine). This date, as has been shown, is 29 May 1904, not 1894. It would seem evident, then, that the Blooms have indeed had sexual con-

---

9. Adams, pp. 37–38.
10. This is evidently also a "Jesuit jibe." Compare Father Conmee's speculations regarding the first Countess of Belvedere and her husband's brother: ". . . if she had not committed adultery fully, *eiaculatio seminis inter vas naturale mulieris"* (p. 220).

gress through the decade since 1894, but relations carried on under some form of contraception, presumably *coitus interruptus.*

This hypothesis might explain in part why Molly is so dissatisfied with Bloom as a lover. Whether correct or not, sexologists have long asserted that *coitus interruptus* is a technique of dubious value. Dorothy D. Bromley, for instance, reports that "Urologists are particularly severe in their condemnation of *coitus interruptus* as the cause of various functional and nervous disorders in men. . . . But there is no doubt that the practice often causes nervous disturbances in women." [11]

Molly, it will be recalled, will not sleep with the lights out (p. 748), and as for Bloom's technique as a lover "he ought to give it up now at this age of his life simply ruination for any woman and no satisfaction in it pretending to like it till he comes and then finish it off myself anyway" (p. 725). And "I'm not an old shrivelled hag before my time living with him so cold never embracing me . . . a woman wants to be embraced 20 times a day" (p. 756); "he wont let you enjoy anything naturally" (p. 756); and, finally, "its all his own fault if Im an adulteress" (p. 765).

Furthermore, Bloom carries in his pocketbook a "French letter" (pp. 364, 757), the term being an old euphemism for the contraceptive sheath, or, as it is called elsewhere in *Ulysses,* the "preservative." Bloom has a supply of these sheaths in the locked drawer of his desk—a drawer that Molly has thoroughly investigated, of course. They were ordered, it appears, from the same London establishment from which Bloom secured the obscene postcards (p. 706), an association that suggests "perversion," and indeed Bloom himself says of the French letter, "cause of half the trouble" (p. 364). Needless to say, however, any form of contraception in Catholic Dublin would be considered immoral, and this is especially true of *coitus interruptus,* for it is also a true form of onanism.[12]

Lastly, it is evident that Molly herself employs yet another contraceptive technique: "So much the better in case any of it wasnt washed out properly" (p. 727).

Unpleasant as this sort of investigation certainly is, it nonetheless reorders any view of Bloom's "sin against fertility," as W. Y. Tindall puts it,[13] and makes Bloom's motivations even more puzzling. If the nature of the "sin" is clear, then the more urgent question is why, in the face of such devastating consequences, and from no real physical necessity, does he continue to commit it?

In an answer to this question it may be of value to attempt a survey of the Blooms' courtship and marriage.

Their romance, which had begun at Dillon's in musical chairs and vocal solos, was continued at Luke Doyle's in charades, developed in Poldy's love poetry and erotic letters (p. 732), took the form of Bloom's perversity concerning drawers— but then bloomers were *named* after Mr. Bloom (p. 746)—and was physically

11. *Birth Control: Its Use and Misuse* (New York: Harper & Bros., 1934), pp. 70, 72; Sigmund Freud, in 1894, "The Justification for Detaching from Neurasthenia a Particular Syndrome: the Anxiety-Neurosis," *Collected Papers* (London: Hogarth, 1948), 1:88; Victor W. Eisenstein, *Neurotic Interaction in Marriage* (New York: Basic Books, 1956), p. 112.

12. *Ibid.,* p. 67.

13. *James Joyce: His Way of Interpreting the Modern World* (New York: Scribner, 1950), p. 115.

consummated on Howth Hill, presumably, on the 8th of September, 1888, Molly's 18th birthday (pp. 720–21).

They were married a month later on the 8th of October, 1888. Millicent, the daughter, was born on the 15th of June, 1889, though there is no evidence that the augury of Milly in 1888 either hastened the marriage or was a source of trouble between Leopold and Molly. On the contrary, Milly was, from Padney Socks to Silly-Milly, a great joy to Bloom. It is the vision of Milly that frees his mind from the wasteland of Agendath (p. 61), and perhaps from the horrific advent of the beasts, the murderers of the sun, in the lying-in hospital (p. 407). And Molly, too, though characteristically changeable in her attitude, admits that Milly is like herself and rightly belongs in the general female conspiracy against Bloom: when Milly breaks the little statue of Narcissus, Molly has it repaired without telling Leopold (p. 751).

Even so, it is evident in Milly's reports of Bannon and the picnic they are to take on Monday that the pattern of loss is about to be repeated, and with regret Bloom understands that Milly too is slipping away from him.[14]

At this point it would be assuring if the various removals of the Blooms through the years of their marriage could be determined accurately. However, as Adams has shown, it is impossible to untangle the Blooms' affairs.[15] It is certain that in the early days of their marriage they continued on friendly terms with old acquaintances—the Dillons, Mastianskys, Moisels, and Citrons. "Pleasant old times," Bloom reflects (p. 60). And Molly recalls with undiminished pleasure the irritation she was able to give Josie Powell by becoming Mrs. Bloom (pp. 728–29).

Through these years, 1888 to 1894, Bloom was working for Wisdom Hely, "a traveller for blotting paper," as Ned Lambert contemptuously puts it (p. 105). But if Bloom was not particularly successful in impressing Hely with his advertising schemes, he certainly was "happy in his home" during this period.

> Happy. Happier then. Snug little room that was with the red wallpaper, Dockrell's one and ninepence a dozen. Milly's tubbing night. American soap I bought: elderflower. Cosy smell of her bathwater. Funny she looked soaped all over. Shapely too. Now photography. (P. 153)

But in 1894 Bloom lost the job at Hely's, and he and Molly moved, evidently to Holles Street, where they were "on the rocks" and Bloom was reduced to peddling Molly's hair (p. 363), and she herself to selling clothes and playing the piano in the Coffee Palace (p. 738).

Adams has pointed out that Bloom's memory of the decade since 1894 is very hazy, notably lacking in detail, while his recollections of the years through 1894 are remarkably clear and rich in events.[16] Bloom, like anyone else, seeks to avoid the remembrance of events that were painful or humiliating (his characteristic formula is to change the subject by fertile association with something harmless); and, therefore, his fuzziness or downright suppression of memory concerning the decade since 1894 suggests that the "trauma" in his marriage occurred in that year.

---

14. Bannon gives this relationship a sinister turn when he decamps from Burke's apparently because he has learned that Bloom is "Photo's Papli" (p. 416).

15. Adams, pp. 186–89.

16. *Ibid.*, p. 188.

And indeed a calamity did befall the Blooms in the winter of 1893–94, namely, the death of their newborn son, Rudy.

All was well until then, and Bloom was a proud and solicitous expectant father. "Got big then. Had to refuse the Greystones concert. My son inside her" (p. 88). He remembers going down to the pantry at night to get Malaga raisins for Molly, "before Rudy was born" (p. 149). And one of the Bloom-jokes enjoyed by the drunken heroes at Kiernan's is told by Ned Lambert (in the dyed suit): "you should have seen Bloom before that son of his that died was born. I met him one day in the south city markets buying a tin of Neave's food six weeks before the wife was delivered" (p. 332).

The Blooms last had what would be called "normal," not to say "moral" marital relations on 27 November 1893. Rudy was born a month later on 29 December 1893, and died eleven days following, on 9 January 1894 (p. 720). It is significant, surely, that this is the date from which has been calculated the ten-year period of the so-called sexual denial of Molly.

The death of Rudy was a catastrophe of the first order for Leopold and Molly. Bloom did not cease, in all the intervening years, to mourn the lost son. Rudy is always just at the fringes of his consciousness.

Mrs. Thornton, he remembers, "knew from the first poor little Rudy wouldn't live. Well, God is good, sir. She knew at once. He would be eleven now if he had lived" (p. 66). And hearing Simon Dedalus's tirade against Mulligan, Bloom thinks, "Full of his son. He is right. Something to hand on. If little Rudy had lived. See him grow up. Hear his voice in the house. Walking beside Molly in an Eton suit" (p. 88). Later, in the Hades episode, he thinks, "a dwarf's face mauve and wrinkled like little Rudy's was. Dwarf's body, weak as putty, in a whitelined deal box" (p. 94). In the cemetery he calls to mind the location of his own burial plot, where his mother lies, and little Rudy (p. 109). And Ben Dollard's rendition of "The Croppy Boy" forces the comparison: "I too, last my race. Milly young student. Well, my fault perhaps. No son. Rudy" (p. 280).

As Sir Leopold, he grieves for the "only manchild which on his eleventh day on live had died," and recalls that "the good lady Marion . . . was wondrous stricken of heart for that evil hap and for his burial did him on a fair corselet of lamb's wool . . . lest he might perish utterly and lie akeled" (p. 384). Molly remembers this as well: "I suppose I oughtnt to have buried him in that little woolly jacket I knitted crying as I was" (p. 763).

Nonetheless, back of this grief there is a curious ambiguity in Bloom's feelings, a sense not only of loss but also of personal failure as a man, a sense even of guilt. "Our. Little. Beggar. Baby. Meant nothing. Mistake of nature. If it's healthy it's from the mother. If not the man" (p. 94).[17]

At the moment, a funeral coach bearing the body of a child has just passed, and, therefore, it is clear that Bloom is thinking generally about infant mortality—a question he chooses to discuss later at the lying-in hospital. But the thought turns strangely into a kind of dreadful folk-logic, which, whether he believes it or

---

17. Rudy was conceived under characteristic Bloomian conditions, in Raymond Terrace and at an open window overlooking two dogs copulating in the street. Both Leopold and Molly attest to this report, though evidently Molly did not see the "sergeant grinning up" (pp. 83, 763). It is one of the many curious coincidences of the book that the singer to whom Molly hurls a coin is a militaryman-beggar who is described as one who "jerks, growls, and bays" (p. 222).

not, is a superstition he has had to live with: if the child is sickly, or if the child dies, the failure is in the nature of the father. Molly appears to agree with this logic: "that have a fine son like that theyre not satisfied and I none *was he not able to make one it wasn't my fault*" (p. 763, italics mine).

The phrases of Bloom—"dwarf's mauve face," "mistake of nature," "Mrs. Thornton knew at once," "poor little Rudy,"—when paralleled by Molly's "whats the use of going into mourning for what was neither one thing nor another" (p. 759), suggest that Rudy was not only sickly, but perhaps malformed, and therefore that Bloom, in the context of the superstition, has real reason not only for grief but also for guilt and for feeling that a judgment has been passed on his manhood.

Perhaps now the "logic" of Bloom's trauma can be formulated: having failed so horrifically in procreation, Bloom fears the risk of another child, with all its attendant possibilities of death; but this rejection of "something to hope for, not like the past you can't have back" (p. 101) paralyzes him as a viable and virile paterfamilias.

This too is the meaning of the accusation that is made against him in the voice of Carlyle in Oxen of the Sun. Indeed, the principal subject of the episode is that of human fertility; and the major human crime in this regard is "Copulation without population!" (p. 416). Therefore, the praise of Theodore Purefoy is the curse of Leopold: "In her lay a Godframed Godgiven preformed possibility which thou hast fructified with thy modicum of man's work" (p. 416). For all its ludicrous bombast and echo of a drunken Stephen, the judgment has the ring of truth; and as for Bloom, "Has he not nearer home a seedfield that lies fallow for the want of a ploughshare?"—this hypocrite who is "his own and his only enjoyer" (p. 402)? And he must hear Stephen hysterically yet quite ironically assert that the thunder is the voice of the God Bringforth, passing damnation on all who have refused to realize the godpossible by the use of the Preservative Killchild (p. 389). Later, in Circe, Bloom will be accused by Purefoy: "He employs a mechanical device to frustrate the sacred ends of nature" (p. 482). And it should be noted that the black mass in honor of "Dog" is performed by the spoiled priests under the preservative umbrella (p. 583).

Allowing for extravagance and for the hallucinatory character of these scenes, the personal evidence of Leopold and Molly nonetheless confirms their essential truth and makes it clear that the death of Rudy was indeed the crisis in their lives that was not then and has not yet been resolved. "Twenty-eight I was," says Bloom. "She was twenty-three when we left Lombard street west something changed. *Could never like it again after Rudy*" (p. 165, italics mine). And in sad echo, Molly recalls: "I knew well Id never have another our 1st death too it was *we were never the same since*" (p. 763, italics mine).

Indeed they were not. The move from Lombard Street led merely to the inevitable pattern of successive removals and multitudinous jobs that has brought them to Eccles Street and an "Unfurnished apartment to let."

If, as it appears, Bloom's reaction to the death of his son has left him caught in a net of grief and guilt, in fact, one with his father, with Mrs. Sinico, with the "once prosperous cit," even with Athos, the dog, in "the love that kills" (p. 113), it remains to be considered whether any salvation has been effected by his odyssey. And this question most obviously centers on the vision of Rudy that occurs at the conclusion of Circe.

Stuart Gilbert has maintained that the vision is "a tranquil close after the bestiality," and this calm is the signal that the "wave-worn mariner who, riding out a tempest mad with magic, has made at last the haven where he would be."[18] Whether this means that Bloom has "worked through" his own psychic difficulties and has identified "would be" with what yet "could be" is uncertain. It is true that at one point during the day he has thought of the possibility of having another child: "Too late now. Or if not? If not? If still?" (p. 280). And even Molly considers it, though, it must be admitted, with undisguised scorn: "yes thatd be awfully jolly" (p. 727).

But it is more likely that Gilbert, like Tindall and all subsequent critics who have emphasized the "paternity motif" in Ulysses, intends to say that the mystical estate of fatherhood is about to be conferred on Bloom in the person of Stephen Dedalus and that the vision of Rudy is no more than its sign and seal.

And, indeed, the correspondences are remarkable, in that the vision of Rudy seems to be a complex of elements from Stephen's own experience as well as from Leopold's. For instance, it is Stephen who has thought of himself as a "changeling," as Rudy is described: thinking of Dublin in Viking times, Stephen imagines the "horde of jerkined dwarfs . . . I moved among them on the frozen Liffey, that I, a changeling, among the spluttering resin fires" (p. 46). Bloom and Molly both recall seeing Stephen at Dillon's long ago, "in his lord Fauntleroy suit and curly hair like a prince on the stage" (pp. 414–15, 664, 759). Bloom has imagined Rudy in an Eton suit, and has himself appeared so dressed in his memory of his own father (p. 431). The lamb Rudy carries probably derives from the woolly jacket Molly knitted. The ruby and diamond buttons recall Stephen's response to jewelry (p. 238), though Bloom also has had associations enough with "ruby" and has even thought of diamonds: "Jewels diamonds flash better" in the dusk (p. 369). As for the glass shoes, Stephen wears "a Buck's castoffs" (p. 50), and both Stephen and Bloom have been uncomfortable in ill-mended socks (pp. 208, 88). Rudy is reading the Hagaddah, and ironically, we learn later that Bloom's father's Hagaddah has been marked with the old gentleman's glasses at the prayers for Passover (p. 708). The bronze helmet is curious: perhaps it suggests the gear of knighthood, since Rudy is Sir Leopold's son; or perhaps it is a grim jest, continuing the medics' obscenities regarding the French capotes. The violet ribbon on Rudy's ivory cane calls to mind Molly's violet garters (p. 362) and Bloom's purple ones (p. 696). And the cane itself may be a transmutation of Stephen's "familiar" and of Bloom's stick from the beach.

Nonetheless, such a synthesis is not fully convincing; a vision of Rudy is hardly a surprise in the world of Circe. Bloom has thought of Rudy all through the day, and the vision's meaning, aside from being an inevitable idealization, is not clear. Like so many of Joyce's symbols, this one seems indeterminable, ambiguous—as easily the symbol of the irretrievably lost as of the hope conceivably found. At best this ambiguity suggests only that choices are still available to Bloom.

And in fact changes are indicated—not monumental, but significant. Leopold has ordered breakfast in bed, a remarkably bold move for a man who has been a servant for so many years—a bold move, and one undertaken in the most obvious and the most likely field of action.

But, as always, whether Molly will comply is not for mere man to say. "Hopeless thing, sand." A hopeless thing, too, is the task of governing Molly Bloom.

---

18. James Joyce's Ulysses (New York: Vintage Books, 1955), p. 348.

"Death Among the Apple Trees":
The Waves and the World of Things

FRANK D. McCONNELL

Northwestern University

COMMENT BY THE AUTHOR

If I were starting to write "Death Among the Apple Trees" today, I believe I would be a good deal less defensive about the romantic overtones of Virginia Woolf's great novel—a novel, by the way, that rereading and teaching have rendered only more impressive and moving to me—and a good deal more assertive about the perennial importance and growing influence of Virginia Woolf on contemporary fiction. Today I received a prospectus of the English Institute's 1974 program of seminars, one of which is a series of "Revaluations of Virginia Woolf." Quentin Bell's magnificent biography has appeared since I wrote my essay, and has helped us immeasurably to see the profound contemporaneity not only of Mrs. Woolf's fiction but of the agonies and solaces that were the landscape of her psychic life. And, most significantly, what seemed in 1968 to be the new objectivism of post-existentialist fiction, both here and in France, has very largely evolved into just such a delicate, problematic transaction between inner and outer worlds as I find articulated in The Waves.

Robbe-Grillet, whose The Erasers *furnished me my example of a "Woolfian" contemporary passage, has evolved even further toward the "playpoem" atmosphere of* The Waves—*or, perhaps, even more so of* Between the Acts. *His* Project for a Revolution in New York *takes the concerns of the objectivist novel in the only direction, really, they had left to go: into a visionary cinema of the mind, an "objectivism" that is distinguished from free fantasy only by its tough-minded recognition of its own fantastic nature. Muriel Spark, after the hard-edged, ironic triumphs of* Memento Mori *and* The Girls of Slender Means, *has lately given us a*

First published: 16, no. 3 (1968): 23–39. Slightly revised.

49

series of books—The Driver's Seat, Not to Disturb, The House by the East River—*which move more and more toward the determinative and definitive fissure of the modern mind, the articulation of the cleft between the universes inside and outside the head, and the recognition that fiction, if it inhabits anywhere, inhabits the no-man's-land between those warring cosmos. And, of course, in America, the recent work of John Barth* (Chimera), *John Gardner* (Jason and Medeia), *and particularly Thomas Pynchon* (Gravity's Rainbow) *has defined what I believe to be the most romantic and most complex vision of any contemporary national literature—a vision which, while it may not owe any conscious debts to the bitter, broken romanticism of Virginia Woolf's later novels, nevertheless is their most direct inheritor and continuator.*

Virginia Woolf herself, of course—who thought Ulysses *an "underbred" book— would not be happy about being called the progenitrix of novels as rowdy as Barth's or as obscene as Pynchon's. But fortunately—as with her own deep debt to Joyce—a writer is frequently not in conscious control of his literary influence, passive or active. And if the history of contemporary, post-romantic writing is the history of our debates in the silence Shelly imposes at the end of* Mont Blanc—*the resounding silence of mind making itself in the midst of an inhospitable universe—then we may at least say, looking at the fiction of the last six years or so, that Virginia Woolf's manner of filling that silence, her special mode of humanizing it, has come to be a more relevant solace for our own agonies of thought than we could possibly have imagined, even at the time she wrote her best work.*

> And what were thou, and earth, and stars, and sea,
> If to the human mind's imaginings
> Silence and solitude were vacancy?
>
> *Mont Blanc*

Shelley's final question in the Vale of Chamouni, like the apparent cliché that concludes the *Ode to the West Wind,* is not so triumphantly rhetorical as a simple reading suggests. In context, both questions reveal an uncertainty about the relative primacy, in this world, of the human imagination, with its endless train of rich and apparently holy impressions, on the one hand, and the "everlasting universe of things" which, as inhuman and possibly mindless power, presents a chillingly negative version of the intellectual beauty in which the mind craves to believe, on the other hand. If the apocalyptic wind of change and revolution, like the "Necessity" of Shelley's tutor Godwin, is in fact *not* a power benign to and consonant with the mind's imaginings, then a humane spring may be very far indeed behind the winter it brings on. The questions reverberate in the silence they impose with that curious and profound self-criticism that is characteristic of Shelley's best poetry.[1] But of course they are only an extreme manifestation of one of the most permanent dilemmas of the romantic imagination: the terrible ambiguity, Coleridgean in origin, implied by the autonomy of the creative mind, the fear that what seems an imaginative transfiguration of the world of matter

---

1. James Rieger, *The Mutiny Within* (New York: Braziller, 1967), pp. 200ff., refers to this quality as Shelley's "polysemism."

may in the end be only the vaudeville trick Edward Bostetter calls it: ventriloquism.[2]

Virginia Woolf, writing about Shelley in 1927, at about the time she envisioned the novel that was to become *The Waves,* seems to have been aware of this distinctively romantic problem:

> He loved the clouds and the mountains and the rivers more passionately than any other man loved them; but at the foot of the mountain he always saw a ruined cottage; there were criminals in chains, hoeing up the weeds in the pavement of St. Peter's Square; there was an old woman shaking with ague on the banks of the lovely Thames. . . . The most ethereal of poets was the most practical of men.[3]

It is an odd conflation of Shelley with Wordsworth and with Virginia Woolf herself; for certainly the "ruined cottage" is an unconscious reminiscence of *The Excursion,* and the old woman on the banks of the Thames seems remarkably like the grimly prophetic figure, "a tall quivering shape, like a funnel, like a rusty pump, like a wind-beaten tree for ever barren of leaves," that Peter Walsh encounters in *Mrs. Dalloway.*[4] But as an evaluation of Shelley it is enlightened, accurate, and, for the era of the "New Criticism," courageously generous. And by one of those tricks which literary history seems delighted to play on authors, it ironically anticipates the critical fate of Virginia Woolf's own work, particularly her strangest and richest novel, *The Waves.* For while criticism, both enthusiastic and dyslogistic, of Virginia Woolf has taken it more or less for granted that she is "the most ethereal of novelists," indications have been rare—if indeed there have been any—that she is also "the most practical of women.": that the aestheticism of her "stream of consciousness" includes the qualifying and fulfilling countermovement toward things in their blind phenomenalism, a countermovement that is an essential energy of the profoundest romantic and modern literature.

The reasons for Virginia Woolf's reputation as ethereal are, of course, both apparent and inevitable, with a perverse kind of inevitability. The very violence with which she inveighed against a double critical standard for women writers, and her vast scorn for the characterization of herself as "lady novelist," have insured for her an enduring attractiveness to people who hold precisely the values she contemned: a hypersensitive feminist apartheid, a concern for the obsessively "mystical" element in literature, and a kind of narrative introspectionism that has less to do with the mainstream of twentieth-century fiction than with the neurasthenia of the suffragette who insists on the vote but swoons at the editorial page. The inaccuracy of such a view finally results in the domesticated "Mrs. Woolf" of a book like Dorothy Brewster's *Virginia Woolf,*[5] a mixture of the tough-minded narrator with her own heroines, a book much like one that would result if one were to take as the final authoritative voice in *The Rape of the Lock* Belinda rather than Pope; or the Virginia Woolf-guru of N. C. Thakur's *The Symbolism of Virginia Woolf,* which in an access of mystagogy identifies as analogues for *The Waves* the Persian mystic Malauna Rumi, the Christian Trinity, the Hindu

2. *The Romantic Ventriloquists* (Seattle: University of Washington Press, 1963), pp. 3–7.

3. *The Death of the Moth* (New York: Harcourt, Brace, 1942), p. 125. Later citations refer to this edition.

4. *Mrs. Dalloway* (New York: Harcourt, Brace, 1925), p. 122.

5. *Virginia Woolf* (New York: New York University Press, 1962).

Trimurti, a misreading of Shelley's "Hymn to Intellectual Beauty," and the sayings of Buddha—in a single page.[6]

It is finally "mysticism," as a kind of exalted subjectivity, that is the *ignis fatuus* for Virginia Woolf's commentators, and particularly for commentators on *The Waves.* For *The Waves,* as both Brewster and Thakur inform us, was the novel that the author called her "abstract mystical eyeless book," her "playpoem." The reference is to a 1928 entry in Virginia Woolf's diary, one of the earliest pertaining to *The Waves,* at that time still to be called *The Moths.* But the passage, read more fully, puts a significant bias on the aura of "mysticism." Virginia Woolf writes:

> Yes, but *The Moths?* That was to be an abstract mystical eyeless book: a play-poem. And there may be affectation in being too mystical, too abstract; saying Nessa and Roger and Duncan and Ethel Sands admire that; it is the uncompromising side of me; therefore I had better win their approval. . . . I rather think the upshot will be books that relieve other books: a variety of styles and subjects: for after all, that is my temperament, I think, to be very little persuaded of the truth of anything—what I say, what people say—always to follow, blindly, instinctively with a sense of leaping over a precipice—the call of— the call of—now, if I write *The Moths* I must come to terms with these mystical feelings.[7]

It was, in fact, in one sense precisely the "coming to terms" with the mystical feelings that accounted for the long and complex growth of the book and its transformation from *The Moths* to *The Waves.* An earlier entry, from 1927, in Virginia Woolf's diary explains the relevance of the first title as she again mentions "the play-poem idea; the idea of some continuous stream, not solely of human thought, but of the ship, the night, etc., all flowing together: intersected by the arrival of the bright moths."[8] She obviously thought of this book as the *chef d'oeuvre* of her distinctive fictional talents, and obviously identified the initial impulse of its writing as a quasi-mystical revelation of what the completed whole would be like—the prophetic "fin in a waste of waters" that finds its way into Bernard's Roman vision. But in the very writing of the book, in the "coming to terms" with its subjectivist origin, it seems to have grown into something that Virginia Woolf herself could not have recognized at the beginning, something both tougher and more profoundly relevant to her own best gifts than the triumph of affectiveness the book has often been thought to be—something whose insignia is in fact the difference between the bright and evanescent moths who were first to "intersect" the book's plot and the inhuman, terrifying neutral waves that have the last inarticulate "word" in the final novel and give their ambiguous benediction to the human sense of a personal immortality.

"Coming to terms" with mysticism—at least in the English imaginative mainstream—is precisely a matter of translation, which implies necessarily eradication of the full subjective flower of mysticism, of *writing it down,* turning contemplation into verbalization, vision into version. From Walter Hilton's medieval *Scale of Perfection,* which in making the mystic's way a ladder refuses to leave out the lower rungs of unrefined experience, to Wesley's "methodizing" of the Evangelical

6. *The Symbolism of Virginia Woolf* (London: Oxford University Press, 1965), p. 105.
7. *A Writer's Diary* (London: Hogarth, 1953), p. 137.
8. *Ibid.,* p. 108.

Inner Light; and from the Red Cross knight's descent from the mount of vision to the self-conscious and quizzical apocalypse of *Prometheus Unbound,* the massive common-placing bias of the English mainstream is clear: a mainstream to which Virginia Woolf irrevocably belongs, as her earliest diary entries indicate, with their unflattering comparison of Christina Rossetti to the Byron of *Don Juan.*[9]

One of the most important "translations" of the mystic into the fictive is the passage already referred to, describing Bernard's experience in Rome:

> These moments of escape are not to be despised. They come too seldom. Tahiti becomes possible. Leaning over this parapet I see far out a waste of water. A fin turns. This bare visual impression is unattached to any line of reason, it springs up as one might see the fin of a porpoise on the horizon. Visual impressions often communicate thus briefly statements that we shall in time to come uncover and coax into words. I note under F., therefore, "Fin in a waste of waters." I, who am perpetually making notes in the margin of my mind for some final statement, make this mark, waiting for some winter's evening.[10]

There is something remarkably Wordsworthian about this passage, not only in the gratuitousness with which the vision, the moment of escape, comes, but also in its spareness, the deliberate and nearly abstract simplicity of it. What gives it its peculiar force, however, is the determination of Bernard to "coax into words" the phenomenon whose irrational, unawaited appearance defeats his present effort at description. The fin, he says, springs up suddenly, like a fin in a waste of waters.[11] And with the romantic phrasemaker's characteristic faith in his own failures, he duly notes the phenomenon in his mental chapbook for later working into the story he is trying to make of his life and the lives of his friends.

It is, in fact, precisely the befuddlement of the vision that makes it important to Bernard. For if the vision of the fin in a waste of waters is a "moment of escape," the escape is *from* words themselves, with their implicit "plotting" of human life and with their pretensions to causality and coherence. Bernard simultaneously welcomes and forestalls the defeat of his language since this defeat, by revealing a tension between word and world, insures his liberation from the possible "mysticism," or absolute subjectivity, of his perpetual storytelling. He is the most pretentious and self-conscious of cataloguers, noting this purely phenomenological and nonhuman revelation under "F" for "fin"; but it is just this pretension, anxious to take risks with experience yet willing to be made absurd by the experience itself, that is his imaginative salvation.

Is there a story to tell at all? asks Bernard a moment before he has the vision of the fin. Confronted with the teeming and massively undifferentiated sight of a Roman street, he realizes that he could isolate any figure or grouping within range and "make it a story":

> Again, I could invent stories about that girl coming up the steps. She met him under the dark archway. . . . "It is over," he said, turning from the cage where the china parrot hangs. Or simply, "That was all." But why impose my arbitrary

9. *Ibid.,* pp. 1–4.

10. *Jacob's Room* and *The Waves* (New York: Harcourt, Brace, 1959), p. 307. This edition is cited throughout.

11. This is remarkably like W. K. Wimsatt's famous definition of Romantic metaphor as the "tenor" generating its own "vehicle" in *The Verbal Icon* (Lexington, Ky.: University of Kentucky Press, 1954).

design? Why stress this and shape that and twist up little figures like the toys men sell in trays in the street? Why select this, out of all that,—one detail? (P. 306)

It is a question directly relevant, not only to the internal coherence of *The Waves* and, indeed, of all fiction, but to the specific situation in which Bernard finds himself. For his Roman monologue is, among other things, his first speech after the death of Percival, the strange, mute seventh figure about whom the other six characters of *The Waves* weave so much of their discourse. And whatever the similarity between Percival and Virginia Woolf's brother Thoby Stephen, his importance for the novel cannot be mistaken.

If Percival's death is a rupture in the hopes and sensibilities of the other characters, it is equally a rupture in the serial organization of their monologues: a delicate and highly subtle instance of imitative form. In the manner of serial music, each set of monologues by the six characters begins with a speech by Bernard and runs through the speeches of the other five before Bernard initiates a new "movement." But at the beginning of the fifth large section of the novel, the section introducing the news of Percival's death, Bernard for the first and only time does not begin the series: the first speaker is Neville, the closest of the six to Percival: " 'He is dead,' said Neville. 'He fell. His horse tripped. He was thrown. The sails of the world have swung round and caught me on the head. All is over. The lights of the world have gone out. There stands the tree which I cannot pass' " (p. 280). Throughout the fifth and sixth sections, Bernard does not appear, and the order of speakers is Neville—Rhoda—Louis—Susan—Jinny—and again Neville. Six speakers, but no Bernard. With that kind of mathematical aesthetic puzzlement which is common to *The Waves* and serial music, we can ask whether Bernard when he begins section six with his Italian monologue is initiating a new series or ending the previous one; whether he is reacting to Percival's death or continuing (subsisting) in Percival's absence; whether, in fact, this most articulate of the six has overcome or been overcome by the sheer datum of the body's end. The narrative placement of his voyage to Rome imposes on the reader the same kind of casuistry he imposes upon himself in his crucial vision of the fin. And in forcing us to ask, with and about Bernard and his friends, Is there a story?—or, Does the form hold?—the book also forces us to question, again with Bernard, the subjectivity that is its own inmost structure.

All this, of course, depends upon Percival, the silent, physically impressive character whose nearly Sartrean role in *The Waves* is *to be present* and *to be seen* by the others. "But look," says Neville, seeing Percival in the school chapel, "he flicks his hand to the back of his neck. For such gestures one falls hopelessly in love for a lifetime" (p. 199). And the lonely Louis, in his vision of fields and grass and sky, sees that "Percival destroys it, as he blunders off, crushing the grasses, with the small fry trotting subservient after him. Yet it is Percival I need; for it is Percival who inspires poetry" (p. 202). As the figure who is, resplendently, *there,* both conscious and yet definitively the object of all the other consciousnesses in the book, Percival is necessarily the inspirer of poetry as transaction between the inner and outer worlds. He is also necessarily mute, since the fullness of his presence in his own body is a plenum of self-consciousness that does not require the kind of speech the others constantly perform: their continual effort at pontification, or bridge-building between consciousness and experience.[12] Neville notes this essential "in-himselfness" of Percival at the crucial dinner party in section four of *The Waves*. "Without Percival," he says, "there is no solidity. We are silhouettes, hollow phantoms moving mistily without a background" (p. 259). And Bernard; least affected yet most perceptive about Percival, puts the matter in the precise terms, not only of the characters' experience but of the book's own highly self-conscious structure:

> "Here is Percival," said Bernard, "smoothing his hair, not from vanity (he does not look in the glass), but to propitiate the god of decency. He is conventional; he is a hero. The little boys trooped after him across the playing-fields. They blew their noses as he blew his nose, but unsuccessfully, for he is Percival. Now, when he is about to leave us, to go to India, all these trifles come together. He is a hero." (P. 260)

Much in the manner of the window-turned-mirror, in the first chapter of *To the Lighthouse*, Percival by his presence organizes the other six into a "party" in the fourth section of *The Waves*, and again organizes them—this time by his absence—in the final gathering in section eight. For the unity he represents, the impossible—for the six and for the book itself—full transaction between subject and object, is a unity no less primary in its negation than in its assertion. Susan realizes this when she addresses the dead Percival: "You have gone across the court, further and further, drawing finer and finer the thread between us. But you exist somewhere. Something of you remains. A judge. That is, if I discover a new vein in myself I shall submit it to you privately. I shall ask, 'What is your verdict?' You shall remain the arbiter" (p. 283).

Percival is a "hero" of acclimatization, of that at-homeness in both the world of things and the world of self-awareness whose loss is the creative trauma of the romantic imagination. He represents in his self-containment, his absolute visibility, the sense that the other characters can never quite attain or resign themselves to, the sense that "I am (rather than I have) this body," which implies that "I am of (as well as in) this world." Bernard's summing-up of the final gathering of the six at Hampton Court is, in this context, an immensely poignant coda to the book's career: "We saw for a moment laid out among us the body of the complete human being whom we have failed to be, but at the same time, cannot forget" (p. 369). For the body is at once the body of the dead Percival, impossible of attainment for these modern children, the stunted corpses of each one's potential self, and of

---

12. Sartre, in speaking of the incompatibility of conscious and "phenomenal" being, makes the following point:

> If we suppose an affirmative in which the affirmed comes to fulfill the affirming and is confused with it, this affirmation cannot be affirmed—owing to too much of plenitude and the immediate inheritance of the noema in the noesis. It is there that we find being . . . in connection with consciousness. It is the noema in the noesis; that is, the inheritance in itself without the least distance.

(*Being and Nothingness*, trans. Hazel Barnes [New York: Washington Square Press, 1966], p. lxv.) It can be readily seen how Percival in *The Waves*, as both "hero" of consciousness and full objective corporeality, is precisely this self-creating and therefore "silent" affirmation.

course the shattered and diminishing continuity of the six sensibilities taken as a single *gestalt.*

That the six speaking characters do form a kind of *gestalt,* not only in their common relationship to Percival, but in their sustained effort to see clearly the world around them and each other, has long been a commonplace of commentary on *The Waves.* But we must not confuse the *gestalt*-narrative with either lyricism or allegory; we must not assume, with Jean Guiguet, that the monologues of *The Waves* are a sustained single voice only factitiously differentiated by character names,[13] or, with Dorothy Brewster, that the six characters are a code for different aspects of a single massive human personality. Both interpretations, which end by more or less totally "subjectivizing" the book, fail to take account of the range of complexity and phenomenological subtlety of the grouping of the six.

Perhaps the most useful commentary on the organization of *The Waves* is Virginia Woolf's brief sketch, "Evening Over Sussex: Reflections in a Motor Car," published posthumously in *The Death of the Moth.* In this remarkable performance, Virginia Woolf not only projects a set of six "personalities"—six separate yet complementary reactions to the world of things—but explicitly links them to the central romantic and modern problem of breaking out of the subjective into a real resonance with the phenomenal: the selves are "six little pocket knives with which to cut up the body of a whale" (p. 8); and although she may not have had Melville in mind at the time, the "whale" involved is obviously of the same mysterious and absolute objectivity, terrible in its purity, as Moby Dick. Driving through Sussex at evening, when incipient darkness has obliterated all but the most permanent rock-face of the landscape, Virginia Woolf notes (again in noticeably Wordsworthian terms) that: "One is overcome by beauty extravagantly greater than one could expect . . . one's perceptions blow out rapidly like air balls expanded by some rush of air, and then, when all seems blown to its fullest and tautest, with beauty and beauty and beauty, a pin pricks; it collapses" (p. 7).

The pinprick, the sense of despair at the fecund exuberance of the world, introduces the first of the "selves": for "it was allied with the idea that one's nature demands mastery over all that it receives; and mastery here meant the power to convey . . . so that another person could share it" (p. 8). Such despair, however, generates the second self, whose counsel is to "relinquish . . . be content . . . believe me when I tell you that it is best to sit and soak; to be passive; to accept . . ." (p. 8). As these two selves hold colloquy, a third self is detached, and observing the other two aloofly, reflects that: "While they are thus busied, I said to myself: Gone, gone; over, over; past and done with, past and done with. I feel life left behind even as the road is left behind. We have been over that stretch, and are already forgotten. . . . Others come behind us" (p. 9). The first three selves seem to have reached a point of exhaustion in each other's counsel and in the melancholy at imminent death that the third self articulates. But suddenly a fourth self, which "jumps upon one unawares . . . often entirely disconnected with what has been happening," says, " 'Look at that.' It was a light; brilliant, freakish; inexplicable" (p. 9). It is a star; and as soon as the star is named as such, a new self attempts to find the "meaning" of the star in its prospects for human progress: "I think of Sussex in five hundred years to come. I think much grossness will have evaporated. Things will have been scorched up, eliminated.

---

13. *Virginia Woolf et son oeuvre* (Paris: Didier, 1962), p. 281.

There will be magic gates. Draughts fan-blown by electric power will cleanse houses. Lights intense and firmly directed will go over the earth, doing the work" (p. 9).

With this, the sunset is complete, and a sixth self, presumably dormant all the time, arises to coordinate the other five:

> Now we have got to collect ourselves. . . . Now I, who preside over the company, am going to arrange in order the trophies which we have all brought in. Let me see; there was a great deal of beauty brought in today: farmhouses; cliffs standing out to sea; marbled fields; mottled fields; red feathered skies; all that. Also there was disappearance and the death of the individual. . . . Look, I will make a little figure for your satisfaction; here he comes. (P. 10)

The "bringing in" of beauty, with its homey touch of "bringing in" produce at the end of the day, strikes precisely the right note: for this extended *gestalt* activity of assimilation, energetic as it is, is still a kind of factitious "bringing in" whose origin is the insuperable otherness of the phenomenal and whose end-product is the deliberately ambiguous placebo of the "little figure." [14]

Working back from the sixth "self" of "Evening Over Sussex," it is a fairly simple matter to see in each of the selves a close parallel to the six speaking characters of *The Waves*. The sixth, making his little figure against the onset of night, is obviously very like Bernard, the inveterate phrasemaker who "sums up," or attempts to, in the last section of the novel. The fourth self, with its quick and inarticulate cry of "Look!" resembles Jinny, who says to herself, "Every time the door opens I cry 'More!' But my imagination is the bodies. I can imagine nothing beyond the circle cast by my body" (p. 264). And the fifth, who in reaction to the fourth attempts to describe and to project into the future the world of appearances, is like Louis, the man of business, ashamed of his past and his father, the banker in Brisbane, who imagines himself forging in iron rings the world to come. Rhoda, the most ethereal of the characters, for whom life is "the emerging monster" (p. 219) and whose career is a calculated disappearing act, is the full-blown version of the third self, in love with death and the approaching dark. The second self, with its counsel to resign and accept, is like the country-bred, self-contained Susan, probably the most chthonic of Virginia Woolf's characters. And the first self, whose need to master and to articulate sets off the procession of the other selves, is like Neville, the poet and precisian whose terrible need for communication seems almost to skirt a desperate homosexuality.

But more important than these striking parallels of mood is the light thrown by "Evening Over Sussex" on the basic phenomenological impulse of *The Waves*, which, as I have tried to indicate, is a compelling effort to subvert the subjective or the comfortably "mystical." For as it is the discomfort—highly Wordsworthian or Shelleyan—of the first self at the *intransigence* of the nonhuman world that necessitates the procession of "selves," so Neville's crucial version in the first chapter

---

14. Jean Piaget in chapter 1 of *Play, Dreams and Imitation in Childhood,* trans. C. Gattegne and F. M. Hodgson (New York: Norton, 1962) notes that the child's imitative accommodation *to* the external world arises from the growing impossibility of his assimilation *of* the external world; these are exactly the dichotomies of "Evening Over Sussex" and *The Waves.*

of the man with his throat cut seems to "begin" the movement of the novel. The version must be quoted at length:

> His blood gurgled down the gutter. His jowl was white as a dead codfish. I shall call this structure, this rigidity, "death among the apple trees" for ever. There were the floating, pale-grey clouds; and the immitigable tree; the implacable tree with its greaved silver bark. The ripple of my life was unavailing. I was unable to pass by. There was an obstacle. "I cannot surmount this unintelligible obstacle," I said. And the others passed on. But we are doomed, all of us by the apple trees, by the immitigable tree which we cannot pass. (P. 191)

The tone of this passage is inescapably related to one of the most important apprehensions of things in the English language, Wordsworth's despairing sight in the Intimations "Ode":

> —But there's a Tree, of many one,
> A single Field which I have looked upon,
> Both of them speak of something that is gone:
>   The Pansy at my feet
>   Doth the same tale repeat:
> Whither is fled the visionary gleam?
> Where is it now, the glory and the dream?
>   (ll. 51–57)

The doom is, of course, the doom of consciousness-in-the-body, the "dying animal" of Yeats or the "ghost in the machine" of Gilbert Ryle. And this is the essential context for the italicized passages describing the waves, the house, and the birds at the beginning of each chapter. For these passages are not simply, as Joan Bennet and others have described them, compelling prose-poems paralleling human life with the cycle of the day and of nature. They are, on the other hand, deliberate and highly effective attempts to present a phenomenal world without the intervention of human consciousness, a world of blind things that stands as a perpetual challenge to the attempts of the six monologists to seize, translate, and "realize" their world. And although full of lyrical and "anthropomorphic" metaphors, it is difficult not to see in these passages an anticipation of the concerns and predispositions of contemporary novelists like Alain Robbe-Grillet and Nathalie Sarraute:

> *The sun fell in sharp wedges inside the room. Whatever the light touched became dowered with a fanatical existence. A plate was like a white lake. A knife looked like a dagger of ice. Suddenly tumblers revealed themselves upheld by streaks of light. . . . The veins on the glaze of the china, the grain of the wood, the fibers of the matting became more and more finely engraved. Everything was without shadow. (P. 251)*

The sense of preternatural (or preconscious) clarity, the way in which the precision with which things appear actually jeopardizes their stability as "this" thing—everything Robbe-Grillet most desires for the so-called new novel is there, and profoundly assimilated to the central theme of *The Waves.* In fact, the obvious parallel between the "day" of these descriptions and the lives of the characters may well be quite too obvious. The connection is such a ready commonplace that the ease with which we adopt it may be a deliberately planted instance of our own willingness to assume an overeasy mastery of the universe of things. Certainly the very end of the book is disturbingly ambiguous: Bernard's final ecstatic resolve to assert the human, to fling himself, "unvanquished and unyielding" against death itself is followed by the chilling line: *"The waves broke on the shore"* (p. 383). To ask whether this is an affirmation or a denial of Bernard's resolve is nugatory: it is simply and sublimely irrelevant to Bernard, as Bernard to it, and therein lies its enormous power. For the "nature" of the italicized passages is neither the anthropomorphic and sympathetic nature of the pastoral nor its malevolent but equally anthropomorphic contrary in a view like Gloucester's: "As flies to wanton boys, are we to th' Gods;/ They kill us for their sport." It is rather the nature of sublime and self-sufficient *un*humanity that finds articulation in the dirge from *Cymbeline* (an important "hidden theme" for both *Mrs. Dalloway* and *The Waves*), in Shelley's confrontation with Mont Blanc, or in Sartre's conception of the forbidding and impenetrable *être en-soi.*

Each of the characters, in lifelong quest of a fully articulate existence, reflects in one way or another the inherent tension between the words of subjective consciousness and the irrecoverable otherness of both things and other people. Only Bernard, in a moment of vision near the end of his final summing-up, achieves a perception that "redeems" him and his five friends precisely by bringing the terms of their failure to full consciousness: "For one day as I leant over a gate that led into a field, the rhythm stopped: the rhymes and the hummings, the nonsense and the poetry. A space was cleared in my mind. I saw through the thick leaves of habit. Leaning over the gate I regretted so much litter, so much accomplishment and separation, for one cannot cross London to see a friend, life being so full of engagements" (p. 373). As the life of intrasubjectivity, "so full of engagements," grows finally to the proportions where it chokes off the possibility of even the most minimal actions, Bernard momentarily shunts off personality and sees "the world without a self":

But how describe the world seen without a self? There are no words. Blue, red— even they distract, even they hide with thickness instead of letting the light through. How describe or say anything in articulate words again?—save that it fades, save that it undergoes a gradual transformation, becomes, even in the course of one short walk, habitual—this scene also. Blindness returns as one moves and one leaf repeats another. Loveliness returns. . . . But for a moment I had sat on the turf somewhere high above the flow of the sea and the sounds of the woods, had seen the house, the garden, and the waves breaking. The old nurse who turns the pages of the picture-book had stopped and had said, "Look. This is the truth." (P. 376)[15]

---

15. Interestingly, one anticipation of this oceanic world-without-human-consciousness may well be the last vision of the Time Traveller, of the final disappearance of man eons in the future, in H. G. Wells's *The Time Machine.*

It is a vision of absolute phenomenality, where "there are no words" or, in Bernard's earlier terms, "there is no story."[16] And as such it is not an absolutely beautiful vision, since "beauty" is a product of the affective consciousness.[17] "Loveliness" and "blindness" return together as the vision fades and becomes habitual—literally as it again becomes a vision subject to the *use* of language. But what is most startling about this passage is what Bernard does see in his moment of enlightenment. What "the old nurse" (who may very well be a reminiscence of the foster-mother Nature of the Intimations "Ode") *shows* Bernard is precisely the world of the italicized chapter heads, "the house, the garden, and the waves breaking"—precisely, that is, the world of unobserved, nonconscious things in the full ambivalence of its relationship to the characters of *The Waves* so that in a moment of almost perfect representative form, Bernard simultaneously breaks out of subjectivity into a phenomenological perception, and breaks into *The Waves* in its inmost narrative structure. Her lyrical tough-mindedness will not allow Virginia Woolf to take the way either of aestheticism or of "objectivism," but insists even here that narrative form and the formless world mutually condition each other. The way out and the way in, like the way up and the way down, are one and the same.

Finally, what *The Waves* gives us is something very like the world of Jorge Luis Borges's fable, "Tlön, Uqbar, Orbis Tertius," where an attempt to project a fictive, totally Berkeleyan and subjective world ends by taking over and transforming the "real" world. Virginia Woolf's mystical and eyeless book achieves a subjectivity so total and so self-conscious that it finally becomes a radical criticism of "mysticism" and of the subjective eye itself in the face of sheer phenomenalism. It is a kind of Hegelian paradox of "purity" whereby the subjective carries itself through a mirror reversal, entering a new and strange style of the insuperably nonhuman and "other":

> People go on passing; they go on passing against the spires of the church and the plates of ham sandwiches. The streamers of my consciousness waver out and are perpetually torn and distressed by their disorder. I cannot therefore concentrate on my dinner. "I would take a tenner. The case is handsome; but it blocks up the hall." They dive and plunge like guillemots whose feathers are slippery with oil. (*The Waves*, P. 240)

> Soon unfortunately time will no longer be master. Wrapped in their aura of doubt and error, this day's events, however insignificant they may be, will in a few seconds begin their task, gradually encroaching upon the ideal order,

---

16. One of the earliest essays on *The Waves* is that of Floris Delattre, *Le Roman psychologique de Virginia Woolf* (Paris: Vrin, 1932), containing the following comment:

> The successive monologues are long asides which the actors pronounce before the stage-set, without distinguishing themselves from each other, and in which we see only far-off reflections of the drama playing itself out. (P. 199, my translation)

It is interesting to compare this with Robbe-Grillet's ideas of eliminating "the illusion of depth" from the novel in *For a New Novel,* trans. Richard Howard (New York: Grove Press, 1965).

17. This is much like the purely "phenomenal" and hence terrifying vision of the Marabar Caves in *A Passage to India.*

cunningly introducing an occasional inversion, a discrepancy, a confusion, a warp, in order to accomplish their work: a day in early winter without plan, without direction, incomprehensible and monstrous.[18]

The first passage is Louis's monologue in a London restaurant; the second is Robbe-Grillet's description of a day in a small café. The remarkable resemblance between these passages, from novels normally assumed to represent polar schools of contemporary literature,[19] is an index not only of the substantiality of a "modern tradition" of narrative but also of the profound contemporaneity of Virginia Woolf's greatest novel. Far from being the *sui generis* masterpiece of a hyperaesthetic "lady novelist," *The Waves* is a tough-minded and sobering examination of the chances for the shaping intellect to shape meaningfully at all. And far from being a "dead end" for fiction,[20] it is a novel whose penetration to the roots of a distinctly modern and crucially humanistic problem is human and humanizing as few other books can claim to be.

18. Alain Robbe-Grillet, *The Erasers,* trans. Richard Howard (New York: Grove Press, 1964), p. 7.

19. See R. M. Adams, "Down Among the Phenomena," *Hudson Review* 20 (1967): 255–67.

20. See Arthur Koestler, "The Novelist's Temptations," in *The Yogi and the Commissar* (London: Hutchinson, 1965); and John Edward Hardy, *Man in the Modern Novel* (Seattle, Wash.: University of Washington Press, 1964).

Beyond the Lighthouse: *The Years*

HERBERT MARDER

University of Illinois

COMMENT BY THE AUTHOR

The Years is a novel in which everything moves toward a single point, a climactic scene in which the action is summarized and images converge. Virginia Woolf was aiming at an effect of unity in diversity, of stasis within motion. She wished the reader to retain in his mind a large number of naturalistic details and simultaneously to perceive these details as part of a single complex design. The novel resembles a series of concentric circles, each one presenting the essential imagery in more condensed and heightened form than the one that preceded it, till all finally reach an ideal point at the center. Thus Woolf hoped to capture a moment out of time, Eliot's "still point of the turning world."

But if the reader is to reach that ultimate stillness, the pattern must crystallize at the crucial moment into a perfect figure without irrelevancy. All the elements of the novel, all the lesser patterns, must be connected and nothing may be left out or left over. This is an effect more often sought by poetry than by fiction. To achieve it, Woolf, like Joyce, had to renounce the conventions of plot. She had to be free to order symbols and images without the constraints imposed by a developing story line.

The Years has always been a puzzle to critics who tried to read it as an Edwardian family chronicle, that is, as if it were a conventional story. There has recently been a tendency to recognize affinities between The Years *and Woolf's other symbolic fiction, but it still remains her least understood and most underrated work. The essay reprinted below describes some of the ways in which* The Years *presents interconnections between consciousness and the external world. It deals with Woolf's treatment of the Self and the not-Self or, as she termed it, of "solitude and society." More remains to be said along these lines. We still need*

First published: 15, no. 1 (1967): 61–70. Slightly revised.

to learn from Woolf about the freeing of the consciousness from obsession and its gradual ascent toward enlightenment. That is the theme of The Years. *A full account of the novel as a protest against the tyranny of clock time and as an epic of consciousness remains to be written.*

Virginia Woolf's *The Years* has never, since its brief emergence as a best-seller in the late thirties, been a popular book. Most critics consider it a failure. The consensus is that it is formless, incoherent, a "patchwork quilt" of episodes without aim or continuity.[1] It is charged with lacking precisely that characteristic tension and balance of opposites which distinguishes her other fiction. Some writers hold that *The Years* is a reversion to conventional realism. According to this view, the book is a "weather report," a traditional narrative, dwelling lovingly on the outer surfaces of things, presenting beautiful tableaux, but never penetrating to the inner life.[2]

It seems to me that these judgments are mistaken. *The Years* is symbolic fiction, a lineal descendant of *To the Lighthouse* and *The Waves*. Like these earlier works, it demands close reading, which it has rarely received.

The theme of *The Years* is related to a problem that concerned Virginia Woolf throughout her career: the conflict between the inner life and outer forms or conventions. This conflict was the subject of a key passage in an early novel. The heroine of *Night and Day* asked why there should be a "perpetual disparity between thought and action, between the life of solitude and the life of society, this astonishing precipice on one side of which the soul was active and in broad daylight, on the other side of which it was contemplative and dark as night. Was it not possible to step from one to the other, erect, and without essential change?"[3] Virginia Woolf returned to this subject in *To the Lighthouse* and *The Waves,* but both these books stress the inner life at the expense of outer reality. In *The Years* she wanted to achieve a perfect balance between solitude and society, to join the lyrical, visionary mood of the earlier novels with a comprehensive epic of English social life. Her aim, she said in her diary, was to encompass "the whole of human life . . . to give the whole of the present society—nothing less: facts as well as the vision." Further on she reflected that the "discovery of this book . . . is the combination of the external and the internal. I am using both, freely."[4]

Precisely what did she mean by "the combination of the external and the

1. Bernard Blackstone, for instance, writes that in *The Years* "there is no pattern. . . . The rhythm has been deliberately destroyed. Order and coherence have vanished." *Virginia Woolf: A Commentary* (London: Hogarth, 1949), p. 194. J. K. Johnstone says that "there is no centre around which the whole novel coheres, no principle of organization which sets it apart from life as a self-supporting work of art." *The Bloomsbury Group* (New York: Noonday Press, 1954), p. 369. See also Joan Bennett, *Virginia Woolf* (Cambridge: Cambridge University Press, 1949), pp. 97–98; Deborah Newton, *Virginia Woolf* (Melbourne: Melbourne University Press, 1946), p. 55; W. H. Mellers, "Mrs. Woolf and Life" (review of *The Years*), *Scrutiny* (June 1937), pp. 71–75.

2. See R. L. Chambers, *The Novels of Virginia Woolf* (Edinburgh: Oliver & Boyd, 1947), pp. 45–46; D. S. Savage, "Virginia Woolf," *The Withered Branch: Six Studies in the Modern Novel* (London: Eyre & Spottiswoode, 1950), p. 97.

3. *Night and Day* (New York, 1920), pp. 338–39. All quotations of Virginia Woolf's work are from the Harcourt, Brace editions, to which the page numbers in parentheses refer.

4. *A Writer's Diary* (New York: Harcourt, Brace, 1954), pp. 186, 191, 229.

internal?" How could it be accomplished? One answer immediately suggests itself. *The Years* begins by dwelling on the appearances of things. The physical environment in which the characters live is described in great detail, and so sensitively that the whole mood of an age is evoked. The part played by these details in the larger pattern emerges only gradually. It is some time before Virginia Woolf begins to probe the minds of her characters; when she does so, however, it becomes apparent that the objectively described scenes form the basis of our psychological knowledge, that all the solid objects among which the Pargiters moved, the rooms through which they walked, were presented not only as magic photographs of times gone by but as symbols of mental states. And this has been done without compromising the solidity, the material reality, of the objects themselves. Nothing is included casually or at random. The spotted walrus on Eleanor's desk, the cab that stops next door, the coins for which Colonel Pargiter fumbles with the hand that has lost two fingers—all the details of the opening come back to us hundreds of pages later. Take the Colonel's deformity, for instance, the hand like "the claw of some aged bird," which we first notice when he clumsily caresses his mistress, and again when he rewards one of his children with a sixpence. That truncated hand sticks in one's mind with the vividness of a sight remembered from childhood. On page 372 North wonders why old Eleanor never married, and we understand him perfectly when he speculates: "Sacrificed to the family . . . old Grandpapa without any fingers." Externals like this constantly illuminate the inner lives of the characters. To borrow Henry James's famous metaphor, what seemed all surface one moment seems all depth the next.

There is a related sense in which Virginia Woolf was combining the external and the internal in *The Years*. It has to do with the way in which she drew her characters. She never for a moment permits us to forget the surroundings in which these people move, never invites us to retreat into a world of fantasy, as she did in her earlier novels. We are always conscious of the flux of events by which each individual, with his burden of self-awareness, is influenced at every moment. There are no extended flights of lyricism, as in the "Time Passes" section of *To the Lighthouse* or the interludes in *The Waves*. Instead we have countless lyrical moments diffused throughout the book, always combined with the prosaic circumstances out of which they have arisen. Similarly, our knowledge of the inner lives of the characters comes to us in the form of brief vivid impressions. We are never in anyone's mind long enough to follow the twisting and winding of his thoughts. The result is a kind of narrative pointillism, a constant shuttling back and forth between the external and the internal, between prosaic observation and visionary experience. Ultimately, a sense emerges that outer and inner have blurred and combined. The various characters arise like emanations from the mass of details, seeming both part of their surroundings and distinct from them.

This feeling is echoed in the experience of the characters themselves. It is expressed at a crucial moment by Eleanor, reflecting about the atomization of her life, and gripping coins in her hands, almost as if to reassure herself of her own existence. "Millions of things came back to her. Atoms danced apart and massed themselves. But how did they compose what people called a life?" (pp. 366–67). Eleanor's cousin Maggie asks a similar question. Riding in a cab on her way to a dinner party, she glimpses a beautiful sunset. Later that night she recalls her vision and the mood it evoked. " 'What's I?' " she asks. "Am I that, or am I this?

Are we one, or are we separate? . . ." (p. 140). The sunset seems, momentarily, to have become part of Maggie and she of it, but this transport is interrupted by her mother, with some trivial remark. In Maggie's vision "the lights—the sunlight and the artificial light—were strangely mixed." After the interruption, which reminds Maggie of the presence of her parents, and of her destination, the light grows "more and more artificial; yellower and yellower" (p. 131). The image of the mixing lights, natural sunlight and artificial lamplight, is symbolic. "Are we one, or are we separate?" The answer is that the natural light and the artificial light—solitude and society—can be mixed. We must be neither one nor separate, but both.

Maggie is able to discover only a vague glimmering of this idea; it moves across her horizon and then is lost. Much later in the novel her cousin's son, North, succeeds in making the idea explicit. Just returned from a solitary sheep ranch in Africa, North has gone to visit his Aunt Eleanor and has found a question raised by one of her friends—"If we do not know ourselves, how can we know other people?"—highly interesting (p. 309). He likes "serious talk on abstract subjects. 'Was solitude good; was society bad?'" (p. 310). To this question North, in spite of his years of loneliness, has been inclined to answer Yes. But now he begins to doubt the validity of his former assumptions. He considers another fragment of the conversation: "'Solitary confinement is the greatest torture we inflict.'" From Eleanor's flat he crosses London to dine with his eccentric cousin Sara and to remind her that family and friends are having a party that night. Sara, who lives to a great extent in the fantastic world of her imagination, would prefer to stay at home. She feels that society is corrupt; it is a Wasteland, a "'polluted city . . . of dead fish and worn-out frying pans'" (p. 340). She shares her bath with a Jew, she explains, who leaves a line of grease and hairs on the tub. They can, in fact, hear the bath water running in the next room. This reminder of our common humanity strengthens Sara in her feeling that the life of solitude is best. But North cannot agree. Later in the evening he reflects that "thinking alone [ties] knots in the middle of the forehead" (p. 414).

North goes to Delia's party because he wants to stop "thinking alone." The image he uses to describe the ideal life contrasts with Sara's images of a greasy tub and polluted river. He wants "a life modelled on the jet . . . on the spring, of the hard leaping fountain . . ." (p. 410). This thought comes to him while he drinks a sparkling claret cup to celebrate the family reunion: he is watching the bubbles rise. Are we one, or are we separate? North's thought, like Maggie's vision, suggests the combination of the external and the internal. He aspires "to keep the emblems and tokens of North Pargiter . . . but at the same time spread out, make a new ripple in human consciousness . . . to be the bubble and the stream . . . myself and the world together" (p. 410). This is just what he cannot do. North remembers how far he is from this ideal of integrating self and world. "What do I mean, he wondered—I, to whom ceremonies are suspect, and religion's dead; who don't fit . . . don't fit in anywhere?" Suddenly his sentences refuse to flow. His mind seems to have dried up because of his uncertainty about "what's solid, what's true; in my life, in other people's lives" (p. 410).

At this point he turns instinctively toward the one person who has achieved the balance in life that he lacks. As he looks at her, old Eleanor unties a knot in her handkerchief. Her act symbolically reveals the solution to North's dilemma.

All through the finale this sleepy old woman who asks fundamental questions is demonstrating that there need be no conflict between solitude and society, that it is "possible to step from one to the other, erect, and without essential change." Her very being embodies the ideals toward which Maggie and North have been painfully groping. She shows them how outer and inner elements of the personality can be made to nourish and support each other at every moment. Her untying of the knot in her handkerchief is an example of the way in which she does this. The knot was there for a purpose—to remind Eleanor to do a favor for the son of the porter at her flat. Now she asks her brother, an Oxford professor, to help Runcorn's boy get into college. She has found the path between two extremes, turned this knot, which stands for the forces of egoism in her life, into an act of kindness. The knot is also related to Eleanor's self-realization in another way—in its connection with an inner experience that has colored the evening for her—a dream and vision of felicity, a heightened sense of identity—which has come and gone as she dozed off amid the hubbub of the party. It belongs to the same order of symbolism as the coins she holds in her hands.

When Eleanor arrived at Delia's flat, she took money out of her purse to pay her share of the cab, but Peggy refused to accept it. Then the sight of old friends brought back the past and made her ponder the significance of her life. Her musings have already been quoted in part: "Millions of things came back to her. Atoms danced apart and massed themselves. But how did they compose what people called a life? She clenched her hands and felt the hard little coins she was holding. Perhaps there's 'I' at the middle of it, she thought; a knot; a centre; and . . . she saw herself sitting at her table drawing on the blotting-paper, digging little holes from which spokes radiated" (p. 367). Here the solitary, inner dimension of the personality is symbolized in three ways: by the coins, the knot, and the dot with spokes radiating from it—a child's image of light. The thought that "perhaps there's 'I' at the middle of it" is comforting to Eleanor, who feels that she has grown old without having had anything one could properly call a life. Perhaps, after all, there is something within the individual that survives, a hard core within the perishable body, like the coin within the soft cup of her hand. Her mind continues to wander between sleep and waking, and again "she shut her hands on the coins she was holding, and again she was suffused with a feeling of happiness" (p. 426). She exultantly contrasts her vision of a self that endures with the disappearance of a solid object, the spotted walrus that had once stood on her mother's desk, where she had kept the family's accounts—an object that Eleanor had believed would go on existing after they, the Pargiters, were gone. Now she realizes that "this had survived—this keen sensation (she was waking up) and the other thing, the solid object . . . had vanished." Eleanor's euphoria verges on a religious sense of immortality.

But there is another side to the coin symbolism. We are speaking, after all, of pieces of money. There is an ambiguity here, suggested by Eleanor's hatred of keeping the family accounts. Emphasis on the ego (associated with the coins) may lead toward inner freedom; it may also lead in the opposite direction, toward self-indulgence and a kind of moral constipation. The coins in the grasping fist are an appropriate symbol of this spiritual disease. Eleanor is perhaps not altogether free of it. When she thinks of a self that endures she clenches her hands, feels "the hard little coins," and envisions this self as a "knot." The image is revealing. The fact that she has escaped the danger and found a way to freedom is shown by the contrast between Eleanor and her brother Edward, who has succumbed to egoism. While Eleanor asks the scholarly Edward to help Runcorn's boy, North, looking on, ponders the effects of Edward's cultivation of "the past and poetry." In many ways Edward's life represents an admirable achievement. Nevertheless, North reflects, there is "something sealed up, stated about him" (p. 407). Then he sees more clearly what is wrong. Edward has mastered the classics, but in the process he has become incapable of sharing what he knows with others. He is imprisoned within himself. "Why can't he flow?" North asks himself. "Why can't he pull the string of the shower bath?" (pp. 408–9). This homely image is a reference to North's visit to Eleanor earlier in the evening; she took him into her bathroom and showed off her shower bath, of which she was very proud. We must call to mind that Eleanor grew up in a Victorian house with one bathroom for a family of nine. Virginia Woolf emphasizes the point: a single bathroom and a basement for the servants "and there all those different people had lived, boxed up together, telling lies" (p. 223). Sara's greasy tub and polluted city are the direct legacy of this late Victorian decadence. Eleanor's possession of a new shower bath, which sprays pure jets of water, symbolizes her inner purification and freedom.

Eleanor's absentmindedness about the knot in her handkerchief and her tendency to doze and dream during Delia's party are further indications that she is free of compulsive grasping. She can let go of the coins in her hands, and we find her searching for them amid the cushions of her seat. When the dawn comes they are still scattered about her: "She gathered together her gloves, her bag and two or three coppers and got up" (p. 431). Virginia Woolf intended originally to make this symbolism of inner freedom the conclusion of *The Years*. "It's to end," she planned, "with Elvira [Eleanor] going out of the house and saying, What did I make this knot in my handkerchief for—and all the coppers rolling about."[5] But she later changed her mind and closed by emphasizing the social rather than the personal side of Eleanor's vision.

The image of the taxicab, which refers to the outer, social being, stands over against the image of the coin. As we have seen, the coin is, at least potentially, a symbol of illumination. (Compare the dot with spokes radiating from it.) By its light all things can be simplified, reduced to unity. In this respect it is akin to the light imagery in Virginia Woolf's earlier novels, especially *To the Lighthouse*. But in *The Years* Virginia Woolf wished to "give the whole of the present society . . . facts as well as the vision." The taxicab in the street that Eleanor sees as the book closes does not lend itself to simplification or reduction in quite the same way as do the images of coin and lighthouse. By complementing the coin symbolism it makes us aware of a state of fulfillment deeply rooted in the "here and now," although it reaches toward the transcendental.

It is important to remember that the book opened with a scene in which Delia was bitterly disappointed when a cab, which she thought was bringing a young man to call, passed the Pargiter house and stopped down the street. The final scene is an inversion of this opening. The cab, which revealed Delia's frustration, has become a symbol of social communion. The fiery sunset of 1880 has

---

5. *Ibid.,* p. 214.

been succeeded by a peaceful sunrise. Eleanor goes to the window as the party is breaking up and the last guests are getting ready to depart. The morning light has made everything look ethereal, unearthly. Maggie is holding a bunch of many-colored flowers, and Delia calls to Eleanor to look at how beautifully she has arranged them. But Eleanor is watching a taxicab, which has stopped two doors down to let off a young man and woman.

" 'Aren't they lovely?' " said Delia, holding out the flowers. Eleanor started. " 'The roses? Yes . . .' " she said. But she was watching the cab" (p. 434). The roses that Maggie has arranged stand for the cultivation of the inner life. Eleanor agrees with Delia that they are beautiful, but her answer also refers to the scene in the street below where the young couple—are they newlyweds?—are on the verge of entering the house together. She includes them both—the flowering within, the communion without—in a single affirmation. " 'There,' Eleanor murmured, as [the young man] opened the door and [the couple] stood for a moment on the threshold. 'There!' she repeated as the door shut with a little thud behind them." "There"—it is a word of fulfillment from the past, a word that Maggie's mother had repeated, many years earlier, showing her daughters a stately circling dance to the sound of distant music. "In and out among the chair and tables [she had danced] and then, as the music stopped, 'There!' she exclaimed. Her body seemed to fold and close itself together . . . and [she] sank all in one movement on the edge of the bed" (p. 143). Now Eleanor, like the opulent Eugenie Pargiter, is achieving her own fulfillment, symbolically casting off her spinsterhood. She turns round into the room, toward the others. " 'And now?' she said, looking at Morris [her brother], who was drinking the last drops of a glass of wine. 'And now?' she asked, holding out her hands to him."

In its emphasis upon the future, upon motion rather than stasis, the ending of The Years differs from the endings of most of Virginia Woolf's novels. James Hafley, who believes that The Years "overcomes . . . a fairly serious limitation of Virginia Woolf's earlier novels" precisely as a result of this difference, has pointed out that "To the Lighthouse concludes when Lily Briscoe, exhausted but triumphant, says, 'I have had my vision' and puts aside her paintbrush. The Years, on the other hand, concludes with Eleanor reaching out, asking 'And now?' The present moment is no longer simply an end in itself; it is at once an end and a means."[6] Hafley's statement sums up the two-fold symbolism in The Years. Like so much else in the book, this symbolism is connected with the "combination of the external and the internal." The coins in Eleanor's hands are the share she wanted to pay for the cab that brought her to Delia's party. That is, her holding them is symbolically a social as well as a private act. Virginia Woolf is saying that we must first discover "what's solid, what's true" within ourselves, and then share it with others. If we fail to penetrate to the inner substance, we will have nothing to give. But if we try to hoard the treasure, like Edward, it will turn into dust.

In The Years Virginia Woolf went beyond the purely retrospective, visionary symbolism that concludes To the Lighthouse. By making Eleanor's vision grow directly out of the most commonplace incidents she demonstrated that fact and vision are not necessarily incompatible. The life of solitude and the life of society

---

6. *The Glass Roof: Virginia Woolf as Novelist* (Berkeley, Calif.: University of California Press, 1954), p. 144.

can be brought into harmony with each other. That is the significance of her choice of symbols like Eleanor's shower bath, the coppers in her hands, the taxicab in the street—all homely objects. Visionary elements no longer stand boldly outlined against the sky, as they did in the earlier book. They are integrated with other events, joining in the broad stream of life. They accost the reader amid familiar surroundings and insinuate themselves into his mind by their naturalness. The practical and the visionary are shaped into one of those "globed compacted things" which were, for Virginia Woolf, the ideal in art.

The Masks of Conrad

MAURICE BEEBE

Temple University

COMMENT BY THE AUTHOR

When I wrote "The Masks of Conrad" and speculated on the nature of multiple selves, I had no idea that I would be asked some twelve years later to confront the earlier me who wrote that article. It is a rather disconcerting experience. On the one hand, my present self takes a strange, almost fatherlike pride in the ability of my younger self to anticipate the change in direction of Conrad studies during the past decade. Yet today's I is rather annoyed by the failure of the earlier me to realize that critical interpretation is even more relative and subjective than I thought. Throughout my paper I emphasized three Conrads. I now realize that there were many more.

My essay was written at about the time New Criticism reached its peak. Explication, analysis, and interpretation dominated literary studies to such an extent that the excessive weight of numerous "readings" helped bring about the collapse of the movement. There was a tone of excited discovery about many of the early new critical interpretations, and the best critics were those who offered their readings as hypotheses rather than proven conclusions. Unfortunately, too many other critics insisted with dogmatic certainty that they had made the last turn of the screw, conveniently ignoring the existence of a tremendous number of equally convincing but contradictory readings of the same works of literature. In our eagerness to avoid the biographical heresy and the intentional fallacy, we were not sufficiently aware of what I have described elsewhere as the selective fallacy. We learned that any reasonably well-trained critic can find in any reasonably complex work of literature just about anything he may be looking for, and there is a natural tendency therefore to select evidence that supports the critic's thesis while ignoring everything that conflicts with it. As Marvin Mudrick put it, "Eye to eye, the critic confronts the writer, and astonished, discovers himself."

First published: 11, no. 4 (1963): 35–53. Unrevised.

70

My own readings of Heart of Darkness *and* Victory *are to a degree subject to that same failing. I have since read studies of those particular works that would cause me to modify my interpretations. Yet I think that I am more right than wrong. Subsequent work that I have done on Conrad, especially on that most misunderstood of his novels,* Lord Jim, *has convinced me that his artistic vision was perhaps even darker and more nihilistic than I thought twelve years ago. The prevailing tendency of Conrad criticism since 1963 tends to substantiate that view. But the work of still other Conradians has forced me to acknowledge the shadowlike presence of a lighter and more affirmative Conrad who served as "my" Conrad's secret sharer. I realize now more clearly than before that Albert Guérard was correct in finding the essence of Conrad's art in his impressionism—that most wary and cunning of fictive techniques by means of which the author effaces himself and places the burden of understanding upon the reader. We should credit Conrad himself with the realization that the ultimate self of an artist is the many selves who confront his work.*

When critics write about Joseph Conrad, they assume that readers know who Conrad is. But, to judge from the profusion of conflicting interpretations of his works, there are many Conrads. How many new readings of *Heart of Darkness,* for example, must we have before we concede that this story is precisely what the first narrator promised us—yet another of "Marlow's inconclusive experiences"?[1] Perhaps the advantage of an inconclusive story is that it forces each reader to conclude it for himself; the more readings available, the more the story is enriched. Nevertheless, behind most of our interpretations is the unspoken assumption that the author knew what he was doing, that for him one reading would be more valid than another, and that he carefully planted clues within the story that would lead us to the right conclusion. Playing detective, we pick up these clues, put them under our critical lenses, and follow a trail that we hope will lead us to the culprit, who is always, of course, the doer of the deed, the maker of the work. It is for this reason, I think, that one reaction to the excesses of the New Critics has been renewed faith in biographical research. Of late we have heard little about "the biographical heresy," and books like Richard Ellmann's *James Joyce* and Mark Schorer's *Sinclair Lewis* are almost universally acclaimed. We are now told that the critic must rely on biography if only to the extent that it sets *"the limits of rational interpretation* by laying down cautionary principles: This particular writer, being the kind of man he was, working as he did, living in the age in which he lived, could *not,* whatever he meant, have meant *that."*[2]

True enough, but if we see now that there are dangers in ignoring the maker of the work, there are equally strong dangers in too uncritical an acceptance of biography. The life of an author is as subject to individual interpretation as are his writings. The Conrad of Jean-Aubry is not quite the Conrad of Jocelyn Baines or Jerry Allen. Yet each of these biographers assumes that to know the man Conrad is to know the writer. They go further and equate the fiction with the experience. Thus, Jean-Aubry can tell us solemnly that *Youth* narrates "the exact, authentic

---

1. Bruce Harkness, ed., *Conrad's* Heart of Darkness *and the Critics* (San Francisco: Wadsworth, 1960), p. 4.
2. Patrick Cruttwell, "Makers and Persons," *Hudson Review* 12 (1959): 504–5.

circumstances of the wreck of the *Palestine"* and that *Heart of Darkness* is "nothing but a detailed account of his [Conrad's] ill-fated Congo adventure."[3] Baines is not quite so literal-minded, but his impatience with the critics of Conrad gives away his conviction that because the man Conrad—that is, *his* Conrad—was a rather simple fellow, the fiction must be simple too. "I do not believe," he tells us, "that Conrad intended 'The Secret Sharer' to be interpreted symbolically,"[4] and any reader who sees something beneath the surface of a Conrad story is dismissed as "alchemical" or "fantastic." The biographers' premise is that if we just knew everything about Conrad's experiences the mysteries in his writings would be solved. Allen, in a recent essay, describes the long search by scholars for the real river where Almayer lived.[5] That river has been found at last—in Borneo—and in an overgrown cemetery on a nearby hill the grave marker of a Charles Olmeyer. Unfortunately, we do not know enough about the life of the real "Almayer" to say with sureness that Conrad's first novel is a true story; but how does a scholar justify traveling halfway around the world in search of a river and a grave marker unless he equates source with result and assumes that to know the Pole, Captain Korzeniowski, is to know Conrad the writer?

Somewhere between these two extremes—the many Conrads of the subjective interpreters and the several Conrads of the literal-minded biographers—there is another Conrad who is neither the man nor the writer but the creative spirit that functions like a Holy Ghost in joining the creator with the creation, and may also be interpreted variously. Or, to put the matter differently, there was first the man, Korzeniowski, who was born in 1857 and died officially in 1924, though he virtually disappeared from life sometime in the 1890s when Joseph Conrad, the British man of letters, was born. Just as we cannot determine the exact birthdate of Joseph Conrad, the date of his death is uncertain, for he remains alive in the works he wrote. We use the past tense in writing of Korzeniowski, the present tense in writing of Conrad; but the latter was also a citizen of public record who died officially in 1924. Joseph Conrad married, fathered sons, paid taxes, had literary friends, and conducted business with publishers. Sometimes in fact the man of letters was ready to receive personal as well as financial credit for the products of his pen, but a study of his correspondence and memoirs reveals that he did not often pretend fully to understand what he had written and that he liked to maintain the pose that he was but an agent for still another Conrad, a creative force that operated through him, making use of the physical energy of the mortal Conrad but remaining somehow apart from the man.

Consider Conrad's own account of how he began to write. In *A Personal Record* he tells us that one morning, while he was between voyages and residing in a London boarding house, he ordered the breakfast dishes removed from the table, called for paper and pen, and then almost unconsciously, without intention, wrote the first lines of *Almayer's Folly*.

It was not the outcome of a need—the famous need of self-expression which artists find in their search for motives. The necessity which impelled me

3. Gerald Jean-Aubry, *The Sea Dreamer: A Definitive Biography of Joseph Conrad*, trans. Helen Sebba (Garden City, N. Y.: Doubleday, 1957), p. 238.

4. Jocelyn Baines, *Joseph Conrad: A Critical Biography* (New York: McGraw-Hill, 1960), p. 358.

5. Jerry Allen, "Conrad's River," *Columbia University Forum* 5 (Winter 1962): 29–35.

was a hidden, obscure necessity, a completely masked and unaccountable phenomenon. Or perhaps some idle and frivolous magician . . . had cast a spell over me through his parlour window as I explored the maze of streets east and west in solitary leisurely walks without chart and compass. Till I began to write that novel I had written nothing but letters, and not very many of these. I never made a note of a fact, of an impression or of an anecdote in my life. The conception of a planned book was entirely outside my mental range when I sat down to write; the ambition of being an author had never turned up amongst those gracious imaginary existences one creates fondly for oneself at times in the stillness and immobility of a day-dream.[6]

It makes a good story—this account of a man of thirty-eight suddenly cast under a mysterious spell that turned him into an author in spite of himself—but, unfortunately, it is not a true story. Baines has shown that Conrad began writing much earlier than he claimed and that he had literary pretensions from an early age. But what interests me here is not whether or not the story holds up factually, but why Conrad bothered to invent it. Perhaps because, as his friend Ford Madox Ford would have said, even if the facts are false, the "impression" they carry is true. For, after all, Conrad was not the first or the last writer to suppose that he was the vehicle of a force greater than himself, and though "inspiration" is out of fashion, novelists as unlike each other as Kipling and Faulkner have insisted that not their public selves but their "demons" must assume credit and responsibility for their writings. Conrad took pains to maintain the myth of his other self. When asked to revise one of his works, he replied, "I shall try without faith, because all my work is produced unconsciously (so to speak) and I cannot meddle to any purpose with what is within myself.—I am sure you understand what I mean—it isn't in me to improve what has got itself written."[7] And on another occasion, "You know I take no credit to myself for what I do—and so I may judge my own performance. There is no mistake about this. . . . It [*Nostromo*] is a very genuine Conrad."[8]

We may well ask why Conrad insisted so firmly on the myth of the second self. One explanation may be found in the literary scene at the time he began to write. He could not, of course, become a literary artist without knowing what an artist is. By the 1890s an archetype of the artist had established itself so firmly that it may well have seemed binding. One aspect of that archetype was the insistence that the true artist could stand aside even from himself. The theme of the divided self has been repeated again and again in portrait-of-the-artist novels from Goethe's time to ours, but never so often as during the period from 1880 to 1920. Many of the French writers known to have influenced Conrad insisted on a division between man and artist; it is a theme found frequently in Henry James; and by 1920 had become such a commonplace that Aldous Huxley was able to satirize the concept in his "Farcical History of Richard Greenow." From midnight to early morning the body of the intelligent, sophisticated Greenow was occupied by the sentimental Anti-self, "Pearl Bellairs," whose gushing best-sellers supported, embarrassed, and ultimately destroyed the man through whom

6. *A Personal Record* (New York: Harper & Bros., 1912), pp. 114–15.
7. Baines, p. 160.
8. *Ibid.*, p. 287.

she acted. Richard Ellmann, in his brief discussion of the phenomenon, relates the popularity of the *doppelganger*—found in works as various in type as Stevenson's *Dr. Jekyll and Mr. Hyde,* Wilde's *Picture of Dorian Gray,* Beerbohm's *The Happy Hypocrite,* and Valéry's *Monsieur Teste*—with the vogue of pseudonyms among late nineteenth-century writers.[9] W. K. Magee became "John Eglinton" to avoid the provincialism suggested by his too-Irish name; George Russell derived "AE" from Aeon, the name of a heavenly personage who came to him in a vision; Oscar Wilde adopted the name "Sebastian Melmoth," perhaps after Maturin's hero, in the hope that it would eliminate "amiable, irresponsible Oscar" entirely; Ford Madox Hueffer changed his name to Ford Madox Ford when he felt that he had become a new person; and so thoroughly did William Sharp become "Fiona Macleod" that "he wrote under her name books in a style different from his own, sent letters for her to friends in a feminine handwriting, complained to friends who wrote to her that they never wrote to him, and eventually almost collapsed under the strain of double life."[10] We should remind ourselves that "Joseph Conrad" is also a pseudonym.

The theme of the divided self is not the only idea Conrad may have derived from the archetype of the artist dominant at the time he began to write. Behind the idea of the divided self is the ideal of detachment, the view that the artist can create only by standing aloof from life, looking down upon it from the vantage point of an Ivory Tower. Since the early nineteenth century this ideal has had to fight its way against an opposing tradition, the view that art may be equated with experience and that therefore the artist is a man who lives not less but more fully than other men. This tradition holds that the artist must continually tap the Sacred Fount of experience, but there is always the danger that he will dissipate his creative energy in life and love; like the heroes of *Sentimental Education, Roderick Hudson,* and *Maurice Guest,* he may be trapped by life to such an extent that he can no longer produce art at all. This point is hammered home in novel after novel of the late Victorian period, and explains in part why the ideal of the Ivory Tower became dominant.

Conrad may well have felt the lesson with peculiar force, for here was a man who had accumulated more than his share of romantic experiences, who had traveled to exotic places, and, for a while at least, had loved so passionately that when he lost the woman in question, he may have attempted suicide. Conrad undoubtedly knew that his experiences gave him a rich fund of material upon which he could base his fiction, but he knew too that there was something suspect about an artist who became entangled with life. Add to this an innate shyness, a reluctance to expose the self, and consider too that what is most significant about Conrad's early life is that he rejected it. After the romantic years in Marseilles, when he lived the adventurous life of a Carlist smuggler, fell in love with a beautiful woman, gambled, fought, and presumably tried to kill himself, Korzeniowski seems gradually to have become more and more detached and aloof. The Congo experience a few years later seems to have verified his suspicion that life is innately corrupt and all action tainted by selfishness. From James and Ford

---

9. Richard Ellmann, *Yeats: The Man and the Masks* (New York: Dutton, 1948), pp. 70–73.

10. *Ibid.,* p. 73.

he may have learned that if the artist is essentially the detached observer, no one can see clearly that with which he is too intimately involved. James envied Conrad his experiences, but Conrad's attitude toward them is not without a secret guilt and shame.

Even if there were no biographical evidence that Conrad rejected the past to help us understand the appeal of the second self, we would have only to consider the anomalous situation of a man who changes courses radically at the midpoint of his life. If such a man entirely denies the past, he admits that half his life was wasted; but if he exalts it, he implies that it is the present half that is empty, like a bitter old Mark Twain looking back nostalgically on the days of childhood. Unlike a Twain or a Proust, Conrad did not attempt to discover a lost self by recovering past time; rather, he attempted to destroy the past by transforming it into art. The life-stuff he used was the same life-stuff that must often have seemed to be in control of the young Korzeniowski when he was submerged in experience, but the artist in Conrad could use or reject what he pleased. He could control experience and thus master it. Conrad's second attempt to kill off Korzeniowski was successful, but he hid his guilt by insisting that the murderer was not the British man of letters, Joseph Conrad—a respectable married man, a father, a man with friends, a citizen willing to speak out publicly for the values held by society—but that mysterious, godlike, "very genuine Conrad" who just happened to occupy the same body as the man.

Recognition of the second self is, I think, essential to an understanding of Conrad's fiction, for it lies behind the many doubles and secret sharers of his fiction, it explains the use of Marlow as one of his masks, and it finally justifies the intended ambiguity of his "inconclusive" tales. But if Conrad's biographers make much of the sharp, chronological division in the life of their subject, they tend to ignore the implications and to go on assuming that to know the man is to know the writer. And Conrad has been almost as unfortunate in his critics, most of whom assume that the meaning of a Conrad tale can be expressed in terms of the man's allegiance to those values of service, fidelity, and courage which we expect to find in "one of us." But there is more to Conrad than this, as we can see by examining the two works in which he came most firmly to grips with the nature of detachment and experience. Whereas *Heart of Darkness* is, I think, a bitter indictment of life and an affirmation of art, the novel *Victory*—contrary to the traditional interpretations—is a defense of detachment.

Because *Heart of Darkness* is an indictment of life, Conrad had to protect himself by standing behind the mask of Marlow. Perhaps too much has been made of Conrad's use of Marlow as narrator, for he appears in only a few of the stories and may be easily enough understood as a simple technical device—a heritage from that oral tradition of the storyteller that lies behind the art of fiction. Patrick Cruttwell tells us:

> Conrad invents a teller of his own stories called Marlow; "his own stories," some of them, meaning things which had really happened to the person Conrad, as in *Heart of Darkness* and *Youth*. These stories, which were true, are presented as if they were fiction by a personage who *is* fictional but who is close to the true protagonist of the real events. An odd complication: what were its motives, what its effects? Conrad, as a writer, had some special problems. He

was a Pole who wrote in English about Englishmen; he was a highly sensitive ingenious contemplative writer, who (at least in the stories told by Marlow) was using the convention of the oral anecdote spontaneous and unformed. Marlow solved some of these problems for his creator. He was English, not Polish; being represented as a former sailor who had retired from the sea— here he "is" Conrad—he could, as it were, hide Conrad's personal experience even while narrating it; and the pretence that he is merely telling a tale to a group of friends excuses—in fact, necessitates for artistic reasons—a certain vagueness at the centre, a doubt of what it all really means—for the doubt can be given to Marlow, not to Conrad.[11]

If Marlow is a protective device, it is easy to understand why he is used in the stories most directly related to Conrad's own experience as a man, for we have seen that the writer in him rejected that experience.

We need not agree with Jean-Aubry's assertion that *Heart of Darkness* is "nothing but" an account of Conrad's Congo experience, but on the evidence of the Congo diary, the biographical basis of the story is too obvious to be denied. What matters is that it was an episode in Conrad's life that had a profound, transforming effect upon him. It was the bitter realization of a childhood anticipation. There in "the heart of an immense darkness," as Jean-Aubry tells us, "he could no longer feel between his white companions and himself that innate solidarity, that common conception of human dignity, that fidelity to few very simple and, so to speak, tacitly assumed principles which throughout his childhood and his fifteen years at sea had been the constant atmosphere of his life and, at the bottom of his heart, his safeguard and his pride."[12] Conrad himself implied this in one of his *Last Essays*:

> Away in the middle of the stream, on a little island nestling all black in the foam of the broken water, a solitary little light glimmered feebly, and I said to myself with awe, "This is the very spot of my boyish boast."
> A great melancholy descended on me. Yes, this was the very spot. But there was no shadowy friend to stand by my side in the night of the enormous wilderness, no great haunting memory, but only the unholy recollection of a prosaic newspaper "stunt" and the distasteful knowledge of the vilest scramble for loot that ever disfigured the history of human conscience and geographical exploration. What an end to the idealized realities of a boy's daydreams! I wondered what I was doing there, for indeed it was only an unforeseen episode, hard to believe in now, in my seaman's life. Still, the fact remains that I have smoked a pipe of peace at midnight in the very heart of the African continent, and felt very lonely there.[13]

After the Congo experience, Conrad fell into what he called "a long, long illness and a very dismal convalescence."[14] Later he told Edward Garnett that "before the Congo, I was just a mere animal," and we may suppose, with Jean-Aubry, that it was this experience more than any other that brought him a sense

---

11. Cruttwell, pp. 489–90.
12. Jean-Aubry, p. 169.
13. "Geography and Some Explorers," in *Last Essays* (London: J. M. Dent & Sons, 1926), pp. 24–25.
14. Jean-Aubry, p. 175.

of death-and-rebirth that enabled him to bury Captain Korzeniowski and become the novelist Conrad.[15] His surrogate Marlow tells us that the trip up the Congo represented his "furthest point of navigation."

But if *Heart of Darkness* were only a memoir, it would be too personal and individual to serve as a comment on life in general. It is for this reason that we have in the story not only the mask of Marlow but the elaborate frame by means of which we achieve detachment even from the storyteller. The frame, like the mythic parallels, serves to increase the universal implications of the story. Actually, we as readers are auditors of the storyteller Marlow, and if the Thames also "has been one of the dark places on the earth," we may say the same of wherever we are. As many critics have noted, the heart of darkness is within us; but we know this only by means of Conrad's technical devices. Without them we would seem to have in the story only a rather special and particular experience, and *Heart of Darkness* would be only an elaborate, picturesque travelogue.

What does Marlow discover in the heart of darkness? I think that we can accept Albert Guérard's contention that this is one of Conrad's secret sharer stories and that Marlow discovers in the appalling depravity of Kurtz an aspect of himself which, once seen, forces him to assume an attitude of only looking on.[16] But we read the story superficially if we merely equate darkness with evil—it is not a matter of darkness out there and lightness here, but darkness forever corrupting the lightness. If Kurtz was "man enough to face the darkness," man enough to be damned, it is because he had within himself the capacity of a saint or a universal genius and could never be satisfied with the middle way of mediocrity. Like Satan, he fell through pride—"exterminate the brutes!"—but he fell from a height, whereas the other exploiters in the Congo are mere lowly agents of the "flabby devil" that runs their show.

Because the darkness extends far beyond the Congo, Conrad wisely ends Marlow's story at the home base of the Company, in Belgium, and in the apartment of Kurtz's Intended. That Marlow has not fully learned the significance of Kurtz is shown by the fact that he allows himself once again to be deluded by anticipation: "Thus I was left at last with a slim packet of letters and the girl's portrait. She struck me as beautiful—I mean she had a beautiful expression. I know that the sunlight can be made to lie too, yet one felt that no manipulation of light and pose could have conveyed the delicate shade of truthfulness upon those features. She seemed ready to listen without mental reservation, without suspicion, without a thought for herself."[17] If she can prove the force of sunlight, then Marlow need not accept the darkness. Yet "she came forward, all in black, with a pale head, floating towards me in the dark. . . . The room seemed to have grown darker, as if all the sad light of the cloudy evening had taken refuge on her forehead. This fair hair, this pale visage, this pure brow, seemed surrounded by an ashy halo from which the dark eyes looked out at me." Immediately he perceives her intense pride and thus seems to see her with Kurtz at the moment of his death. "I asked myself," Marlow says, "what I was doing there, with a

---

15. *Ibid.*

16. *Conrad the Novelist* (Cambridge, Mass.: Harvard University Press, 1958), pp. 33–43.

17. Harkness, p. 65. Subsequent quotations from *Heart of Darkness* in this paragraph may all be found on pages 66–69.

sensation of panic in my heart as though I had blundered into a place of cruel and absurd mysteries not fit for a human being to behold." Just as the light and dark imagery is fused in this final scene, Marlow comes to see a resemblance between the pale Intended and Kurtz's dark jungle mistress: "I . . . see her too, a tragic and familiar Shade, resembling in this gesture another one, tragic also, and bedecked with powerless charms, stretching bare brown arms over the glitter of the infernal stream, the stream of darkness." Then follows the often-discussed "benevolent lie" of Marlow, his assurance that the last word uttered by Kurtz was the name of the Intended. But if this is factually a lie, it is, like Conrad's story of how he became a writer, "impressionistically" true, for this final scene shows that there is as much horror, as much darkness, in the apartment of the Intended, in the dark-eyed girl herself, as in the depths of the Congo. With this realization, Marlow has few choices: he can participate in the folly and the evil, he can care only for himself like the neat and orderly accountant in the jungle, or he can merely look on with sympathetic but horrified detachment. He chooses the last course.

In the Axel Heyst of *Victory* we have a Marlow-like hero whose defense against life is "to drift without ever catching on to anything,"[18] for he believes that "he who forms a tie is lost. The germ of corruption has entered into his soul" (p. 188). Before the crisis Heyst, like Marlow before his Congo experience, has been fortunate in not having to really test his detachment. "I don't know myself what I would do," Heyst tells Lena, "what countenance I would have before a creature which would strike me as being the evil incarnate" (p 196). After Marlow faced the heart of darkness in Kurtz and himself, he retreated from all ties, lest he be corrupted, but though Marlow shared the experiences of Captain Korzeniowski, he also represents the storyteller Joseph Conrad. By learning to transform his experiences, by telling "benevolent lies" that were actually not lies at all, he affirmed the vision and imagination of the artist even while indicting raw experience. Heyst, on the other hand, is put in such a position that he cannot retreat before the evil incarnate in the diabolic Mr. Jones, and *Victory* ends in the annihilation of the hero. *Victory* appeared at the beginning of the First World War, and in its symbolic depiction of the detached man forced to commit himself in action, it provides a fitting climax to the Ivory Tower tradition. Yet it does not repudiate that tradition, for the message of Victory is more nihilistic than affirmative.

If I am right in reading *Heart of Darkness* as a bitter comment on the nature of existence and if also valid are the standard interpretations of *Victory,* we would have to assume that Conrad changed his mind radically between 1899 and 1914. Again and again we have been told that the meaning of *Victory* is summed up in the final words of Axel Heyst: "Ah, Davidson, woe to the man whose heart has not learned while young to hope, to love—and to put its trust in life!" (p. 383). I find it hard to believe that the subtle and ironic Conrad could have attached so simple a tag-moral to the end of a complex story, particularly since it is at odds with the view of life expressed in his other works. And is that

---

18. *Victory,* Modern Library edition (New York, 1932), p. 89. Later references to this edition are incorporated in the text. I have taken the liberty of correcting several typographical errors in citing passages from this edition.

lesson what *Victory* really teaches? It would make more sense, I think, to read *Victory* as a tragedy of inadequate detachment, for if Heyst had not become involved with life, if he had resisted the impulse to play the rescuing knight, he would not have fallen at all. If the author of this novel is on the side of active participation as opposed to detachment, how do we explain the fact that the representatives of life depicted in this novel are so singularly unattractive? Jones says, "I am the world itself come to pay you a visit" (pp. 354–55), and earlier he and his confederates were identified as "the worthy envoys, the envoys extraordinary of the world" (p. 327). Perhaps Jones, Ricardo, and Pedro are only "the embodied evil of the world" (p. 279), but which characters can be said to represent the goodness? The benevolent but blundering Morrison? The sympathetic but quickly retreating Davidson? The victimized and scarred Lena? Surely not the Schombergs or Zangiacomo? And finally, if *Victory* demonstrates the evils of detachment, how do we reconcile this with the praise of detachment in the "Author's Note," where the writer Conrad tells us that "the unchanging Man of history is wonderfully adaptable by power of endurance and in his capacity for detachment" (p. ix) and that this "faculty of detachment born perhaps from a sense of infinite littleness . . . is yet the only faculty that seems to assimilate man to the immortal gods" (p. x)?

Part of the difficulty in interpreting *Victory* comes from the inconsistent point of view. Because the author's voice in the novel is never clearly established, we are too likely to let Heyst be the interpreter of his own story. In fact, the several narrators of the story seem to have an attitude toward life not unlike that of the aloof Heyst. In the first paragraph of the novel the human narrator of the first part tells us that we are "camped like bewildered travellers in a garish, unrestful hotel"—and when we meet Schomberg, we learn who is the hotel-keeper. Later, the omniscient narrator tells us that "every age is fed on illusions, lest men should renounce life early and the human race come to an end" (p. 91). If it is Heyst who says "all action is bound to be harmful" (p. 52), the omniscient narrator echoes his opinion with the statement that action is "the barbed hook" (p. 164). Because there is no Marlovian mask in this novel, the distinction between teller and hero is dangerously obscured, and we come to suspect that in this novel Conrad did not trouble to disguise himself.

Yet the difficulty we have in determining the author's voice in *Victory* is matched by our difficulty in understanding Axel Heyst. At one level he is simply a man—a man, like all men, made up of contradictions and caught, like Hamlet, in indecision: too sympathetic and lonely to remain entirely alone, too reserved and reflective to participate effectively. Much of his detachment seems unnatural, a heritage from an embittered father that has been imposed upon him against his will. He is at once introverted and friendly (he writes to many friends in Europe), and his many contradictory nicknames suggest that Conrad tried to make him represent all types of mankind. Symbolically, however, he carries an additional weight of meaning. First, he is an artist: he arrives in the islands with a portfolio of sketches under his arm, and though we hear nothing more about his practicing art, his temperament is certainly that of the late nineteenth-century archetype of the artist. His name "Axel" may well have derived from the Axel of Villiers de l'Isle Adam's drama—that epitome of the artist-as-exile who was willing to leave his living to his servants.[19] Conrad changed the last name from Berg to Heyst, perhaps to suggest "highest," perhaps because "Heyst" rhymes with "Christ," for in the early pages of the novel Conrad clearly attributes godlike qualities to this "strange being without needs" (p. 190). He is out of everybody's way, yet conspicuous, and his most frequent visitors are shadows. To Morrison, he seems to come in answer to prayer, and for a man supposed to hold himself aloof, he does a remarkable amount of saving of other people in this novel. He saves Morrison, he saves Lena, he saves even Jones, Ricardo, and Pedro. Is it too much to suggest that in this single figure Conrad tried to sum up all his selves—the man, the artist, and that godlike, creative force that neither Captain Korzeniowski nor the respected man of letters Joseph Conrad could fully understand? If so, it is only the man who utters the famous "moral," and it is only the man the critics seem to hear.

What may those other selves be saying? Perhaps because some critics find this novel, unlike most of Conrad's, too easy to understand, they have been rather harsh on it. We are told that the inconsistent point of view suggests uncertainty by Conrad, that the style is weaker than in his earlier works, and that he could find no way to resolve the action except through coincidences. Yet Conrad is known to have taken pride in this work—to have felt that his reputation as a literary artist would stand on *Nostromo* and *Victory*. Perhaps he felt this so strongly that he decided to retain the title because of its personal relevance for him. His explanation in his note to the first edition is weak. There he tells us that he realized that the public would be likely to associate the word with the war and that "the word Victory, the shining and tragic goal of noble effort, appeared too great, too august, to stand at the head of a mere novel." Yet he decided to retain it because "Victory was the last word I had written in peace time. It was the last literary thought which had occurred to me before the doors of the Temple of Janus flying open with a crash shook the minds, the hearts, the consciences of men all over the world. Such coincidence could not be treated lightly. And I made up my mind to let the word stand, in the same hopeful spirit in which some simple citizen of Old Rome would have 'accepted the Omen'" (p. vii). That statement has the proper rhetorical ring and reveals the voice of the man of letters as dutiful citizen. But because the "very genuine Conrad" is a more cunning being, I prefer to take more seriously the brief first paragraph of the note: "The last word of this novel was written on the 29th of May, 1914. And that last word was the single word of the title." For if we like coincidences, we may be struck by the fact that actually the last word of the story is the word "nothing":

> Davidson took out his handkerchief to wipe the perspiration off his forehead.
> "And then, your Excellency, I went away. There was nothing to be done there."
> "Clearly," assented the Excellency.
> Davidson, thoughtful, seemed to weigh the matter in his mind, and then murmured with placid sadness:
> "Nothing!"

---

19. See Katherine H. Gatch, "Conrad's Axel," *Studies in Philology* 48 (1951): 98–106.

The novel seems to exist between poles of nothingness and victory, and is therefore more complex, ironic, and ambivalent than is generally recognized. If so, it is in the total balancing of a pure work of art that the artist's triumph is to be found, for ultimately the poles merge into one. Perhaps, in fact, there is an affirmative progression from an awareness of the horror at the heart of existence to the realization, as in Poe and Mallarmé, that when the darkness pervades everything a oneness is finally achieved that is equivalent to nothingness. There is a precedent in Conrad for the equation of triumph with final insight. Of Kurtz's last utterance in *Heart of Darkness* Marlow said, "It was an affirmation, a moral victory paid for by innumerable defeats, by abominable terrors, by abominable satisfactions. But it was a victory!"[20] As Conrad completed the story of Axel Heyst, life at its most evil and violent welled up around him in the form of the world war, and the creative spirit in him may have insisted that he retain the title because it knew that it was superior to all that, for it could see clearly the evil at the heart of life, yet transform it into a strange, artistic beauty.

As a surrogate for the artist who wrote *Victory* Axel Heyst also achieves triumph by acknowledging the nothingness at the heart of existence. In most interpretations of the novel the final victory is accorded to Lena, for she "breathed her last, triumphant, seeking his glance in the shades of death" (p. 380). But if her motive was to balance the scales by saving Heyst, as she had been saved, she is victorious only in achieving a proud martyrdom, and Heyst makes her victory a pyrrhic one when he voluntarily destroys the self she has saved. I would argue that the real victory is Heyst's. Some critics feel that he achieves a partial triumph in the self-awareness shown in his final statement to Davidson, but even before the trio of villains arrived on the island, he knew and regretted his incapacity to act, to let himself go. No new insight is reflected here, but if there were, it would seem strange that he should kill himself after making the statement. Another partial victory may be found in the fact that he discovers courage in himself only when he learns to become afraid. It was easy to be brave earlier, he tells us, for he scorned life. When he formed a tie, however, "all his defenses were broken now. Life had him fairly by the throat" (p. 209). With something at stake now, he finds himself weaponless and hesitant until, too late, with the girl dead and with her what was at stake, he takes his revenge upon the world.

In one of his symbolic roles, we have seen, Mr. Jones represents "the world itself." One of the unsolved mysteries of *Victory* is the manner of Jones's death. Davidson says, "I suppose he tumbled into the water by accident—or perhaps not by accident" (p 384). One possibility is that Jones killed Heyst, as he killed Ricardo, then set fire to the cottage and committed suicide. But in another of his symbolic roles Jones is the devil, and because the devil ought to die in a fiery blaze, it seems wrong for Jones to end his life on the wharf. Did he shoot himself, then jump into the water? It is equally difficult to visualize his drowning, accidentally or intentionally, in shallow water within reach of the wharf. Perhaps Mr. Wang, the Chinese houseboy, killed Jones as he killed Pedro, but we are specifically told that it was Wang who discovered the body. This leaves Heyst as the most likely killer. Earlier Conrad drew a connection between killing and loving. Heyst told Lena, "I've never killed a man or loved

---

20. Harkness, p. 63.

a woman—not even in my thoughts, not even in my dreams," and a moment later, "To slay, to love—the greatest enterprises of life upon a man! And I have no experience of either" (p. 200). The repetition suggests that Conrad wanted us to assume that if Heyst could learn to love a woman, he could also learn to kill.

But why would he kill Jones? One reason would be that he sees in Jones a double of himself. Just as Jones represents the world—even his name suggests any man—Heyst has to acknowledge that there is a lot of "the original Adam" in himself. Heyst and Jones are both exiles, but whereas Heyst's aloofness is the result of his temperament and his father's skepticism, Jones had been "hounded out of society" (p. 357) and "having been ejected . . . from his proper social sphere because he had refused to conform to certain usual conventions he was a rebel now, and was coming and going up and down the earth" (p. 297). With his effeminate eyebrows and his obsessive hatred of women, Jones is apparently homosexual, whereas we can only assume that Heyst was not sexual at all until he met Lena. Nonetheless, Jones perceives an affinity between himself and Heyst, and recent critics of the novel have had no difficulty in documenting the similarities.[21] Driven by his perverted love for Ricardo, Jones tries to kill his secretary rather than lose him to a woman, but the shot goes astray and wounds Lena. Actually, Heyst is responsible for her death, not only because he failed to defend her against "the world," but because, "towering in the doorway" (p. 376), he failed to heed Jones's request that he "stoop a little" (p. 368) as Jones took aim at Ricardo—a minor culpability perhaps, but characteristic of the hesitating Heyst and symbolically appropriate, for if Jones and Heyst are doubles, the passive Heyst and his aggressive counterpart must come to act as one. Then Heyst realizes that the power to love gives him the power to kill, and we can assume that he finds the means to destroy Jones. After that, he must kill himself also, just as the original Axel thought that he could retain a pure love only by killing himself and his beloved. At the moment of her death Lena receives a vision of "divine radiance" as she imagines Heyst "ready to take her up in his firm arms and take her into the sanctuary of his innermost heart—for ever!" (p. 380). By voluntarily accepting oblivion, she and Axel Heyst achieve at last a complete detachment—"the only faculty," we recall, "that seems to assimilate man to the immortal gods."

To return to the three basic selves of Conrad, the man Korzeniowski is obviously less significant for an understanding of *Victory* than for works like *Heart of Darkness*. Conrad tells us in his preface that there were real-life originals for the major characters in *Victory,* but he stresses the fact that he had but fleeting glimpses of them and that they crossed his life only casually. If there is merit in this novel, Conrad seems to be saying, it will be found not in a transcription of his experiences as a man, but in the craftmanship and imagination that can take the most insignificant germs and make them expand into a whole fictive world. But perhaps it is because Conrad did not have a firm base of personal experience on which to build *Victory* that we can find in this novel a clear example of how the craftsmanship of the writer and the imagination of the demon may come in conflict.

---

21. See, for example, Frederick R. Karl, *A Reader's Guide to Joseph Conrad* (New York: Noonday Press, 1960), pp. 258–60.

The ending of the novel has been frequently criticized. As the action moves toward the final holocaust, the omniscient narrator steps aside and forces us to see the last events through the eyes of an all-too-human narrator who is inadequate to the task of interpretation and was not even present to witness many of the occurrences. The craftsman in Conrad may have felt that the switch in point of view near the ending completed a circle begun by the first-person narration of the first part. He may have realized too that a direct depiction of the final violence would seem melodramatic. There is a suggestion of melodrama in the scene of Lena's death, but Conrad stops at the proper moment and instead of showing us Jones killing Ricardo, Wang killing Pedro, Heyst killing Jones, and Heyst finally committing suicide, he forces us to see some of these events at second hand and to surmise others for ourselves, thus achieving an ironic distance that modifies the violence. But if the second Conrad was a craftsman, he was also a public-spirited citizen who may well have realized that the demon in him had set in motion certain forces that could only destroy one another. To show Heyst killing Jones, then himself, would be to reveal too clearly that if Heyst and Jones are doubles and if Jones represents the mortal, loving, yet evil self of Heyst, then Heyst voluntarily destroys in himself the capacity to act just after he has found it. That was hardly a proper message for wartime, and we can sympathize with the author of the patriotic note to the first edition for refusing to present dramatically such a nihilistic conclusion. Several generations of critics, by continuing to maintain that *Victory* is a repudiation of detachment, a spirited defense of man's need to commit himself in action, have testified to the success of the second Conrad.

Yet those same critics have refused to look closely at the ending of the novel or to face squarely the ultimate implications of the clues placed there by the third Conrad. To do so would be to admit that we are on dangerous ground when we try to interpret the "very genuine Conrad" as if he were only "one of us."

Conrad's Menagerie: Animal Imagery and Theme

STANTON DE VOREN HOFFMAN

Sir George Williams University

I

Conrad's villains are often absurd, like the man at the central station in *Heart of Darkness* who puts out a fire with a pail that has a hole in its bottom, and as such they are sometimes puzzling in the larger contexts of the novels in which they appear. In other words, one does not always know exactly what they are. They appear as caricatures or as effigies cut out of something; they are two-dimensional and hollow; they seem to be "pasteboard figures,"[1] figures that are overdrawn, exaggerated, fantastic, and fantastically mean; but they often seem more, something beyond their villainy and wrong choices. They have one major trait in common—irresponsibility, and a perfect "unattachment for anything but the self."[2] But more than this selfishness, they represent states of anarchy and chaos related to the themes and temptations of the novels in which they appear. One might even think of the fallen angels in Milton's *Paradise Lost,* where their disorder at one place is rendered through an image of goats,[3] an image that relates their moral to physical corruption, their disobedience to lust. This is to say that in Conrad, goats and their kind often prevail. One critic has remarked about

First published: 12, no. 3 (1964): 59–71. The author did not wish to make any comments or revisions.

1. Douglas Hewitt, *Conrad: A Reassessment* (Philadelphia: Dufour, 1952), p. 109.

2. Edward Crankshaw, *Joseph Conrad: Some Aspects of the Art of the Novel* (London: John Lane, 1936), p. 24.

3. See *Paradise Lost* VI, 856–58. It is not inappropriate to speak of Milton in reference to Conrad, for there are to be found Miltonic parallels in his work such as the evil trinity and Edenic imagery in *Victory,* the restless activity of the fallen in *Heart of Darkness,* and the "wrong-headed lucidity" of Kayerts in "Outpost of Progress," which suggests an Adam lost in wandering mazes.

Victory that a heavily recurrent diabolic and bestiary imagery dominates the presentation of the modern world's moral evil.[4] This is true elsewhere. Sailors make reference to Satan and hell in the form of nautical curses, and villains appear as part of an underworld of bestial life. DeBarral in *Chance* comes from this underworld; Donkin in *Nigger of the Narcissus* is a bird of prey. In works such as *Lord Jim, Victory,* and *Nigger of the Narcissus* there are recurring similes and metaphors of the animal and the irrationally bestial. They relate to themes woven into the wholes of these works.

All these animals, birds, amphibians, and serpents of Conrad's fiction represent a lower order of being, a regression into a meaningless chaos that is made clear through a series of "burlesque" and slapstick actions identified with these same characters.[5] They further indicate the closeness to the Conradian protagonist of the temptation to regress to lower orders of being—the instinctive and irrational—for no matter what the hero falls into—the unconscious, the disordered dream, the other self, moral cynicism, detachment—he falls into the animal; and while he never quite barks, his sometimes comic and always absurd doubles do. Like Jim, he sometimes goes down to a chorus of yelps. Jim plunges into the sea that is called the dream, and this plunge is accompanied by the officers of the *Patna,* each one reduced to an animal symbol-image, all together simulating the comic fury of inappropriately matched beasts; and Heyst's indifference is supposedly reflected by the catlike fury of Ricardo as well as by the corpse and gravelike hollowness of Jones.[6] But there is still some difference between Jim's case and Heyst's case and the case of the crew members of the *Narcissus,* for there are many kinds of beasts, some more dangerous or more foul than others. The bestial imagery of *Lord Jim* can be viewed as a furthering of that novel's "burlesque" and low comic elements, for elephants, horses, and yelping dogs that do not bite are a bit laughable.[7] But for the most part, and most important, this type of imagery serves as the symbol that suggests to us that in all the temptations that Conrad's heroes encounter, there is the threat of the irrational, the bestial that defines all the types of disordering that are Conrad's concern.

II

In *Lord Jim,* the characters who are identified with Jim's fall and temptation, and, more specifically, those who accompany his plunge, characters who are objects

---

4. Kingsley Widmer, "Conrad's Pyrrhic *Victory*," *Twentieth Century Literature* 5 (1959): 127.

5. The low comic has much unnoted importance in Conrad—especially in *Lord Jim,* but also in *Heart of Darkness, Falk, Youth,* and elsewhere. The *Patna* scene, for instance, is marked by the antics of the officers as they struggle to get the lifeboat undone. Marlow refers to these things as "farce," "low comedy," and "burlesque." In *Lord Jim* this slapstick comedy identified with Jim's abandonment of the *Patna* seems to serve as a kind of objective way of illuminating certain characteristics of the fallen state. Burlesque is often a symbol for disorder. It is characterized by violent incongruities, repetitions and mechanical patterns and a general dehumanization of the individual.

6. Conrad has identified death with the excesses of his heroes.

7. It also can be viewed as serving this function in *Victory,* for the catlike frame of Ricardo allows for some absurd gestures, and Conrad can move from kitty on the hearth to leaping jaguar with comic virtuosity. But the cat is still a beast of violence.

of low comic slapstick, are the figures of this bestiary. The officers of the *Patna,*
groveling on all fours, trying to get their lifeboat free, snarling and huddled later
in the same boat, are horses, bullocks, elephants, owls, and crows. They are also
dogs. The engineer has the head of an old horse; the captain, like a "trained baby
elephant," and called a "hound" by the harbormaster, snorts "like a frightened
bullock." In the lifeboat scene, one finds "one bleated, another screamed, one
howled," "a couple of mean mongrels," "they screeched together," "the other
beast was coming at me," "like three dirty owls," "hoarse as a crow," "he glared
as if he would have liked to claw me to pieces," "greasy beast," "fishy eyes," "drew
in like a turtle," and so on. Later, Robinson is a "worn-out cab horse," Blake of
Blake and Egstrom a man who screams in the manner of "an outraged cockatoo,"
Cornelius a man who walks with the creeping "of a repulsive beetle," a man
"mute as a fish," verminlike, catlike, henlike, wormlike. Even Gentleman Brown
has fierce crow-footed eyes—he claws the air, and is bowed and hairy, and like
some man-beast of folklore.

All these characters, in one way or another, are related to Jim's fall. The
Patna scene (which has the greatest concentration of "burlesque") has the greatest
concentration of animal imagery—after his leap, Jim sits in a lifeboat surrounded
by three beasts that hoot, roar, and yelp. He himself is able to emphasize the
doglike aspects of his situation. For as he relates his fall, he comments: "If I
had opened my lips just then I would have simply howled like an animal," and
Marlow, as he listens to Jim and is frightened and forced to act and to become
involved in a struggle that is analogous to Jim's struggle, remarks: "I can't say
I was frightened; but I certainly kept as still as if there had been something
dangerous in the room, that at the first hint of a movement on my part would
have been provoked to pounce upon me."[8]

The scene on the deck of the *Patna* represents a fall on several levels, for it
is not only the plunge into the dream and the failure to order it, the leap from
the world to the unconscious, but also the escape into the disordered personality,
neurosis, and evil. To be perceived, through the animal, is that the disordered
personality involves the movement away from Morton Zabel's ethical fact, and
a discovery of chaos, which is a portion of all being and which somehow must
be formed and ordered, possibly through tradition, discipline, code, or art—even
though these are sometimes suspect. The evil committed and the flight toward
rest and repose and away from responsibility are not merely a case of officers
abandoning a ship. They are more, for these officers suggest an entire world of
beasthood. In them is contained everything, indicative of not only the disorder
that is the subject of the novel but also the impermanence of role and of being
that is part of disorder, and that is made significant through one of these
creatures being many creatures. In choosing the dream without form and
external parallel, in choosing one's egotistical illusions, one leaps into formlessness.
What has happened is that a lower order of existence has been "chosen," and
when the hero feels he could have "howled," he is creating an internal analogue
to the actions aboard the *Patna* and afterwards. Marlow, the second hero, feels
something ready to pounce. This can be two things: Jim as animal, but, more
likely, the lower self of Marlow, which is about to be revealed through his associ-

---

8. *Lord Jim*, Modern Library edition (New York, 1931), p. 171.

ation with Jim's actions and justifications, and which remains close to him at all times. Stein's butterfly, which suggests that one must live with dirt, with corruption, has a meaningful relationship to this feared animal that is about to pounce.

III

In *Victory,* except for an occasional metamorphosis into a viper and serpent, Martin Ricardo remains a cat throughout, and he is everything from a house cat to a jungle beast. His servant is a dog-ape-bear. As the grunts and savage snorts are accompanying motifs in *Lord Jim,* here also the catlike purrs and motions are the accompaniment for Ricardo, and thus for Heyst. They are used with an equal intensity and greater consistency, and Ricardo, named death and the serpent, appearing as a figure for lust, seems completely dehumanized. An image has been made a person; his nature overwhelms him—true of all Conradian villains, for they become less men as they become more image—and his nature is to be seen through a convenient metaphor worked over and over again, with variations, rendering him somewhat absurd, as the mad bunching together of animals (dogs, owls, crows) in *Lord Jim* renders also its officers absurd. But a cat is more dangerous than an owl, an ape more frightening than an elephant. These images are everywhere.

"Mr. Jones got up spectrally, and Ricardo imitated him with a snarl and a stretch." Ricardo shows his teeth, he emits a grunt of "astonishing ferocity, as if proposing to himself to eat the local people," his moustaches stirred by themselves in an "odd, feline manner," he is a deliberate "wild-cat turned into a man," his expession is that of "a cat which sees a piece of fish in the pantry out of reach," he is an enormous savage cat, a rather "nasty, slow-moving cat," he has a catlike grin, is like a "cat watching the preparation of a saucer of milk," and he has "the placidity of a domestic cat dozing on the hearth rug," complete with a satisfied sound of purring. Ricardo "retracted his lips and looked up sharply at Schomberg, as if only too anxious to leap upon him with teeth and claws"; his motions as he rises are curious sideways movements, with glancings and unexpected elongations of his thick body; like a cat, he purrs and prowls, has greenish irises, an excitement "such as a wild animal of the cat species, anxious to make a spring, might betray," has a "vicious cat-like readiness to get his claws out at any moment," darts from tree to tree, and has a strange air "of feline gallantry." Pedro, "looking more like a performing bear," is also a man-beast: "The lower part of his physiognomy was over developed, his narrow and low forehead, unintelligently furrowed by horizontal wrinkles, surmounted wildly hirsute cheeks and a flat nose with wide, baboon-like nostrils. There was something equivocal in the appearance of his shaggy, hair-smothered humanity." Schomberg, an earlier figure for lust, passion, and disorder, has a thick paw and gnashes and grinds his teeth in a mock-bestial manner.

As in *Lord Jim* this heavily worked and recurrent animal imagery does several things. Basically, it dehumanizes, and this has, in this novel, double significance, for dehumanization is necessary for allegorical characters and also for a theme that surrounds them. What the animal represents is the great danger. This could refer to Ricardo's lust. He who gives in to violent and unpurged passion is clearly dehumanized, just as he who plunges into the uncontrolled unconscious, the dream, the illusion, is dehumanized. Ricardo, Pedro, and Schomberg appear to represent a lack of restraint, a failure to integrate passion—to live with dirt, to refer to Stein's butterfly again—and only Lena seems to make a partially successful attempt at integration (at least symbolically). As representatives of this lack of restraint, they are ferocious, violent, and predatory. But they are also excessive and exaggerated, and the bestial images are applied in a slightly ridiculous manner—Ricardo sees a fish out of reach, rests on a hearth rug, etc.—a manner involving possibly too many variations upon a basic cat metaphor.

The animal imagery in *Victory* creates some problems in interpretation. In *Lord Jim,* the bestial imagery, representative of an aspect of Jim's fall and also representative of a human "choice" and possibility, implies that certain elements are part of allowing the unconscious to master us. Jim's problem, as interpreted by Stein, is a problem of being, of living with the dream that a man must live with, and of ordering this dream and all its implications of a destructive element. The bestial imagery seems directed toward this destructive element, toward what seems to be the major problem of the hero—and his explainer, Marlow. But in *Victory* the case is different; the bestial imagery, important in the novel, does not seem to be clearly an intrinsic part of the major character's major temptation. In *Victory* the theme seems to be about the failures and sins of an isolated romantic skeptic (implying no discernible element of disorder); yet, the animal imagery suggests again a lower order of existence, violence, disorder, the irrational (consider the end of Jones), the primitive. This makes sense in relationship to Ricardo, but less so in the case of Heyst (although Conrad is certainly implying the dehumanization that belongs to his disavowal of involvement). Heyst's sin seems less a case of disorder than of the wrong kind of order. In *Lord Jim* the animal imagery explained and reinforced something occurring within Jim. But in *Victory* Heyst is supposedly suffering from indifference and detachment—the romping beasts do not seem to belong, although they do belong to an underlying theme of passion and its purgation. The trouble is that Conrad, then, has given great emphasis to an imagery that implies the great importance of one kind of fall, while his primary or stated theme in this novel seems concerned with another kind of fall, not needing the correlative of burlesque and the figures of predatory beasts, though the theme does need the the corpse-spectre imagery associated with Jones. All these symbols and directions of this novel work one way, Heyst another way.

Thus *Lord Jim* and *Victory,* approximately fifteen years apart, represent variations in the use of a type of imagery that is to be found with some frequency and consistency elsewhere in Conrad—in one case the menagerie is an integrated part of theme and total action, the theme of Jim's fall and the theme of Jim as a man caught between two selves and two possibilities of being, a man struggling to be; in the other case, animal imagery is still part of a Conradian mode of presentation and revelation but is poorly integrated into the novel. Furthermore, the menageries of both novels are slightly different; the difference is between elephants and dogs on one hand, and cats and apes on the other. The underworld of emotions seems more vicious in the latter case. But no matter how he uses it, Conrad has his image and his symbol for the disorder that is part of his subject. Disorder and chaos are the tumbling of clownish grotesques, revealed as snorting animals, animals making human gestures, undercutting human gestures, bringing us closer to our elemental and bestial selves. The various falls of these novels are the steps to the lower order of existence. The officers of the *Patna* and Martin Ricardo, as he slinks by, are to show us what might be, what might happen. It is a little bit like Circe and her island.

IV

In *Chance,* after Powell falls from innocence through his cavernous journey to the underworld of Saint Katherine's Dock House, and begins to see mankind in a light he had not seen it in before, he goes to his ship, the *Ferndale,* and the street by the docks becomes a foul place of vision, a further step in his education, and his fall:

A mean row of houses on the other side looked empty: there wasn't the smallest gleam of light in them. The white-hot glare of a gin palace a good way off made the intervening piece of street pitch black. Some human shapes appearing mysteriously, as if they had sprung up from the dark ground, shunned the edge of the faint light thrown down by the gateway lamps. These figures were wary in their movements and perfectly silent of foot, *like beasts of prey slinking about a camp fire.*[9]

This is the city of night and the grave, the slimy city of *The Secret Agent* and the prison-house city of *The Return,* the dead and sepulchral city of *Heart of Darkness.* In *The Nigger of the Narcissus,* as the *Narcissus* loses its life and makes port, docking, the city and the land become a place of confused and horrible clamor, foul and suggestive smells, huge objects, bestial shapes. The smoking steamboats that hug the coast are like migrating and amphibious monsters, windows seem the eyes of overfed brutes, and the bow-lines that connect the *Narcissus* to the land hiss and strike, like a pair of snakes. Much earlier, the tugboat, which is a child of the land and its confusions, is short and black, recalling an enormous and aquatic black beetle "surprised by the light, overwhelmed by the sunshine, trying to escape with ineffectual effort into the distant gloom of the land." It leaves behind a round black patch of soot, the "unclean mark of the creature's rest."[10]

Donkin, who is the prototype of Ricardo and Chester and the second engineer, and of other carriers of disorder, is also a child of the land. He is the only character in *The Nigger of the Narcissus* who seems to belong there; and he is imaged as a creature, a brute, a foul bird. He creates and spreads rebellion and anarchy; a child of gloom, he also leaves an unclean mark of his own rest, and he perverts many things—Wait's illness, the commands of Mr. Baker, the sailor's responsibility. He appeals primarily to the irrational sentiments, the underground of sentiments accompanying a fear of death. He is always as close as a bird of prey. His shoulders are "peaked and drooped like the broken wings of a bird"; he advanced "confidentially, backed away with great effect; he whispered, he screamed, waved his miserable arms no thicker than pipe-stems—stretched

---

9. *Chance* (Garden City, N. Y.: Doubleday, 1957), p. 22. (My italics.)
10. *The Nigger of the Narcissus* (London, 1950), p. 27.

his lean neck—spluttered—squinted." He flourishes a "hand hard and fleshless like the claw of a snipe," and:

> Jimmy considered the conical, fowl-like profile with a queer kind if interest; he was leaning out of his bunk with the calculating uncertain expression of a man who reflects how best to lay hold of some strange creature that looks as though it could sting or bite . . . his big ears stood out, transparent and veined, resembling the thin wings of a bat. . . . The other [Donkin] stretched out his skinny neck, jerked his bird face down at him as though pecking at the eyes . . . Donkin, crouching all in a heap against a bowsprit, hunched his shoulder blades as high as his ears, and hanging a peaked nose resembled a sick vulture with ruffled plumes . . . sat down heavily; he blew with force through quivering nostrils, he ground and snapped his teeth, and, with the chin pressed hard against the breast, he seemed busy gnawing his way through it, as if to get at the heart within.[11]

Donkin shows yellow teeth over his shoulder and goes after the dying Wait's biscuits with a vulturelike swoop. Wait refers to him as a "screechin' poll-parrot," and to his chatter as the chatter of a "dirty white cockatoo." He also appears as a bird in Wait's brief dream.

The Nigger of the Narcissus presents a kind of field full of folk in various stances and poses upon a death journey. At times this little world threatens to dissolve into chaos, and the image given is one of a babel of voices, pokings and hittings, and inexplicable crankiness. The novel has striking images of a world in disorder, moments of doubt, egoism, pride, and complacency. Always near is Donkin, the animal symbol for the fall that surrounds and taunts these men, the animal symbol for the irrational aspects of their self-pity and corrupting humanity. The bird imagery defines Donkin and defines the disorder that he carries with him and that he attempts to transmit to the ship's crew. He is a major figure in Conrad's bestiary, and the accompanying figure in what seems to be a great morality of the life cycle with seasonal imagery and a perpetual black-white identification, suggesting the two-sided aspects of experience and illumination. One always travels with his shadow. And part of this shadow is Donkin's underground, the temptation to escape, the desire to sink into a sea and to drown in one's disordered self, the desire of self to destroy, and to restore chaos. Wait himself is the pivot for this disorder-order conflict, but it is Donkin who is the explaining symbol of what can really happen. It is significant that when the crew becomes disordered over Wait's desire to return to work and to create the illusion of living, their noise and mutterings resemble the sounds of beasts, for they emit "mixed growls and screeches," and when, after their abortive mutiny, they return to their berths, they return as beasts; for, we are told, "others dived head first inside lower bunks—swift, and turning round instantly upon themselves like animals going into lairs." Even Belfast, Wait's protector and advocate, in defending Wait pants like a dog.

The land, like the city, whose creature Donkin is, is a place of corruption. Like the city Powell encounters, it is foul and reminiscent of a lower world of bestial life. The landing of the *Narcissus* is accompanied by a great clatter of

---

11. *Ibid.,* pp. 110, 111, 128, 132.

noises—of screams, voices, splashes, of wheels over stones, "the thump of heavy things falling," the racket of feverish winches, the grinding of strained chains—and a confusion of odors—perfumes and dirt, spices and hides, of "things costly and of things filthy." This is the analogue to the disorder aboard the *Narcissus,* and it is, in a sense, its source. Here we have a mass of noises and smells (and confusions) that are suggestive, but also veiled in a great hovering cloud, never clear, and quite frightening. Everything somehow suggests the monstrous: the smokestacks, the steamships, the houses, the cranes—in a word, a city of great and horrible animals. The *Narcissus* must dock and must return, and the land must make its claims; as aboard the ship one is always near to and toying with chaos, so is there chaos in the relationship of the ship to the land. The problem is to live somehow, even in this nightmare.

The Secret Agent is the last few pages of *The Nigger of the Narcissus,* the city of *The Return,* the dockside vision of *Chance* fully amplified. The city, which is slime and emptied aquarium,[12] is also the jungle, and there is a constant suggestion of characters described in corresponding bestial imagery.[13] Many of the characters are hence "grotesque as though they expressed in deformity of body a perversity of soul, caricature of the same order as . . . the captain of the *Patna.*"[14]

Verloc reminds us of a fat pig; he is "burly in a fat-pig style," and when Stevie's hearing about the cruelty of a German officer would cause him to have stuck that officer like a pig, we recall that his carving knife will kill Verloc, sticking him like a pig. Verloc emits grunts of assent, animal notes; and Winnie in her final moments, as she turns on her husband, is described in terms of animal gestures. She springs up from a crouching position, assumes a wild aspect, and becomes cunning, stealthily grasping the knife, moving like a beast. Verloc in his attempts to forgive and be generous is not a monster—"he paused, and a snarl lifting up his moustaches above a gleam of white teeth gave him the expression of a reflective beast, not very dangerous—a slow beast with a sleek head, gloomier than a seal, and with a husky voice." And Winnie wrestles with Ossipon—as a beast struggles, frantically and irrationally, creating a mock love-bout, where she becomes a serpent twined about his whitened body. Conrad's Yundt has a clawlike hand, and Sir Ethelred's room suggests the forest's deep gloom (the

---

12. See Elliot B. Gose, Jr., " 'Cruel Devourer of the World's Light': *The Secret Agent,*" *Nineteenth-Century Fiction* 15 (1960) : 39–50.

13. The jungle is merely one of many images worked into patterns here—the entire strategy seems to be one of dehumanization, and each character, passion, relationship is presented as an abstraction, coldly and in the barest and most rigid form. The animal imagery is more of a secondary imagery here—although it emerges clearly in the serpent image applied to Winnie, and as part of a possible theme relating to "madness and despair" (one of the novel's many repeated motifs), the necessity of bringing out into the open one's destructive self (thus through a knife and a pig image, Winnie is identified with Stevie, the only character who is pure and uncontrolled passion)—and it is tied to many other things that suggest corruption and anarchy, for instance, the corpulence imagery. This latter imagery, applied to Ossipon, Michaelis, Sir Ethelred, Verloc, Vladimir, Winnie's mother, a policeman, seems a major symbol and correlative; wallowing, uncleanness, disorder are reinforced and amplified by fatness.

14. Paul Wiley, *Conrad's Measure of Man* (Madison, Wis.: University of Wisconsin Press, 1954), p. 107.

home for these animals, since it contains the anarchy underlying the more apparent anarchy of the revolutionist, criminal, and police), which it is, in a sense. The world of anarchy is presented through all kinds of images of disorder; the suggested bestial background and identification accompanying some of the gestures of these characters is merely part of a general definition. But it is enough to suggest again the animal and the irrational nature of men, no longer ordered or striving for balance with their rational and ordered selves.

V

Thus Conrad's bestial imagery is a far-reaching thing. It is a major part of *Lord Jim, Victory,* and *The Nigger of the Narcissus;* it is important in *The Secret Agent* and in "Outpost of Progress," where Kayert's and Carlier's romp around the house is porcine, and in *Falk,* where it seems to be parodied (or a strange variation)—man-beast becoming man-boat—with centaur images, among others. It appears only incidentally elsewhere—the manager's uncle in *Heart of Darkness,* De Barral in *Chance,* and in *Under Western Eyes,* where the revolutionists appear as grotesque and exceptional buffoons, fools, and "apes of a sinister jungle."[15]

Generally, the animals of this menagerie are creatures of disruption, disorder, and prey. When an ape fights with a cat, it is not only the Punch and Judy aspect that is significant, but also the fact that two beasts are fighting, and in a bestial manner. The same is true for the romp of an elephant and a horse on the *Patna's* deck. Conrad shows his evil in terms of elephants, mongrels, bears, apes, cats, owls, crows, vultures, parrots, snipes, cockatoos, pigs, beetles, worms, and snakes. He creates an underworld of animals to define an underworld of desires and actions and to show us not only how close this underworld is to us but also what it is and what happens to the one who falls. The fallen man in Conrad becomes abstract, dehumanized, an image, a variation upon an image (suggesting no permanence of being), a caricature, and a beast. The city of *The Secret Agent* is the world after the fall, and its characters are abstract, bare, bestial, and unwholesome—corpulence serving as a figure for a kind of moral pestilence. In "Outpost of Progress," ridiculous through pathetic clichés, Kayerts and Carlier are less than human; and the implied animal image at the end is merely another way of saying what they are and what they have become.

Conrad's menagerie, then, is always part of a vision of evil, part of a theme that explores man's relationship to dirt. In our dreams we often wander in dark forests and jungles; the Great Personage's study is this dark forest, as it should be, for the city is a jungle, its inhabitants beasts, and the gloom pervades everywhere. When Conrad at the end of chapter eight of *Outcast of the Islands* has Almayer's Nina, at her father's instruction, shout "Pig! Pig! Pig!" at Willems, we find a central symbolic scene that is to be woven into the fabric of later works, becoming a symbolic and recurring motif, used with complexity and multiplicity of purpose and result.

---

15. Albert J. Guérard, *Conrad the Novelist* (Cambridge, Mass: Harvard University Press, 1958), p. 246.

The Secret Agent and the Mechanical Chaos

DAVID L. KUBAL

California State University

COMMENT BY THE AUTHOR

The political events that have preoccupied us since this essay was published cannot but bring us closer to The Secret Agent. *The opposition of the force that seeks a rigid stasis in society and the force intent upon mere disruption has constituted the most alarming political drama of these intervening years, just as it forms the dialectic of Conrad's novel. This is not to say that the novel was waiting in the wings of history for sixty years for confirmation. We must take care not to fall into the zeal for "relevancy" that frequently characterizes contemporary literary criticism. Such short-sightedness leads inevitably to a solipsism that grants unwarranted value to those works which seem to "speak" to us and distorts their historical importance in the process.*

Indeed, the drama of The Secret Agent *is at one with the central concern of the English novel. A genre that arose out of and along with the middle-class, democratic surge in the eighteenth century, the novel treats the negotiations of the individual demanding freedom and a social system dedicated to preserving itself against change. Defoe, Fielding, and Sterne initiated the theme, which was most forcefully carried out in the nineteenth century by Jane Austen, Dickens, George Eliot, James, and Hardy. Conrad wrote directly in that tradition.*

Yet, if Conrad does not handle a new idea in The Secret Agent, *he does treat the theme of his forerunners in a significantly different manner. It is true that beginning with Dickens's late fiction, and particularly in* Bleak House, *the*

First published: 15, no. 3 (1971): 65–77. Slightly revised.

interplay between the self and the system began to break down; the latter gradually became more reluctant to parlay. Esther Summerson and her husband, along with Mr. Jarndyce, for example, were forced out of society and into a suburban sanctuary. Increasingly in subsequent fiction, freedom for the hero, if possible at all, became a hole-in-corner affair, like that of Dorthea Brooke. Within that corner, of course, a private life was often possible in which the self, if its demands on the larger society were modest enough, could find a measure of liberty.

Not merely is this alternative unavailable in Conrad's novel, however, but the whole conception of the self that had given such dramatic vitality to the novel of the previous two centuries has disappeared. It is not only, then, the metaphor of "mechanical chaos," but also a radical departure from the traditional conception of the individual that distinguishes The Secret Agent *from its predecessors and links it to* 1984. *In commenting on Orwell's novel Irving Howe says, "The whole idea of the self as something precious and inviolable is a cultural idea, and as we understand it, a product of the liberal era; but Orwell has imagined a world in which the self, whatever subterranean existence it manages to eke out, is no longer a significant value, not even a value to be violated." In this matter Conrad also anticipated Orwell as well as those twentieth-century novelists terrified of the modern state.*

Although there is no doubt that The Secret Agent *springs from the darker niches of the Victorian mind—and more clearly arises out of such European imaginations as Dostoevski's—it also represents one of the first full expressions of our civilization's political despair. That its pertinency and power should remain convinces us of Conrad's genius; still, the fact that it is a part of an entire tradition concerned with a political experience much like our own should in an odd way console us. For at least we know that we are not alone and that we have other resources besides our own with which to confront our culture.*

In *The Secret Agent* Joseph Conrad creates a chaotic world. It is not simply a society in which values are declining or disintegrating, a society such as we find in *Vanity Fair.* Thackeray's vision includes characters who have, at least, a rudimentary sense of a moral system. And if the moral sense is not acute in the characters, the narrator supplies a standard of judgment. In *The Secret Agent,* on the other hand, neither the characters nor the narrator, whose judgment is muffled by heavy irony, reveals any concrete positive *or* negative standards. Conrad's creations exist in a normal vacuum where nothing is clear, where the actions of both the police and the anarchists are indistinguishable. A moral sense implies the ability to distinguish, to recognize degrees of goodness as well as evil. But everything and everybody in the novel appear essentially the same under the narrator's ironical gaze, so that the reader is left without any solid basis for judgment. Stevie graphically imitates this chaos when he draws "circles, circles; innumerable circles, concentric, eccentric; a coruscating whirl of circles that by their tangled multitude of repeated curves, uniformity of form, and confusion of intersecting lines suggested a rendering of cosmic chaos, the symbolism of a mad art attempting the inconceivable."[1] Like a mirror, the idiot reflects the jumbled

---

1. *The Secret Agent* (New York: Doubleday, 1953), p. 49. All subsequent references are to this text.

chaos of society, a chaos where there is no identity, where everything has the same monotonous design, and in front of which we, like Stevie, are confused, befuddled, and only able to utter not a judgment but a weak sigh, "Bad world for poor people" (p. 146).

But a final and complete chaos is inconceivable. I am using the term to describe a state in which, relatively speaking, there is no order or structure. A society, no matter how chaotic it may appear, must have some design to continue. Holding the world of *The Secret Agent* together is the machine. Looking back to the description of Stevie's "mad art," we notice that within the confusion there is an organizational principle. It is the circle, which offers some concrete, familiar means by which we can recognize the outlines of what the boy is doing. Without the circle we could not begin to talk about his "art." But the circle, at best, is a monotonous, static, and mechanical figure. It never varies or grows toward anything; it is an inorganic, insular design, an image of infinity without purpose, which begins and ends at the same point.

Such is London in *The Secret Agent,* where there is, as Conrad says in the "Author's Note," "darkness enough to bury five millions of lives" (p. 11). The society is a confusing maze that maintains its tenuous order through mechanics, where its characters, "somnambulists," a recurring image in the novel, gyrate without purpose, possessed by single ideas; either nameless or designated by geometric figures, they exist as isolated entities, unable to communicate with each other, dedicated to the destruction or the protection of the social mechanism. It is an absurd universe that finds its meaning in the everlasting motion of the piston; if the machine stopped, the society would dissolve.

Conrad achieves thematic and structural unity through the paradoxical images of mechanism and chaos. Not only does he present the characters, their ideas, and London as formless matter directed by machines, but he organizes the novel itself on this basis. The sequence of the chapters reflects the confusion of the characters and their existence. Conrad disregards chronological time almost totally to indicate further that time itself is without purpose. Like Stevie's circles, time here is nothing more than a circular movement, the path of the clock that does not point to either the past or the future; it is enclosed and repetitious. When time present originates from nothing and moves toward nothing but merely rotates, the concept of time lacks reason, and hence to place events in a logical sequence makes no more sense than to dislocate them. In short, this is a world that can no longer give the word *destiny* meaning. Therefore, the attempt to blow up Greenwich is irrational in a double sense. It is not, as R. W. Stallman says, an attempt "to destroy Time-Now, Universal Time, or life itself,"[2] but a senseless charge on the meaningless. The plan to bomb the Observatory, an arbitrary place that regulates clock time, if accomplished, would have succeeded only in momentarily upsetting mechanical time, which hardly would have disturbed "Universal Time" much less "life itself."

The first break in chronological time comes after chapter 3. The first three chapters introduce the Verlocs, the anarchists, and Mr. Vladimir of the Russian embassy. Serving as a prologue to the action, this section outlines the reasons behind the explosion. Chapter 4, beginning the next section, jumps forward in

---

2. "Time and *The Secret Agent*," *The House That James Built* (East Lansing, Mich.: Michigan State University Press, 1961), p. 112.

time to a point after the explosion and introduces the Professor, who is informed of the bombing by Ossipon in the "renowned Silenus beer-hall." Chapters 5, 6, and 7 also take place after the explosion and follow chronological time except for the flashback in 5, in which Heat examines Stevie's body. After Conrad presents the reaction of Heat, the Assistant Commissioner, and Sir Ethelred to the disaster in these three chapters, he switches in 8 to about two weeks before the explosion and Winnie Verloc's mother's trip to the poorhouse. Between the end of 8 and the beginning of 9 there is a gap of ten days where Verloc goes to the Continent. Then after the first part of 9, which occurs immediately before Stevie's death, we are brought back to the end of 7, where the Assistant Commissioner was left standing outside Verloc's shop. From the last half of 9 until the end of the novel the action follows the clock.

Conrad solves the problem of unity by establishing the thematic pattern of mechanical chaos, which I will discuss later, and through a circular pattern in the structure. The gap between chapters 3 and 8, for example, is narrowed by their identical endings. In both chapters Winnie and Adolf are in bed and the last words, spoken by Verloc in answer to her question about the light, are "put it out" (pp. 61, 153). Through this very obvious and mechanical device the artist suggests the banality and monotony of their existence. Thus we see here the chaotic structure, unified in a mechanical way, substantiating the theme. Further, the chapters not only culminate in the same way but are also parallel in atmosphere and imagery. In both, the husband and wife feel a great sense of isolation and are unable to communicate. Again, through each chapter the "lonely clock" continues its senseless ticking, which supports the mood and carries out the mechanical imagery. Conrad uses much the same device in tying together 4, the actual beginning of the action, and 13, the final chapter. Both take place for the most part in the Silenus, where the Professor and Ossipon are discussing a tragedy. In the former they talk about Stevie's death and in the latter about Winnie's suicide. As in the first example, these chapters share a common imagery. The "mechanical piano," a nickelodeon, haunts the atmosphere of the bar, and Ossipon is primarily interested in his "much-folded newspaper." The circular structure along with the imagery again implies the wearisome, automatic uniformity that dominates an existence that even horror and violence cannot interrupt. And thus, with the establishment of the relationship of these two chapters, the action of the novel as well completes a circle, like a clock, ending where it began.

Besides these illustrations of cyclical form in *The Secret Agent,* Stallman notes still others. In order to support both the theme of automation amid chaos and the unity of the novel, Conrad has also designed particular chapters in an insular and repetitive manner. In 2, for example, Verloc begins his trip to the embassy from Brett Street and ends there; 3 is also a self-contained unit, consisting mainly of the anarchist's conversation; 8 starts off with Winnie, her mother, and Stevie leaving for the poorhouse and culminates at the Verlocs'; and, finally 9, somewhat more complicated, commences with Verloc's return from Europe, continues with his circular walks with Stevie and with his homecoming after the boy's death, and ends with the secret agent coming back after his confession to the Assistant Commissioner.[3]

---

3. *Ibid.,* pp. 120–21.

Yet, as we have seen—the structure of the novel is not divorced from the setting, characterization, or theme. Indeed, Conrad's achievement consists primarily in the integral unity of these elements: they are all interdependent, reflecting upon, illuminating, and substantiating one another. On the first page of the novel, with the description of Verloc's shop Conrad introduces the image of confusion mixed with the mechanical figure:

> The shop was small, and so was the house. It was one of those grimy brick houses which existed in large quantities before the era of reconstruction dawned upon London. The shop was a square box of a place, with the front glazed in small panes. In the daytime the door remained closed; in the evening it stood discreetly but suspiciously ajar. (P. 17)

Not only is the shop a "square box," but we learn later that it is situated off "an open trianglar space" (p. 129) and is operated by a man whose alias is Λ. The shop's window, however, displays a "dingy blue china bowl," pornographic material, and "badly printed" newspapers. Inside the shop hangs a "hopelessly cracked" bell "on a curved ribbon of steel" (p. 18).

A metallic imagery pattern appears throughout the novel, suggesting the machinelike gloss of the city. But this is only a highly polished veneer, unsuccessfully hiding the underlying filth and desolation. Our first glimpse of the city is on the morning that Verloc goes to the embassy.

> The very pavement under Mr. Verloc's feet had an old-gold tinge in that diffused light, in which neither wall, nor tree, nor beast, nor man cast a shadow. Mr. Verloc was going westward through a town without shadows in an atmosphere of powdered old gold. There were red, coppery gleams on the roofs of houses, on the corners of walls, on the panels of carriages, on the very coats of the horses, and on the broad back of Mr. Verloc's overcoat, where they produced a dull effect of rustiness. (Pp. 23–24)

London, an opulent, "fat" city, another recurring image of disintegration, appears brilliant in the sunshine; its streets are covered with buses, vans, and carriages that contain wealthy women, dressed in "the skin of some wild beast." When the sun disappears the "rustiness" and the bestial quality become more apparent. In the alley where the Professor and Inspector Heat first encounter each other, the houses have a "moribund look of incurable decay—empty shells awaiting demolition" (p. 78); and when Ossipon leaves the Silenus it is "a raw, gloomy day of the early spring; and the grimy sky, the mud of the street, the rags of the dirty men harmonized excellently with the eruption of the damp, rubbishy sheet of paper soiled with printers' ink. The posters, maculated with filth, garnished like tapestry the sweep of the curbstone" (pp. 75–76). The best illustration of the nether world of London is the hackney carriage, its horse and driver, that takes Winnie's "bloated" mother away. "The Cab of Death," a symbol of the city itself, approaches the Brett Street shop, "crawling behind an infirm horse . . . on wobbly wheels and with a maimed driver on the box" (p. 134). The cabbie himself is partly a machine with his "hooked iron contrivance."

Indeed, machines of all kinds dominate the novel. Clocks are constantly intruding upon the characters: Winnie and Verloc fall asleep to one's rhythm;

Stevie draws his circles while sitting under a clock; Sir Ethelred, "The Great Presence," is constantly watching and regulating his actions by the clock; and Winnie, again, is amazed that the clock does not measure accurately the time she thinks it took to murder her husband. We recall, besides the incessant traffic on the street, that Winnie was transported to her death by a locomotive. Telegrams and newspapers play a major role in supplying the characters with information. But the most ominous machine remains the mechanical piano that accompanies the conversation of Ossipon and the Professor. It is an image of the machine gone out of control. It stops and starts apparently without reason: "The piano at the foot of the staircase clanged through a mazurka with brazen impetuosity, as though a vulgar and impudent ghost were showing off. The keys sank and rose mysteriously" (p. 66).

To say that machines themselves are "ominous" or threatening is misleading. Yet, when we understand the mechanical as an extension of the human in the society, then the machines assume this significance. The only way that the automatic can posses power of its own is through man's permission. This occurs when the person, out of greed or ignorance, cedes his authority over the machine to the device itself. The transaction completed, a process of dehumanization takes place. Cut off from his sphere of influence, from his duty to organize nature, man becomes subservient to the machine and thus begins to take on its characteristics. In short, dehumanization begins only when man fails or voluntarily surrenders his responsibility to control his own creation.

This is why Conrad's "doctrine of work" assumes so much meaning in his "answer" to the modern dilemma. The isolation and the consequent moral corruption of Kurtz in *The Heart of Darkness* happen because he fails in his responsibility to control nature and the machinery of imperialism. And this is the reason why Marlow so conscientiously dedicates himself to his vocation of captaincy. He realizes that if he had not devoted himself to his steamer, he might have lost his humanity. By making sure that his machine does not blow up, he maintains his control over it and guards himself against the encroaching "darkness." He says:

> "You wonder I didn't go ashore for a howl and a dance? Well, no—I didn't. Fine sentiments, you say? Fine sentiments, be hanged! I had not time. I had to mess about with white-lead and strips of woollen blanket helping to put bandages on those leaky steam-pipes—I tell you. I had to watch the steering, and circumvent those snags, and to get the tin-pot along by hook or by crook. There was surface-truth enough in these things to save a wise man."[4]

And later,

> "The earth for us is a place to live in, where we must put up with sights, with sounds, with smells, too, by Jove!—breathe dead hippo, so to speak, and not be contaminated. And there don't you see? your strength comes in, the faith in your ability for the digging of unostentatious holes to bury the stuff in—your power of devotion, not to yourself, but to an obscure, backbreaking business."[5]

---

4. In *Three Great Tales* (New York, n.d.), p. 257.
5. *Ibid.,* pp. 272–73.

The characters of *The Secret Agent,* on the other hand, have no other devotion than to themselves. In fact, there is no "backbreaking business" as such done in the novel. Both the anarchists and the police are principally engaged in conversation and theorizing. Mr. Vladimir's censure of Verloc, "As far as I can judge from your record kept here, you have done nothing to earn your money for the last three years" (p. 34), could very well be directed at everyone in the novel. Even the menials, the constables who lurk everywhere, the hackney driver, and the washwoman, Mrs. Neale, seem to be either doing nothing or finding an excuse to get away to a pub. Any kind of labor demands cooperation, but in a society in which the individual is completely shut off from his fellows, even communication, not to mention cooperation, remains impossible. Verloc, the secret agent, has worked alone for eleven years; Michaelis writes his illogical book in seclusion; the Professor of course is dedicated solely to the perfection of the detonator; Inspector Heat and the Assistant Commissioner proceed at odds without exchanging vital information. Ironically, the only productive work is done by Stevie, the idiot. He at least cleans floors and picks up boots.

Like self-contained but uncontrolled machines, then, these characters move in their insular worlds. Set apart not only from each other, they are separated from other nations. As it occurs to Ossipon, "The insular nature of Great Britain obtruded itself . . . in an odious form. 'Might just as well be put under lock and key every night'" (p. 231). They do, however, have a common interest in the social mechanism. The anarchists as well as the police and the embassy people, in their own unique ways, devote themselves to society. Michaelis, the fat ticket-of-leave apostle, a revolutionary who cannot converse with anyone "because the mere fact of hearing another voice disconcerted him painfully, confusing his thoughts at once" (p. 49), posits an entirely mechanical view of history. Although he has no logic and cannot think consecutively, he proposes as a good Marxist that "history is made with tools, not with ideas; and everything is changed by economic conditions—art, philosophy, love, virtue—truth itself" (p. 52). Ossipon, too, who is described as if he were a steam engine—"he raised to his lips a cigarette in a long wooden tube, puffing jets of smoke straight up at the ceiling" (p. 48)—subscribes to a thoroughly scientific concept of man and believes he can categorize the human by his physical characteristics. Like the Belgian doctor in *The Heart of Darkness* who measures Marlow's cranium before he leaves for Africa, Ossipon views man as simply another purely predictable machine. The nihilistic Professor, besides dedicating himself to the creation of the "perfect detonator," recognizes the absurdity of the social mechanism. He advocates chaos in its place.

Another aspect that these irrational automatons, except for the Professor, have in common is their dependence on women: like Verloc, the Assistant Commissioner, Sir Ethelred, and Mr. Vladimir have made themselves subservient to the feminine. The "lady patroness" supports Michaelis, controls the Assistant Commissioner, and supplies along with other prominent London women a sounding board for Vladimir's wit. Yundt, "the terrorist" as he calls himself, must lean on an old woman for support, as Sir Ethelred, "The Great Presence," must hold on to Toodles, an epicene secretary, to get to the House. Ossipon is entrapped by the wiles of kitchen maids, and Verloc, betrayed by another woman in France, is eventually murdered by his wife. This inversion further indicates the confusion in society: all the men are emasculated and the women have assumed the dominant role. The question remains, and Conrad implies it throughout the novel, how long can a society, controlled by women and run on habit and memory, and devoid of any balanced, moral structure, be sustained?

The representatives of the respected ruling class (Sir Ethelred, the lady patroness, and the two policemen) are entrenched in themselves and their own private interests. No better than the anarchists, they employ their own devious means, deceit and manipulation, in pursuit of their fixed idea. Sir Ethelred, another "vast bulk" of a man, as divorced from reality as the lady patroness, refuses to deal in anything but generalities, leaving the details for Toodles, and is so enamored with his bill for the fisheries that the activities of the anarchists exact only a casual interest. Heat and the Assistant Commissioner, another character left without a name, use the Greenwich affair either as a game or as a means to protect their own interests. The latter, afraid that his inspector will accuse Michaelis and thus alienate the lady patroness, enters the investigation to make sure that it goes "properly" and "to get away from the desk." He is more pleased when Winnie mistakes him for a foreigner than when he persuades Verloc to confess. Heat, also obese, is intent upon maintaining his private lines of communication with the underworld and even advises Verloc to leave the country before he is arrested, so that Heat's source of information will not be revealed.

The Verloc family is the focal point in the novel, and their activities reveal the other characters. Within the person of Adolf Verloc all the aspects of the society concentrate. Or to put it another way, he reflects and personifies the civilization itself. He seems to have no past, no roots; he eats most of his meals with his hat and coat on; he lives a completely separate existence and appears always to have lived in this way. Not only is he shut off from his wife and all other people, but nature itself eludes him: he "felt the latent unfriendliness of all out of doors with a force approaching to positive bodily anguish" (p. 58).

His principal concern, his fixed idea, is with security and with the maintenance of the status quo. We remember that immediately after he tells Winnie of Stevie's death and the possibility of a prison sentence, he says, "Look here, Winnie, what you must do is to keep this business going for two years" (p. 204). A mechanical man, the secret agent finds his only purpose in being of use to others. In reply to Winnie's command to answer the shop bell, he "obeyed woodenly, stony-eyed, and like an automaton whose face had been painted red. And this resemblance to a mechanical figure went so far that he had an automaton's absurd air of being aware of the machinery inside of him" (p. 165). And yet unlike a machine, or perhaps like an uncontrolled machine, he is disheveled, inconsistent, and without purpose. Aimless meanderings occupy the major part of his daily routine, and when one evening Winnie asks him, "Are you going out tonight?":

> He shook his head moodily, and then sat still with downcast eyes, looking at the piece of cheese on his plate for a whole minute. At the end of that time he got up, and went out—went right out in the clatter of the shopdoor bell. He acted thus inconsistently, not from any desire to make himself unpleasant, but because of an unconquerable restlessness. It was no earthly good going out. He could not find anywhere in London what he wanted. But he went out.
> (P. 150)

His idea of security and his belief that he can be loved for himself cause his death. Believing that his wife had no other thought than for him, he is unable to fend off her feeble approach with the knife. Confronted with an idea he never considered, his inner mechanism could not react to the new stimulus, and he "expired without stirring a limb, in the muttered sound of the word 'Don't' by way of protest" (p. 216).

Winnie Verloc, too, is guided by a single idea. Her devotion to the protection of her mother and especially to Stevie and her conviction that "things don't bear looking into very much" seem to guard her from the chaotic world, to allow her to maintain an "unfathomable indifference." When her purpose is removed, however, when her ineffectual, old mother is safely settled at the poorhouse and Stevie dies, she erupts with her "new freedom" and, like an untracked locomotive, murders her husband and is driven by fear into her alliance with Ossipon and finally into despair and suicide. When the society fails to offer a moral structure, fails to provide guidance and direction, the individual must fall back upon his own devices. But Winnie, whose mental ability is questionable, can only construct weak, wooden habits that have the barest instinctual bases. And when the reasons for the habits are taken away, a new and awful liberty descends upon her. At this time, when all civilized restraint is removed, Winnie's darker nature, like Kurtz's, reasserts itself: "Into that plunging blow, delivered over the side of the couch, Mrs. Verloc had put all the inheritance of her immemorial and obscure descent, the simple ferocity of the age of caverns, and the unbalanced nervous fury of the age of bar-rooms" (p. 216). Winnie does not know how to deal with an alien experience, and in trying to cope with it she disintegrates.

This leaves us with Stevie, who comes the closest to being the moral center of the novel. Yet, his crippled mind weakens his gestures toward reform in much the same way that his sister's mechanical devotion lessens the quality of her personal sacrifice. Stevie is neither the artist of the novel nor the moral agent. Stevie does not shape but rather is shaped himself. His circles are a mere reflection of his own mind and the world. And his outcries against brutality and injustice are easily pacified and redirected. His demonstrations in behalf of the horse and driver and his "ideal conception of the metropolitan police" are forgotten when Winnie asks him to stop the bus. Finally, Verloc's careful training totally wipes away Stevie's ideal. Although Stevie's moral instincts are initially sound, they are clay in the hands of anyone who gains his confidence. Even so, he is more human than anyone else in the novel. That is, he does react to something beyond himself, outside his own self-interest and can recognize, however weakly, that something has gone wrong. At least when he utters "Bad world for poor people," he rises, despite his own mind, above the mechanical chaos.

The Secret Agent discovers its logic and unity in the relationship of images and thematic similarities. While characters are distorted and stylized, its action and settings tend toward the melodramatic, controlled only by the irony. It is then a symbolic novel, which treats human existence below the facts of history and politics. Conrad ignores the veneer, the appearance of civilization, to plumb once more the depths of darkness. This time, however, the subject is London and not Africa. The differences remain slight. The trip up the Congo and the journey through the London streets are both "weary pilgrimage[s] amongst hints for nightmares."[6]

Succinctly, Conrad's vision is one of desolation, chaos, and hopelessness. In a state where man has relinquished his right of self-government in exchange for security and where he has failed to control the machinery he has developed to harness natural powers—in this particular case symbolized by the bomb—the disintegration that follows is a moral one. Devoted as Verloc, Ossipon, the Professor, Michaelis, Heat, the Assistant Commissioner, Vladimir, and Sir Ethelred are to self-aggrandizement, in one form or the other, the isolation of man and the destruction of Winnie, Stevie, and Mrs. Neale are to be expected. The dedication of one's life to the self alone and its creature comforts ultimately brings about spiritual death. When this avocation becomes the sole end of a society, all other purposes are lost, and any moral system, which would necessarily be in the way, must be eliminated.

But if a civilization's moral structure disintegrates and its institutions and its means of restraint and guidance crumble, what is to prevent absolute anarchy, chaos, the free rule of people like the Professor? The only answer in Conrad's mind is the machine. Not a solution but a ballast, mechanism is an inevitable result of the destruction of an organic society that was once rooted in a belief in man's moral nature. One must recall that in the novel anarchy does not succeed but the machine does. Because of the incompetence and impotence of the revolutionaries and the ability of the social mechanism—despite the bumblings of the police—to quickly smother the psychological effects of the bomb, the masses are not disturbed: "The trade in afternoon papers was brisk, yet, in comparison with the swift, constant march of foot traffic, the effect was of indifference, of a disregarded distribution" (p. 76). Not only is London well protected in its self-imposed isolation from any disturbing intrusion, but its protectors make sure that nothing does upset it.

Nonetheless a tension is sustained between chaos and the machine in this society; if the balance should be upset, and this is Conradian irony at its most devastating, the result would be nonexistence. And the anarchists and the police, like chaos and the machine, need one another for survival. It is a sport, like the war between Oceania and Eurasia in *1984*, to keep each other alert. If Heat captured the Professor or the Professor accomplished his end, there would be nothing in society to prevent final atrophy on the one hand or complete chaos on the other. At last, then, neither the machine nor chaos triumphs. The Greenwich affair stands as just another "border war." At the end it is the Professor who "passed on unsuspected and deadly, like a *pest* in the street full of men" (p. 253, italics mine). The distance between *The Secret Agent* and *1984* is not so great as one might suppose.

---

6. *Ibid.*, p. 230.

The Two Lawrences

ELISEO VIVAS

COMMENT BY THE AUTHOR

An artist of the stature of Lawrence—and as the reader recedes in time from the Himalaya he was, his overtowering stature emerges—is not only the two persons I found in him in 1958 or even the three that Katherine Mansfield found: he is as many persons as there are readers of his work, each serious reader finding in his texts objectively what interests him consciously and unconsciously. The majority find in Lawrence, as they find in whatever falls under their eyes, subjective matter that they thrust into the text, matter that is often no more than a grotesque caricature of what Lawrence was concerned with. If we bear in mind that Lawrence himself sometimes perpetrated caricatures of what he passionately and sincerely espoused, we need no further explanation of the diverse and mutually exclusive Lawrences that continue to elicit our attention.

All these Lawrences, perhaps even some of the absurd caricatures of the Himalaya he is, have their diverse uses. It would take a contemporary Savonarola (he usually comes today wearing the tunic of a Commissar of Culture) to do to Lawrence's works what the priest and the barber did to Don Quixote's library, and what has been done since then even outside the borders of Communist Russia or Nazi Germany—burn those of his works he does not approve of.

We must be tolerant. But tolerance does not demand of me that I sympathize with the meddler in people's lives that in my essay I more politely called "the prophet." Nor does it demand of me that I value everything that has been written about him. Some of his readers simply do not know how to read. A bishop of the Church of England declared in court that in Lady Chatterley's Lover *Lawrence portrayed sex as something essentially sacred. He overlooked the fact that one of*

First published: 7, no. 3 (1958): 113–32. This essay, with revisions, is the first chapter of Vivas, *D. H. Lawrence: The Failure and the Triumph of Art* (Evanston, Ill.: Northwestern University Press, 1960).

103

Mellors's ways of making love was then (I do not know whether it still is) considered by his Church a sin contra natura. *Let me hasten to add parenthetically that I have long believed that the notion of natural law is pious nonsense.*

Furthermore, the tolerance I have the right to demand of others allows me to insist on the validity of my view: In order to read Lawrence au fond, *one must first read him as an artist. Some readers may take his reformer's intrusions into our lives to be more important than his art. That is their right. But it can be shown that fully to grasp the prophetic element in Lawrence one must first read him seriously as what I call "the poet." I stick with Lawrence:*

> *Oh, give me the novel. It's the novel I want to hear.*
> *As for the novelist, he is usually a dribbling liar.*

I

Can there be doubt at this late date that D. H. Lawrence is one of the most important writers in the English language in the first half of the twentieth century? Whether he has a permanent place in the history of English literature only those endowed with the power of prophecy can say with assurance. I believe he has; but I do not take my attitude as anything more than a belief grounded on hunches and endowed with no authority. We can, however, say with authority—the authority of a judgment that has by now the backing of critical consensus—that with Yeats, Eliot, Faulkner and one or two others—perhaps Pound and Joyce, but who else?— Lawrence was one of the constitutive writers of our generation. I use the word "constitutive" in somewhat the same sense that contemporary neo-Kantian philosophers employ it: the world in which we live is not entirely made up out of our own minds, but the character that it appears to have for those who have read Lawrence seriously, it has in part by virtue of his work.

Leavis has recently written that *The Rainbow* and *Women in Love,* which he correctly considers Lawrence's best novels, "have had essentially no recognition at all." But a less ardent admirer of Lawrence would acknowledge that if we judge by critical interest Lawrence has at last come to occupy the place in English literature that he unquestionably deserves. Father Tiverton may be right when he points out that Lawrence did not compel his successors to write like him; what he did was to make it impossible for them to write like his predecessors. But a writer's importance cannot be exclusively judged by his literary influence. As we look back on the first half of our century and consider the changes that have taken place between the year 1911 (when Lawrence's first novel appeared) and the present, it would seem that this is as much Lawrence's century as that of any other writer of the period. For he was one of the writers who helped give form to the sensibility we now possess and who helped define the values and concerns that are the substance of our lives. If it is true, as Ezra Pound has put it, that artists are the antennae of the race, we can say of Lawrence that early in our century he thrust his long, tremulous filaments into the future and brought back to us a report of what we were gradually to find there as the years went by.

But we shall miss Lawrence's positive value as well as overlook the serious threat to a healthy moral life that he represents if we center our critical interest exclusively on the biographical or psychoanalytic aspects of his work: the gossipy game of discovering who were the originals for the characters of his novels, or of finding the neuroses that are expressed in them; the dreary and often trivial game—in certain quarters considered "scholarly research"—of ascertaining whether Lawrence did or did not read Zelia Nuttal or Bernal Diaz del Castillo. If we are to take Lawrence seriously, we must read him as Mr. Leavis, Father Tiverton, Mr. Hough, and only a very few others have read him: as a writer who discovered by means of the creative act the structure of experience and, by embodying it in his art, achieved a vision of life.[1]

Not that we can afford to do without the biographical labors of his friends and enemies, or that we can ignore the literary psychoanalysis that is so freely practiced on him. There is urgent need, as I shall indicate below, for these kinds of investigation. But the essential task is that of examining Lawrence's art and not his sick soul. The latter is of importance objectively only when it becomes the source of traits discernible in the work itself. What is of undisputed importance is the work itself. Do we have an adequate knowledge of Lawrence's vision of the world; do we know how perfect or imperfect it was? The critics mentioned above have in the last few years addressed themselves to this question. But I do not believe that these men have said the last word on Lawrence, simply because on such a subject there is no last word. If a man be a poet of his stature, no age no critic, no reader definitively "places" him. It is a job that has to be done again and again—a job that we must do, not for the sake of the poet, but for our own sake. In the process of this continued critical definition and redefinition, we may not arrive at a final estimate of his value, but we do something at least as important: we redefine our heritage and, insofar as it is given to us to do so, we enlarge our vision. No doubt in doing so we run the risk of inflicting a radical injustice on the poet, hastening to read into his work our own inchoate aspirations and our fears. But this is inevitable and, in any case, the dialectic of criticism tends to make the necessary corrections.

When we try to read Lawrence objectively, in order to discover the nature of his gift to us, we do not find it easy to do. The best of contemporary criticism rightly frowns on the facile separation of substance and form. Sophisticated critics

---

1. This essay was already in its second draft when two noteworthy books on Lawrence were published in close succession: F. R. Leavis, *D. H. Lawrence: Novelist* (New York: Knopf, 1956), and Graham Hough, *The Dark Sun: A Study of D. H. Lawrence* (London: Duckworth, 1956). Leavis's book I reviewed in the January 1957 number of *The Sewanee Review*. My reaction to Hough's book is not fully registered by the references that I introduced into this manuscript after reading his discriminating, thorough, and scholarly examination of the whole range of Lawrence's work. I recommend it highly, although if I were to review it I would have to register my disagreement with him on a number of important points. These two books are in the same class with Father Tiverton's *D. H. Lawrence and Human Existence* (London: Rockliff, 1951). They approach Lawrence objectively and essentially as an artist. Mark Spilka in *The Love Ethic of D. H. Lawrence* (Bloomington, Ind.: Indiana University Press, 1955) attempts the same objective approach, but he does not realize that to find an "ethic" in a poet is to turn the poet into a moralist and to deny him his role as poet.

today quite automatically harness the word *message* with quotation marks. They shun the word *moral* when used as a synonym of *message*. It is a basic assumption of contemporary criticism, and a fully justified one, that poetry with an intrinsic moral is bad poetry and that if it it good poetry the moral has been artificially tacked to it by the writer. No critic well grounded in contemporary aesthetics would find an "ethic" in genuine poetry. (I employ the word *poetry* throughout in its widest sense.) If he found it, he would suspect the quality of the poetry. Nevertheless, the first and the most difficult problem that the critic of Lawrence has to face is that of distinguishing in his work poetry from prophecy, art from message; of distinguishing aesthetic vision authentically revealed from propaganda, of distinguishing the world he discovered in and through the act of creation from his criticism and his turgid lucubrations. The created world will be found at its best to be a powerful aesthetic organization of the values and disvalues, the matter of experience as grasped by a gifted mind and transmuted and in-formed by it. What the poet gives us is what he brings up from the depths of his creative imagination, in the ideal isolation of his perfected form and in-formed substance. True, the matter the poet works with is the stuff of his experience of life and of art; but if he be an artist, the act of creation adds to his experienced matter to make up a literally new product: the in-formed substance of his poetry. The addition makes this product more than an imitation or reflection of what exists; it is literally an addition, the manifestation of the freedom of his spirit. The vision the poet offers us has order and splendor, whereas the objects of our vision are incomplete, opaque. The first and most important step in arriving at knowledge of ourselves and of the world is to apprehend both immediately in their own terms as objects of the act of aesthesis. It is at this point that the work of the poet comes to its full nonresidential utility: we do not see the world reflected in it, we see the world by means of it. And the difference between the alternatives is radical. It is in this special sense that the poet's world is normative.

II

Father Tiverton asserts that it is not possible to separate art from message in Lawrence, and in a sense he is right. But he himself has noted adversely certain features of Lawrence's thought and called attention with sympathy and sensitiveness to others. Again, the refusal to make the separation overlooks two facts. The first is that Lawrence did not always produce "pure" art; and the second is that Lawrence himself advised us to make the separation and gave us essentially valid reasons for doing so. The reader will probably remember the last two lines of the essay on "The Novel":

> Oh give me the novel. Let me hear what the novel says.
> As for the novelist, he is usually a dribbling liar.[2]

This statement represents no mere passing thought with Lawrence but a considered insight, as fundamental to his aesthetics as it is to any aesthetic worth serious consideration. All we have to do to verify the first part of Lawrence's

---

2. The essay on "The Novel" is to be found in *Reflections on the Death of a Porcupine and Other Essays* (Philadelphia: Centaur Press, 1925).

assertion is to remember the first chapter of *Studies in Classical American Literature:*

> Art speech is the only truth. The artist is usually a damned liar, but his art, if it be art, will tell you the truth of his day. . . . The old American artists were hopeless liars. But they were artists in spite of themselves.

That art tells "the truth" is something that a reader acquainted with contemporary aesthetics would hesitate to assert in the facile way in which Lawrence asserts it. But then, any one who wants to read Lawrence with profit has to learn to overlook the nonsense in him. Nor is it impertinent to remember that Lawrence often showed very little concern for the truth: he stuck to the solar plexus, as he tells us in *Fantasia of the Unconscious.* Having pointed out the impropriety of the use of the word *truth* in this connection, however, we need not scruple to employ it; the word stands for something real and important, although it would take close and prolonged analysis to define it. But that the intention of the work, if it be art, will often be in conflict with what the artist takes to be his intention—this is as well known as it is easy to prove. Over ten years ago, two young men made a reputation by baptizing this principle "The Intentional Fallacy." In the same chapter of *Studies* from which the above quotation was taken, Lawrence writes that "the proper function of a critic is to save the tale from the artist who created it." Agreed. But there is a catch to the statement. For a critic can save the tale only if he recognizes art, and he cannot recognize it unless he has an idea of what art is prior to his recognition that a particular thing is indeed art. All this we have long known, for Plato made it perfectly clear in one of his most popular dialogues, *The Phaedo.* But it is not a truth that many critics are fond of, since it entails the job of coming to terms with abstract and difficult problems of aesthetics.

The distinction between the dribbling liar who is the novelist and the truth of the novel applies to Lawrence as much as it does to "Old Leo" and the others against whom Lawrence employed it so brilliantly in his essay "The Novel." But before we apply it, it is desirable to take a closer look at it, for it expresses the basic distinction with which I shall be working in this essay.

In "The Novel" Lawrence traces the distinction to a conflict between "the passional inspiration" of the artist, as he calls it, and his didactic purpose or philosophy. He writes:

> It is such a bore that nearly all great novelists have a didactic purpose, otherwise a philosophy, directly opposite to their passional inspiration. In their passional inspiration they are all phallic worshippers . . . yet all of them, when it comes to their philosophy . . . are all crucified Jesuses. What a bore! And what a burden for the novel to carry!

Although Lawrence's thesis cannot be accepted at its face value, there is in it an important insight. The terms in which the insight is couched are not theoretically felicitous, and the assertion that what makes a novelist a dribbling liar is the conflict between his philosophy and his phallic worship is one of those irresponsible generalizations that frequently open Lawrence to easy attack. But we often find novels that contain conflicting intentions, and this is the important point. Exactly how these intentions are to be defined is something to be found by an analysis of each novel.

It is, then, in the work itself that we shall find the clash between the liar and the poet. What turned so gifted an artist into a liar is the subject of biographical inquiry. That there are two Lawrences has long been known: indeed, one could without artifice distinguish more than two. Katherine Mansfield found three. But for our purposes two are enough. How shall we explain this conflict? From the objective point of view the conflict can only be a failure of integration between form and substance; or, more precisely, a fault in the transmutation of the matter of experience into the in-formed substance of art. The matter is whatever the artist uses—passion or ideology or anything else, if there is anything else; in any case, we recognize the fault when the work fails to function in the aesthetic mode, when it arouses emotion or insinuates questions as regards matters of fact or of value that prevent the intransitive contemplation that is the proper reaction to art as art. The objective failure is, of course, finally to be traced to subjective sources: to divided vision, to a clash of allegiance in the artist himself between the creative act of aesthetic apprehension and his own narrow commitments as a moralist or a political or religious man or a sectarian of some sort. Here we cross the field of objective into that of biography. A complete explanation demands that we furnish cause for the aesthetic fault. And ultimately it is in the stresses and strains between the espousals and the commitments of the artist as practical man and as artist that we find the objective conflicts expressed in his work. That the account of such clashes and stresses is bound to be only speculative and is not susceptible of verification is unfortunate; but it is not a state of affairs over which any one can have control. In general terms, the subjective clash is to be accounted for in the following manner: the matter of experience attempts to reveal itself in the creative act, but the nonaesthetic demands of the artist predominate or at least are strong enough to prevent a fully adequate aesthetic transmutation of matter into in-formed substance. The moralist or the practical man or the religious or the political man is offended or bruised by what the poet is on the verge of creatively discovering and attemps to bring it into harmony with his nonaesthetic commitments. In a genuine artist the clash is never radical; it is never a question of unconditional surrender. Nor does it appear to him as a conflict between aesthetic and nonaesthetic demands. It appears as the travail and turmoil of the creative act.

This is the reason the artist has a hard time against the dribbling liar. His business is to submit, with humble docility, all that comes up as matter for his work to the demands of the whole. The liar adds his own matter, and the artist in his humility and his impersonality does not recognize what the liar offers and fails to see the manner in which it is offered. For the artist is capable of an impersonality that the dribbling liar in him resents; it ignores his pet notions, his wounds, his vanities, his loves and hates, in favor of something that, gestated in the depths of his mind, seems nevertheless alien to him—and, indeed, is, since it possesses a self-sufficiency all its own. To the degree that the artist fails to digest his experience aesthetically and that bullying passion and autocratic ideology take over, the product is a "dribbling lie"—or, as I shall call it, impure art, the work of the prophet. In Lawrence we find both forms of impurity: excess of passion and the autocracy of ideas, both of which are the result of his failure to bring the prophet to heel. There are other faults in his work, but the more serious faults are caused by the dribbling liar.

It follows from what has been said that, properly speaking, poetry is not a medium for the communication of "ideas," for the exposition of a "philosophy." We can, of course, speak of a philosophical poet. We can expound the philosophy of Shakespeare's plays, of Conrad's novels, of Eliot. But we then use the term in one of two senses: we mean that the poet's revealed vision is grounded on a number of presuppositions, either moral or cosmic, which he takes for granted and which function as principles by means of which he selects the matter he chooses to transmute into in-formed substance. Or, probably more often, we mean that more or less automatically we evaluate the revealed vision in terms of our own standards. In the latter sense, Shakespeare, say, is a philosophical poet. But he expresses as many philosophies as there are critics who interpret him.

Essentially the same distinction was drawn by Lawrence between poetry and message from a different point of view when he wrote in a well-known passage of the "Foreword" of *Fantasia and the Unconscious* that his verse and novels are pure passionate experience and that his philosophical ideas "are inferences made afterwards from the experience." Had this always been the case he would always have been a poet. Up to the writing of *Women in Love* this was, by and large, the case; he was a "pure" artist and his novels did not drag with the useless impediments of philosophical messages. The claim that the matter that became the substance of his art was "passionate" experience is best overlooked, as we overlooked the "phallic worship" above, because by implication the claim denies to his response to the world a factor it always contained in abundance: Lawrence responded to his environment and his own experience with one of the finest intelligences produced by our century. But note that I did not say, one of the best philosophical intellects, for that faculty he almost entirely lacked. For this reason, when we use the term *philosophical* in respect to Lawrence's work, we must think of it as permanently under the harness of quotes. Lawrence's lucubrations lacked the clarity and the coherence that are required of a piece of philosophical intellection. Be that as it may, the impurities we find in the pure poetry he wrote prior to *Aaron's Rod,* and we find many, are relatively minor. But after *Women in Love* his prophetic urge took over. This is not to say that his later work is entirely unpoetic. Some of his short stories—whatever their relative merit as compared with his major novels—are pure poetry.

These observations require a careful qualification. Lawrence wrote, and the preceding discussion has been carried on, as if the relation between poetic substance and conceptual content were a simple matter of either-or, whereas it can only be one of degree. Actually, the matter of experience that goes to make up the substance of a poem must already be conceptually structured to some extent. Even the best of poets—a poet so pure that what Eliot said of Henry James would apply fully to him: one with a mind so fine that no idea could violate it—cannot help acquiring in his practical nonpoetical living more or less rudimentary or finished "philosophical" notions by means of which his experience is given some sort of order prior to its substantiation and information by the creative act. Even when young Lawrence was living in his parents' home, visiting Jessie Chambers at the farm, he was reading a great deal, as we know, and he was "thinking" after his fashion, which is to say that he had ideas of all sorts, had already begun to pick up a philosophical attitude toward life. His mind was not, it could not be, so fine that it was ideologically virgin in an absolute sense. The ideas that serve as matter for the making of his poetry perform two legitimate functions: one, already indicated, is that of serving as principles of selection. But they may perform this function wrongly: when they reject matter on moral rather than on aesthetic grounds, they turn the poet into a dribbling liar or prophet. The ideas themselves may also function as matter to be transmuted into in-formed substance and to be revealed in the poetry in the opinions of the "actors" or in the principles of their actions. In his poetry Lawrence's ideas are not merely dressed up in false dramatic face: Mr. Pessimism, who is bound to commit suicide at the end of the tale, or Miss Chastity who, being naive, is victimized by Sir John the lecher.

If Lawrence wants to call his art "pure experience," there is no law to prevent him from so doing, nor is there any harm in it so long as we make clear that the expression is being used in the sense gathered from the considerations I have tried to elucidate. But neither Lawrence nor any one could take his art as "pure" in the sense that it was altogether free from conceptual structure. That it could never be. In this sense, "pure" experience is utter mindless chaos: the blooming and buzzing confusion of which we used to hear when William James was still read by American philosophers.

III

The difference between Lawrence's pure art and his prophetic work is not difficult to perceive in the concrete. Take for instance his deep and early-rooted rejection of our industrial society, his attitude toward "the machine," toward the world of his father. His hatred of industry seems to have been an attitude acquired early in life, before he began his career as a writer. Expressed discursively, this attitude makes up an idea, a bit of philosophy. In *The Rainbow* (chapter 12, entitled "Shame") we find the attitude in those passages that record Ursula's reaction to the colliery her Uncle Tom managed, and it is an important although a subordinate theme in *Women in Love*. The chapters on the Critches' management of the mines are written out of Lawrence's hatred of the machine. But however deep and implacable that hatred was in *The Rainbow* and in *Women in Love*, it is not merely a dramatized abstraction; it is consubstantial with the drama.

Contrast with this the hatred of the machine that he expressed in *Lady Chatterley*, and you will see the difference in concrete terms and will appreciate, I hope, how radical and all-important it is. In *Lady Chatterley* we are given a more or less mechanical, a more or less factitious illustration of an ideological commitment. In *Women in Love* Gerald first appears as a strong man, successfully managing his mines and the men. But his weakness manifests itself early, in the episode in which he tries to prevent Gudrun from driving the cattle mad. In what seems at the time an almost purely unmotivated, a gratuitous act, Gudrun slaps his face.

"You have struck the first blow," he said at last . . . "And I shall strike the last," she retorted involuntarily, with confident assurance.

From that point on Gudrun, taking advantage of his weakness, is bent on his destruction, although she is not aware of what she is after. The reader finally comes to realize that Gerald, for all his appearance to the contrary, is a weak man, whose weakness is deeply rooted. But in spite of it he is not held up for scorn by the poet; he is presented as an amiable person. The school-inspector does not run off with all the virtues, leaving the industrial magnate all the vices. Gerald is not a mere foil to Birkin or to Gudrun. Nor are he and Gudrun a foil to the other couple. Although they are living two different types of lives that contrast with each other, each is revealed as authentic drama. Gerald's upper-class point of view is authentically expressed by himself in word and action; it is not a social trait or a statistical datum; it is Gerald's expression of stances and attitudes of his own that the reader can take to be generic class traits if he is willing to do without the benefit of elementary logic.

Within the novel Gerald's point of view constitutes a viable attitude toward life—up to a point, the point being that at which his emptiness leads him to catastrophe. His conception of himself, his men, and the mines, as means to the abstract end of production, is one of which he gives a good account. His life "does not centre"; it is held together by the social mechanism, as he acknowledges; but for all its lacks, it is a way of life. If we judge it inferior to Birkin's (remembering that it is not a matter of either-or), it is we who introduce moral criteria of our own, or in the case of a conflict between poet and poem, choose the former's criterion, not the latter's. But if we do, we must allow others with different criteria to judge Birkin's life (in spite of or because of his worship of the "Eros of the sacred mysteries") to be considerably inferior to Gerald's. In Gerald's favor it could be pointed out that he contributed to the creation of a viable social system, such as it was. But what did Birkin contribute after leaving his job?

Here we come upon the reason that Gerald's weakness is more convincing than Clifford's. It is the weakness of inward vacuity that Gerald seeks desperately to remedy by his dedication to "the ethics of productivity." But he fails. The ethics of productivity cannot give his life direction, and he is not the kind of man who can drift without a goal. Whether other men can or not is not a question that a reader of the novel needs to drag into his transaction with it, unless he wishes to turn the novel into sociology of doubtful value. When Gerald leaves England and goes with Gudrun to the Alps, he is destroyed by the woman who manipulates his emptiness pitilessly and not altogether consciously. The drama is completely coherent in terms of its own presuppositions and within its own boundaries.

Clifford Chatterley, on the contrary, is a mere mechanical illustration of a point of view. Everything about him is contrived, not excluding, of course, his emasculation. I know that Lawrence stated that this was the way the story came to him and that the "symbolism" was "inevitable." But his claim does not obviate the criticism; for the dribbling liar did not give himself away to the poet during the composition of the novel or later. We have external evidence to back this contention. In "A Propos of *Lady Chatterley*" he writes, without shame or even awareness of what he is doing, that "the point of the book," is that he wants "men and women to be able to think of sex fully, completely, honestly, and cleanly." But this statement is merely supporting evidence. The decisive evidence is internal. Clifford has several roles in the novel, all of them contrived. He serves, first of all, as the goat for Lawrence's hatreds—the clever successful novelist, the capable industrial manager, the well-born gentleman, the master of the miners. But he also justifies Connie's adulterous affair with the game-keeper and, by contrast, brings to our attention Mellors's vitality.

All of this is but the illustration of a thesis inferred from previous novels, very likely from *Women in Love*. The will of the prophet is ostentatiously in dominance. Lawrence intends that we should despise the emasculated cripple. His gifts are presented as contemptible talents. The intimacy that, in spite of his prejudices, he allows to grow between himself and his nurse and the way in which he allows her to lead him by the nose emphasize his weakness again by a mechanical device. The novel is full of what Isaac Rosenfeld used to call "plants." I do not mean that the picture of the nurse is a mechanical creation. Hough has called attention to the superb quality of the sketch. Once noticed, it becomes self-evident. But the role the nurse plays in the story is thoroughly factitious. This is not true of the relationship between Connie and Mellors—a theme Lawrence had exploited frequently before but always freshly and poetically. Take what attitude you wish toward *Lady Chatterley* and take it on whatever grounds you choose: abhor it as sinful or reject it because it is an example of the worst taste that can be exhibited; think up whatever excuses you can for it; say with Hough (whose attitude toward it, however, is anything but simplistic) that "the freedom to present any aspect of experience is always a gain," or side with his indefatigable biographer and editor, Harry T. Moore, who dismisses those who object to it as "censor-morons"—you cannot deny that the love affair between the lady and the game-keeper is genuine, authentic, that, in Lawrence's terms, it came out of pure experience and not out of a philosophy.[3]

The same is true of the ugly relationship between Mellors and his wife. That the love affair between Connie and Mellors does not represent the best that there can grow between a man and a woman, as Lawrence the prophet would have us believe, is, in my opinion, an important truth to notice; but here it is irrelevant. That Lawrence intruded his prophetic will into the account in order to prove that love-making, to be completely satisfactory, must involve elaborate love-play carried on in four-letter words there is no doubt. But when we look at the affair as a whole we cannot charge it with being manufactured. For these reasons the book is neither a complete failure nor a complete success; exactly how much of one or the other is a delicate question of degree and one on which it would be a pure waste to put dogmatic energy. On the whole, I believe, we must grant that, viewed from a different perspective, *Lady Chatterley* is a "well-made novel"—a coherent story, the parts of which are skillfully joined and proportionate to one another. It is not, like much of his work—and in this class fall such ambitious projects as *Aaron's Rod, Kangaroo, The Plumed Serpent,* and such short novels as *St. Mawr* and many others—an incoherent, padded, poorly joined conglomeration of themes. But at its heart there is a fatal fault: Clifford Chatterley is a fabrication perpetrated by Lawrence the prophet.

It is not at all difficult to show that Lawrence preaches a ridiculous and pernicious philosophy; that his attitude toward our society, insofar as he expressed it positively in the form of prescription for the cure of its mortal illness, was

---

3. I refer to Moore's Introduction to his edition of some of Lawrence's essays, entitled *Sex, Literature and Censorship* (New York: Twayne, 1953).

shallow and irresponsible. But the central question for us, here, is not whether Lawrence's doctrines are right or wrong; the central point is that *Lady Chatterley* is an incongruous mixture of genuine poetry and dramatized philosophy and that the latter is found in those parts of the novel in which Lawrence vents his spleen at Clifford and in which he, impertinent meddler that he is, tells us how to live and love. The meddling makes up those aspects of the novel which Lawrence wrote from conclusions inferred from pure experience that had been embodied in earlier novels. Lawrence was pulling a van Meergeren on himself, and the forgery was not so good as the original. Forgeries seldom are.

IV

I stated above my conviction that the effect of the deterioration of poetic energy is to be discovered in the works themselves and that the immediate causes are purely aesthetic ones, found objectively in the texture of the composition, but that if we are to attain a complete account of the aesthetic failure we have to go, ultimately, to the poet's biography. This is the point at which criticism must perforce cease to be autotelic. If there is a fault in the vase because the hand of the potter trembled, we shall find the original cause in the relations of the potter to his society or to himself, in short, in data that are not "purely" aesthetic. In the case of Lawrence the causes of failure of his poetic skill after writing *Women in Love* are obscure and can only be put forth diffidently, for they are speculative interpretations of facts that are complex, vague and, at this date, beyond adequate authentication. A complete account of them would involve the writing of a critical biography. Here all I can do is to give a succinct outline of several of the factors that I take to be the most important. But I must make it quite clear that in broaching the topic I am undertaking a job of critical spelunking. I am inviting the reader to go down with me into a cave where we shall be lighted by the dim and wavering flame of a quasi-psychoanalytic candle. If the image be objectionable, let me put it more literally by saying that we are about to enter a region of pure speculation in which facts, such as they are, are inherently susceptible to the most conflicting and weird interpretations.

The biographical data required are already at hand: what the task calls for is diffident interpretation. Everywhere we pan in Lawrence material we strike pay dirt. But it would be folly to forget that the word "perhaps" darkens the whole discussion. Speculations of this sort are necessary, they are often illuminating, but they can neither be converted into uninterpreted fact—if there is any such thing—nor be put forth as scientific hypotheses.

The investigation would begin with an analysis of Lawrence's childhood, interpreting along orthodox lines Lawrence's attachment to his "genteel" mother and his intense hatred of his working-class father. The investigation would next emphasize the alienation that this relationship probably generated. His alienation, his acute sense of social inferiority, and his ambivalent attitude toward the upper classes, of which he speaks with candor and pathos in the "Autobiographical Sketch" published in *Assorted Articles,* are probably allotropic manifestations of a complex reaction. To this alienation his superior talent and his mother's ambitions for him no doubt contributed. The investigation would then move on to an examination of later events: his protracted and unsatisfactory love affair with Jessie Chambers, the death of his mother, the final brutal break with his childhood sweetheart, and his relatively easy success as a writer at the beginning. From here the investigation would take up the central event of his life—Frieda. None of these experiences could be expected to lead to a facile "adjustment" to his world. On the contrary, they all tended to intensify his acute sense of difference between himself and others. Then comes the suppression of *The Rainbow,* with its immediate consequences and the threat it carried to his future as poet. All of these events are taking place at the time when many educated people are reacting from the aestheticism of the nineties—the business of the gemlike flame and the pallid art for art's sake. If I am not utterly wrong, this aestheticism was to evolve by a devious process into the hedonism of the Russell-Keynes group, of which the economist has left us an unconvincing apology. Lawrence, when he came into contact with the followers of G. E. Moore, sized them up immediately and accurately and reacted with deep repugnance toward them. But those who could not accept the aesthetic hedonism of G. E. Moore's disciples did not have at hand an adequate aesthetic that would provide them with something they badly needed—a sharp definition of art and a clear distinction between what is art and what is something else. Nor did the times allow them to realize the need for such an aesthetic. The need for it was not perceived and the hammering out of it did not take place until twenty-five years later, counting, of course, in good round numbers, when the problems of paraphrase, of the intention of the work as contrasted with that of the artist, and of intrinsic as against extrinsic criticism, and the like, came up for serious and protracted discussion. It is incidentally of interest to notice that many critics who today command respect have not yet realized the need for this aesthetic or given evidence that they know it is available.

At any rate, when Lawrence began his career as a poet, in spite of his shrewd distinction between the dribbling liar and the poem, he takes art as a means and considers, with the majority of his contemporaries, that any thing is art that can be called art—and, of course, there is no human product that cannot be called art. The end of art, furthermore, is for him and his contemporaries the good life, and anything is good that can be defended as such on more or less plausible grounds, with but one exception: nothing is good that is traditional and well established; but anything that is revolutionary, anything that appears to be an innovation, anything that can be claimed to be a release from Victorian norms is good. Lawrence, although he had very little respect for most of his fellow artists, was to "The Pompadour Café" born—the Café in *Women in Love* in which the scene of Gudrun's snatching Birkin's letter from Halliday took place. He was part of the avant-garde; he did not need an introduction to it, he required no initiation; never has a duck taken to water as readily and naturally as Lawrence took to the group of more or less well-born and not so well-born men and women whom he met after the publication of his first novel and whom he used as matter for some of the actors of the books. In *Point Counterpoint* Huxley pictures Lawrence—if my memory does not betray me after more than a quarter of a century—as ill at ease and antagonistic to the London bohemians from whom he is distinguished by his vitality. This is no doubt true to the biographical fact. But it does not contradict the contention that Lawrence was a bohemian. What else can we call this rootless, wandering expatriate, living into the twenties on a shoestring, if not citizen of that demi-republic of letters that had and, I am told, still has, enclaves in London, Paris, Florence, and Taos? When the war ended he escaped from England and the Pompadour Café—again, so to speak—and started a tour that finally took him completely around the world: to Italy, to Ceylon, to Australia, to Taos, "old Mexico," and finally to Europe to die. But what good did it do him to escape physically?

But I am going too fast and am in danger of losing my trail. The war brought the great trauma, the slow, pitiless, and final break with his world. During a war everybody feels the urge to do something in some way or other—or nearly everybody. In 1914 the youth of England went to the trenches to die, and died—or, like Middleton Murry, found useful work to do at home. But Lawrence would not help. He was opposed to it although he was no pacifist. He refused to serve nor would he keep quiet about his refusal—and with a German wife he could not get by unnoticed. Why did he take the position he did? One word seems to account for it—*alienation.*

But there are darker aspects to this alienation than are usually recognized. In the painful twelfth chapter of *Kangaroo,* entitled "Nightmare," we have a clue to these darker aspects. It is not possible to read the chapter as anything but autobiography, and not because we know from other sources that it is but because of its tone. The chapter reveals among other things the reaction of Lovat-Lawrence to the medical examinations to which the army doctors subjected our fictional-real character. The Lovat-Lawrence reaction is not normal, in either of the two chief senses of the word:

> And because they had handled his private parts, and looked into them, their eyes should burst and their hands should wither and their hearts should rot. So he cursed them in his blood, with an unremitting curse.

This is neither the usual reaction to a medical examination nor what the reaction should be. Am I hopelessly wrong is assuming that the intense sense of outrage wells up from a suppressed fear of homosexual tendencies that, happily, his marriage with Frieda had enabled him to conquer—although not altogether, as we have good reason to suspect?

Whatever was back of his attitude toward the war, Lawrence opposed it with intense passion and intense terror in his soul. But he could not stand idly by. Something had to be done. But what can a poet who is married to an enemy alien do when the world is out to destroy him or, what adds up to the same thing, when he thinks it is, when it pushes him around, snoops into his private life, denies him the means of making a living, and forces him to undergo degrading medical examinations? There is nothing to do but become a social reformer and attempt to flee. But Lawrence was not allowed to leave England while the war was going on. He escaped, neverthless—in imagination: he planned a Utopia and discussed it, apparently seriously, with friends whom he appointed as disciples. Most of the prospective pioneers knew better than to submit their lives to his management: Katherine Carswell had a good excuse—she had a husband. Middleton Murry had another; and so for the rest but one. Bret was ready to follow him. One can without impropriety say, since she herself left us the account of her relation to Lawrence, that she was ready to chase him to the end of the world with a yearning heart and a trumpet ready to the ear to catch his every word. It would all be hilarious had it not involved so much gratuitous pain.

In the meantime, while waiting to ship to Florida and start his happy little colony—in the swamps, among the noble Seminoles, one supposes—he undertakes the reform of England in collaboration with Bertrand Russell. The brief friendship and quarrel with Russell appear to the reader today as pathetic and comic— but not so to Russell, who tells us today in dead earnest that at the time he thought seriously of committing suicide, so strong was the impact of Lawrence on him. Something like thirty-five years later one of the world's foremost philosophers, renowned publicist, social critic, and popular moralist is still burning with hatred of Lawrence. Another man, more secure in his superiority over the meddling poet turned reformer, or at least more secure in his sense of the worth of his own talents and ambitions, would have laughed at himself and at Lawrence's impertinence and presumption of long ago. What can we conclude but that he must know in his heart that Lawrence had something of infinite value that he, the famous philosopher, utterly lacks?

Once Lawrence, forced by his opposition to the war, became a reformer, he never gave up the role. Give a man who has a deep need to boss others the chance to lead the world out of its mess, and the need refuses to down. It seeks satisfaction by any means at hand. Having tasted that kind of intoxicating blood, our bengal is never satisfied with anything else. Art, pure art, is by comparison an insipid quarry. He tells us somewhere that he used his novels as means to shed his sickness. This is true. But he also puts his novels to other uses. He will reform mankind, just as he will tell Bertrand Russell what and how Russell may think.

Because *Women in Love* had been conceived earlier than the brutal trauma he underwent during the war (originally, as everybody knows, *The Rainbow* and it made up one single novel), the prophet did not meddle with this book as he did with subsequent novels. But from *Aaron's Rod* on this statement does not hold. *Kangaroo* is hardly a novel. It is at best an effort, a futile effort, to solve a problem. After *Women in Love* he is not able to in-form the matter of his experience with the success he had achieved earlier. We find a continuous development in stylistic gifts—in his mastery of the language as a means of expression and communication. Some of the short stories are quite successful, and in everything he writes are to be found in profusion vignettes and even expository paragraphs that are evidence of his mastery over the language: pure poetry. Several chapters of *Morning in Mexico* are magnificent, although it would not be astonishing to me if anthropological students of the Southwest found his interpretations of the Indian dances offensive to their scientific conscience and utterly fantastic. And as late as the posthumous *Apocalypse,* we find whole paragraphs that constitute triumphant evidence of what a gifted man can do with the English language. But on the whole the poet has lost control. He is too deeply involved in a bitter struggle against forces that he feels threaten him to handle them as he handled his experience up to *Women in Love.*

This passionate desire of his to do something about the world was not subject matter that could be transformed into substance—or at least that he could transform. It was, for him, too definitely oriented toward practical ends. What he could and did do was to handle with a messianic fervor subjects he had formerly handled aesthetically. He changed settings. He took Aaron and Lilly to Florence, he took Lovat and his foreign wife to Australia, he went with Kate to "old Mexico." He added to his interest in love a strong sociological and political interest that he had not shown in his earlier work. And from his observation of the Indian dances in the Southwest he achieved a clearer grasp than he had previously had of a profound insight, namely, that one of the needs of modern man is a religion that will reestablish his broken connection with the Cosmos. And thus, he managed to give himself and those of his readers who do not clearly grasp the distinction between quasi-art and art in the most exacting sense the impression that he was growing, prodigiously and in depth, in an aesthetic sense. But the rate of growth, *exception fait* of his increasing mastery over language, was negligible.

A detailed examination of the work that Lawrence did after *Women in Love* will show that, whatever its incidental aesthetic excellences, and they are many, and whatever its ideological value, on the whole it fails to come up to the purity exhibited in his two greatest works, *The Rainbow* and *Women in Love*. I do not put *Sons and Lovers* in the class of these two novels because it is not the expression of his mature vision. The contrast between *Women in Love* and *Lady Chatterley* sketched above could be considerably extended and refined. The upshot would be the same. It would show that there is nothing in the notorious novel that is not to be found in the earlier and greater work—unless one is prepared to argue that those passages that have kept the latter work from legitimate circulation in the United States and England in the original edition are an important contribution to our grasp of human experience. The same holds for Lawrence's grasp of his other major theme, religion. Compare *The Rainbow* with *The Plumed Serpent*: the earlier book is by far the more successful. In the Mexican novel he knows more, he is a better informed, a more traveled, and a better-read man. But what he has learned since the publication of the earlier book is something that a sociologist or a philosopher of religion could have expressed more precisely and with greater clarity than the novelist can or, at any rate, than our novelist did. But, of course, to substantiate these generalizations we shall have to turn to these novels and examine them in detail.

The Development of Gide's Concept of Personality

LESLIE A. SHEPARD
Washington State University

COMMENT BY THE AUTHOR

The essay below constituted an attempt on my part to utilize what I considered noteworthy in the approach of the French nouvelle critique, while at the same time testing the validity of certain traditional concepts in the light of the insights gained by recent methods and theories. I demur at the premise that literary works are purely verbal contructs lacking all reference to reality, or even that critics should regard them exclusively as isolated texts, self-generated and pointing to nothing beyond their transparent entity; the reader is cautioned that my essay has such limitations. But if I am not drawn to a stance that examines writing as if it were in a void, I have found conventional critical procedures of literary analysis also somewhat unsatisfactory. I wondered whether, rather than cutting off the channels leading from life to art, or explaining a composition in terms of biographical, social, and literary influences in the orthodox manner, it might not be more enlightening to adopt the view that there obtains no dividing line between life and literature, that in effect both are subject to the same laws, for a basic dialectic characterizes all human activity, and the elements of the same structure have equivalents on the moral, psychological, and artistic levels capable of being expressed almost like mathematical proportions and translatable into one another's values like the symbols of an equation.

The genesis of this concept followed my reading of Barthes, Doubrovsky, Picard, and others, and I am grateful to acknowledge my indebtedness to them, for my position can be defined to some extent with respect to theirs, even though at times in a negative sense; however, it actually began to take shape while I was doing research on Gide with the intent of establishing the development of his

First published: 17, no. 2 (1969): 47–66. Slightly revised.

theory of personality. It seems likely, therefore, that Gide's works, particularly when viewed through their treatment of personality, favor such an approach: indeed the dynamic interpenetration of life and literature characterizing Gide may be a relatively infrequent phenomenon. The correspondence between childhood repressions, artistic restraint, the choice of a classical style, and the conviction that appearances must be passed through the sieve of interpretation on the one hand, and revolt, poetic freedom, the cult of sincerity, and the ambition to mirror all of life on the other hand clearly suggests relationships that represent different projections of a fundamental pattern. The development of the concept of personality throughout Gide's fiction is intimately bound up with the kinetics of his self as well as the tension he recognized as existing between style and subject matter. If my assumption is correct in that style lends itself to conversion into such general terms as significance, meaning, and sense, it would appear that the notion of content, which we have come to distrust and relegate to memories of the past as far as works of art are concerned, may get a new lease on life, although not in its static Aristotelian denotation; instead of being reducible to technique, it will be seen as the indispensable constituent of a dialectical opposition that would lose its functional role without its antithesis, form.

Pygmalion engraving his ideal of perfection in marble, crystallizing the amorphous substance of his fancy into plastic permanence—such is the metaphor the Gidean activity calls to mind. But this Pygmalion lovingly follows the contours of his own mirror image; he constitutes the subject of his dream. Rather, perhaps, than Gide's life, what seems to emerge from the sizable corpus of his works is a Life of Gide, a new gospel, a *legenda aurea* inspired by Goethe. Yet this figure reminds us of an animated statue; it is not mere waxwork. For the legend has a great amount of pulsating experience sealed in it; the imposing outlines hide an inner tension. Pygmalion, who poses as Narcissus, wants to chisel an easily identifiable, classical profile that will fire the public imagination, while Walter-Werther wishes to pour out the contents of his overflowing ego.

The correspondence between, on one side, the Gide intent on creating a striking public image and the classicist determined on restraint and, on the other side, the author who demands the highest sincerity of himself and Gide the Romantic is far from perfect, yet I think that this contrast is functionally useful and valid within certain limits. Significantly, one finds that the dialectical struggle may be transposed to several different levels. Whereas the field may change from the stylistic to the moral and psychological, the structural relationships frequently remain constant. A detailed analysis of the psychic dynamism at work in Gide's personality falls outside the scope of this inquiry; however, the problem of motivation is not irrelevant, for in his case the fictional and autobiographical are constantly intertwined. The Gidean work is a *galerie de glace* with the author in the center, his image refracted countless times by the deceptively shimmering walls.

The earliest manifestation of a conflict must be searched for in the twilight of his "somnolent" childhood and, if we are to accept Gide's own interpretation, even in the antinomies of his heredity. The author was fond of envisaging the ambivalence of his personality as the product of a deep chasm between the paternal and maternal heritage. The father's side appeared to him to stand for the permissive, creative, playfully intellectual temper; the Rondeaux he associated with restriction, stifling narrowness, and self-denial. What Gide indentified as the divergent atmospheres of the *Midi* and of Normandy may well have characterized only the personalities of Paul Gide and Juliette Rondeaux.[1] Still, this opposition casts its shadow on his first childhood reminiscences. What we call the mother's sway should not be understood merely as a force acting upon Gide from the outside. It is or soon becomes an internalized element, one of his inner voices, a part of his superego. For the motherly injunctions have been planted into the child surrounded by the protecting humus of love. Their seed will not die. When he thinks he has overcome them we notice that all he did was to change his deck of cards. The rules of the game still apply. The war still has to be fought. Only toward the end of his sojourn on earth will this latter-day Saint George put down his lance to allow himself a brief respite. For one glorious moment before his life is snuffed out he becomes Theseus, contemplating the slain Minotaur under a clear Attic sky. But for the rest of the time his puritanical conscience pursues him. Life has to be conceived as a relentless strife, an uninterrupted vigilance. The avowed enemy changes at a relatively early stage. The signs themselves are ultimately reversed; good and evil are interchanged: the new creed enjoins a struggle for, not against, sensual gratification. But one would be mistaken in imagining that his vindication of the pleasures of the flesh will turn André Walter into a quiet eudaemonist or hedonist; nothing could be farther from the truth. On the contrary, Gide becomes an ascetic more than ever; with superhuman effort he chains himself to his desk to formulate the tenets of the new faith. Rather than embracing his philosophy, he preaches it to others.

Essentially the fatal maternal bequest may be envisaged as guilt, the awareness of original sin, of the tainted human condition that prompts the Jansenist to speak of *le moi haïssable*. The Protestant practice of *libre examen* has the function of exposing the lurking evil. This method of soul-searching, which was encouraged in the Gide household, is held responsible for the Huguenot's general penchant for introspection and favors a tendency to divide the ego into judge and accused.[2] Bad conscience is a foe that can never be definitely cornered and destroyed. It survives, it gathers substance on any level. The search for the "real" underlying cause of Gide's mental *déchirement* is therefore rather a futile wild-goose chase. Once his environment had transmitted, probably at the very dawn of his life,

---

1. Albert J. Guérard in *André Gide* (New York: Dutton, 1963) has called attention to the questionable accuracy and possible reversibility of the influences ascribed to these two regions of France (p. 5). Guérard, like a number of eminent contemporary French essayists, such as Maurice Blanchot (in "Gide et la littérature d'expérience," *La Part du feu* [Paris: Gallimard, 1949], pp. 216–28) and Sartre (in "Gide vivant," *Situations* 4 [Paris: Gallimard, 1964]: 85–89) before him, treated Gide's production in terms of an inner dialectical struggle. The latest publication espousing this approach is Daniel Moutote's *Le Journal de Gide et les problèmes du moi* (Paris: Presses Universitaires de France, 1969). Though it does not attempt to examine the transposition of structural relationships from level to level, so far Moutote's approach resembles most closely that adopted by the present writer.

2. For an incisive discussion of this matter, see Jean Delay, *La Jeunesse d'André Gide*, 1 (Paris: Gallimard, 1956): 261–77.

a susceptibility to guilt, once he had discovered sin in himself through an examination of his conscience, it mattered little which form of socially censured activity he would seize on to expose the *other* in himself.

Les Cahiers d'André Walter, the author's first published work, is still a stuttering and confused piece of writing. It suggests, though does not openly admit, guilt, which at this particular stage Gide identified in himself as the vice of onanism. The André Walter phase, whose coincidence with the author's preoccupation with his mirror image has been generally recognized, is characterized, first, by an effort on Gide's part to seize himself from the outside, to eliminate his self-doubts by watching himself act as a corporeal entity. Second, self-observation represents a social impulse, a process of self-building *vis-à-vis* the public. Thus besides helping Gide-Walter to solidify himself, at least retrospectively, the *Cahiers* is written with one eye on the reader, as the first installment of the Gide myth. As an aesthetic phenomenon, the Narcissus pose is directed at his environment. Far from being a solipsistic tendency, it is the bond linking him with the external world, the thread that allows Daedalus to feel his way out of the labyrinth, to a point where communication becomes possible.[3] The appearance of Narcissus signifies that Gide has found "himself," that is, the platform on which he can face humanity. This platform is based on his newly found status as artist, a creature abominable in its depravity, *maudit,* yet in a sense the Chosen One, the elect, as broker between the transphenomenal idea and the world of appearances. In order to regain his balance, to compensate himself for the humiliation of acknowledging his guilty otherness, he has hit on a solution by discovering the germs of genius in himself. Walking on the street, a canary alights on his hand—no doubt a sign from heaven. To his mother's prosaic query about his vocational objectives, he is tempted to answer, "N'as-tu donc pas compris que je suis élu?"[4]

Gide's second work, Le Traité du Narcisse, announces the terms according to which Gide consents to play the social game. The poet, contemplating the flux of phenomena, can catch a glimpse of the eternal truths, the ideas. He must isolate himself like Moses and, instead of preferring himself, should manifest the idea. In this appeal of devotion to the work of art Gide embraces, under the influence of Mallarmé, a classicistic aesthetic: indeed, the style of the *Traité* itself shows him forsaking the diffuse manner of André Walter.[5] But this stands for only one half of the message. The poet is urged to *suppress* his individuality in favor of the work of art; however, he is also told to *reveal* himself. Gide's

---

3. See Jacques Lacan, "Jeunesse de Gide ou la lettre et le désir," *Critique,* No. 131 (April 1958), pp. 291–315. For Lacan both what he calls the *stade du miroir* and language constitute rejections of reality.

4. *Si le grain ne meurt* (Paris: Gallimard, 1955), p. 190.

5. Critical opinion attributes considerable significance to the *Traité* as a turning point in Gide's career. See, e. g., Germaine Brée, *André Gide, l'insaisissable Protée* (Paris: Belles Lettres, 1953), pp. 41–42, 64, 65–66. Because of its impact on Gide scholarship in this country, it may be worth pointing out that Brée's study, after identifying the significance of Mallarmé's symbolism for Gide as a withdrawal from realism and suggesting that Mallarmé's influence will be particularly perceptible in *Paludes* and *Les Nourritures terrestres,* goes on to assert (p. 77) that in precisely these two works Gide at last freed himself from the impasse of symbolism. The glaring error is inherent in Germaine Brée's premise that each Gidean work constitutes an answer to some previous one. In truth, antipodal tendencies are found in each of Gide's books taken separately as well.

hesitancy or ambiguity is significant, because it already indicates the dilemma he will never be able to resolve between the desirability of stylizing or representing life. I have portrayed this as the conflict between the classicist and romantic, where by the latter term I understand the tendency to render experience in its unbounded, chaotic, unassorted wealth and immediacy. The fact that, unwittingly or not, Gide is on both sides of the fence becomes clear when, shortly after exhorting the poet not to prefer himself to the idea, he adds, " 'Malheur à celui par qui le scandale arrive,' mais 'il faut que le scandale arrive.' "[6] We already sense in this enigmatic statement the first indication of the personal message to come, of self-revelation and reformist fervor despite the classicistic premises.

Having accepted his culpability and transformed it into a claim to being the Chosen One in the context of Romantic Satanism, Gide now felt ready to undergo the scathing experience that would bring to the surface the hidden splendors of his unconscious. He chose to designate his trip to North Africa in 1893 as the catalyst disclosing his real personality. The Algerian and Tunisian journey assumed symbolic proportions as a sort of voyage to the underworld, a story of illness and rebirth under the pagan brightness of the Mediterranean sun. But Gide was not yet ready to preach the lesson he had purportedly learned. *Paludes* (1895) only obliquely hints at it, through its images of stagnation and frustration associated with learning and intellectual life. The first real intimation came with *Les Nourritures terrestres*, a hymn to the world of the senses. His reading of Nietzsche contributed perceptibly to the philosophical underpinning of *L'Immoraliste*, the novelistic counterpart to *Les Nourritures*.[7] Here the protagonist, Michel, embraces a philosophy according to which civilization is an illness one must be cured of in order to bring to light the authentic man, the primitive who is not cluttered with social taboos and inhibitions:

> Ce fut dès lors *celui* que je prétendis découvrir: l'être authentique, le "vieil homme", celui dont ne voulait plus l'Evangile; celui que tout, autour de moi, livres, maîtres, parents, et que moi-même avions tâché d'abord de supprimer.[8]

His motto is: find out who you are, and realize yourself, develop your faculties, particularly the physical ones, to the full. Self-realization is the supreme law; you are the measure of everything.

Le Prométhée mal enchaîné, which chronologically precedes *L'Immoraliste,* constitutes another defense of individuality. The eagle devouring the Titan's liver symbolizes the cross one has to bear, one's particular thorn in the flesh, the specific difference distinguishing each of us from our fellows. Our tormenting sores make us human, they give content and meaning to our lives. What is worth preserving in man is his originality, his idiosyncrasy. Gide obviously protests here against mass-produced culture, against a standardized ideal of human happiness, a society whose members conform to the degree of becoming interchangeable.

During this period in Gide's career the emphasis is primarily on discovering,

---

6. *Le Traité du Narcisse.* in *Romans, récits et soties, oeuvres lyriques* (Paris: Gallimard, 1958), p. 9. All subsequent quotations from Gide's novelistic works will refer to this edition.

7. Nietzsche's influence on Gide is a contested point. Gide always claimed that he had discovered the author of *Also sprach Zarathustra* during the composition of *L'Immoraliste.* See Renée Lang, *André Gide et la pensée allemande* (Paris: Egloff, 1949), pp. 81 ff.

8. *L'Immoraliste,* p. 398.

asserting, and developing the *real* personality and self, after the artificial layers composed of upbringing, civilizatory influences, and social restraints have been peeled off. The author is after true nature, even if it has to be, as Michel thinks, that of a gross and brutish specimen. Noble or ignoble savage, his existence behind the gloss of social convention is always taken for granted. Yet ever since *Paludes* Gide was interested in the problem of freedom as well. In fact, the concepts of nature and freedom are rather undifferentiated in Gide's lexicon at this stage. The cult of *déracinement* and *disponibilité,* which starts with *Les Nourritures terrestres,* itself has something to do with liberty. If the former implies no more than a break with tradition, it prepares the ground for the latter, receptivity and avoidance of attachment. The person who is *disponible* must be unfettered by ties and allegiances and open to influences. However, this type of freedom is a state that presupposes total inactivity. The slightest deed upsets it. All action must remain in the field of speculation; as Monsieur Teste found out, even artistic execution shackles freedom; in the *Tentative Amoureuse* (1893) Gide himself showed that the work can "retroact" upon its author. The person wishing to adopt *disponibilité* as his rule of conduct would find that he is free only to "be" in the abstract, but not to do anything. "Savoir se libérer n'est rien; l'ardu, c'est savoir être libre."[9] More than difficult, it is in practice impossible.

But what about free actions? Can we assert our independence through an autonomous movement of the will? This question too intrigued Gide from the very first; it assumes major proportions in *Le Prométhée mal enchaîné* and in *Les Caves du vatican.* In each work, famous passages describe actions without apparent rhyme or reason. Nevertheless, Gide did not believe in the unmotivated act as a philosophically valid concept. Time and again he stated that to suppose that man could escape the chain of cause and effect was absurd; the *acte gratuit* could not be performed in the strict sense.[10] The only point he made was that narrowly interpreted self-interest does not always explain the actual motivation. People of imagination and pluck are capable of transcending mere practical interest. Accordingly, the actual meaning of freedom in the Gidean *oeuvre* is provisional. Both *disponibilité* and the *acte gratuit* should be seen as terms that need to be qualified. Instead of real freedom, they imply only a subjective state, a lightness of touch, a willingness to gamble. The attitude of the "free" man is one of playfulness, for he has understood that life is a game.

Though Gide never ceased to be a creature of ambiguity, his production lends itself to three chronological divisions: the short neo-romantic and symbolist period, under the influence of German idealism and the French *fin de siècle,* characterized by introspection and contempt for the external world; early manhood, with its affirmation of the senses, extramental orientation, and assertion of self; and maturity, when a balance is achieved between the two points of view. It was in connection with his Dostoevski studies that the questions of personality gained a sharpened profile in Gide's mind. In 1908 he published an article entitled *Dostoïevski d'après sa correspondance,* where he recognized some similarities between his and the Russian

9. *Ibid.,* p. 372. A recent study, Henri Freyburger, *L'Evolution de la disponibilité gidienne* (Paris: A.-G. Nizet, 1970), dicusses at some length (pp. 97–129) the contradictory aspects of the concept of freedom at this particular stage in Gide's development.

10. See, e.g., *Oeuvres complètes.* 15 vols. (Paris: Nouvelle Revue Française, 1932–1939), pp. 841–42.

novelist's handling of certain themes. Then, on the occasion of the Dostoevski centennial, he delivered a series of incisive lectures at the Vieux-Colombier. He attributed great importance to these, describing them as a profession of faith. Together with *Journal des faux-monnayeurs* the Dostoevski study may be regarded as a companion volume to *The Counterfeiters,* which, written between 1919 and 1925, constitutes the mature Gide's view on the subject of personality.

Gide's *Dostoïevski* emphasizes the difference between Dostoevski's procedure and the method of most French authors. The Frenchman instinctively tries to organize the data at hand. He must present the person he is depicting as a logical, cohesive whole. If he finds that in reality the model diverges from the pattern it should follow, the French novelist will suppress these divergencies. Even in life, Gide observes, Frenchmen fashion themselves, their conduct, after an ideal. They behave as they think persons like them *should* behave.[11] The inconsistencies, the deviations from the norm appear ridiculous to them. By contrast, Gide points out, Dostoevski shows us characters that yield to contradictions. In fact, it is the negations and inconsistencies that interest the Russian writer the most. Dostoevski's creations experience emotions that are each other's opposites, almost simultaneously. This is an aspect of the ego's duality. But the duality Dostoevski describes is not the pathological split personality of the medical textbook. He espies the contradictions that all of us have inside us, but that we try to deny in order to resemble the model. This is disconcerting and downright embarrassing to the Western reader. We who live on the basis of established conventions are perplexed to find our secret thoughts brought to light in the Russian writer's characters.[12] While most if us live imitative lives, Dostoevski gives the unwelcome truth behind convention.

The capital importance attributed by recent criticism to *Notes from Underground* in Dostoevski's treatment of personality was already recognized by Gide. "Je crois," he notes, "que nous atteignons avec *l'Esprit souterrain* le sommet de la carrière de Dostoïevski. Je le considère . . . comme la clé de voûte de son oeuvre entière."[13] The element of the underground man is the perfidious, demonic realm of the intelligence. Hell, to Dostoevski, is the region of the intellect. It is opposed to God's kingdom, where only those who have renounced their individuality can enter. It is also morbid, because it freezes action in us. The fact that the intellectual looks at all sides of each problem makes him incapable of action. It follows that, conversely, the man of action is intellectually inferior: " 'Celui qui pense n'agit point . . . ,' et de là à prétendre que l'action présuppose certaine médiocrité intellectuelle, il n'y a qu'un pas."[14]

Up to this point, Gide has on the whole faithfully interpreted Dostoevski. But here he adds a touch of Mallarmé and Valéry. He claims that according to Dostoevski the intellectual disdains practical action, "car l'esprit altier est empêché d'agir lui-même; il verra dans l'action une compromission, une limitation de sa pensée."[15] Now, in fact Dostoevski envisaged the underground man's hesitancy

---

11. *Dostoïevski* (Paris: Gallimard, 1964), pp. 143-45.
12. *Ibid.,* p. 153.
13. *Ibid.,* pp. 164-65.
14. *Ibid.,* p. 195.
15. Gide admitted that, to some extent, he had used Dostoevsky to illustrate his own thought rather than elucidate the Russian writer's works. *Gide, Freedom and Dostoevsky* (Burlington, Vt.: Lane Press, 1946) by Mischa H. Fayer stresses Gide's eclecticism or bias in this matter (pp. 143–44).

as a debilitating disease, not a haughty refusal to have anything to do with sordid reality. Significantly, Gide reverses the publication dates of *Notes from Underground* and *Crime and Punishment,* claiming that "dans *Crime et châtiment,* Dostoïevski n'avait pas encore établi cette division entre le penseur et l'acteur."[16] But actually *Crime and Punishment* was written two years *after* the *Notes.* He then proceeds to misquote Dostoevski, asserting that according to the Russian author the man of action of the nineteenth century is a characterless creature. In truth Dostoevski says that it is the man of acute consciousness who lacks character. These slips are illuminating, because they illustrate the difference between the Gidean and Dostoevskian perspectives. At this stage Gide no longer regarded intellectuality as a mere shortcoming. The period of Dionysiac fervor had passed; he was now striving for a synthesis and harmonious coexistence of the spiritual and physical.

The Dostoevski study indicates that by the time of the composition of *Les Faux-monnayeurs* Gide began to wonder whether it was as simple to unearth "old Adam," that is, the basic, authentic man, as he had supposed when writing *L'Immoraliste.* Sincerity remained his highest ideal; however, he was now willing to admit that even with the best of intentions sincerity cannot come up with a cut-and-dried inner reality as a result of its probings. As early as December 3, 1909, at what one might consider the halfway mark of life, he observes in the *Journal* that the word *sincerity* is one of those that are becoming harder for him to understand. Every young man thinks he is sincere when he has convictions, he adds. In another jotting, dated October 9, 1927, the fifty-eight-year-old author further limits the efficacy of sincerity. There is in every human being a little bit of the irresistible, he admits; but the share of "as you will" is much greater; it is foolhardy to assert at the age of twenty that you know yourself thoroughly.

Gide had traded the obscure, indistinct sense of guilt he felt in his childhood for an admission of his otherness; with Rousseau, he had said, "j'ose croire n'être fait comme aucun de ceux qui existent; si je ne vaux pas mieux, au moins je suis autre." This had been a bargain with society, concluded in keeping with the requirements of the romantic role of genius: he was to be recognized as a sacred monster, a depository of society's sins, an accredited horrible example. This solution had the advantage of isolating, objectifying, defining the will-o'-the-wisp origin of the culpability burdening his conscience. Once the culprit had been identified in his anomaly, Gide could trust himself to be skillful enough to turn things around and prove that his wickedness was really virtue. It was an ingenious scheme for getting rid of his guilt; but unfortunately the psyche cannot be out-maneuvered in such a fashion. With *Corydon* he had gone as far as possible in both accepting a well-defined, concrete otherness, and justifying it. By the early 1920s he must have realized that he was indeed winning his case. With typically Gidean mistrust, however, he reexamined the terms of the bargain he had struck with his fellows, and found that the role of sacred pelican was too high a price to pay. The part of Prometheus performing an exhibitionist self-vivisection was beginning to irk him, even though the audience was appreciative. His Dostoevski readings had momentarily reawakened in him an awareness of evil as a palpable reality in the world, but he refused to cast himself as archculprit, and ultimately minimized the part of the demon in *Les Faux-monnayeurs.*

That personality is changeable Gide never denied and had already acknowledged

---

16. Fayer, pp. 143–44.

in *L'Immoraliste*. The Wildean Ménalque admonishes Michel not to cling to the past:

> "C'est du parfait oubli d'hier que je crée la nouvelleté de chaque heure. Jamais, d'avoir été heureux, ne me suffit. Je ne crois pas aux choses mortes, et confonds n'être plus, avec n'avoir jamais été."[17]

Michel discovers that one year has sufficed to turn his friendship for Charles into indifference: "C'est que mes occupations et mes goûts n'étaient plus ceux de l'an passé."[18] As a matter of fact, the cult of *disponibilité* largely follows from the premise that, because the self and ego undergo a constant metamorphosis, one should not be bound by the commitments and obligations of yesterday. The notion that man is in the process of becoming, that he is not stationary or immutable, can be found throughout the Gidean *oeuvre*. The "river of time" in *Le Traité du Narcisse* already has a certain Bergsonian flavor. Beginning with *Les Caves du vatican* the theme of the changeableness of personality becomes a persistent one. Even the "crustaceans"—Anthime, Julius, and Amédée—experience temporary dislocations of ego, and it is unnecessary to stress Protos's mutability. True enough, in some of these cases one might argue that the changes merely stand for disguises, or that they do not correspond to the intimate core of personality. But the following quotation should leave no doubt as to the mature Gide's position on this issue. Speaking of Edouard, Laura says:

> "Il n'est jamais longtemps le même. Il ne s'attache à rien; mais rien n'est plus attachant que sa fuite. Vous le connaissez depuis trop peu de temps pour le juger. Son être se défait et se refait sans cesse. On croit le saisir . . . c'est Protée. Il prend la forme de ce qu'il aime. Et lui-même, pour le comprendre, il faut l'aimer."[19]

Later in the novel Edouard himself observes, "Et je ne prétends pas que l'inconséquence soit l'indice certain du naturel . . . mais, le plus souvent, cette conséquence de l'être n'est obtenue que par un cramponnement vaniteux et qu'au dépens du naturel."[20] Consciousness is thus in constant flux, and personality changes with it. It is interesting to note that whereas for the younger Gide the modifications that the social environment causes in man were invariably regarded as detrimental and as having a stifling effect on the ego, the author of *Les Faux-monnayeurs* takes being for the other to be one of the almost inevitable ground rules of human existence. Ménalque still comments bitterly on those who fashion themselves after their friends' requirements: "Lois de l'imitation; je les appelle: lois de la peur."[21] In *Les Faux-monnayeurs* the sarcastic, scornful tone is gone when Edouard refers to the same phenomenon in relation to his love for Laura:

> "Il me paraît même que si elle n'était pas là pour me préciser, ma propre personnalité s'éperdrait en contours trop vagues; je ne me rassemble et en me définis

---

17. *L'Immoraliste*, p. 436.
18. *Ibid.*, p. 443.
19. *Les Faux-monnayeurs*, p. 1099.
20. *Ibid.*, p. 1207.
21. *L'Immoraliste*, p. 431.

qu'autour d'elle. . . . Ou plutôt: par un étrange croisement d'influences amoureuses, nos deux êtres, réciproquement, se déformaient."[22]

A few weeks later he records a similar psychic process in connection with Olivier: ". . . sans tenir compte de lui, je ne pourrais ni tout à fait bien m'expliquer, ni tout à fait bien me comprendre."[23]

The Gide of 1920 admits that, abstracted from its relationship with others, the ego is hardly definable at all. This is a far cry from Philoctetes, who found his true personality in the solitude of his desert island. Nevertheless, the author does not consider personality as revealed through others indicative of what is most authentic in man. Though he does not deny that without Laura he would lose his contours, he uses the verb *déformer* to characterize their mutual relationship; and at the end of the paragraph he confesses, "Quiconque aime vraiment renounce à la sincérité."[24] Such cases of deep interpenetration between human beings cannot be set down, though, as *mere* hypocrisy. In the Edouard-Laura relationship it is difficult to separate the genuine from the meretricious: their love was sincere, and one might argue that their mutual "deformation" was the result of changes in their true personalities. Their case is clearly different from the deliberate disguise Michel is forced to assume in his dealings with his former friends. Yet Gide maintains that absolute sincerity cannot be achieved within any social framework. This idea is stressed in the process of *decrystallization*, the tragic recognition of a married couple that their union was based on mutual errors and self-deception: ". . . au bout de quinze ans, de vingt ans de vie conjugale, la décristallisation progressive et réciproque des conjoints."[25] The *Journal des faux-monnayeurs* indicates that Gide originally intended this to be the main subject of the novel. In the actual execution it became only a minor theme, highlighted in the estrangement of La Pérouse from his wife and in the Molinier couple.

Closely related to the mutability of personality is its dialectical, self-contradictory nature. I have summarized the author's views on this issue in connection with his Dostoevski essay. A striking example of the hidden springs in the psyche is provided by the behavior of Gontran Passavant at his father's bier. Trying in vain to join the corpse's hands in a gesture of prayer,

il entend soudain un brutal "Nom de Dieu," que l'emplit d'effroi, comme si quelqu'un d'autre . . . il se retourne; mais non: il est seul. C'est bien de lui qu'a jailli ce juron sonore, du fond de lui qui n'a jamais juré.[26]

Little Boris is certainly the most self-contradictory character in *Les Faux-monnayeurs*. When we first hear him, he answers the question whether he feels like taking a walk in the following manner: "Oui, je veux bien. Non, je ne veux pas."[27] Even here, though, Gide's contention is not that personality cannot be analyzed and explained in terms of causes and effects. The explanation may

---

22. *Les Faux-monnayeurs*, p. 986.
23. *Ibid.*, p. 997.
24. *Ibid.*, p. 986.
25. *Ibid.*, pp. 988–89.
26. *Ibid.*, p. 967.
27. *Ibid.*, p. 1071.

elude us, because we do not have all the facts, but it can be found. When Edouard rejects Mme Sophroniska's appeal to an ultimate mystery, we feel that we have Gide's last word on this matter. The "inconsequent" behavior of the Gidean characters results from their complexity and mutability: the author does not believe in simple and fixed human beings; however, he does not hold either that personality is refractory to logical explanation: he equally refuses to have recourse to the irrational.

A third kindred question is the duality and multiplicity of personality. Armand, apparently the fictional counterpart of the Armand Bavretel described in *Si le grain ne meurt,* was chosen by Gide to exemplify the type of duality often manifested in romantic irony. The resumpticn of this theme signifies a return to the inspiration of *André Walter.* Gide was a keen student of Baudelaire who, of all French poets, had lent greatest importance to the ego-splitting function of irony.[28] *Le Traité du Narcisse* contains reverberations of *L'Héautontimorouménos,* the poem in which Baudelaire attributes his torments to the voice of irony within himself. The sentence, "Tout était *parfait* comme un nombre et se scandait normalement; un *accord* émanait du rapport des lignes; sur le jardin planait un constant *symphonie,*"[29] depicting the paradisiac state before the fall, sounds like the counterpoint to Baudelaire's lines, "Ne suis-je pas un *faux accord/* Dans la divine *symphonie,*" characterizing the sad human condition resulting from the thirst for (self-) knowledge. In *Les Faux-monnayeurs* Armand formulates the problem as follows:

> Quoi que je dise ou fasse, toujours, une partie de moi reste en arrière, qui regarde l'autre se compromettre, qui l'observe, qui se fiche d'elle et la siffle, ou qui l'applaudit. Quand on est ainsi divisé, comment veux-tu qu'on soit sincère? J'en viens a ne même plus comprendre ce que peut vouloir dire ce mot.[30]

While the changeableness and complexity of personality render the task of sincerity difficult, Gide considers that this form of duality makes it almost impossible. We are condemned to lying about ourselves no matter how hard we try to tell the truth, or at least a shadow of insincerity, a lack of perfect coincidence remains with us as an inseparable companion.

As I have pointed out, in Gide's opinion social interaction always falsifies the true personality to some extent. It is consequently only in solitude and through introspection that we can reach the substratum: "Ce n'est que dans la solitude que parfois le substrat m'apparaît et que j'atteins à une certaine continuité foncière. . . ."[31]

But, not unlike other introspective protagonists, Edouard finds that continued self-examination leads to a gradual evaporation of the ego. At best therefore we may succeed in catching an occasional glimpse of what we are, or rather, what we are in the process of becoming.

However, the *fundamental* difficulty of finding ourselves does not lie in human

---

28. An entry in the *Journal,* dated June 14, 1905, notes, apropos of Baudelaire, the great importance of the notion of irony as a source of torment. Gide's essay on Baudelaire, written as a preface for *Les fleurs du mal,* contains some incisive observations on this subject.

29. *Le Traité du Narcisse,* p. 5.

30. *Les Faux-monnayeurs,* p. 1229.

31. *Ibid.,* p. 987.

changeableness, complexity, duality, falsification through social contracts, or in the fact that introspection tends to blot out the content of consciousness. The real hitch is that, to a large extent, particularly in the realm of emotions we are what we think we are. "Je ne suis jamais que ce que je crois que je suis."[32] On the emotive level reality cannot be distinguished from imagination. It may suffice to fancy that we love in order to fall in love; conversely, by telling ourselves that our love is imaginary we can reduce the intensity of the emotion. It must be admitted that in the formula "I am what I think I am" Gide summed up the predicament of the modern fictional hero or anti-hero more succinctly and strikingly than anyone before him. Yet the purport of this maxim is not so radical as it would seem at first glance. If it is true, on the one hand, that emotive reactions depend greatly on our intellectual assent, on the other hand what we think we are is influenced by our reading, our associates, the capacity of our brain, that is, in the final analysis it still comes down to the interplay of heredity and environment. I have emphasized that, when the chips were down, Gide always acknowledged himself to be a determinist. It may be taken for granted therefore that he considered the freedom suggested by his maxim to be only subjective. Nevertheless, the various factors I discussed above as contributing to the difficulties of sincerity demonstrate beyond doubt that the mature Gide, the author of *Les Faux-monnayeurs,* no longer regarded nature in man as a readily decipherable and transparent force that automatically takes over when the artificial impediments of civilization have been removed. Though he believed that ultimately all life, vegetable, animal, and human, is subject to immutable laws, he realized that the functioning of these laws is executed in a very different manner when we speak of human beings. It is not enough to encourage people to dare to be themselves; the first and probably greater problem is to decide just what this self consists of.

Gide's quest would seem to suggest that sincerity does not suffice, because life has to be, at least subjectively, in large part a creative effort. The concept of man must be constantly reinvented. The novelist is a creator of human reality; the Gidean *oeuvre* itself adds up to a sum total of whatever lent itself to invention in the author's personality as well as its more easily definable aspects. There exists an area in the ego that is open to interpretation and a variety of definitions. In this sense the monument Gide created to himself, the new gospel he fashioned, by taking raw material from autobiographical data, and by interpreting these data in such a manner as to produce a splendid effect on the reader, should not be censured as merely spurious or self-complacent. The dilemma Gide faced can be envisaged as an aspect of the duality of style and subject matter. Throughout *Les Faux-monnayeurs,* there is ample evidence that the author was himself cognizant of this dilemma; in fact, the effort to resolve it may be said to be the central theme of the novel. An entry dated January 11, 1892, in the *Journal* speaks of the conflict between the rules of morality and the rules of sincerity. Morality, Gide states, is substituting for the natural creature, "old Adam," a fiction one prefers. Old Adam is the poet; the "new man" is the artist. The work of art results from a struggle between the poet and the artist. This was the time when Gide had just transposed the conflict from the moral to the aesthetic sphere, yet his phrasing

---

32. *Ibid.*

shows the correspondence that existed in his mind between the two. The poet wants to pour the content of consciousness on paper; the artist realizes that the data must be given some form—he restricts, interprets, stylizes.

Gide saw an irreconcilable opposition between the exigencies of what he had termed, in his youth, the poetic and artistic impulses respectively. The one, still partial, way to overcome it, he thought, lay in the device of the *composition en abîme* or novel within the novel: he would portray a writer coping with the hardships of transforming the liquid stuff of experience into a finished novel. Successive entries in *Le Journal des faux-monnayeurs* attest to the fascination this idea exercised on the author. It may be noted that the terms in which he visualized the conflict were modified in every single entry. Nevertheless, they tend to revolve around the reality-life-sincerity v e r s u s imagination-art-stylization polarity. In August 1921, he sets down that the novel is to have two foci: on one side, the event, the fact; on the other side, the effort of the writer to make a book of it all. In *Les Faux-monnayeurs* the issue is most clearly presented in a conversation between Edouard, Mme Sophroniska, Laura, and Bernard. Edouard tries to make his thesis palpable to the others by formulating the basic problem several times. Talking of his writer-protagonist, he says, "le sujet du livre, si vous voulez, c'est précisément la lutte entre ce que lui offre la réalité et ce qui, lui, prétend en faire."[33] A little later he phrases it thus: "A vrai dire, ce sera là le sujet: la lutte entre les faits proposés par la réalité, et la réalité idéale."[34] After this conversation Edouard records in his diary:

> Je commence à entrevoir ce que j'appellerais le "sujet profond" de mon livre. C'est, ce sera sans doute la rivalité du monde réel et de la représentation que nous nous en faisons. La manière dont le monde des apparences s'impose à nous et dont nous tentons d'imposer au monde extérieur notre interprétation particulière, fait le drame de notre vie.[35]

As I indicated at the outset, the purpose of the Gidean literary effort is at least two-fold: he wishes to capture himself by petrifying the elusive substance of life on paper, and wants to build a bridge to other human beings. Actually, the two can be seen as facets of the same basic aspiration, for the aim of asserting oneself to the public is to strengthen the reality of one's own existence. The extreme importance for Gide of the need to solidify his self-image has been brought out in Jean Delay's *La Jeunesse d'André Gide*. That the same problem did not cease to occupy him at the time of the composition of *Les Faux-monnayeurs* may be illustrated by the following quotation: "Il me semble parfois que je n'existe pas vraiment, mais simplement que j'imagine que je suis. Ce à quoi je parviens le plus difficilement à croire c'est à ma propre réalité. Je m'échappe sans cesse. . . ."[36] In the field of artistic expression Gide's dilemma consists in creating a myth that will attract and fascinate the public without at the same time removing fiction from reality to an extent where he can no longer recognize himself in the image he has fashioned. In other terms, Gide must keep the ideal picture within the bounds of the

---

33. *Ibid.,* p. 1082.
34. *Ibid.*
35. *Ibid.,* p. 1096.
36. *Ibid.,* pp. 987–88.

possibility to identify with it. The moment he cannot establish the basic equation between himself and the fictional character, the work lapses into a literary exercise. It is not a useless effort, for it contributes to his fame, but it ceases to advance the personal legend; it only indirectly serves his purpose of self-realization. Edouard registers this danger at one point in writing his novel:

> Désormais, entre ce que je pense et ce que je sens, le lien est rompu. Et je doute si précisément ce n'est pas l'empêchment que j'éprouve à laisser parler aujourd'hui mon coeur qui précipite mon oeuvre dans l'abstrait et l'artificiel.[37]

And he concludes with a sigh, ". . . heureux, ai-je pensé, qui peut saisir dans une seule étreinte le laurier et l'objet même de son amour."[38]

Author and work are indeed so closely bound together in Les Faux-monnayeurs that all the major male characters bear some resemblance to Gide. Edouard, Olivier, Bernard, Vincent, Passavant, Boris, Armand, and La Pérouse each embody traits, express views, and undergo experiences borrowed from Gide's life. It is not necessary to dwell on the resemblance between Edouard and the author. La Pérouse is Gide's mouthpiece in describing the positive existence of evil in the world. Vincent voices the theories of Gide the naturalist. Armand shares the author's ironic dédoublement. Bernard parallels Gide's quest of sincerity. In his conversations with Armand, Olivier doubles for the author, who describes himself in Si le grain ne meurt as conducting approximately the same verbal intercourse with young Bavretel. Passavant belongs to a special category, for he appears to be a zamostvanec or double in the Dostoevskian sense: he represents chiefly what at the same time tempts and repulses Gide: social success, sexual scheming, the unscrupulous exploitation of innocent victims. Boris is a likeness of thirteen-year-old Gide, sensitive, persecuted by his schoolmates, and struggling against the vice of onanism.[39] Many more examples could be cited to show that in the charmed Gidean landscape the author has carved his face on every stone and let the mountains echo his voice and the streams mirror his image. An intricate network of replicas attempts to ensnare the elusive reality of spectral Proteus.

The mature Gide has the courage to admit that in a sense we are all counterfeiters; we all lead vicarious lives. Old Adam cannot be exhumed undamaged, because human nature is not a voice calling out loudly and clearly as soon as the confusing din of the external world has been eliminated. The puzzling uncertainties of our predicament cannot be disposed of by identifying ourselves with a race, nation, subculture, group, deed, or disposition. This is what Bernard learns from the angel toward the end of the novel. The analysis of Boris's neurotic ailment discloses that at this stage the author was beginning to suspect that it is misleading to single out one specific event or accident as the cause of a person's mental afflictions. Armand's words, "mon mal vient de plus loin," might serve

---

37. *Ibid.*, p. 1003.
38. *Ibid.*
39. Pierre Lafille in *André Gide, romancier* (Paris: Hachette, 1954), p. 252, suggests that Boris's figure was modeled on the Russian boy whom Gide describes as one of his schoolmates in *Si le grain ne meurt*. Nevertheless, Delay is probably correct in conjecturing that Boris is substantially Gide's double.

as the summation of the lesson the older Gide has learned. Though the intensity of guilt feeling may vary from individual to individual, Gide makes it clear enough that everything is interrelated in society. The Borises of this world are assigned a larger share of the guilt, because they are more sensitive, more vulnerable. They get sacrificed on the altar of mankind's yearning for redemption. But Boris's death was a symbolic act on Gide's part as well, one of his many catharses that permitted him to avoid the fate of his fictional characters in real life.[40] The Gidean career is an ascent from the gesture of Oedipus who plucks out his eyes in deference to a society eager to deposit its vices on his shoulders, to Theseus, who returns the stares of his fellows with the imperturbable smile of experience and wisdom.

We are counterfeiters inasmuch as the ideal of absolute sincerity is impossible to achieve. There remains an area in us that is susceptible to suggestion, seizes on the opportunity of imitation, and welcomes ready-made structures of behavior. These tendencies presuppose an underlying liberty; in fact the area I referred to has traditionally been called that of freedom. What Gide saw as the irreconcilable conflict between experience and interpretation can in fact be resolved through the realization that the (subjectively or objectively) undefinable region in us exists as a legitimate field of operation for the inventive powers of the novelist. If the term *creative writing* is not devoid of sense, its deepest significance must be that the artist shapes the concept of man to the extent that man has to be invented. The Gidean assessment of sincerity was tending toward this conclusion; it may be the privilege of the critic to draw in the final inch of the line the author has already sketched before his death. For this slight completing touch allows us to recognize in André Gide the coiner instead of counterfeiter.

---

40. An entry dated March 30, 1924 in *Le Journal des faux-monnayeurs* (Paris: Editions Eos, 1926) states that the author's autobiographical heroes lack the common sense that has always kept him from carrying their follies as far as they do.

Malraux and Nietzsche's
Birth of Tragedy

THOMAS H. CORDLE

Duke University

In the 1886 preface to *The Birth of Tragedy,* Nietzsche wrote: ". . . conceived in terms of *art* . . . this book addressed itself to artists or, rather, to artists with analytical and retrospective leanings: to a special kind of artist who is far to seek and possibly not worth the seeking. It was a book novel in its psychology, brimming with artists' secrets, its background a metaphysics of art. . . ."[1]

I have a picture in mind of André Malraux reading these lines some thirty-five years later and catching his breath as though he had been addressed by name. For his leanings were precisely "analytical and retrospective," if one understands these terms to be more or less equivalent to "psychological and historical," and he was no doubt already possessed by that curiosity about artists' secrets and about the radical function of art in human life which was to dictate the course of his mind's labor for decades to come.

It is perhaps a little too fanciful on my part to imagine that Malraux saw his own career prefigured in just these lines of Nietzsche, but there is even so a great probability that the essay played a preeminent role in the formation of his aesthetics and his historical vision, and it would be a fine thing if we found one day in his intimate papers a record of his first reading of the book comparable, in its tone of enthusiastic recognition, to those written by Nietzsche when he discovered Stendhal and Dostoevski.

In the meanwhile, one needs no special pretext today to juxtapose the names of Nietzsche and Malraux. Their affinity has been declared in general but certain

First published: 8, no. 2 (1959): 89–104. The author did not wish to make any comments or revisions.

1. My source for quotations from Nietzsche is Francis Golffing's translation of *The Birth of Tragedy* and *The Genealogy of Morals* (Garden City, N.Y.: Doubleday, 1956).

terms by Malraux himself, and practically every critic who has written on Malraux in the last ten years has had something to say of the influence of Nietzsche on his work. If a pretext were needed, it could readily be found in *The Birth of Tragedy*. The brief discourse in chapter 23, where Nietzsche speaks of the creative function of myth in culture and diagnoses the illness of modern Europe as one resulting from its loss of myth and its counter-effort to view itself historically, may reasonably be regarded as the primary source of one of the controlling ideas in Malraux's long and intense scrutiny of the nature and history of art, in *Les Voix du silence,* and in *Le Musée imaginaire de la sculpture mondiale,* and in *La Métamorphose des dieux.* And there is also an intimate association of tone between this first book of Nietzsche and Malraux's early writing. The exhortation, in chapter 28, that begins: "Let us imagine a rising generation with undaunted eyes, with a heroic drive towards the unexplored . . ."—the very lines that Nietzsche picked out to ridicule in his later preface as extravagantly romantic—strikes a rhetorical note that Malraux echoes in his essay "D'une Jeunesse Européenne" (1927) and again in parts of *Les Conquérants* (1928) and *La Voie royale* (1930).

Resonances of Nietzschean ideas, vocabulary, and accents are to be found throughout Malraux's work, but without overlooking in the least their importance, I should like to direct attention to another kind of evidence of Nietzsche's thought that penetrates Malraux's novels through and through.

The effects of Nietzsche's essay on the origins of the Attic tragedy were, we know, several. Most important perhaps was the radical reorientation it gave to historical studies of Hellenic civilization. Its philological perceptions, backed by a fertile intuition, revealed aspects of the Greek mind that had not been hinted at by other critics, not even by Aristotle. But for anyone who reads the work today, and who has wondered, however idly, about the means and ends of poetry, its most attractive and compelling face is that "metaphysics of art" (*Artisten-Metaphysik*) mentioned in the preface and the theory of literature which necessarily derives from it. Looked at from this point of view, tragedy is a perfect emblematic expression of the "metaphysics"; but it is by no means its last expression. In other words, Nietzsche opens an enchanted path to the literature of the future.

If, as I think may have happened, Malraux encountered *The Birth of Tragedy* in the moment when, already certain of his vocation and of his imaginative and linguistic powers, he was seeking the ways in which a work of art conceives and makes explicit the relationship between a man's inwardness and his outwardness, between the one and the many, between past and present, and present and future, he found in Nietzsche's work a clear explanation and illustration of how a few poets had reduced their own similar interrogations to parable without sacrificing the alternatives that they proposed. He discovered, in short, the form of the tragical, which reposes in turn on the musical phenomenon of dissonance. The intention of my paper is to see that outline in his novels and to discuss the manner of its embodiment.

I

In Nietzsche's view, all art springs from two radical, and radically dissimilar, poetic impulses: *dream* and *intoxication.* The dream poet, whose utterance is inspired by the god Apollo, projects of himself a luminous image of individual triumph over the discordant forces of nature. He is the poet of the invincible illusion, of the individual will, of the will to comprehension, order, and serenity. His is the voice of culture, morality, and civilization; and his song, in its perfected form, is the heroic epic.

His brother, the lyrical poet, is at heart the creature of the god Dionysus. In the rapturous state of intoxication, he loses his individuality and becomes the instrument of a universal will, which expresses musically the wholeness and the unity of life. All is pain and discord within the poet, but his pain is also joy at being embraced by the indestructible principle of life. When the god Apollo touches him, he discharges in dream images the music that strains within his soul. The "I" of his utterance is not that of his individual self. It is a voice that springs from the very center of all being.

The Dionysiac poet is the poet of truth, since the music within him is the true image of the world. Life is torment and sorrow, and better unlived when it is experienced in the separateness of individuality. It is unfettered joy when that bond is broken and the one becomes in spirit a reflection of all.

Unchecked, the Dionysiac spirit manifests itself in popular orgies that are only a little this side of madness. The Apollonian poet, and the Apollonian spirit, are born of the need men have to be delivered from the truth of their condition and from the hysteria that it produces in them. The Apollonian illusion seeks to restore their shattered faith in the efficacy of individual undertaking, while at the same time imposing limits upon their enterprise. It frowns upon all excess, even that occasioned by the noblest sentiments. The Apollonian illusion is one of well-being and equilibrium.

In order to live fully, a people needs to behold in rhythmic alternation the Dionysiac truth and the Apollonian illusion. Its vital force derives from the tension of a spirit extended between these two poles, and it not only lives well but in beauty when it sees before it, in addition to the two polar images, an image of the tension itself.

This, as Nietzsche apprehended it, was the origin and the meaning of tragedy. The Apollonian and Dionysiac urges are constant and universal. The art in which they are most perfectly combined belongs to the Hellenic fifth century. The tragedy was at bottom a Dionysiac orgy that had yielded to the magic of the Apollonian vision. With Aeschylus and Sophocles, at least, it contiued to be the Dionysiac rite from which it had descended, the Apollonian spirit of elevation and measure having redeemed it from anarchy and transformed a popular festival into a drama of redemption.

Before a chorus of bearded satyrs there appears the figure of an epic hero. Together they relate and act out the tale of the hero's effort to deliver a community of men from a curse that lies uopn them. The hero succeeds in his enterprise, but only at the cost of assuming the burden of the curse himself. What he set out to conquer and destroy is, therefore, not destroyed; it is intensified and rendered more certain by being concentrated in one victim. The chorus, which has viewed the hero's recklessness with alarm and foreboding, sees its fears fully justified in the suffering he brings upon himself. The latter, in turn, has won a victory in that he has forced the issue of fate, drawn it into the clear, and shown that it is dreadful but bearable if only it be consciously accepted. And the fatality has, of course, justified itself by its indifferent choice of victims.

For Nietzsche, the power and the beauty of the tragedy lay in the play and counter-play of timidity and assertiveness in the face of an unalterable evidence. The awe and unease of the chorus at the hero's early success is changed to pity and satisfaction in his downfall. "The transcendent genius of culture and morality" goes down before the wisdom of "archetypal man, cleansed of the illusion of culture." The hero appears to sin in his pretentious will to dominate, but he is really guiltless, because "a truly noble man is incapable of sin." The fate is cruel but not vindictive, because it punishes indifferently. "Whatever is, is both just and unjust and equally justified in both." The sureness of the tragedy lies precisely in its *not* being a moral drama. It offers an "aesthetic justification" of the pain and contradiction that men suffer in their relations with the world. The spectator of the drama is cleansed and restored in spirit by the compound effects of "aesthetic delight"—produced by the concentrated image of myth and the miracle of the stage—and "metaphysical solace" at seeing realized before him his deepest intuition of human sorrow and futility.

II

There is no doubt that we recognize instantly in Malraux's novels the heroic face of the tragedy. His heroes are, in the fullest sense, protagonists, because they *think* their drama in the terms that their civilization has conceived to articulate its most pressing questions. In their utterances, in the analysis of their situation and their feelings, and in the imagery that conveys the tone of their existence, the novelist employs a language that tends to lift their action out of the particular and state it in the concepts of a universal dialogue between man and his destiny. He readily sacrifices something of the individuality they have gained through trait and gesture in order to endow them uniformly with rationality and facility in theoretical discourse, because thereby he establishes their indenticalness on a level above that of the individual and makes them representative of their culture.

They achieve *tragical* stature—in the Nietzschean sense of the word—by virtue of an aesthetic effect of disproportion that exists between the purpose and intelligence that they display in action and the ephemeral, contradictory nature of the conflicts in which they are engaged. Seen from this angle, the world with its ruthless indifference appears unworthy of these glorious creatures it has spawned. But there is equal disproportion between the passionate intensity of the emotions aroused in combat and the relative serenity of the epic dream for which it is waged. There always comes a moment when blood begins to flow and death becomes a real presence, and then the hero loses his superiority for a time and becomes one of the crowd, experiencing its joys and fears and clinging to other men merely for the warmth of their comradely bodies. In that moment there is disclosed to him what one of them calls "the banal mystery of life," an inexplicable urge to fellowship, compassion, and sacrifice, which surpasses the dream of culture and, by contrast, renders morality insignificant. This is appropriately a fleeting vision, intended not to supplant the heroic ethic, but to counter it momentarily and to alter radically its perspectives—to evoke, in short, that substrate of Dionysiac wisdom which the tragedy revealed behind the epic illusion. In Malraux's novels, as in the Greek tragedy, the two visions, or movements, are coefficient. The hero, with his will to justice and human dignity, can materialize only against a background of contradictions and cross-purposes. And the simple, unchanging wisdom of "fundamental man" can appear only as transcendence of the hero's dream of civilization.

The brightest images of Malraux's fiction are those which constitute the "heroic epic." There are certain personal histories, declarations, and scenes that seem, in our memories, to preponderate over the rest. In *Les Conquérants,* they are Garine's biography of rebellion against a bourgeois society, his extraordinary success in political and military organization, his struggle for a decisive victory over Hong Kong, and finally his departure toward an obscure death somewhere away from the scene of his triumph. In *La Voie royale,* the same rebellion and the same gift for military conquest are joined in Perken with the will "to leave a scar on the map." He risks his life to save another man from a brutal servitude and dies slowly and painfully, with his "kingdom" crumbling around him. The career of Vincent Berger in *Les Noyers de l'Altenburg* (1943), follows essentially the same course of rebellion against his own civilization (less vociferous than the rebellion of his predecessors) and distinguished service to a foreign revolution. His role in the gas attack on the Eastern Front deflates his heroic character just as Garine's forced departure from Canton and Perken's infected wound had done. He is reduced to the level of a commoner humanity and is humbled, bewildered, and improved by the experience.

Out of the profusion of *La Condition humaine* (1933), I select the revolutionary biography of Kyo Gisors, his adherence to the "will" of Marxism rather than to its "fatality," and his determination to restore to dignity the masses of the deprived and the humiliated. There is a Communist insurrection that succeeds and a political betrayal that condemns the victors, and then a scene of mass execution in a schoolyard, where a cyanide pellet passed from hand to hand becomes the concrete symbol of brotherhood and sacrifice.

In *L'Espoir* (1937) it is more difficult to particularize because the prestige of heroism belongs in some measure to everyone, but in bits and pieces the same story comes forth: the battle waged against heavy odds, the development of military leadership under fire, the generosity of volunteer combatants, and the passionate espousal of ideals of freedom and brotherhood (which here unite, in a tenuous fellowship, orthodox Christians, Anarchists, Communists, and Socialists of the left and the right). Single-handed, a career officer covers the retreat from Toledo of a group of militiamen, and is then captured and executed. A passionate Frenchman, a fireman by profession, by the very loftiness of his sentiments inspires courage and obedience in a ragged mass of surly and ill-trained riflemen. He is machine-gunned by a low-flying aircraft as he stands atop a ladder fighting a blaze in the heart of Madrid. Some injured airmen are tenderly carried down a mountainside by the entire populace of a remote village. Defeat at Toledo is followed by victory on the Manzanares, but at the end there remains the menace of ultimate destruction.

Viewed in this synoptic manner, there is a striking uniformity in the elements, and in the movement, of the epic. The scene changes only superficially: it is always one of armed strife. The hero is always allied with an underdog cause (even Perken was training his hill tribesmen to resist Siamese and French colonial expeditionary forces), and he is distinguished above all by his technical proficiency and his will to conquer. Some defeats are more complete than others, but in one form or another defeat is always there. The redemptive gesture of sacrifice and succor passes from the hero to the crowd, but its sense remains the same: it is an affirmation of human solidarity in the midst of pain and defeat.

The relative constancy of the design is an evidence of its primacy in the novelist's vision, and if it tends to stand forth in our memory of the novels, it is probably because it appears each time with increased clarity and certainty. Heroism, the generosity of great causes, and the brotherhood of man are inescapable in Malraux's fiction, as inescapable as charity, humility, and repentance in Dostoevski's.

But for all that, this particularly luminous current represents only a part—and sometimes a rather small part—of Malraux's creation. If we reject our selective memory of the novels and go back to all that is really in them, we find that these noble aspects of human endeavor and behavior are accidental features in a landscape that accommodates equally well images of solitude, terror, cruelty, and mania. For Malraux's version of the tragic myth would be no more than an adolescent dream (it is that, of course, at bottom) if he had not succeeded in projecting it against the background of a Dionysiac vision of the world that is, as nearly as his art could reproduce it, an analogue of that "music" which Nietzsche held to be the "true image of the world."

The central image in Malraux's fiction is war. All of the novels—even *La Voie royale* to a degree—are born in an atmosphere of political unrest and armed conflict. In three of the books, *Les Conquérants, La Condition humaine,* and *L'Espoir,* the rhythmic progress of story and scene is identical with the stages of a military campaign. Even in those moments when their combat is not the first concern of the characters, when they allow themselves the luxury of private reflection or intimate conversation, their voices and thoughts are orchestrated with the pounding of cannon, the explosion of bombs, and the rumble of military vehicles. The pervasiveness of this music of war is one of the remarkable aspects of Malraux's art. Already a powerful accompaniment in *La Condition humaine,* in *L'Espoir* it becomes an overmastering presence before which individual human figures seem to materialize for just an instant and then to fade away.

The war is, in itself, not a thing that might, or might not, have been. It is the world as it is, an image of the human situation raised to the highest intensity. It is the ground upon which human possibilities are realized. It brings forth, as nothing else can, extremes of conduct and feeling: fear and suffering are compensated by courage and love, while around them bloom those rarer flowers, extreme cruelty, extreme indifference, and extreme initiative. When war chances to be called revolution it becomes a vision of the future that commands passionate hopes and allegiances, and its present is marked by a chaos of organization that encourages unorthodox modes of authority and obedience.

Viewed through the prism of this primary image of Dionysiac frenzy, the proportions of the novels become, in fact, truer. The heroic career is seen as one type of response among several to the pressures of a world that is, at bottom, an impossible contradiction. Beside Kyo, and on equal footing with him, stand Tchen, Ferral, Clappique, Katow, and old Gisors; beside Garine, Hong, Tcheng-Daï, and Rebecci. And only a little behind them appear those necessary but loathsome creatures, the police inquisitors: Nicolaïeff, Chpilewski, Koenig. All are prey to the same Dionysiac urges. Some convert them to noble expressions;

others find for them only bizarre and abject modes of realization. But in the last analysis, each one is justified by his "biography," by the peculiar conjunction of his own person and the events and conditions haphazardly offered him by the world. These are not the faces of good men and evil men that Malraux offers to our scrutiny. They are the manifold masks of a single being, man, whose condition is everywhere the same.

"Each man dreams of becoming God," says old Gisors. He dreams of mastering and resolving in his unique self the world's disorder. But each man dreams also of losing himself in the warm stuff of life to become the simple, indistinguishable creature of an unknown god. These are the two poles of human seeking. Nietzsche would have called both Dionysiac because of their extremism. The one sees the world and all within it as a matter to be manipulated by a single individual will; the other denies outright the existence of that will. It is in relatively simple portraits that Malraux most strikingly illustrates this dualism. Ferral, for example, conceives an empire created and ruled by the force of his intelligence; and he very nearly realizes it. But he also seeks self-annihilation in contemplating the sexual pleasure of his mistress and is humiliated by the abjectness of his desire and by its failure. Clappique's mythomania is a way of incorporating the world into himself in order to deny its existence and his own with it. Grabot, in *La Voie royale,* dominates a savage world through brute courage, but he compensates by having a woman bind him, naked and alone in an attitude of subjection (a condition at which he arrives authentically as a prisoner of the Moïs).

One of Nietzsche's most arresting insights into tragedy was that the role of hero was always played by the god Dionysus, who borrowed the mask and the legend of an epic hero in order to clothe in parable his own drama of suffering and redemption. Behind epic features Malraux's heroes only half conceal the Dionysiac forces of their characters. They are not radically different from Ferral, Clappique, and Grabot. The heroes too are inhabited by an extravagant will to conquer, by mythomania, and by courage. The endowments of persuasiveness and tactical vision simply permit them to pursue their careers of domination through and in the midst of a mass of their fellows; and the warm vitality of that community they have created sometimes envelops them and bears them toward the other pole of their human nature, that of nonidentity. Garine does not love the people for whom he is going to fight, but he is one with them in their struggle. Perken does not want to be a king, but "to live in the midst of a great number of men, perhaps for a long time." Kyo finds it easy to die because he is dying with other men who are giving their lives in the same cause.

However, every one of these men begins as a stranger to the domain and to the action in which he realizes his capabilities as a commander; and that was one of the Dionysiac characteristics that Nietzsche pointed to in all the great tragic heroes. They were unnatural in wisdom and power, and also in their origin. Garine is of mixed European parentage, Russian and Swiss, and he engages himself in a Chinese revolution. Perken was born a German but became a Dane with the peace treaty of 1919. He stakes out his empire in Siam and Cambodia. Kyo is of French and Japanese parentage, and his career as a revolutionist is pursued in China. Vincent Berger belongs to an Alsatian family which, in one generation, has been both French and German, but he discovers his capacity as a revolutionary planner and leader in Turkey. On the surface, there is an air of generosity in the aid they all offer to the revolution and in the risks they take on behalf of it, but in reality each of them—even Kyo—has seized upon the foreign revolution to resolve a personal drama that is only poorly explained by his conflict with a society based on traditional prerogatives and exploitation.

The terrorists, Hong and Tchen, are perhaps the most haunting examples of Dionysiac personality. At the outset, they are more at home in the revolution than the leaders: they are on their native soil and have experienced the tangible effects of the injustices they are combatting. It is true that Tchen's intellectual formation, begun by a Protestant clergyman and completed by old Gisors, is more complex than Kyo's, and that Hong's ideological instruction was received from an Italian anarchist; but initially their relationship to the revolutionary action is simple and straightforward. It is a matter of executing orders destined to accomplish immediate objectives. The shock and the blinding revelation of their first experience of bloodletting convert them from political murderers to priests of a cult of assassination. Hong, drunk with his suddenly discovered power, goes on killing, choosing his victims according to his hatred and with no thought of political expediency. Tchen, a more disquieting personage, finds in death—in dying with his victim—a total comprehension of life and a communion with his fellows that he cannot reach by any lesser act.

The intoxication of authority and success in the leader, the ecstasy of administering sacrificial death in the terrorist, the endless satisfaction of cruelty in the policeman are replaced in *L'Espoir* by the Dionysiac face of the crowd; and there is, so far as the scope and intensity of the image are concerned, more gain than loss in the exchange. The rare greatness of the novel reposes far less in the individual figures who people it than in the sustained vision of a people at war. The rapturous outbursts at the beginning, the distribution of arms and the headlong rush into death, turn to surly disobedience and mass defection at Toledo. These chaotic movements induced by hopes and fears, which Garcia names "the Apocalypse," are reminiscent of the hysterical dances of St. John and St. Vitus that swept over great areas of Europe in the Middle Ages, and in which Nietzsche saw a survival of the Dionysiac frenzies of ancient times. Patience and unrelenting effort have, by the end of the story, succeeded in turning some of the mob into an effective military force, but the impression of a vast disorder is indelible. The state of war has here made men and women express their fundamental human nature in unreasoning emotions and uncalculated acts of courage, treachery, and cravenness.

Meanwhile, there is in each of the novels a figure and a zone that remain uncompromisingly Apollonian. The old men—Tcheng-Daï, Gisors, Alvear, Dietrich Berger—bear the burden of culture and civilization, and nothing succeeds in making them relinquish it. They are in every case the moral force behind the struggle that is going on. The revolution has in fact originated in them. Tcheng-Daï's philanthropy is older than the revolution in South China and has created a model for its social aspirations. The teaching and the slogans of Gisors have formed the young revolutionary party in North China. Alvear's insistence upon preserving "the quality of man" is at the bottom of every resistance to the hierarchical spirit of fascism. Dietrich Berger's rigorous example of honesty is in itself a rebellion against the ecclesiastical, political, and social institutions of his world. These old men refuse whatever is uncivilized, beginning with the conflict waged in defense of their own notions of humanity. They know war for what it is: a madness, an evil greater than the one it would correct. They are not altogether alone, for a part of every man engaged in the struggle belongs to them. But they are powerless before the overwhelming Dionysiac forces turned against them. Destroyed by the grief of seeing sons and the sons of friends maimed and killed, they protest and then seek a refuge in oblivion. Tcheng-Daï is resolved to commit suicide, and only assassination keeps him from it. Gisors turns to opium. Alvear withdraws into his library with a bottle of brandy and looks toward his fate with curiosity. The suicide of Dietrich Berger is never explained, but one may reasonably ascribe to him the motives of the others. His act anticipates a dreadful war by just a few months.

The hero inherits this dream of civilization in greater or lesser degree (little enough in Garine, totally in Kyo) and harbors it somehow with his Dionysiac urge to power and expenditure. The tragic myth begins in this uneasy synthesis of ideal and force. Together they form an enchanted mantle that permits the hero to instigate and engage in combat without seeing all the horror that it is. Redemption from this visionary isolation is accorded him in a number of more or less fleeting perceptions of the frailty of his fundamental nature and the depth of his attachment to other human beings. The first of these is usually humiliation: Garine is humiliated by imprisonment in Europe; Perken, by sexual impotence; Kyo, by May's infidelity; Vincent Berger, by the attack of a madman in the bazaar of Kabul. Later on there comes what might be called a compassionate revolt. Garine experiences it when he looks at the mutilated body of Klein; Kyo, when he sees a feeble-minded prisoner beaten by a jailer; and Perken, when he discovers Grabot blinded and harnessed to a millstone. The revolt does not originate in Vincent Berger, but when he sees the soldiers carrying their stricken foes back to their own ambulances, he falls in with the mass sentiment and takes up one of the enemy himself. Finally, each one has to face in unequivocal terms the fact of his own death. Perken and Kyo die quite wretchedly; Garine departs to die somewhere along the way to Europe; Berger is gassed, but survives. In each case death is, or appears to be, inevitable, and the dream of supremacy necessarily collapses with the fear engendered by its approach. These reversals in the hero's career bring us back into the domain of the tragic myth, properly speaking. They constitute, in the terms of Nietzsche's analysis, the intrusion of Dionysiac feeling into the Apollonian epic.

Altogether, the hero is a complex characterization since, in the last view, he is seen to reflect the whole range of human responses to the acute condition of war. He embodies the idealism that lends to the struggle another face than that of horror, and to this he joins the aptitude for conquest and the obsession with accomplishment that make war a continuing reality. But he is also the expressive medium of the lowly creature emotions—pity, shame, and fear—that lift the veil at last and reveal the human condition for what it truly is. There is a large element of gratuity in this, as well as one of fatality. The effects of intelligence upon events are in truth quite limited. Nietzsche noted something similar in the Greek tragedies and in *Hamlet*: however much the hero may inquire and explain, his situation and his acts remain clearer and more certain than his words. This is an observation to be retained and studied by the reader of Malraux's fiction, because those intense discussions on psychology, politics, history, theology, and art which contribute so much to the physiognomy of his books very often produce views that are refuted or seriously altered by the events of the story. It is wiser to take them for what they are, an essential dimension of fictional character, and not seek in them an explanation of the novels as a whole.

That explanation is of another nature and is best conceived in terms similar to those of Nietzsche's theory of tragedy. Its fundamental element is the Dionysiac image of the world as horror and madness, suffering and contradiction. This image is no discovery of Malraux. The literature of our time is more or less filled with it from Conrad, Gide, and Mann to Kafka, Faulkner, and Camus. Nor is it a discovery of the twentieth century: among the nineteenth-century novelists most loved by contemporary writers are Dostoevksi, Tolstoy, the Balzac of *La Recherche de l'absolu* and *Les Illusions perdus,* and the Melville of *Moby Dick.* And one could appeal further, if need were, to the prestige of Baudelaire and Rimbaud.

If Malraux is to be distinguished from his contemporaries, and from a number of his predecessors, that distinction imposes itself first in the manner in which the Dionysiac is evoked in his novels. Every reader has felt, sometimes acutely, the ambiguity produced in his books by conjunction of historical reality and creative imagination, an ambiguity that Gaëtan Picon expresses so well in his essay on Malraux:

> Evoking the objective reality of an era, Malraux does not cease to speak of himself: his era is in harmony with his drama as it is with his style. A harmony so profound that the events of history unfold in the work as would the most personal fiction, and that those revolutions and wars whose tumult each of us has heard, whose external countenance we have glimpsed, receive here something of the unreality of nightmare, as if the poet were drawing them forth from his deepest and most isolated reveries.[2]

It is as though the Dionysiac substructure had been given to Malraux, impressed upon him, much as it was impressed upon the Greek tragic poet; and he shares with the latter a certain independence with regard to that world that allows him the more freely to transfigure it. The tragic myth is of course the form of that transfiguration. It betokens the redemption from chaos through heroic action and nobility of character.

It has been remarked that ours is an age without heroes, an age marked even by the will to be done with classic heroism. There are a number of ways to interpret this phenomenon, not the worst of which is that it fulfills the desire of our culture to see an image of its own impotence before a world of contrarieties and imponderables and of its plunge into the underworld of doubt and despair. Our secret hope is perhaps that the plunge will prove refreshing, and that we will emerge fortified with the strength of ancient certitudes recaptured in the bowels of human experience. The accent upon heroism in Malraux's novels is in apparent conflict in contemporary literary thought. His heroes begin with certitudes—their own lucidity and the efficacy of their action—and though these certitudes are later displaced by others, which spring from the undifferentiated

---

2. Gaëtan Picon, ed., *Malraux par lui-même* (Paris: Editions du Seuil, 1953), p. 21.

mass of humanity around them or from that part of themselves which belongs to it, they are still not annulled.

It has been easy to attribute the presence of the heroic figure in Malraux's fiction to a temperament which, as his "biography" so amply suggests, has sought to realize itself heroically. But there is some possibility of error in such a judgment. The novels demonstrate clearly that the greater part of his effort has been to evoke a Dionysiac vision of the human situation. The heroic epic which, to paraphrase Nietzsche, is heard as a fine, clear melody against the polyphony of the dithyramb, is perhaps as much a product of conscious aesthetic choice as of temperament.

It is a fairly safe assumption that a writer's earliest work reveals his deepest and most pressing preoccupations, and Malraux's fiction begins with *Lunes en papier* (1921), *La Tentation de l'Occident* (1926), and *Royaume farfelu* (1928). The abrupt transition to a work of the character of *Les Conquérants,* and the recurrence of its elements and its design in all of the succeeding novels, suggest an intense reflection upon the nature of fiction and upon what constitutes its possible perfection. Nietzsche's essay on the tragedy would have provided an incomparable basis for such a reflection because its notions were applicable to imaginative literature in general and because it sought to define the work of art (and human life underlying it) in terms purely aesthetic. The triumph of tragedy, in Nietzsche's view, was that it seized and held firm the dissonances of human existence and still cast over them an illusion of harmony and beauty. The accomplishment of Malraux's novels could be stated in much the same way. They join together indissolubly humiliation and failure with proficiency and the will to conquer and endow their union with an air of indisputable rightness.

From *Jean Santeuil* to *Time Regained*

GERMAINE BRÉE

University of Wisconsin

COMMENT BY THE AUTHOR

The article I wrote in relation to Bernard de Fallois's thesis shows the uneasiness it had caused, an uneasiness subsequently corroborated by the facts. What Fallois provided was a theory of the genesis of the first-person narrator that turned out to be drastically simplistic when the manuscripts became available. The question has not as yet been fully elucidated. Interpretation here outran scholarly caution. Thereby my article is dated. On the other hand, speaking more generally, the publication of fragments of what was obviously a first version, or one of several versions of Proust's work, was an exciting literary event, as the essay shows. It was largely among scholars in the United States that the note of caution was sounded, taking a little longer to echo in France itself. The whole episode certainly proves that enthusiasm and genuine dedication—such as M. de Fallois showed— can be the most dangerous of qualities in a researcher unless they are rooted in meticulous scholarly criticism and careful methodology.

The decade of the fifties will be a memorable one in the annals of Proustian scholarship. For one thing it brought to Proust's readers the three-volume critical Pléiade edition of *A la recherche du temps perdu.* True, nothing can ever replace for a certain generation the excitement of plodding through volume after volume of the current Gallimard edition, unhampered by any critical apparatus, by variants, et cetera. But the Pléiade edition is nevertheless precious. Besides this publication we are now in possession of two hitherto unknown works by Proust: *Jean Santeuil* (1952) and *Contre Sainte Beuve* (1954). Between Proust's

---

First published: 6, no. 3 (1956): 16–21. Unrevised.

rather tenuous first volume, _Les Plaisirs et les jours_ (1896) and his massive _A la recherche du temps perdu_ (1913–1927) there now stands a considerable bulk of writing and a gap is filled both in the chronology of Proust's development and in our knowledge of his work.

The publication of two sizable volumes over a quarter of a century after Proust's death raises many questions. One of these is easy to answer: there is no doubt at all as to the authenticity of the manuscripts. Others are more complex. In his introduction to _Contre Sainte Beuve_ Bernard de Fallois—the brilliant young scholar who painstakingly and devotedly edited both volumes—starts out in the following way: "The unpublished work of Proust does not exist. The word 'fin' that he wrote after the last lines of his book (_A la recherche du temps perdu_) definitely marks its end. The thousands of pages that he devoted to the preparation of his work are no more than a preparation." In other words the volumes we now have are successive drafts, preliminary attempts at expression that Proust discarded because he found them unsatisfactory. For a reader familiar with Proust's great novel, they raise fascinating questions: What is their value in themselves? Why did Proust toss these thousands of pages carelessly into a carton? What are the relations between these volumes and the later work? The scholar will find in them a mine of documents to be carefully scrutinized and studied. Problems concerning the structure, the origins, the transformation and reworking of materials, the various stages of the work, the creative processes that finally produced _A la recherche du temps perdu_ will have to be reconsidered in the light of the manuscripts published.

Here, however, certain difficulties appear, particularly in the case of _Contre Sainte Beuve_. They are inherent in the very nature of the manuscripts found. _Jean Santeuil_ is an unfinished novel that was written, it would seem, almost entirely between 1896 and 1899, though some pages seem to have been added later. The manuscript, in spite of the strange array of loose leaves on which Proust wrote, was found in fair order, bore a pagination written in Proust's hand and indications as to the order of chapters.[1] The volume therefore keeps pretty close to the manuscript and is fairly coherent. The order of the episodes as established by the editor contains some discrepancies that might have been avoided and are not due to Proust himself.

Contre Sainte Beuve on the other hand presents many an enigma to the inquiring mind. M. de Fallois's excellent preface states them and does not attempt to solve them. His task here as editor was extremely difficult since he found hundreds of fragmentary passages, only a few of which seem related to the _Contre Sainte Beuve_ essay. The others were short drafts of passages many of which reappear, often in a somewhat modified form, in _La Recherche_. "Certain passages," he writes in the preface, "offered a great resemblance with _La Recherche:_ we left them aside deliberately. . . . Among the very abundant manuscripts, containing as many as eight or nine versions of some fragment, we had to make a choice." Moreover, in order to give a coherent development whenever he could, M. de Fallois completed certain fragments by adding to them passages from other fragments. As for the dating, that was an impossible task. And M. de Fallois appeals to the

---

1. Philip Kolb, "From _Jean Santeuil_ to _A la recherche du temps perdu._" Paper read at the 1954 meeting of the Modern Language Association.

enlightened reader to support his method as against the "professors" and "fussy critics." We are fairly warned.

The text we have, therefore, is incomplete—very incomplete—reorganized with genuine care, but reorganized, and it weaves together various versions into a plausible but arbitrary whole. The enlightened reader may well thank the editor, but the scholar is dissatisfied. He can work fruitfully only with far more accurate data.

On the whole, however, we can rely on the dating of one fragment of the *Contre Sainte Beuve,* the ninety-six pages (out of some four hundred) that give the book its name, since Proust, in some of his letters, in particular in those to his friend George de Lauris, spoke of his project and of its development. These seem to have been written roughly between 1900 and 1909.

In spite of these many baffling uncertainties, the two publications clearly establish at least one fact: there was no break in Marcel Proust's literary activity. Instead of the effete, young snob that biographers liked to depict, we find a persistent writer and a writer who was willing to lay aside without a word hundreds of pages because he judged them unworthy of publication. The line is unbroken that leads from *Les Plaisirs et les jours* (1896) to *Jean Santeuil,* to the translations and annotations of Ruskin, to the *Contre Sainte Beuve,* thence to *La Recherche.* Proust never stopped writing. It is questionable whether he ever gave up his initial project of writing a novel. Only the apparently impossible dating of the fragmentary "cahiers," many of which are still unpublished, would answer that question. But a pattern seems established. After Proust abandoned *Jean Santeuil* he turned to Ruskin and to a meditation on art that strengthened his approach to aesthetic problems and his ideas on the nature of creative activity and on the relation of the work of art to its creator. This led to his attack on Sainte Beuve's critical method. His article on Sainte Beuve is the direct outcome of this meditation, but strangely enough, as M. de Fallois points out, it persistently refuses to remain an article and, almost in spite of Proust, turns into a novel. Proust literally writes himself out of his essay into his fictional world. Whereas in *Jean Santeuil* passage after passage recalls *Le Temps perdu,* and yet we can find no passage that is actually reproduced in the later novel, entire pages of the *Contre Sainte Beuve* will be incorporated into the later text. There is no break between the two works: Sainte Beuve merely disappears, or rather he is metamorphosed; his critical approach to literature as Proust sees it becomes a component of one— of more than one, even—of Proust's fictional characters. The *Contre Sainte Beuve* thus appears as the very pivot of an evolution that leads from the rejected *Jean Santeuil* to the "grand oeuvre," *A la recherche du temps perdu.*

Much can be said—much has been said and will be said—on the relation between the three works. One of the many paths that can be followed from one to the other is through the study of the central figure and of his relation to the author.

In *Jean Santeuil,* Proust writes an apparently objective tale, centered around the figure of Jean Santeuil. He takes great pains to detach Jean completely from himself in the mind of the reader by interposing, at the beginning of his book, the burly figure of the writer C. C. is a great swimmer, an outdoor man in complete contrast to Proust himself. Proust then uses a rather worn literary device: the fiction of the manuscript lent to the two admiring young disciples of C. and published by them at the time of C.'s death. The book is purportedly the auto-biography of C., whose fictitious name is Jean Santeuil. The device is transparent and quite unconvincing and Proust, after the introductory pages, makes no further use of it. There is nothing at all in common between C.—a figure inspired, we are told, by the American painter Harrison—and the Jean of the story.

This lack of cohesion is characteristic of the whole book. The story develops in the traditional linear way and, somewhat as in a picaresque novel, the episodes are strung together by means of the personality of Jean. Though Jean has a personality, it does not often come to life. There is no relation between Jean's love affairs and Jean's involvement in the Dreyfus case, between the family scenes and the story of Jean's success in society. In other words the novel as a unified whole refuses to take shape. And yet the episodes taken separately are well told; they are, it soon appears, infinitely closer to giving us a straight auto-biography of Proust than *La Recherche* ever will. It has been said that all the Proustian themes are in *Jean Santeuil*. Yes and no. The experience of involuntary memory, for example, is described over and over again—too often, the reader is tempted to say. It is described—but as an episode among others. It bears no relation at all to other themes, and plays no part in the ordering of the novel. *Jean Santeuil* offers no architecture of any kind and fails to become a fictional re-creation or transposition of reality. On the other hand it reveals an exceptional maturity in the writer: Proust in 1896 was, it would seem, in possession of most of his ideas, ideas that he will not greatly modify. What he will modify are his techniques as a novel writer.

This, therefore, is Proust's first attempt: to pour directly into his novel the total content of his own life, but to transpose it by means of an objective narrative and through the creation of a "double," Jean, seen from the outside, objectively. The attempt fails.

When Proust starts to work on his Sainte Beuve, the rigid framework of a critical article is distasteful to him. He needs an auditor, someone to whom he can talk. Proust often proceeds that way, and so does his narrator in *La Recherche*: to develop certain critical points of view the narrator talks with Albertine. In a sense it would seem that for Proust the art of criticism is linked to the art of conversation, an art that, as we know, he considered wasteful, because it disperses the forces that would be better employed in creative activity. And it is obvious that criticism makes sense to him only as conversation. It is an attempt at explanation, and why explain unless there is someone to whom one wishes to explain?

At the same time—and as M. de Fallois suggests—Proust seemed desirous to preserve the visage of the mother he had lost in 1905. He starts his essay in the form of a conversation between himself and his mother. It is logical here that he should drop all attempts at objectivity: he is not writing a novel but merely giving his own reaction to Sainte Beuve. Moreover, the conversational pattern precludes the editorial objectivity of the scholar. The "Je" has entered the scene, a "Je" that is supposedly Proust himself, speaking directly of his own experience and ideas.

The theme that Proust develops in the *Contre Sainte Beuve* is controversial, or at least partial and therefore open to attack. Sainte Beuve, as is well known, is the author of the type of criticism that goes from the author to the work: find out all about the tree and you will know its fruit. "You will find out nothing at all," answers Proust and he holds a proof: Sainte Beuve's complete lack of understanding of three great writers whom he knew—Balzac, Nerval, and Baudelaire and his total blindness to the value of their work. And Proust goes on to explain that the writer we observe, the man we see moving like others in society, is not the man who writes. It is another hidden "moi" whom we should reach if we wish to know the creator, and the only way to reach him is through his work. No reader of Proust familiar with Vinteuil, Elstir, and Bergotte, to say nothing of the narrator himself, can be surprised by this assertion.

It is not my purpose to discuss here the value of this essay with regard to criticism, but it does seem to be one of the major keys to the world of *Le Temps retrouvé*. For in the *Contre Sainte Beuve* is not the "Je" rapidly to become that other "moi"? He detaches himself from Proust and begins to lead his own life. It is a surprising and strange metamorphosis and it seems that here Proust holds his major theme: he will tell the story of that other "moi," the creator within himself.

The last stage is here reached in the creation of the narrator. Proust is now engaged in giving an objective projection of a totally subjective world, the world of that inner "moi," that is not directly the "Je" of the conversations. As M. de Fallois points out, he has found simultaneously the "tone," the "voice" that blends together and unifies the vast and heterogeneous world of *La Recherche*.

Though we thus see the narrator emerge, bringing with him the mother who becomes the grandmother—just as the direct "Je" of Proust becomes the "Je" of the narrator—and many another character, we cannot claim that the *Contre Sainte Beuve,* as we now have it, brings the key to other important facets of the work: its architecture, for example.

Perhaps, however, we can risk one other guess. It has often been said that Proust "got" the idea for the overall structure of the novel around 1908. The fragments we have, and the information M. de Fallois gives us about the many many versions that Proust wrote and discarded seem to indicate one thing: the idea came slowly; it was worked out by trial and error. The "pattern" developed from within: it was not superimposed from outside. Proust worked for many long years with "fragments," episodes or descriptions or analyses that remained as they had remained in *Jean Santeuil,* insulated from each other. And Proust was long unable to unify them into a whole. The creation of the narrator, by chance—or might we say by necessity?—was slowly arrived at, emerging as he does from the depths of Proust's meditations on art and the artist and their ambiguous relationship to the world of appearances. He contains within himself the rest of the Proustian world, this "moi" bearer of an extra-temporal world, enclosed within that other, outer "moi" that Sainte Beuve saw only. But nothing in the pages we have shows us as yet by what process he drew in his wake the complete Proustian universe.

Kafka and Proust: A Contrast in Time

MARGARET CHURCH

Purdue University

Two theories of time to be found in contemporary writing are well illustrated by Marcel Proust and Franz Kafka. The first one, represented by Proust, is the sense of continuous duration, which M. Poulet in his recent book on human time traces back to the period of pre-Romanticism to such figures as Senancour and Joubert. The second one, represented by Kafka, is the Platonic concept of time that has given rise to individual experience presented in general form, seen in German literature in works of such figures as Stifter, or to the desire for abstraction, seen more recently in the Expressionist dramatists like Reinhard Sorge.

For to accept the concept of duration means that an author attaches importance directly to the inner continuous atmosphere of the mind and uses this concept to couch his subject matter in. The durational writer redefines time as a continuum; what is time for the physicist is for him space. Proust, Joyce, Gertrude Stein, to mention only a few examples, treat time as duration. In fact, the stream-of-consciousness technique springs from this source.

To adopt the Platonic concept of time, however, means that an author does not attach the first importance to the individual psychological process. Thus, he attempts, as does Kafka through his dream-parable technique, to deal with an area that defines man in general rather than the individual man. The "doctrine of ideas" implies that the timelessness of an idea is more important than the experience of time. Thus, man is more important than an individual man for the Platonic thinker, and the techniques of myth or parable with their general applications to all human life are preferred to the painstaking analysis of Leopold Bloom or M. de Charlus. Although all great literature may be applied to man in general (and Proust's, of course, is no exception), I am interested in showing in this essay how a basic attitude toward time influences a writer's method.

First published: 7, no. 2 (1957): 107–12. The author did not wish to make any comments or revisions.

Proust and Kafka represent clear-cut examples of the results of these two traditions in European literature, one an ancient one having its seeds in Europe in the Everyman genre and the other a comparatively recent one that may be connected roughly, one suspects, with the birth of interest in the individual in other areas—economic, social, and political.

According to Max Brod, Proust and Kafka had never heard of each other. Nevertheless, Goronwy Rees, in the preface to his translation of Gustav Janouch's conversations with Kafka, draws some comparisons between them. Rees points out that both writers exhibit heroism in the overscrupulousness of their attempts to discover truth—"the same power of observation and penetration, the same mastery of a psychological calculus for measuring the smallest, most fatal of human actions."[1] But to speak of Proust's analyses without mentioning his conception of time is dangerous. As a means of invoking a sense of duration, Proust uses involuntary memory and, thus, causes time to be reconstructed; for Kafka memory is almost nonexistent—his tools being parable, symbol, and dream. Therefore, the observations of the authors take place on two entirely different levels. In one passage in the conversations (although this volume must not be taken too seriously), Kafka states that "the actual reality is always unrealistic." In the light of this quotation, Rees's comparison may be seen to be a superficial one, for the past with all its intricate detail is of paramount importance to Proust.

In the diaries, in which Kafka mentions his interest in Plato, we find no trace of Proust's absorption in the past and its connection with the present. "Was hält mich für eine Vergangenheit oder Zukunft? Die Gegenwart ist gespenstisch. . . ."[2] One sees in Kafka almost a fear of remembering, which accounts in part for the technique in his novels. He writes: "ich fürchte, wie ich merke, die förmlich physische Anstrengung beim Sicherinnern, den Schmerz. . . ."[3] At one point in the diaries he does remark that the future is, in a sense, already past, for "das Ende der Zukunft ist mit allen unsern Seufzern eigentlich schon erfahren und Vergangenheit."[4] But this entry is an anomaly, for in general he solves the question of the relationship between past, present, and future by eliminating them through symbol and parable.

In some of Kafka's short stories, such as "Forschungen eines Hundes" or "Der Bau," the emphasis in technique is not on external events, which are minor ones, but on the processes of the mind—giving time at first glance a durational quality. Kafka, however, generalizes about human experience, and the specific event is not important as it is in Proust. The singing dogs or the burrow are symbols, not creations from a living past. Kafka's focus in these short stories is on the concept derived from the event; since for Proust duration is important, however, the experience of the *madeleine,* for instance, is of significance in itself.

Another difference in the two methods may be seen in the story "Beim Bau der Chinesischen Mauer." Here long-dead emperors are set on the throne and proclamations of mythical emperors read. The living present is ignored and

1. Gustav Janouch, *Conversations with Kafka,* trans. Goronwy Rees (New York: Praeger, 1953), p. ix.

2. Franz Kafka, *Gesammelte Werke. Tagebücher 1910–1923* (New York: Schocken Books, 1948), 5: 475.

3. *Ibid.,* p. 324.

4. *Ibid.,* p. 22.

ancient history replaces it. Time in its conventional sense becomes distorted for the villagers, forced by their position to view their emperor through a mist of distance. They fear and distrust the present, recognizing unconsciously that time is a cycle and past symbols as pertinent now as then. By replacing the present, the past frees the individual from conventions and laws in force and sets others in their place, thus enabling the villager to see himself, as it were, from a distance. The simultaneous existence of past and present seems at first glance to bring the time conception here close to the Proustian conception. But the method (distance) by which this state is achieved is not an individual experience as is the method by which the past is recalled in Proust. The villagers' time values are based on their geographical location, a general condition. Kafka merely sets up in his story an interesting hypothetical situation in which he reveals what would happen to the definition of time under certain peculiar circumstances. His entire inquiry is on an abstract level. Proust, on the other hand, applies his theory of time to particular events in specific lives.

In the novel *Amerika*, there are, however, several passages in which a spontaneous creation of the past is brought about. As Karl hears his uncle tell the group on the ship about his affair with the maid, Johanna Brummer, involuntarily he re-creates her. "Im Gedränge einer immer mehr zurücktretenden Vergangenheit sass sie in ihrer Küche neben dem Küchenschrank. . . ."[5] Then for a moment Karl sees and feels all the details of the affair as he had experienced them. Later, as he plays a song of his native country on his piano, there is re-created through the music a scene from Karl's earlier life when he had heard soldiers in the barracks singing to each other from window to window. Superimposed on the great, bustling New York street, over which he has no outward control, is this simple scene from his homeland enabling him to erase the present. And finally there is the passage in which Therese, telling the story of her mother's death to Karl, realizes that: "Sie wusste jede Kleinigkeit, die damals vorgefallen war, jetzt, nach zehn Jahren, ganz genau. . . ."[6]

It is obvious that the extended use of the Proustian technique depends on the coexistence of a conventional story, for in order to re-create the past it is necessary to have a present in which the re-creation takes place. The symbolic technique that Kafka uses in *Der Prozess* and *Das Schloss* is free from past, present, and future. In *Amerika*, in which the story is uncomplicated by extended metaphor, he was able to experiment more readily with past and present. It would seem that Kafka's use of parable in the other two novels is the result of his innate preference for the Platonic conception of time. This also accounts for the fact that his attempts to make past and present coexist in *Amerika* are infrequent, awkward, and not actually integrated into the spirit of the story.

But in *Der Prozess* and *Das Schloss* the time experience is almost entirely on the level of the parable, the symbol, and the dream in which experience exists without relation to time or to simultaneity. For instance, in the scene in the lumber room in *Der Prozess*, K. returns on the second evening to find everything exactly as he had left it the night before. The whipper is still standing in the same position in front of the warders. Time has not moved on this level of

---

5. Franz Kafka, *Gesammelte Schriften. Amerika* (New York: Schocken Books, 1946), 2: 35.
6. *Ibid.*, p. 154.

experience although K. has lived through a whole day of clock time. K. deals with this situation in the realm of action by asking the clerks to clear out the lumber room the next day although he unconsciously recognizes that his experience is an inner one, for he knows that the clerks cannot see the whippers and the warders. The recurrence of the scene is not, of course, an example of Proustian recalling of the past, but rather of the illusory nature of experience, a concept springing from the Platonic theory of time. Duration implies that existence may be made continuous by memory. Here K. does not *recall* an earlier scene, but rather time has stood still in this back room of K.'s consciousness where neither past nor present has any meaning. The scene occurs in the timeless area of K.'s unconscious mind, part of which has remained fixated in the lumber room.

Two exceptions to this technique occur in the scene in the Cathedral Square in *Der Prozess* and in a scene with Barnabas in *Das Schloss*. As K. nears the end of his quest in the Cathedral Square, he is startled by the recollection that even when he was a child the curtains in this square had been pulled down. Inside the Cathedral he watches the verger, whose limp reminds him of his childhood imitation of a man riding horseback. These two simple memories serve, however, not so much to re-create the past as in Proust, but to act as touchstones of the world of objects "in der das Leben zwar sein natürliches schweres Fallen und Steigen bewahre. . . ."[7] As links, their existence in the passage is important, for through them Kafka reminds us that his purpose is to mirror life as well as a life so disguised that it is in the semblance of all lives.

In *Das Schloss* K. re-creates a scene from childhood when, dragged on by Barnabas, he finds it difficult to "keep up." He remembers an old church surrounded by a graveyard, in turn surrounded by a high wall. K. had failed to climb the wall until one morning, in an empty marketplace flooded by sunlight, he succeeded. The sense of triumph of that moment returns now to succor him. Evoked by a chance experience, the past becomes present. This is very close to the Proustian recalling of the past except that K. is a figurative character, whereas Proust's hero, indicated by the pronoun *I,* is an individual. Therefore, we are dealing here not so much with a specific relationship of past and present as with a general one.

Furthermore, the characters in *Der Prozess* and *Das Schloss,* unlike Proust's hero, are for the most part without childhood or ancestors. K.'s uncle appears in *Der Prozess* and in an uncompleted chapter K.'s mother is mentioned, but their reality stems entirely from K.'s inner life. As individuals in their own right, they do not exist; for instance, K.'s uncle understands, without being told, the facts of K.'s case. And K.'s mother, in her blindness, represents that which is suppressed in K.'s own mind: for many years she has thought him to be the director of the bank in which he is employed. In *Das Schloss,* with the exception of the story Olga tells K. or the hints of the landlady's affair with Klamm, there is little perspective concerning even the recent past. The officials have no memory, and Kafka seems to imply that too much concern with the immediate and individual past clutters the mind.

Here it should be mentioned that Proust like Kafka is interested in applying his theory of time to man in general. The distinction is that in achieving this Kafka through his parables does so directly, whereas Proust begins with an

---

7. Franz Kafka, *Gesammelte Schriften. Er,* 5: 281.

individual experience, like the one with the *madeleine,* which in itself represents no general truth until interpreted and extended by the author. Thus, in this regard the difference between the two authors is one of technique rather than of purpose.

Kafka derives his story from the unconscious level of experience, whereas Proust analyzes human experience on the conscious level. Kafka employs parable and symbol in order to deal with this submerged area of existence; the Platonic background of his thinking leads him to deal with a general area of experience. The durational background of Proust's thinking leads him to deal with a specific area. We find in Proust's hero an individual, one beset by complex emotions and a complex past. Proust, because he sees time as duration, gives us the experience of living and thinking, whereas Kafka, because he sees time as an idea, gives us the algebraic equation for life, which he leaves us to solve as we may.

Kafka's *The Trial*:
The Assailant as Landscape

FREDERICK J. HOFFMAN

*   *   *

Where I spat in the harbor the oranges were bobbing
All salted and sodden, with eyes in their rinds;
The sky was all black where the coffee was burning,
And the rust of the freighters had reddened the tide.

But soon all the chimneys were hidden with contracts,
The tankers rode low in the oil-black bay,
The wharves were a maze of the crated bombers,
And they gave me a job and I worked all day.

And the orders are filled; but I float in the harbor,
All tarry and swollen, with gills in my sides,
The sky is all black where the carrier's burning,
And the blood of the transports is red on the tide.
                    Randall Jarrell, "The Metamorphoses"

The opening scene of Kafka's *The Trial* describes a quite unexpected interruption in the life of its hero. An upstanding, virtuous, and efficient man, he has reached his thirtieth birthday and is well established as an Assessor at the Bank. This morning, however, instead of being greeted with good wishes and his breakfast, he is confronted by a stranger, who announces his arrest. This introductory shock is of the utmost importance to the impression the novel will ultimately have. It suggests the intrusion of the absurd into a world protected on all sides by familiar assurances and securities. Joseph K. is especially well acquainted

First published: 9, no. 2 (1960): 89–105. Unrevised. Professor Hoffman died in 1967.

154

with these comforts; his life is dedicated to an almost endless calculation, by means of which he helps to assure that society will function smoothly. The break in routine at first seems a trick, perhaps a birthday joke, which he will surely soon discover and dismiss. The strategy of this opening scene is to give the reader a brief acquaintance with an unfamiliar world. After all, he understands K., sympathizes with him, and is in many ways his double. There are rules, there is the law; people have long known how to take care of unexpected intrusions. It is unreasonable to expect that the disruption is more than temporary.

This is the first contribution of the novel to Kafka's analysis of modern circumstance. The element of surprise in human relationships may last only so long; it cannot in any case be permitted to alter the design of human security or that design will change. Surprise is an indispensable element of the fact of violence in modern life. A carefully plotted pattern of expected events has always been needed to sustain a customary existence. A sudden break in the routine challenges the fullest energy of man's power of adjustment. Suddenness is a quality of violence; it is a sign of force breaking through the design established to contain it.

Another oddity of Kafka's opening scene is that the interruption is not a distortion of the setting in which it takes place. It is the same lodging house in which K. has lived for some years. The arrest takes place in the rooms, and the warders are ordinary citizens. No monster crashes into the scene, to split it to fragments. Instead, Kafka describes the warders' appearance with the meticulous care that is one of his trademarks. One of the essentials of modern literature is that it should define and describe the violent disruptions of conventional life in a conventional way. No work of Kafka lacks this precision. This quality of style means that the enormity, the incredible event, in modern life is represented in conventional terms. The unexpected is therefore "usual." It needs no Gothic trickery, no monstrous or surreal properties, to make its effects.

Kafka's skill in presenting the scene as precisely recognizable has another important effect. The scene and the personality at its center are in no genuine sense disparate. They possess a reciprocal status. The hero makes the scene possible; the scene reflects the hero's status. This interaction of scene and hero suggests a profound way of explaining the source of modern violence. We are in a real sense the heirs of the nineteenth century, in that modern attitudes toward force were originally formed then, and the illusions of protective containment of force were gradually established in that time. The only way to understand violence— beyond superficial devices for merely admitting it as a fact of modern life—is to assume it as somehow the result of our willed interference with the balance of force and power in the human economy. We live constantly in a world in which this power is being extended. Many decades ago the instruments used for propelling force first exceeded the strength of man physically to contain or endure it. Almost daily now the means are improved to increase the disparity of force and personality and to lengthen the distance between assailant and victim.

The warders who have come to inform Joseph K. of his arrest are persons like him. They are, as K. is to discover much later, phases of himself, parts of the intricate conscious and subconscious pattern that is the totality of K. In any scrupulous analysis of K.'s situation, we shall have to say that K. has been interrupted by— K., that his neatly efficient life has been interfered with by himself. In the spirit of a half-recognition of this shared impulse, K. takes his stand on a question of protocol, of form: by what right do these men invade his privacy; on whose orders? The warders as well manage the arrest in terms of rules: K. is supposed to stay in his room, he is not allowed to wander about the house, he must wait for the Inspector to arrive. (Politeness is the ironic tone throughout. In the end K.'s executioners bow ceremonially and fastidiously attend to protocol.) This is to suggest that the rules for order are not vastly different from the rules for disorder. They are both a part of the same man, of his will and of the way he exercises it in society. Manners are flexibly pertinent to each expression of human motive. One of the most persistent challenges to literature in an age of violence is that of accommodating human manners to violent occasions. The grammar of violence is achieved through a realignment of the grammatical terms of peace. In the modern war novel, for example, both the descriptions of violence and the matter of accommodation to it are given within the same range and scope of human intercourse.

I have suggested in other essays that modern literature of violence may best be seen in terms of the metaphor of the assailant and his victim. The economy of this relationship may be defined as the distance achieved between the two. It is generally true that the range of psychological resources is best and most clearly employed in violent situations in which the distance between the assailant and the victim is so limited that the two protagonists are within sight of one another. In any violence there is a form of collaboration of the two involved in committing the act. The assailant strikes with force; the victim receives the force. The basic changes in the relationshp occur when the distance becomes too great to allow for moral and emotional visibility as an element of the experience. It is only when that visibility is no longer possible that violence can be called "surprising." K. is surprised by his arrest, not because the warders are invisible but because they are not the real assailants. He finds it all but impossible to adjust to the rules and regulations governing his arrest because he cannot see the source of it or the motive for its having happened. *The Trial* is made up largely of scenes in which K. searches energetically for his assailant. He never knows who he is, and dies without a glimmer of comprehension of his complicity as victim. This desperate circumstance is repeated in a thousand ways in modern literature. The great energy of modern tragedy lies not so much in the carnage that is its established feature as in the uncertainty about causes and motives, the extreme difficulty in determining the victim's relationship to the act of violence.

K. is at liberty in the days following his arrest. The initiative of establishing the reality of his case is left to him. And at first he tries to hold to the idea that the whole thing is after all a hoax, or at worst so flagrant an injustice that he will need only to be firm and honest to have the affair exposed. His new role of criminal is at first only moderately recognized by the men and women around him. The *idea* of criminality is communicated at first in terms of atmosphere and scene. There are no machines at present at the disposal of an assailant. Since the assailant is not known, to the Court, to K.'s friends, or to K. himself, nothing is specified in the usual sense. The elaborate devices used for criminal detection, with which any reader or viewer of murder mysteries is familiar, do not exist. Instead, the Court and its subordinate functions are found in rooms, located in buildings not unlike K.'s rooming house.

On one Sunday morning K. makes his way to such a house and is surprised that the scene provides no sign of its function as a court building. Once inside, he is again puzzled and annoyed that they should not have given him more definite information: ". . . these people showed a strange negligence or indifference in their treatment of him, he intended to tell them so very positively and clearly."[1] This dismay over the absence of conventional signs is closely related to the bewilderment over the accusation itself: who made it, why has it been made, how can he defend himself if he is so vague about its character? "His mind played in retrospect with the saying of the warder Willem that an attraction existed between the Law and guilt, from which it should really follow that the Interrogation Chamber must lie in that particular flight of stairs which K. happened to choose" (pp. 44–45). This is his first real insight into the nature of the crime; it is of the very substance of himself, and therefore the course of his discovering what it is follows the line of his will and choice. He is, however, by no means convinced of his guilt, as his speech in the Chamber attests. Innocent persons are accused of guilt, he tells his audience, "and senseless proceedings are put in motion against them, mostly without effect, it is true, as in my own case" (p. 57).

No great exercise of the imagination is needed to grasp the significance of this remark, made as it is in a crowded room, the atmosphere "fuggy" and unclear, the audience divided in its view of the case. It stresses once again the role of the irrational in modern literature. The majority of literary reactions to the First World War were primarily expressions of shock, disbelief, extreme anger over the "unreasonableness" of the proceedings. This literature is clear at least on the question of the sources of violence. They are linked closely to the "fuggy" atmosphere created by force employed in the functioning of our economy. But beyond that, and more subtly, the mist, fog, smoke of the scene are of our own making. K. is talking into the dim and dirty atmosphere of his own mind as he strikes out at the unreasonableness of his circumstance. But he speaks as the Bank officer, setting that aspect of himself off from the other selves that may inhabit him. The scene of his protest is thus unreasonable: he finds it difficult both to see into it and to determine what if any part of his audience is sympathetic to him.

Moral tragedy has two major determinants: the matter of the hero's complicity, as assailant or victim, or a fusing of both; the matter of his state of awareness of his complicity. Hemingway's Lt. Henry, at first maddened by the irrationality of the Caporetto front, ends by saying that the war did not have anything to do with him. The worst fear haunting the protagonist of the *Waste Land* is that of his involvement as a sacrifice to the necessities the scene describes. Anger and fear are variously interrelated in modern literature, to suggest the deep bewilderment of the modern soul over the question of his precise relation to the criminal circumstance in which he lives. In his own confident expansion of the possibilities of force, he has pushed assailant and victim further and further apart, until the instruments of violence have acquired such overwhelming force as to make the distinction all but impossible. The scene of the violence becomes the sole remaining evidence of motive and its relation to force; the assailant is the scene itself, and the scene includes the victim. The most extreme of our literary efforts to encompass a violence so shockingly out of hand describes painstakingly the deterioration of the victim, to the point where he resembles the assailant and is

---

1. *The Trial,* trans. Willa and Edwin Muir (New York: Knopf, 1937), p. 44.

to all intents and purposes indistinguishable from it. This condition is in part revealed by the fact that the modern hero is not distinguishable from his fellows; or, if he is different, it is only in the degree and detail in which he externalizes his inner violence. The hero is a man of inner and outer violence, moving from one to the other according to the disposition of the author toward the scene. Throughout there is a sense of the dim, strange, "fuggy" atmosphere that defines the condition at the same time as it prevents a clear grasp of the meaning of the violence.

The progress of Kafka's hero is in terms of such a metaphoric scene of diffused violence. K. steadfastly refuses to admit the scene as part of himself. He comes back one day to the Interrogation Chamber and, finding it unoccupied, looks about him. He picks up a volume of what he assumes are law books, but finds in it an indecent picture, crudely drawn, of a man and woman sitting naked on a sofa; another bears the title, *How Grete Was Plagued by Her Husband.* Surely, he thinks, the Courts must be more corrupt than he had guessed; to give his own case more than the most perfunctory and contemptuous attention would surely mean contributing to an already bad situation, He turns to a woman in the room and finds her also involved in the corrupted scene. Quite without clearly recognizing the irony of his position, he is shortly engaged in wooing her support for his case, in terms of the very corruptive influence he has just recently scorned: "And probably there could be no more fitting revenge on the Examining Magistrate and his henchmen than to wrest this woman from them and take her himself" (p. 70). He is at once the outraged victim and the conniving collaborator of the situation. Throughout the progress of the novel, this dual role suggests itself in trivial acts and gestures; K. makes his way toward his death, never fully suspecting the force of his own role in causing it.

The most brilliantly revealing scene in this connection is the episode of the flogging. The two warders who had first arrested K. have been sentenced to be whipped because of a complaint he is said to have made about their behavior (they had tried to appropriate some of K.'s private belongings). But, K. insists, he hadn't intended to have them whipped; he was "only defending a principle." In any event, he is shocked that the scene should be taking place in the Bank building, and most disturbed that the noise might rouse the attention of the men still there. Here he is directly forced to see that he can be an agent of violence, and the sight disgusts him. In what way is a man involved in the sufferings of others? The disparity of principle and human incident is here eloquently presented. The intricate and complex wavering of principle and chance in our moral life causes incidental and sometimes violent pain to others.

This universal enigma is especially and compellingly evident in the literature that attempts to explore the intricacies of motive in modern violence. How much may we say of the degree of responsibility for great violence done many persons, for destruction on a vast scale? The modern hero often quickly loses sight of the question, or is distracted from it by the impact of violence itself. There is an especially vivid illustration of the confusion this question leads to in a French novel of the Second World War, Robert Merle's *Weekend at Dunkirk.* The hero, Maillat, from the beginning observes scores of violent scenes; his own friend is quite suddenly, "unreasonably" destroyed, almost before his eyes; he himself narrowly escapes being violently killed on a British ship that has suffered a direct hit from a Nazi bomber. When he enters a room in a partially destroyed home, he finds two fellow soldiers engaged in raping a French girl. Outraged by the scene he kills the two men; as he confesses later, he had "enjoyed" the experience of seeing them cringe before him, "obeying" his power over them. The will, strongly roused by the incident, exerts itself violently shortly thereafter, and he takes the girl himself.

Not only is the will to violence stimulated by the act itself; the force within us is nourished by the exigencies of a violent scene. Ernst Jünger, a German officer of the First World War, whose record of trench warfare is perhaps superior in the strength of its unornamented factuality to any other war literature, describes again and again the progress of warfare in transforming men into powerful instruments of violence.[2] Kafka's scene merely suggests that the will to violence exists, that it may set off physical action despite the strongest of expressed desires to contain it. Kafka's hero is deeply involved in the flogging scene, and not only because he has initiated the action. His reasons for protesting it are primarily selfish; he does not wish to admit himself capable of such a will and, when a cry of pain rises from one of the victims, he is distressed, but only because someone might hear the ugly sound. As two clerks of the Bank come up to inquire if anything is wrong, K. turns them aside with the remark, "It was only a dog howling in the courtyard" (p. 110).

The meaning of this detail expands beyond itself, to the pattern of the novel itself, but beyond that to the phenomenon of the wound. A short story by Kafka, "A Country Doctor," contains a series of weird mischances, the worst of which is the sight of an incurable wound. The patient, a young boy, had not at first seemed very ill, only mildly feverish, so that the wound made its appearance shockingly and without discernible cause: "In his right side, near the hip, was an open wound as big as the palm of my hand. Rose-red, in many variations of shade, dark in the hollows, lighter at the edges, softly granulated, with irregular clots of blood, open as a surface mine to the daylight."[3] This is the open wound of the human disposition to pain, and the doctor discovers upon closer examination that it also contains the consuming worms of death.

The meaning of this weirdly shocking detail is not easy to grasp; but it would not be too much to say that the boy had willed the wound, or that—in the light of his relationship to the shock of life—he had welcomed it, at any rate that he was scarcely indifferent to it. Ben Belitt, one of our underrated new poets, speaks in one of his war poems of the wound as "Terror's unique enigma, the time-serving will." The will, imprisoned in the landscape of violence, bends the victim toward his wound, "the compassionate image."[4] In Kafka's story, it is the doctor who suffers the worst calamity; the wounded boy submits to death as in a most revealing way the victim of a self-willed affliction. Once again the strange paradox of the assailant as landscape confronts us. For, as our indifference (as in K.'s thoughtless complaint) involves us morally in the suffering of others, we move with even more force of anger and desire across the landscape of violence, to participate in our undoing. Kafka's novel above all stresses both

2. See my essay, "The Moment of Violence," *Essays in Criticism* 10 (October 1960).

3. *The Penal Colony*, trans. Willa and Edwin Muir (New York: Schocken Books, 1948), p. 141.

4. Ben Belitt, *Wilderness Stair* (New York: Grove Press, 1955), p. 61.

our journey across this landscape and our unwitting share in its malevolent character.

This effect persists throughout. K. is gradually brought to a partial awareness of the seriousness of his circumstance, but he does not relinquish 'the privilege of righteous immunity. There are always extenuations: the corruption of the Court, the venality of lesser officials, the protective images of the security his position in the Bank provides, and so forth. At no time is the crime specified; at no time are the officials or minions of the Law made to look like monsters or grotesques. They are common variants of the human condition, of which K. is himself the central image. *The Trial* is in this sense a parable of man's grudging journey to moral awareness. Above all, it stresses the fatal deficiency of common moral safeguards. We are aware of their failure only when, suddenly and without warning, they fail us. One of Kay Boyle's recent novels, *The Seagull on the Step,* describes a busload of passengers on a routine journey in southern France soon after the end of the Second World War. Her attention is dispersed throughout the crowded bus and only occasionally focuses upon the driver, who strikes one as the most trustworthy of the tribe. A brake failure at the last plunges the vehicle down a cliff to destruction and death.

This melodramatic instance simply points up an obvious fact that is all but willfully neglected. K.'s concern for his innocence is only gradually moved from the center of his belligerent confidence in conventional rectitude. His uncle arrives from the country, profoundly disturbed over the news of K.'s arrest and even more upset that he should not have more scrupulously attended to his case. On one of his visits to the Advocate whom his uncle has engaged on his account, K. finds a commercial traveler, named Block, already there and apparently in constant, eager attendance upon the Advocate's every word. Block is an example of the force of unrelenting piety, the parody of a narrow, moralistic self-concern. His submission to the most ludicrous of requirements does not testify to his being in any sense a righteous man, but rather suggests an energetic passivity, almost a ruthless drive toward self-involvement in guilt. While K. holds the Court guilty of a malicious miscarriage of procedure, Block submits to whatever may be with a diligent persistence. His action suggests a soldier hurrying from skull to skull, in search of whichever one had once been his head. When K. visits the Advocate, it is with the intention of telling him he no longer wishes his services, that he feels he will now go on his own. The contrast of Block and K. describes the range of earnestness in the moral life. Surely the political implications of this range are obvious enough.

If only because the demands upon his time have made him weary and listless in his performance as Bank Assessor, K.'s quest of definition shows obvious signs of absorbing his attention more and more. Without relinquishing his firm belief in innocence, he nevertheless improves strategies of self-defense. On one occasion he visits a painter, Titorelli, who makes a poor enough living doing portraits of minor officials. The scene of Titorelli's quarters is itself a revealing image of the moral landscape. It is even a poorer neighborhood than that in which the Court holds its meetings.[5]

---

5. Of course, there are courtrooms everywhere; there would have to be, if the scope and the mind of the hero are considered phases of one search for guilt.

the houses were still darker, the streets filled with sludge oozing about slowly on top of the melting snow. In the tenement where the painter lived only one wing of the great double door stood open, and beneath the other wing, in the masonary near the ground, there was a gaping hole out of which, just as K. approached, issued a disgusting yellow fluid, steaming hot, from which a rat fled into the adjoining canal. (*The Trial*, p. 177)

Like many other Kafka scenes, this may be taken to suggest a variety of meanings. Surely it is in itself identifiable as a disheartening and disgusting slum, whose chief distinguishing marks most candidly define the body's private functions. As the relationship of men to space diminishes, the chance of either hiding such functions or breathing good air all but disappear. K. may be said here to have undertaken a journey to the ugliest sector of his moral world. Within the tenement he encounters three ugly, bold-faced young girls; one of them "nudged him with her elbow and peered up at him knowingly. Neither her youth nor her deformity had saved her from being prematurely debauched" (p. 178). When K. finally finds his way to Titorelli's room, he finds the air here even more atrociously hot and foul than that of the courtroom he had visited. The entire scene clearly defines the décor of human evil. It is not an evil of commission, but an evil of disregard, of the impurities that the body's efforts for survival create in an imperfect and vulgarized atmosphere.

In another sense it is an atmosphere of purgation. The foul smell, the darkness, the constriction of space are all elements identifying the character of the body, its emission of impurities in the ordinary course of its progress toward inevitable corruption. K., in entering it, may almost literally be said to be journeying toward death, for the smell of death is about him and the space he occupies is not much larger than the space of a tomb. In such an atmosphere, K. discusses his case with Titorelli. He is unregenerately convinced that the whole affair is an elaborate injustice, but he is also aware that the ways of justice are skillful, subtle, and devious: "And in the end, out of nothing at all, an enormous fabric of guilt will be conjured up" (p. 187). This remark and the scene in which it is made are available to numerous interpretations, but none of them is free of some suggestion of the idea the novel as a whole supports. The intricacies of human justice and intelligence are a composite of many fragmented decisions and their underlying motives. Evil is subtly and slyly intermixed with the good; indeed, the good is scarcely to be defined by itself, since a just impulse can easily react painfully upon a weaker self.

The portrait Titorelli shows K. gives an ambiguous impression of Justice and Victory combined, though a trick of light and shadow also bring out the impression of "a goddess of the Hunt in full cry" (p. 185). The passion for "right feeling," for a principled life, might easily be confused in the chance admixture of aggression, so that one portrait reveals all three. The impression should convince the hero that he cannot longer expect surface good will to save him from the crime of which he is accused. One strong impression this scene gives is that the human will is never free of the taint of arrogance or ambition; nor is a human act ever free of the chance of causing pain, however indirectly. Quite aside from the very real service K.'s visit to Titorelli performs, by way of making him more fully aware of the seriousness of his case, the scene is itself the most powerful literary image of the landscape of violence. Here there is no real discrimination between assailant and victim. In submitting to the indignities of this setting, K. is in a real sense examining himself, or seeing the capacity of the self for absorbing the filth of its own making. One of the most obvious of the discrepancies noticeable in modern life is that between the nobility of appearance and the disorder of underlying reality. There have been many Potemkin villages in the history of the modern soul. But the most effectively shocking of modern scenes is that in which the disorder of the soul is imaged in a disarray of objects scattered in space. Man's power of calling forth violence, or of enduring within a landscape of its effects, is suggested again in modern literature.

More than that, the victim of this violence is himself an initiator of it. K.'s will and soul are here set forth most uncompromisingly. As he discusses the legal possibilities of his case, he remains at the very center of the disorder to which the officials ordering his arrest had originally hoped to call attention. In this very effective way, Kafka shows him growing toward an awareness of his situation at the very time when he is most earnestly exploring the chances of evasion. As effective as this scene is, it has many equals in modern literature: the apartment scene in *The Great Gatsby,* where the potential violence of Tom Buchanan and Myrtle Wilson is imaged in the powerful contraction of pretentious objects crowded into a tiny space; the "Cyclops" episode of Joyce's *Ulysses,* where the violence is an expression of both a belligerent anti-Semitism and a self-indulgence; the shafts leading down into the mines of Zola's *Germinal,* with their human cargo and their constant threat of damage and disaster; the violence of Naphta and Settembrini as they duel for power over Hans Castorp's soul, in Mann's *The Magic Mountain.* In each of these details (and in scores of war episodes) the scene itself reveals a potential complicity of victim in the act of violence. In Kafka's novel the violence is implicit in almost every detail of Titorelli's residence—not the least, in the shameless defiance of the neat and circumspect decorum which K. had at the beginning relied upon to save himself. K. is a partner in the scene; he has himself willed the ugly distortions and constrictions of the reality of which he is now in the center.

As it turns out, the world is a prison to the degree that man wills it to be. In the next to last of the novel's scenes, K. finds himself in the Cathedral, where he is awaiting a visitor whom the Bank has asked him to entertain. The event has been carefully prepared, and is eligible to much easy interpretation. One can say that K. has come to the Cathedral to hear still another version of his case; or that he is there because of the connivance of the Law officials, who are after all designers of his conscience. Whatever the meaning of the plans, K. is in the dark interior and, waiting for his guest, looks about him. He is curiously drawn to the altar-piece of a small side chapel, which appears to contain near its outer edge the picture of a huge, armored knight.

> He was leaning on his sword, which was stuck into the bare ground, bare except for a stray blade of grass or two. He seemed to be watching attentively some event unfolding itself before his eyes. (P. 259)

The center of the picture is a conventional enough portrayal of Christ being laid in the tomb, but K.'s attention now aroused, he searches further. His eyes are finally drawn to a small pulpit of plain stone, so small as scarcely to accommodate the preacher whom he now sees for the first time.

The scene is a sharply realistic addition to the parable of K.'s life. Once again he finds himself within a setting that is closely identified with his moral circumstance. The huge armored knight he had examined so curiously guards the tomb; the small side chapel is the site chosen for his meditation on his "case"— that is to say, on his willed intervention in the affairs of men and his resistance to confession of the guilt. The priest who stands in the pulpit is the prison chaplain, there to discuss his present disposition to the case. The chaplain's fable brings the scene into the discourse itself: before the Law stands a door-keeper in guard, he says. This man is specially designated for the moment of death. One must await one's turn and be present at precisely the right spot when it comes. But, while the man of the fable has awaited the moment patiently, he has not actively sought it, and the chance is lost. He had taken no initiative in seeking the way, but had passively assumed his fate would be decided and announced to him. But of course K. considers the tale ridiculous and leaves the Cathedral uninformed. Not only has he not sought out the verdict, but he has throughout resisted going the full way to acknowledgment of guilt.

There is nothing left to do now but send K. to his death. Kafka has conscientiously attended to every conceivable scenic effect, and K.'s soul has been quite exhaustively examined. A year after his arrest, on the eve of his thirty-first birthday, two men call at his lodging. Once again their appearance is grotesquely inappropriate to one's expectation of killers on a mission: "In frock-coats, pallid and plump, with top-hats that were apparently uncollapsible" (p. 281). The circumstances of violence are to the very end the same as those of normality. The men are polite to excess: "Tenth-rate old actors they send for me," K. grumbles. "They want to finish me off cheaply." Still firm in his disbelief, convinced of his innocence, K. walks between and slightly to the front of these grotesquely proper persons, like servants perhaps, doormen or carriage attendants: ". . . the only thing for me to go on doing is to keep my intelligence calm and discriminating to the end." As the walk progresses, K. quickens the pace; and the two executioners, their arms tightly clasped to his, run with him. The death occurs on the outskirts of the town, near an old stone quarry, though there is also "a still completely urban house" nearby. One of the men draws out a long, thin, double-edged butcher's knife, and the two of them pass it to each other across K.'s body. "K. now perceived clearly that he was supposed to seize the knife himself, as it travelled from hand to hand, and plunge it into his own breast." But he does not do so, and the partners collaborate in the death, one of them holding K.'s throat, the other thrusting the knife into his heart.

> With failing eyes K. could still see the two of them, cheek leaning against cheek, immediately before his face, watching the final act. "Like a dog!" he said; it was as if he meant the shame of it to outlive him.

Just before this act, K. had turned his head to one side and in the direction of the distant dwelling. He saw, or thought he saw, a man reaching outstretched arms to him. Even at this moment of extremity, his hopes were stimulated.

Could the man be offering help? Was there still some evidence that might save him? Is it possible that the man was an intermediary, who had the power to call off the execution? But the death does occur, the most ambiguous of conclusions of a baffling case. K. is alert to the end to the shame of his death, to its lack of dignity. It is unworthy of him; it has been committed at the level of an animal cruelly tortured to give sadistic pleasure.

The killing is the final ambiguity that follows correctly from a succession of ambiguous scenes. K. is a superb example of the modern moral hero, whose two great and striking characteristics are that he proclaims his innocence while in the act of willing his guilt, and that as a victim of a scene of violence he conspires with the assailant in the act of his death. There is no clear separation of the assailant from the victim in this case. The elaborate, scenic meditation of which the novel consists portrays modern man willing his guilt as he asserts principle, most tragically of all perhaps unable or unwilling to discriminate between the satisfactory reason and the ambiguous cause. While men have always fought wars for a cause and have invoked principle in defense of violence, they have not been altogether clearly vindicated in either case. Events culminating in violence lead after their conclusion very quickly to retrospective doubt.

The history of violence in the twentieth century is dominated by examples of ambiguous dying. The worst fate a man can suffer is a death that is undignified, "Like a dog!" as K. had said in pronouncing upon his. But modern violence is especially efficient in producing corpses without and beyond the hope of ceremonial mitigation. The narrator of the documentary *The Dark Side of the Moon* speaks in one place of her father, who had died in a Russian forced-labor camp, alone; she hopes but cannot really trust that at the end he had not died without some suggestion of identity with his past. Eugen Kogon, in his horrifying *The Theory and Practice of Hell,* gives hundreds of examples of such unattended, ambiguous killings. The wars have themselves provided inumerable illustrations of the character of K.'s death, both within the limit of legally sanctioned force (*All Quiet on the Western Front; The Naked and the Dead*), and as a result of violent miscalculations of justice on either side (*Paths of Glory; Execution; The Cross of Iron*).

One important generality must be made about modern violence; it is not only applicable in a majority of the literary images of violence but must stand out as a major distinguishing mark. The modern man of violence has at his disposal instruments that increase almost incalculably the hazard of violence. They are capable of sudden, irrational, calamitous disruptions of the landscape. They are also capable of almost absolute annihilation. These instruments are the creation of man, of his mind and of his genius. They have caused several serious dislocations in the moral balance according to which violence had previously been judged and its responsibility allocated. For one thing, the distance between assailant and victim is now irretrievably lost; there is no certain, discernible, charitable relationship between the two. This means that beyond a certain point the *idea* of an assailant has disappeared.

In the many portrayals of war in modern literature, there is a common refrain: the war is inhuman, unreasonable, untenable. But if this refrain is to be the end of our meditations upon violence, we shall have to admit total failure in bringing it within reach of our intelligence and our imagination. The only literature of violence that can convincingly endure is that which attempts to grasp this fundamental ambiguity: that weapons created by the acts of rational and ingenious men have destroyed the power of the reason either to contemplate or to comprehend the results of their uses. Unless we wish to settle for a kind of historical fiction that merely allows the reader to relive the war experience, some variant of Kafka's approach is surely needed. The overpowering image at the end of K.'s struggle is of the victim conniving with the assailant in his own destruction. The assailant is no longer a single, identifiable, fingerprinted criminal, whose act can be related to the clear circumstances of a victim's death; the two, in the complex of moral implications described in *The Trial,* are joined in the landscape of violence itself. It is only in this sense that we can understand the paradox of cruelty committed "without cruel intent," or of Eliot's statement that ". . . Unnatural vices/ Are fathered by our heroism. Virtues/ Are forced upon us by our impudent crimes."

Mann's Portrait of the Artist: Archetypal Patterns

HORST S. DAEMMRICH

Wayne State University

COMMENT BY THE AUTHOR

During the last decade Thomas Mann scholarship has been prolific. Conse-quently the bibliographical references in the essay below are dated. The views expressed in my study, however, are still valid. Mann's concern with an artist-typology explains ambiguous sections in his stories, illuminates many characters in his fiction, and gives thematic unity to his works. It also raises timely and unresolved questions: Is an artist justified in creating a transcendental realm of beauty far removed from the daily concern of a suffering humanity and in effect closing his eyes to the misery of contemporary life? Should he enter the political arena, fan the flames of discontent, and turn into a social revolutionary? Must he tread the narrow path between these alternatives and, as Mann suggests, remain uncommitted to causes but faithful to a high ethos of the affirmation of life?

The focus on the figure of the reflective-analytic artist figure has far-reaching philosophical implications. Mann argues that the increasing specialization in the various fields of knowledge that accompanied the cultural change in Western civilization has led to a crisis, a situation of general disorientation. Only artists can convey a semblance of order through their works to persons living in a fragmented and often chaotic world. Yet Mann's portrait of the artist clearly in-dicates that artists cannot be viewed as isolated from the cultural transformation; their woes reflect society's dilemma.

The artist's struggle with an unyielding subject matter, his will to know, and his

---

First published: 14, no. 3 (1966): 27–43. Slightly revised.

clash with an uncomprehending society reflect his ultimately human quest for identity. Not surprisingly Mann associates the Faustian motif and the traditional coming-of-age theme with artist figures in his novels. Mirrored in the artist's struggle the reader perceives his own search for a meaningful basis of existence. For artist figures and readers alike, the quest for self-realization leads along alternative manifestations, such as saint and fallen angel, to the timeless challenge: how to become a civilized person.

In recent years Thomas Mann scholarship has produced a number of important studies that try to account for Mann's concept of the artist.[1] The essentially different interpretations point to the extremely complex nature of Mann's concept; at the same time, they overlook, first, that Mann conceived of a number of artist types and, second, that he finally crystallized his thinking concerning the problem of the artist's existence. As early as 1901 he worked on an extensive treatise in the tradition of Lessing's *Laokoon* and Schiller's *Über naive und sentimentalische Dichtung*.[2] The scope of his proposed essay, which unfortunately remained a fragment, encompassed the entire field of aesthetic theory. Part of it was finally published in 1913 as a fragment entitled "Der Künstler und der Literat." The material presented in this essay was later immensely expanded, reevaluated, and refined in *Betrachtungen eines Unpolitischen* (1918) and "Goethe und Tolstoi" (1925).

Originally Mann postulates two basic artistic dispositions: naive and the reflective. He then proceeds to analyze positive as well as negative characteristics of artists endowed with either of these dispositions. He first distinguishes between a sensuous-creative artist (*Künstler*) and a reflective-analytic artist (*Literat*). Although the sensuous-creative artist's attributes belong essentially to painters and sculptors, Mann does not exclude the possibility that these traits can also be found in literary artists. He envisions a gay Bohemian who is amoral, childlike, innocent, irresponsible, and interested in "bright aspects of life."[3] As a true son of nature, this artist has retained a balanced position in which senses and reason are not yet in contradiction to each other. He responds empathically to sensuous stimuli and is able to project the immediacy of experience into his creative works, which

---

1. See especially Reinhard Baumgart, *Das Ironische und die Ironie in den Werken Thomas Manns* (Munich: Hanser, 1964); Edith Braemer, "Aspekte der Goethe-Rezeption Thomas Manns," in *Vollendung und Grösse Thomas Manns,* ed. Georg Wenzel (Halle: Verlag Sprach und Literatur, 1962), pp. 162–95; Inge Diersen, *Untersuchungen zu Thomas Mann* (Berlin: Rütten & Loening, 1959); Erich Heller, *The Ironic German* (London: Secker & Warburg, 1958); Peter Heller, "Thomas Mann's Conception of the Creative Writer," *PMLA* 69 (1954): 763–96; Herbert Lehnert, *Thomas Mann: Fiktion, Mythos, Religion* (Stuttgart: Kohlhammer, 1965); Hans Mayer, *Thomas Mann: Werk und Entwicklung* (Berlin: Volk und Welt, 1950); Heinz Peter Pütz, *Kunst und Künstlerexistenz bei Nietzsche und Thomas Mann* (Bonn: H. Bouvier, 1963); William Henry Rey, "Tragic Aspects of the Artist in Thomas Mann's Work," *Modern Language Quarterly* 19 (1958): 195–203.

2. See Mann's letter to Walter Opitz, August 26, 1909, in Thomas Mann, *Briefe* (Frankfurt: S. Fischer, 1961), pp. 77–78.

3. Thomas Mann, *Gesammelte Werke* (Frankfurt: S. Fischer, 1960), 10: 67; this twelve-volume edition is hereafter cited in the text as *GW*. All italics in the quotations are Mann's. The translations are my own.

are deeply rooted in reality and not oriented toward abstract ideals, intellect, or cognition. Consequently he does not experience a conflict between ideality and reality: "Basically creative, neither contemplative nor critical, but productive, *the* productive, creative person, and as such used to concessions to his material, he would never feel that utilitarian considerations and high principles are mutually exclusive. . . . Briefly, the character trait probably lacking in this congenial artist is *morality,* a trait which simply is neither typical of nature nor of the 'naive temperament,' but of intellect and the reflective-critical attitude" (*GW,* 10: 67–68).

Since the sensuous-creative artist judges the excellence of his creative work in terms of a perfect imitation of nature, he must guard against being enslaved by reality. Already in his play *Fiorenza* (1905) Mann had humorously shown what happens when naive artists succumb to utilitarian demands. These artists envision a marriage of art to life. But their public's disregard for ideas has a devastating effect upon them. For after they adapt their art to suit the popular taste they themselves are soon unwilling and finally unable to penetrate beneath the purely visible. It is but one step from their concentration on intense color complementations to their willingness to ornament all aspects of life because a pleasure-loving society asks for it. Their creations extend from a beautiful, sexually stimulating Madonna, who no longer conveys the idea of sanctity and suffering, by way of illustrated texts ("Who would look at a 'naked text?'") to fanciful honeycakes, created by an artist who likes to work with a new material (*GW,* 8: 997–1005). Thus Thomas Mann points to a characteristic weakness of the sensuous-creative artist: he could be satisfied with a naturalistic copy of reality or lapse into triviality and platitude by trying to please his public.

The reflective-analytic artist's conception of reality, as well as his attitude toward artistic creations, stands in marked contrast to that of his opposite. The basic temper of this artist (*Literat*) is analytic and introspective, a disposition that estranges him from naive art, indeed from the rest of society. No longer satisfied with the imitation of reality, he strives for the representation of high but abstract ideals, such as freedom, justice, reason, compassion for mankind, and human dignity. He creates his own idealistic image of the world and fights against the corruption of his ideals by reality. The actual world measured by such absolutes is found wanting and is either satirized or condemned (*GW,* 10: 63). Of necessity, he aften appears moralistic and critical of social conditions. Although it seems as if the reflective-analytic artist strictly adheres to ethical norms, Mann suggests that aesthetic considerations actually precede all others, because the primary force in this artist's life is the aspiration to reach perfection in literary expression (*GW,* 10: 65). Yet even the most careful attention to aesthetic questions never leads to indifference in the face of ethical issues: "He despises inconsistencies, compromises, and intellectual cowardice. . . . His sensitivity to beauty and form coupled with his idealism prompts him to protect *noble* principles against *utilitarian* demands" (*GW,* 10: 66).

In *Schwere Stunde* (1905) Mann paints a portrait of Schiller as such an artist, exclusively dedicated to his art, who "selflessly sacrifices himself and consumes himself in the service of a high ideal" (*GW,* 8: 377). This consecration, in which the artist enriches the world but also lavishly spends himself, accounts for Mann's suggestion that the reflective-analytic artist is at his most exalted level "saintliness incarnate" (*GW*, 10: 69). Since his vision is always directed toward the ideal, he may manifest the desire to ennoble and improve man, but he is also clearly in danger of scorning those who do not measure up to his high standards. Ultimately, he may even betray his calling by giving free rein to the desire of improving man morally through his art. Mann's portraits of Hieronymus in *Gladius Dei* (1902) and the fanatic Prior in *Fiorenza* are excellent illustrations of this temper.[4] The Prior, completely swayed by his feverish vision of a moral society, demands an art that will no longer appeal to the senses but only to intellect. Driven by a furious desire to use art in purging man from sensuousness, he hates and castigates all fine art.

In *Betrachtungen eines Unpolitischen* Mann further expands this reasoning. The reflective-analytic artist who is so infatuated with his ideal that he uses his art for specific limited ends, be they progressive or reactionary, could easily lapse into political pamphleteering. His art would become a tool for social or political progress. Mann's argument also implies that the reflective-analytic artist is menaced by yet another peril: he may divorce himself from reality and create aesthetic objects that transcend all limits of human comprehension. Although the reflective temper may predispose an artist toward either extreme, his reaction invariably depends on his specific view of the function of art. Mann singles out two basically different aesthetic theories: first, art should have either social or political consequences, and second, art conveys beauty and constitutes an autonomous realm.

Mann takes exception to all *littérature engagée* primarily for two reasons: he adheres to the view that a spiritual rebirth of man and his ennoblement must precede political reforms, and he also feels that art is doomed to failure once it is put into the service of political doctrines. Mann's most scathing attack is directed against the literary activist (*Zivilisationsliterat*), a radical intellectual whose major aim is the remedy of social or political injustice. As a result of his orientation, this artist loses the freedom necessary to rise above the constantly changing demands of the day and by confining the role of art to criticism ignores its essential purpose: "A manifesto, if it is powerful can at best arouse and agitate; a work of art alone can make you *free*" (*BeU*, p. 303). A literary activist, who is committed to a definite program and who seems to have an answer to every question, forgets that a doctrine does not yet constitute a work of art. Indeed he is irresponsible as artist, for he ought to know "that *all* oratory remains open to doubt, no matter how apodictically a cause is argued or how absolute ideas are felt to be; aesthetic form alone remains unassailable. Art's marvelous superiority over pure intellectualism rests in her lively ambiguity, profound impartiality, and intellectual freedom . . ." (*BeU*, pp. 220–21).

Substantially different from the theory of a *littérature engagée* are the aesthetic principles of a literature that Mann variously defined as aestheticism, the art of the amoral, objective poet, and playful, form-conscious art. Mann's preference for the latter does not imply an endorsement of the theory of art for art's sake. Instead it should be viewed as indicative of Mann's desire to distinguish clearly

---

4. The two, of course, are literary figures, serving a specific function in works of art and not abstract types. Nevertheless the comparison is useful, especially since Mann himself draws a parallel between the reflective-analytic artist and the Prior in *Betrachtungen eines Unpolitischen* (Frankfurt: S. Fischer, 1956), pp. 84–85. This edition is hereafter quoted in the text as *BeU*.

between the artist's obligation *as artist* to his work and his necessary and often timely participation *as citizen* in the affairs of the day. Despite or perhaps because of his own commitment to political causes, Mann emphasized that the artist must retain maximum possible distance from them in his creative works (*GW,* 10: 302, 397ff.; *GW, 9:* 633). Mann's ideal is a conservative, apolitical, and extremely conscientious artist who is able to transcend the spirit of his age (*BeU,* pp. 277, 306–7, 335).

The aesthete, as he is portrayed in the *Betrachtungen,* has an appreciative perception of man's marvelous deeds as well as his monstrous nature. His outstanding characteristic is his refusal to adhere to any fixed position in his works. Indeed, he conceives literary figures so objectively that we are compelled to sympathize with them, even if they represent evil. Because of his principles of literary creation this artist fully realizes that fictional characters always play specific roles within the design of a composition; the opinions which they express are consequently far more relative than the audience might assume (*BeU,* p. 221). Above all, the aesthete is an artist and as such is more interested in aesthetic effects than in absolute truth: "Art is illusion; her magic is that 'her form consumes material content!' Art is not accountable to reality: she is interested in appearance, beauty, passion, and the artist demands that his truly creative works as well as his ephemeral rhetoric be judged by aesthetic standards . . ." (*BeU,* p. 538). The recognition that he plays with characters, ideas, and artistic forms leaves the aesthete in a self-conscious and cautious position and leads to a profound skepticism toward literary activism, a skepticism that does not preclude, however, that he too wants to affect man. But since he aims at the harmonious development of all of man's capacities, that is, the individual's ennoblement (*BeU,* p. 248), he also runs the risk of becoming biased. He cultivates man but neglects important social and political aspects of life (*BeU,* p. 288). Finally by focusing his attention on the inward spiritual growth of the individual, the aesthete may become completely indifferent to contemporary events. Thus the modern artist must fight the temptation of either losing his identity in the political arena or withdrawing from the conflicts of his age. True art must tread its difficult path between these two extremes that would arbitrarily restrict it.

In "Goethe und Tolstoi" Mann shifts the emphasis to artists who hold a superior position on the scale of artist types.[5] This selective principle enables him to expand and refine his categories of "naive" and "reflective" to "naive-plastic" and "visionary." He contrasts two great visionaries (*Visionäre*), Schiller and Dostoevski, with two equally great naive-plastic artists (*Plastiker*), Goethe and Tolstoy. Since literary criticism lacked the precise term for what Mann wanted to express by the concept of the "naive-plastic artist," he resorted to an analogy between literature and the fine arts. He held that this artist actually succeeds through language in rendering the same impression of reality as do the visual arts. Thus Mann's basic premise is that whereas the strength of the visionary artist lies in his convincing presentation of ideas, the naive-plastic artist is unsurpassable in his ability to create physical beauty. His essential trait is an innate sympathy for nature, which is so strong that it can be viewed as telluric dependence or even compulsion (*GW, 9:* 92–93, 114). From this postulated

---

5. *GW, 9:* 58–173.

bond to nature, now viewed as indifferent, dark, demonic rather than simply joyous and innocent as in *Fiorenza*, Mann derives three distinctive features that characterize this artist's existence, his artistic principles, and his art. The naive-plastic artist exhibits a vitality and power of personality that at times border on brutality (*GW*, 9: 78, 136). Because he lacks faith in causes and seems unconcerned with ethical judgments, the naive-plastic artist appears cool and distant and treats all those who fancy that they hold the key to truth with Mephistophelian sarcasm (*GW*, 9: 115–19). In his works he refrains from all value judgments and maintains such objectivity that it might appear to his audience as godlike indifference to good and evil or icy, amoral neutrality (*GW*, 9: 319). But his works have a vivid, sensuous, plastic dimension that is so striking that fictional characters seem to project a physical reality (*Wirklichkeit des Seins*).

The visionary artist as he is characterized in "Goethe und Tolstoi" must be viewed as a further refinement of the reflective-analytic disposition. This artist inclines so strongly toward critical reflection that Mann sees in him *the* "representative of spirit-intellect," "the force that consistently and progressively estranged man from nature and stands in eternal revolt against her" (*GW*, 9: 79–80). He no longer sees nature as an organic unity but rather as a dynamic, fragmented universe of artificial and arbitary man-made forms. In his view, man has lost his inner harmony, for his senses and dialectical reasoning are in conflict. The reflective-analytic artist, profoundly aware of this dilemma, attempts to remedy it. He may try to project into nature an ideal of the harmony that man has lost, a tendency that accounts partially for the. pronounced interest in nature during certain periods of modern literature. Ideally, however, he would strive to establish a new harmony in man, which can no longer be considered as unconscious but rather as a dynamic balance of dialectic rationality and instincts. The incongruity between his almost religious desire to heal man and his critical, corrective attitude toward a world that is either unwilling or unable to follow him leads to ambivalence in his relation to others.

Although the reflective-analytic artist's emancipation from nature confers upon him a distinctive nobility (*GW*, 9: 80, 97), it also imperils his very existence, for he is predisposed toward illness and early death. Looking at the lives of Schiller and Dostoevski, Mann argues that disease is an essential trait of this artist type. It is the demon that drives him mercilessly to fight against time (*GW*, 9: 78) and stimulates and enhances his sensitiveness and creative power, but it may also inspire his great benevolence and compassion for mankind. The works of those reflective-analytic artists who are motivated by a compelling awareness of their cultural obligation mirror a strong concern for the ethical behavior of man. They abound with value judgments and criticism but tend to fall short in plastic qualities. Fictional characters in such works project a reality of action (*Wirklichkeit des Handelns*) and are convincing and unforgettable because of their brilliant discourse. These works then actually attain their poetic characteristic as a result of their fascinating diversity of ideas.

Common to both types of artist is their mutual desire to be part of their opposite and complementary pole: the reflective-analytic artist longs for a more balanced footing in reality and the naive-plastic artist, though to a lesser extent, yearns for the realm of spirit-intellect (*GW*, 9: 124, 177–78). Actually Mann is forced to conclude that the blithe, carefree, and harmonious world of the sensuous-creative artist is untenable. In modern times a naive-plastic artist also tends toward reason and is a deeply probing person. In turn the reflective-analytic artist has become so overburdened by knowledge that he is nauseated and yearns for a less perplexing existence, a feeling experienced by Tonio Kröger and Detlef. The mutual longing also points to an ideal artist who would successfully synthesize the positive aspects of both types (GW, 9: 138). Since Mann has a tendency to see this mutual longing in terms of the encounter between Goethe and Schiller, he focuses his attention on their "problematical friendship" not only in "Goethe und Tolstoi," but also in Lotte in Weimar (1939) and "Versuch über Schiller" (1955). Especially in these later works he ascribes to Schiller characteristics that were formerly reserved for the naive type (i.e., Schiller is playful, childlike, objective, realistic), and to Goethe those of the reflective-analytic artist (Goethe is portrayed as extremely reflective). This procedure, which may do greater justice to Goethe and Schiller than Mann's previous explorations, should not obscure the fact that it does not reflect a synthesis in Mann's thinking, since his basic dialectic remains unchanged.[6]

The most distinctive difference between the reflective-analytic artist and his opposite lies in their mental reaction to experiences that are suitable for artistic production. The naive type identifies empathically with an experience and subsequently casts his impression into literary form while retaining the immediacy of feeling. Thus emotions portrayed in his art have an immediate correlative in his own experience. Originally Mann must have assumed that this artist actually creates spontaneously and unconsciously. In Schwere Stunde, for instance, he pictures Goethe as an artist who created without effort, did not "torment himself" during the creative process (GW, 8: 372), and only had to "open his godlike lips to give form to the sunny substance of the world" (GW, 8: 378). This view was completely revised in Mann's later essays in which he emphasized that any literary artist is by definition a careful, attentive, and conscientious worker.[7] Still Mann continued to believe that the naive artist creates with greater ease and struggles less with his subject matter than his opposite. He also suggested in Lotte in Weimar that for the naive genius the beginning of literary creation lies shrouded in darkness and that his inspiration remains rooted in the "fertile soil of the unconscious" (GW, 2: 620), no matter how cautiously and conscientiously he may work.[8] In contrast, the reflective-analytic artist examines experiences simultaneously with their occurrence. A psychological process ensues in which every observation is analyzed with respect

6. Mann's dialectic neither prevented him from recognizing reality nor misled him into the fiction that these artists are exponents of a mutually exclusive antithesis. See the statement in "Über Fiorenza" (1912), GW, 11: 564.

7. See especially "Rede über Lessing" (1929), GW, 9: 232ff.; "Die geistige Situation des Schriftstellers in unserer Zeit" (1930), GW, 10: 302–3; and "Goethe's Laufbahn als Schriftsteller" (1932), GW, 9: 334.

8. Mann obviously makes use of Goethe's and Schiller's views. See Schiller's letters to Goethe, July 26, 1800, and March 27, 1801, as well as Goethe's reply of April 3, 1801, in Der Briefwechsel zwischen Schiller und Goethe, ed. Paul Stapf (Berlin: Tempel, 1960), pp. 685, 725–29; also Schiller's letters to Gottfried Körner, December 1, 1788, and May 25, 1792, in Schillers Briefe: Kritische Gesamtausgabe, 7 vols., ed. Fritz Jonas (Stuttgart: Deutsche Verlags-anstalt, 1892–1896), 2: 164–68; 3: 202–3.

to its literary possibilities. Seeing is converted into cognition, which upon further reflection becomes the basis for artistic production (*GW*, 10: 66).

The reflective-analytic artist, convinced that it is never the subject matter but its structuring that leads to superior work, regards the immediacy of feeling as well as inspiration as an insufficient basis for artistic production.[9] He is deeply suspicious of those authors who are unable to reduce their personal involvement to a minimum or refrain from subjective sentiments, because authors who create while overpowered by emotions tend to neglect the form of their works. All those artists in Mann's fiction who exhibit characteristics of the reflective-analytic artist have learned to "put their emotions on ice." Tonio Kröger, for instance, realized early in his career that personal identification with emotions had a negative effect on his works. He reached the conclusion that an artist had to be cool, detached, uncommitted, even "nonhuman" and "inhuman" in order to portray life "tastefully and effectively" (*GW*, 8: 295–96). Gustav von Aschenbach, too, learned in his youth to reflect coolly on emotional experiences in order to gain the necessary distance which guaranteed the high quality of his works (*GW*, 8: 449). But while all of these artists delight in their ability to gain distance, since it enables them to work with utmost precision, they are burdened by it as human beings. They suffer from the conflict between their artistic temperament and the human desire to experience "simple, heartfelt" emotions (*GW*, 8: 267).

This imposed intellectual self-consciousness presents a number of dangers to the reflective-analytic artist. First, his attitude toward the world could be dominated by the question: Is an event useful for literary production?[10] Of necessity, human relationships become difficult. Second, since he is preoccupied with observations in real life, his emotions tend to be confined to the creative process when he intensively relives experiences he ascribes to his fictional characters (*GW*, 11: 17). His life is dominated by adventures of the mind. Indeed, his rigorous self-discipline could reach the extreme of suppressing all instincts. Obviously such an artist is far removed from achieving a dynamic balance between senses and intellect and courts disaster, even if he strives to succeed as heroically as did Gustav von Aschenbach in *Der Tod in Venedig* (1912).

On one level of this novella Mann explores thoroughly a reflective-analytic artist's psychological reaction to the stimulus of beauty. Characteristically, Aschenbach's works appeal through their ideational content as well as their high formal perfection (*GW*, 8: 453–55). Aschenbach has achieved maximum distance from emotions. He also has had to deny himself all pleasure and sensuous enjoyment because his work demands persistent dedication and incessant reflection. Weakened by his struggle during the creative process, he labors under nervous strain and is at the point of physical exhaustion when the senses take their revenge. After experiencing a dream of untamed nature, he encounters a sensuous beauty that casts its spell over him. As the novella unfolds, we witness a gradual decrease of his ability to retain distance and a corresponding lessening of his freedom of reflection. Upon meeting Tadzio, whose appeal lies in his "plastic" beauty, a quality reaffirmed throughout the novella, Aschenbach tries at first to maintain

---

9. See *BeU*, p. 538; *GW*, 8: 295; *GW*, 10: 15–17; and Mann's letter to Hans Brandenburg, December 3, 1906, in *Briefe*, pp. 68–69.

10. See "Bilse und Ich" (1906), *GW*, 10: 20.

maximum distance as artist and spectator, both internally and externally. He rationalizes his desires by projecting them to the level of mythology. Furthermore, reminded of the "finest statues of Greek gods," he attributes to Tadzio the qualities of abstract beauty (*das Schöne*). This encounter of sensuous-plastic beauty inspires him to write a little masterpiece, "a page and a half of polished prose," which adds a new dimension to his work by conveying the immediacy of his experience (*GW*, 8: 492–93). But the creative act completely exhausts him. He abandons all work and assumes the role of an observer. Aschenbach finally attempts to overcome even the physical distance between himself and Tadzio. Intoxication overpowers Aschenbach; he surrenders his critical intellect to passion. His will to endure, his dignity and, above all, his morality (*GW*, 8: 500) disintegrate simultaneously with the loss of distance. He dies unaware that his one-sidedness, namely his exclusive preoccupation first with form and later with exotic experience, has led to his complete destruction.

A third risk for the reflective-analytic artist is the possibility that maximum distance will become a mental state that determines his attitude toward the world and toward his subject matter.[11] He creates works with icy precision and the rigid consequence of a mathematical problem. But though such works are superior in form, they may no longer convey any affection for man, a possibility that is descriptive of Adrian Leverkühn's production.[12] The life and works of Mann's hero in *Doktor Faustus* (1947) mirror in an intensified form all the dangers that Mann foresaw for the reflective-analytic artist.[13] Leverkühn's iciness, the core of his artistic temperament, has irremediably separated him from the sphere of normal life. He does not lack feelings entirely, but instinctively shies away from them. Characteristically, he dislikes physical contact with persons and tends to avoid the familiar form of address. His various attempts to enter into warm human relationships end in disaster. Perhaps they must, because they are no longer a necessity, but only halfhearted efforts to break out of a realm of isolation and frozen landscapes, "eine Welt der Erstarrung, der Öde und des Geistes."

---

11. Detlef in the novella "The Hungry" (1903) observes that artists spend their "brooding days in icy regions far removed from the world" and "spread a cold breath of invincible alienation" (*GW*, 8: 265).

12. That Mann considered a love for mankind an essential prerequisite for truly great artists is evidenced by statements in his essays, his Schiller portrait, and by the manner in which he resolves the novella *Tonio Kröger* (1903). Only the conscious acceptance of a love for humanity that resembles the *caritas* of 1 Cor. 13 will make a "poet out of the reflective-analytic artist" (*GW*, 8: 338). See also *GW*, 8: 270; *BeU*, p. 212; "Anna Karenina" (1940), *GW*, 9: 639; and Thomas Mann-Karl Kerényi, *Gespräch in Briefen* (Zurich: Rhein-Verlag, 1960), p. 146.

13. Mann himself observed in a letter to de Buisonjé that Leverkühn does not represent the artist in general but a specific type threatened by sterility in a time of a general cultural crisis. See J. C. de Buisonjé, "Bemerkungen über Thomas Manns Werk," *Neophilologus* 41 (1947): 192. It is noteworthy that Leverkühn prefers the inner world of intellect and visions to the outer world of senses. He claims to have no desire to see or experience anything in the world and displays no interest in the formative arts. Although parallels between Adrian's problems and recent developments in art suggest themselves, critics who identify the destiny of art with his fate mislead our understanding of modern art. See especially Erich Kahler, "Säkularisierung des Teufels: Thomas Manns Faust," *Neue Rundschau* 58 (1948): 185–202; André von Gronicka, "Thomas Mann's *Doktor Faustus:* Prologomena to an Interpretation," *Germanic Review* 23 (1948): 206–18; and William D. Williams, "Thomas Mann's *Dr. Faustus,*" *German Life & Letters* 12 (1959): 273–81.

Leverkühn's cold attitude is not confined to his relations with people but is also present during the creative process when he alternates between chilly contemplation of his subject matter and feverish seething while he creates (*GW*, 6: 332). This oscillation between extremes is intensified to the highest degree by his disease.[14] Indeed, disease becomes the major factor that activates his innate potentiality, stimulates his creative power, and enhances the alternating feelings of triumph and despair. It is noteworthy that in contrast to the visionary artists who had been prompted by disease to a greater warmth toward mankind (*GW*, 9: 77, 80) Adrian's condition prevents him from expressing such emotion. To be sure, he too has a vision: to "break through" to a new art that is no longer isolated from the rest of the world but once again conveys meaning and plays a vital, almost religious role in society. He makes three attempts to realize his dream, but his task is enormously complicated, perhaps even doomed beforehand, since his method of achieving it is predestined by his extremely analytic disposition. His consciousness has become his fiercest antagonist. Thoroughly acquainted with all previous artistic themes and forms, he finds himself in the desperate situation of either refraining from certain compositions altogether or parodying already existing works thematically, structurally, or stylistically (*GW*, 6: 318–19).

Leverkühn first experiments with parody. But though his compositions are masterpieces of rigorous, logical, and technical precision, he is dissatisfied, since they reflect "aristocratic nihilism." He also concludes that both forms and themes have served their purpose and can no longer be used legitimately. Leverkühn first questions and then rejects aesthetic theories that hold that art constitutes a realm of illusion and play (*GW*, 6: 321ff.). Yet, though he feels that human anguish has become so intense that only its direct and naked expression seems permissible, he rejects the idea that art must become social criticism. What he desires is a breakthrough to a new, daring form of expression, one still objective in form but rooted in a true experience of his age. Since the spirit of Adrian's age is characterized by a rejection of humanistic values coupled with a return to primitivism, the Devil, symbolizing these tendencies, becomes his patron and inspires new compositions that combine striking aesthetic forms and a decided preference for atavistic content. Again these compositions do not measure up to Adrian's almost mystic vision of an art that casts off its self-imposed yoke of isolation and communicates with man, an art neither secular nor religious but on familiar terms with mankind: *"mit der Menschheit auf du und du"* (*GW*, 6: 429). In his final attempt to solve the crisis in art, Adrian succeeds in blending the most rigorous construction with true expression; but expression is confined to sorrow, the only emotion experienced by him (*GW*, 6: 643–47). "Dr. Fausti Weheklag" does not fulfill his vision of an ideal relationship between art and humanity; for the cantata, a revocation of the Good, the True, and Beethoven's Ninth Symphony, no longer affirms *human* values (*GW*, 6: 634). Leverkühn's collapse into insanity demonstrates the destructive tendencies inherent in the existence of a completely autonomous but isolated artist, who thirsts for release from a threatened sterility at any price. Yet Leverkühn too, who sacrifices himself

14. Mann mentions an identical experience during the creative process in a letter to his brother Heinrich on February 13, 1901, in *Briefe*, p. 26.

in his art, is enveloped by Mann in an aura of "saintliness," even assuming the features of Christ at the end of the novel. His "saintliness" is that of a damned ascetic and is reminiscent of the Russian conception of a saint, glorified because he suffered himself, not necessarily because he offered his life in the service of mankind.

Within Mann's overall representation of the reflective-analytic artist, Adrian Leverkühn must be considered a prominent but negative projection, while the portrait of Friedrich Schiller reflects the positive incarnation. In *Schwere Stunde* Schiller had been portrayed as an artist who, faced with a mission that could be accomplished only at the expense of his failing health, heroically pitted his will against weakness and disease and succeeded in conquering the ever-resisting subject matter. Schiller's greatness is brought into even sharper focus in the seventh chapter of *Lotte in Weimar*, when his personality is conjured up by Goethe.[15] From the moment when Goethe first recalls his lost friend he reacts ambivalently, wavering constantly between yes and no, admiration and antipathy, intimacy and strangeness. Surrounded by receptive but limited "friends," Goethe longs for "that other one," whose ability was equal to his; who admired with doubt, was critical yet understanding; who encouraged him, spurred him into action (*GW*, 2: 619); who was the only qualified judge of his work, and the only one who was able to comprehend the deep significance of *Faust* and the *Farbenlehre* (*GW*, 2: 622–23, 629). Indeed, Goethe seems convinced that had he died before Schiller, his friend could have completed *Faust* (*GW*, 2: 619). When Goethe contemplates this possibility, Schiller's figure suddenly looms in threatening proportions as his great antagonist. Narcissism and egotism overwhelm Goethe: "Good God! One should have made provisions in the testament preventing it!" These emotions were perhaps responsible for his "dismal failure" when he attempted to complete *Demetrius* (*GW*, 2: 619). By contrasting defeat and possible success, Mann again raises the question whether the reflective artist is superior to his opposite, a question to which Mann gives no final answer. What remains are doubts, possibilities, and hints, such as that the suffering reflective-analytic artist, pressed for time, a slave to his work, would have succeeded through sheer persistence where the naive-plastic artist failed because he was easygoing and waited for things to mature, fully aware that Mother Nature had allotted to him a long and productive life (*GW*, 2: 622, 629).

Yet, Goethe cannot avoid admiring Schiller's enormous productivity, his idealism, his ceaseless efforts to raise man from his wretched earthbound existence to a more spiritual level, and his willingness to lift up even the mediocre with "the arms of the Savior." And Goethe can never forget his eyes, those "intense blue, gentle and bold eyes of the Redeemer" (*GW*, 2: 620). Thus Mann draws for the first time a parallel between the Savior and Schiller, forging a link between the reflective-analytic artist's existence and the life of Christ. Mann further develops his comparison by alluding to Goethe's planned "Reformation Cantata" and hints that Goethe himself thought of Schiller

15. Schiller's picture, as it emerges from Goethe's stream of consciousness, has a specific literary function: by comparing himself to an equally great artist, Goethe becomes aware of his own eminence, his mode of existence, and his literary principles. It also enables Mann to show the strength as well as the human frailty of both the reflective-analytic and naive-plastic artist.

in these terms.[16] But at the very moment when Mann's fictional Goethe sees Schiller in this glorified light, he hesitates. Vacillating between love and hate, affirmation of Schiller's greatness and aversion to his physical shortcomings, admiration for his tolerance and rejection of his concept of freedom as well as the "horribly masculine" alienation from Mother Nature, Goethe expresses in a steadily mounting crescendo his wonder as well as his profound ambivalence in one great vision: Savior and Speculator. This extraordinary if malicious characterization takes cognizance of Schiller's deep concern for man but also of his diplomatic behavior and worldly "speculations" in his attempts to organize publishing ventures (see *GW*, 9: 878–81). Through this representation, Mann actually taints the pictures of both artists: Schiller's glory is dimmed and Goethe appears to us as all too human.

Thomas Mann gives a final affirmation of his archetypal concept of the artist in "Versuch über Schiller." This essay gives a very detailed and objective description of Schiller's life and works, but it goes far beyond a mere commemoration. Indeed, it appears as if its ternary structure of idealization-reality-idealization is determined by Mann's desire to create a living spirit that will continue to inspire his readers. To achieve that purpose Mann, on the one hand, compares Schiller's earthly struggle against huge obstacles and final triumph to the deeds of Hercules (*GW*, 9: 938–40). On the other, he literally resurrects Schiller and draws a parallel between his spiritual message and that of Christ. The stage for this task is set first by a vivid, naturalistic picture of Schiller's burial, drawing attention to the transitory nature of his material substance and, second, through a glowing description of his ascension to eternal life in the hearts of men, a description that bears a striking resemblance to Mathis Grünewald's painting of the risen Christ on the right panel of the Isenheim Altar (*GW*, 9: 872–73). This glorification enables Mann to establish three related tenets. First, Schiller was not only the prototype of the reflective-analytic artist, but "was and is the apotheosis of art" (*GW*, 9: 873). Second, Schiller labored all his life for the formation of purer principles upon which all progress of mankind ultimately depends. His ideal of a harmonious perfection of man is as meaningful for us as it was during Schiller's time (*GW*, 9: 947). Third, Schiller, who not only mastered his own disease but also diagnosed the ills of society, can become the physician for our sick age and cure man from anxiety and hatred. The application is clear: Mann tried to awaken in us the desire to strive for those high ideals to which Schiller adhered throughout his life (*GW*, 9: 951).

In this Schiller portrait Mann reaffirms his belief, first expressed in *Tonio Kröger* (*GW*, 8: 300) that, at his best, the artist could assume a dignified role as healer of man. Despite his deep-seated skepticism toward the artist's nature, reflected in the examination of the many dangers besetting the various artist types and his ironic-critical portrait of artists in his creative works, he emphasizes again that a true artist is not the enemy of life but its friend.[17] Mann's and

---

16. Goethe enclosed a revised draft of the planned cantata in a letter to Karl Friedrich Zelter on December 12, 1816. He also compared Schiller to Christ in a letter to Zelter on November 9, 1830. See J. W. Goethe, *Gedenkausgabe der Werke*, ed. Ernst Beutler (Zurich: Artemis, 1948–1950), 21: 946.

17. See Mann's unequivocal statement to that effect in "Die Aufgabe des Schriftstellers" (1947), *GW*, 10: 782.

Schiller's *yes* to life stands in marked contrast to the pessimism and alienation of other artist-heroes in Mann's work. But even they, as perhaps the "hope beyond hopelessness" in Leverkühn's last work best indicates, transcend their apparent hostility in their creative works. On this archetypal level of the artist who fatally consumes himself but attains a new consciousness in his creations, Mann establishes a definite bond between his fictional artist heroes. He not only relates their temporal reality to the timeless aspects of the artist type; he also suggests that all artists have characteristics that transcend the limitations of their dispositions. It is hardly coincidental that *Lotte in Weimar* also closes with the thought that Goethe has sacrificed himself in his work. Mann's pictures are charged with an ambivalence caused by the incongruity of the all-too-human characteristics of these artists with their magnified symbolic characters. To be sure, the picture of the reflective-analytic type is blamed by that of the naive-plastic artist, but there is no indication that Mann ever obliterated, by assigning indiscriminately conflicting traits to one artist, the careful distinctions he had worked out.

The significance of Mann's typology is threefold: It forms the foundation for many characters in his fiction.[18] It serves him as a useful method in his studies on Fontane, Lessing, Goethe, Schiller, Tolstoy, and Dostoevski. It is a conscious attempt to formulate a myth of the artist at a time when religious myths seem to have lost their place in society. Mann's lifelong preoccupation with this myth is significant not only for an understanding of his own work but also for the much wider context of modern literature in its attempts to assert a complete autonomy for the artist as well as its intense interest in his personality.

---

18. On September 5, 1920, he wrote, for instance, to Julius Bab: "The literary activist appears personally in *Der Zauberberg*" (*Briefe,* p. 183).

The Real and Fictive Quest of Henry James

MOTLEY F. DEAKIN
University of Florida

COMMENT BY THE AUTHOR

Characteristic of James's concept of the quest is the movement toward a moment of "portentous intelligent stillness." When this climactic moment of stillness is put into the context of the flow of fictive presentation that James late in his life categorized by the terms picture *and* scene, *it increases the potential for complexity in that presentation. For James,* picture *identified the blocks of narrative and descriptive matter that prepare for and join the scenes, those other blocks of material which are dramatic and climactic in nature.*

That a dramatic scene, in which one would expect dialogue to be the medium of revelation and truth, could be conceived instead to be preparation for its antithesis, silence, seems an anomaly. One would expect that the eye would be the dominant sense in the picture *and the ear in the* scene, *if James's critical terms are to convey conventional meaning. Generally they do. But James delighted in ironies and contrasts, and he exercised his preference for the eye rather than the ear whenever it furthered his purpose. So here, at the climactic moment of the* scene *he moves from verbal to visual revelation.*

It can be noted too that the dialogue in James's later novels is characterized by an increasing degree of indirectness and suggestiveness, so that we are forced to intuit, to discern the reality that verbally is only partially revealed to us. Thus already something more than words is necessary, and the lapses between the characters' statements become charged with meaning. The ultimate toward which

First published: 14, no. 2 (1966): 82–97. Essay has been slightly revised to include the work of recent critics.

179

James seems to lead us is a situation in which his characters would peer into each other's eyes and commune mentally. But such an ultimate, if actually realized, would not suit James's purpose, for it obviates mystery, ambiguity, and any distinction in the characters' perceptive capacities. Better art results from the reliance, as we find it in the quest pattern, on the unique perception of the individual. It is enough that he senses what is truth for him. And isolated as we are in our individuality, we find that individual perception closer to the reality we have experienced.

Like his contemporaries Mark Twain and William Dean Howells, the young Henry James accepted the travel sketch as an important form he must master in his apprenticeship to literature. Although this exercise in describing the sensibilities and experiences of the traveler left its mark on the subsequent fiction of all three writers, its effect on the novels and tales of James is the most pervasive and remarkable, and therefore deserves attention. Because of the scope of this subject, however, only one of its aspects can be discussed here.

James wrote his travel sketches during his late twenties when, wandering over Europe in considerable emotional turmoil, he was trying to establish the sense and direction of his life. Revealing intimately, as they do, the interests and predilections of the young James, these travel sketches evidence his success in gradually mastering a form appropriate for his material. They show him developing a means of expressing through meaningful patterns of experience a clearer sense of the significance and vitality that to him infused these seemingly dilettantish wanderings.

One of these patterns was the quest.[1] The travel sketch lends itself naturally to the concept of the quest because both rely for their sequential order on the passing of the individual through the landscape; they both provide some goal, an actual place as well as a state of mind. The quest intensifies certain attributes of the traveler's experience. His solitude increases. He is waylaid by greater hazards, which in turn tend to test him, his endurance, his dedication. Enjoyment he still may find, but it is minimized by the seriousness of his venture, by his continual necessity to assess difficulties, to make judgments of right and wrong, of good and bad. If he does endure, if he does find his way to his ultimate goal, then his reward is the sight of some specific object or scene, but it is also some vision, some realization, some truth, which may perhaps at the moment

---

1. Long ago Van Wyck Brooks, in *The Pilgrimage of Henry James* (New York: Dutton, 1925), detected a quasi-religious quality in the imagination of Henry James. He saw this quality as part of a general psychological urge forcing James into expatriation and artistic disintegration. This quality, however, has also a positive value, for one can see it as actuating a pattern of experience upon which James constructed much of his best work. To identify this pattern one could use Brook's term *pilgrimage,* a term accommodating many of the facts upon which this pattern is constructed, but I hesitate to accept it because *pilgrimage* also implies a foreknowledge, a seeking out of a known reality, that to me seems to run askew from the nature of this pattern of experience as it actually exists in both James's life and his writing. The characteristics of this pattern point, rather, to a searching for an unknown, to a growing awareness, a developing realization on the part of the author and his fictive characters. Therefore, to me an identification that seems more precise is the related religious term *quest.*

seem obscure but still radiates to him who sees it a sense of its power and significance.

Translated into the terms of the travel sketch, this correspondence means that James as a young tourist in Europe traveled much by himself and complained in letters home how for months he had talked to no one but waiters and chambermaids, or related in his travel sketches how in Rome during Carnival he deliberately left crowds on the Corso to pursue his solitary way among the outlying shrines of the city, or described how he could find a special charm in old gardens when

> a racier spectacle in the streets has made your fellow-loungers few, and you have nothing about you but deep stillness and shady vistas, that lead you wonder where, and the old quaint mixture of nature and art—under these conditions the sweetness of the place becomes strangely suggestive.[2]

This equation of religious and aesthetic motivations means that it was not enough for James to enjoy the vivid canal life of Venice or the color and pageantry of Rome playing host to the Ecumenical Council of 1869, but he must also test, evaluate, discriminate, exercise his sensibilities, strain them to the breaking point on those sights sanctified by the high priests of dedicated travelers: Murray, Baedeker, and Ruskin. It means that he was already a serious, dedicated young artist intent on making the most of this trial of his aesthetic and literary qualifications; so at first he labored over his letters home because he knew that they would be read and passed on to discriminating readers of the older generation, readers of importance like Ralph Waldo Emerson and George Curtis, who, if they approved, could help open to him the sacred portals of publication, an achievement that in turn could give him the wherewithal to sustain the pitch and tempo of this initiation. But most important, it means that the pattern of his life was a quest for climactic moments, certainly more frequent and easily obtained than those of the religious zealot, yet still moments significant enough to make the questing tourist, standing before the object of his search, show the emotion he felt by a *frisson* of sensibility, by tears welling into his eyes, by a sinking into a meditative trance—all of these reactions offering evidence that he sought to attune his emotion to the uniqueness of the moment through empathy and surrender of self.

James found these moments by contemplating two general kinds of objects: (1) the prospect or vista of the expansive landscape and (2) the artificially enclosed and framed figure in the shrine. The term *landscape* here is intended to be inclusive, meaning a view seen from a perspective and encompassing relatively great distances. It includes views of the city as well as the country or even the view within a large building. The term *figure in the shrine* is intended to mean a relatively small, solitary object set off by its frame, its surroundings. It can be a picture, a statue, or any artistic object approached with the proper interest. It can also be a living person as long as a setting is there to enhance his appearance and significance, though for James as tourist it generally meant a treasured object of artistic value.

Both kinds of objects had long been revered interests of the traveler. The

---

2. Henry James, Jr., *Transatlantic Sketches* (Boston: Houghton, 1888), p. 312. Subsequent quotations from *Transatlantic Sketches* will be cited as *TS* at the end of each quotation.

landscape was the special preserve of the lover of the picturesque, with his concepts of what was striking and pictorial in nature, a preserve in which many different artists had found delight. As a literary subject the landscape had behind it the traditions of the pastoral and the prospect poem, of the descriptions embroidered into popular fiction, and of the travel sketch itself. Sought out as it was by the Romantics, the landscape had hereby attracted to itself a set of doctrinal precepts and a literature.[3] Its general acceptance in the nineteenth century made it of necessity one important test of James's sensibilities. The other test, the figure, the object, had attracted its share of tourists. However, though always an interest of men of letters, it had not achieved an equivalent transfer into a specific literary mode or format, at least not since the demise of the intricate devices of classical rhetoric. Still, it required literary definition and response, particularly when it was of artistic value, as arbiters of taste like John Ruskin and Charles Eliot Norton had insisted. Its importance to James, the aesthetic neophyte, was conditioned by the way in which the generation of his father, attuned to the significance of seeing and intent on rediscovering "our old home" on their own terms, were peculiarly receptive to an act of visual veneration before those works of art which epitomized to them the achievement of Europe.

Turning to James's travel sketches for illustrations, we find that he seldom presented the object of his search without describing as prelude his journey to it.

> To walk in quest of any object that one has more or less tenderly dreamed of, to find your way, to steal upon it softly, to see at last if it is church or castle, the tower-tops peeping above elms or beeches—to push forward with a rush and emerge, and pause, and draw that first long breath which is the compromise between so many sensations—this is a pleasure left to the tourist even after the broad glare of photography has dissipated so many of the sweet mysteries of travel. (*TS,* p. 25)

This search frequently left the highroad to pass through lanes and crooked byways, down streets "narrow and dusky and filled with misty shadows" (*TS,* p. 310), through gates and turnstiles half hidden in the mass of architecture or obscured by old shrubbery, past custodians and beggars reaching out as if to thwart his passing, up flights of stairs and through mazes of rooms, until finally beyond the last parapet, around the last corner or through the last door, hidden behind the last screen or leather curtain, appeared the long-sought object.

If the landscape was James's goal, he liked it best when it broke from the Romantic predilection for wild, precipitate, Alpine scenery to become instead the

---

3. Precepts distinguishing the landscape are embodied in the concept of the picturesque as promulgated by William Gilpin, Uvedale Price, Richard Payne Knight, and Dugald Stewart. The best modern studies of this subject are Christopher Hussey, *The Picturesque* (New York: G.P. Putnam's Sons, 1927), and W. J. Hipple, *The Beautiful, the Sublime, and the Picturesque in Eighteenth-Century British Aesthetic Theory* (Carbondale, Ill.: Southern Illinois University Press, 1957). The influence of landscape in English literature can be traced from the pastoral and prospect poetry of the seventeenth and eighteenth centuries through Romantic nature poetry and the Gothic novel into all kinds of nineteenth-century literature. In the United States the influence of the picturesque was just as pervasive, beginning with the generation of James's father and continuing into the generation of James himself.

soft, feminine lines of the countryside near Rome, a scene long since immortalized in the classic art of Claude Lorrain.

> The country rolled away around me into slopes and dells of enchanting contour, checkered with purple and blue and blooming brown. The lights and shadows were at play on the Sabine Mountains—an alternation of tones so exquisite that you can indicate them only by some fantastic comparison to sapphire and amber. In the foreground a contadino, in his cloak and peaked hat, was jogging solitary on his ass; and here and there in the distance, among blue undulations, some white village some gray tower, helped deliciously to make the scene the typical "Italian landscape" of old-fashioned art. (*TS*, pp. 136–37)

But James was not satisfied just to describe; he must also explain why this scene appealed to him.

> It was so bright and yet so sad, so still and yet so charged, to the supersensuous ear, with the murmur of an extinguished life, that you could only say it was intensely and deliciously strange, and that the Roman Campagna is the most suggestive place in the world. (*TS*, p. 137)

James could admire such a landscape for just its artistic qualities of line and color, but he preferred to add some associative human element. He sought the vista that retained evidence that it had been lived in, that it carried the burden of man's travail and history. So usually at the center of James's landscapes was an old ruin or an ancient hilltop village, a church, a castle or country manor, or even a human figure interesting to the eye, as we find him in the quotation above; each of these objects is picturesque both in its immediate visual effect and as a record of historic pageantry.

If James sought the art object—the picture, the statue, the figure in the shrine—he came not to the hilltop or the rampart that left him open to the expansiveness of earth and sky, but, rather, threaded his way through the narrower approaches, the corridors, the vistas of rooms that led to the sanctuary contrived by human means to set off properly the venerated treasure. Here he did not struggle for elevation, as he had when he wished to see the landscape; he tried instead to penetrate to a remote, secluded sanctuary. James's travel sketches are scattered with the record of his "finds," some of them, of course, well known, like Michelangelo's *Moses* and Raphael's *Madonna of the Chair,* but more often they exemplify his own preferences, the paintings of Tintoretto and the other Venetian masters of the Grand Style, or the Pre-Raphaelites, who were perhaps less appealing, but still attracted him by their pinched and pale angularity, radiating adoration and meek renunciation. James was a conscientious searcher, and when in a nook of an out-of-the-way church or an obscure corner of a neglected gallery he found a forgotten masterpiece, his pleasure increased, as it did, for example, in a Florentine gallery where he discovered "lurking obscurely in one of the smaller rooms, a most enchanting Sandro Botticelli. . . . Placed as it is, I doubt whether it is noticed by half a dozen persons a year . . ." (*TS*, p. 276). The difficulty of the search added zest to the ultimate success and reflected glory upon the seeker thus set apart by his dedication. For James, though, the important element in any of this art, as it was in the landscape, was its ability to carry him into new realms of suggestive thought and to convey a sense of richness in life, The more emphatic the surge of felt experience, the greater the art.

James could achieve this end by looking at people as well as statues and pictures. While he was in Italy, the vivid life about him presented elements that were artistic and memorable. Soldiers in their bright uniforms, ecclesiasts in their black and scarlet dress, street urchins in rags, visitants to churches, women leaning from windows—all fascinated him and became material for his travel sketches. One of these impressions, the most memorable, occurred in Rome when "by the best of traveller's luck" he saw the Pope pass by in the street, "sitting deep in the shadow of his great chariot with uplifted fingers, like some inaccessible idol in his shrine" (*TS*, p. 112). Though it is life that James sees, his imagination changes it into art; the Pope is transmuted into an idol. This impression so hastily received illustrates how closely James indentified life with the aesthetic experience and how he could infuse a momentary experience with a sense of mystery and awe as well as artistic significance. This glimpse of the Pope, this most apt example of the figure in the shrine, returns significantly to reverberate again and again in the imagery of James's later work.[4]

In this way the quest is realized in the experiences of James as tourist, becoming for him a personal mode of existence with its own pattern and system of values. The effect of these experiences is soon apparent in the short stories written concurrently with the travel sketches. The most obvious evidence is the material James transferred from his letters and travel sketches to his stories.[5] Tales like "At Isella" and "Travelling Companions" are travel sketches strung on thin plot lines, combining the American tourists' pursuit of their aesthetic quests with their misadventures as they confronted unfamiliar and misunderstood social customs.

In an early example of greater interest, "A Passionate Pilgrim," James describes a young American, Clement Searle, who makes his way back to his ancestral home in England, where he comes face to face with all that he had missed in life, and then dies. His journey to Lockley Park, the home of his ancestors, is conceived as a quest ending with his penetration into an inner sanctuary. The climax of the quest begins as Searle and his companion enter the estate through a lodge-gate, pass down a long, winding avenue, go through another gate into the park, then through another gate into the gardens that border the house. Finally arriving at the front door, they are given permission to inspect the

---

4. James first records this experience of seeing the Pope in a letter written to his parents that same evening: Henry James, *The Letters of Henry James*, ed. Percy Lubbock (New York: C. Scribner's Sons, 1920), 1: 24–25. He retold the experience in the passage quoted above from *Transatlantic Sketches* and repeated it with much more color and detail late in his life in *William Wetmore Story and His Friends* (New York: Grove Press, 1903), 1: 109. A fictional example of the carriage's use as a frame for the figure seated in it can be found in *The American* (New York: Houghton Mifflin, 1907), p. 515.

5. To cite two examples: the details of an excursion to Worcester, which James described in a letter dated March 18, 1870 (*The Letters of Henry James*, 1: 28), he used almost verbatim in his story "A Passionate Pilgrim"; his description of the view from the top of Milan Cathedral that he presented in *Transatlantic Sketches* (pp. 80–81) he rephrased for an episode in the story "Travelling Companions."

house. As they are shown the old mansion they pass through many apartments until, at the end of their search, they arrive at "the last room of the suite, a small, unused boudoir over the chimney piece of which hung a noble portrait of a young man in a powdered wig and a brocaded waistcoat."[6] The subject of the portrait, who resembles Clement Searle in appearance, is his great uncle, bearing the same name. The story of this ancestor, who perished at sea, supports and counterpoints the story of Clement Searle. The ghost of the sweetheart he left behind haunts the house, just as Miss Searle, the sister of the present owner whom Clement Searle meets for the first time under the eyes of this portrait, will fall in love with the living Clement and mourn him after his death.

The motifs of the quest and the figure in the shrine persist in other short stories of this period. In "The Last of the Valerii" the count places the exhumed statue of Juno in the deserted Casino, an imitation of a pagan temple, and then makes sacrifices to it. In "Eugene Pickering" Madame Blumenthal sits enthroned in her box at the opera as two men observing her reveal her history. And in "The Madonna of the Future" the narrator must first be escorted to see the artist's venerated model secreted away at the top of an old house in the heart of Florence before he realizes that the artist's dream of painting his madonna is only a delusion.

Turning to the early novels written almost concurrently with the travel sketches, we find that *Roderick Hudson,* read in one way, is only a series of sightseeing junkets to landmarks James had already presented in his travel sketches. This novel, though, has a more emphatic bias, because in it James tends to conceive of the quest as the pursuit primarily of the landscape. At the beginning of the novel, Roderick Hudson, the gifted young sculptor, is first offered an opportunity to study in Rome, the mecca of artists, as he and his benefactor, Rowland Mallet, lie on a "grassy elevation studded with mossy rocks and red cedars" where "just beneath them, in a great shining curve, flowed the generous Connecticut."[7] In this setting, an appropriate subject for the painters of the Hudson River School, a promise is made. Later in Rome Roderick's studio faced on a "mouldy little court of which the fourth side was formed by a narrow terrace overhanging the Tiber. . . . [A]t a distance, were the bare brown banks of the stream, the huge rotunda of Saint Angelo, tipped with its seraphic statue, a dome of Saint Peter's . . ." (*RH,* p. 97). This scene offers a promise of future greatness, associating Roderick, as it does, with great artists. Roderick enjoyed exploring Rome, particularly the gardens and ancient monuments. He would climb the upper portions of the Coliseum in order to see the views that "were as fine as he had supposed; the lights on the Sabine mountains had never so seemed the very blurs of the scroll of history" (*RH,* p. 258). These same mountains appeared "iridescent" to Roderick and his friends as, at the Villa Mondragone, "they strolled, in the

---

6. Henry James, Jr., *A Passionate Pilgrim and Other Tales* (Boston: Houghton, Mifflin, 1917), p. 50. This same quest for the portrait is repeated in the late novel, *The Sense of the Past.* Whereas in "A Passionate Pilgrim" only a similarity of character and portrait is established, in *The Sense of the Past* an actual transposition of character and portrait takes place.

7. Henry James, *Roderick Hudson,* in *The Novels and Tales of Henry James* (New York: C. Scribner's Sons, 1907), p. 31. Subsequent quotations from the novels of James—*Roderick Hudson, The American,* and *The Wings of the Dove*—will be cited in abbreviated form at the end of each quotation.

winter sunshine, on the great terrace which looks toward Tivoli" (*RH,* p. 228). By their nature these landscapes seem to Roderick to complement the great primal forces he tries to embody in his statues. Later, when genius and love forsake him, Roderick tries to reconcile himself to his loss by walking in the countryside about Florence, sometimes seeking out an old "Franciscan convent poised on the very apex of the great hill," where he can contemplate the Arno Valley from a "delightfully steep and tangled old garden" that "hangs in the air, and you ramble from terrace to terrace and wonder how it keeps from slipping down in full consummation of its dishonour and decay, to the nakedly romantic gorge beneath" (*RH,* pp. 315–16). As the novel progresses, Roderick moves to more and more exalted mountain scenery, from the Roman Campagna to the Val d'Arno and finally, at the end of the novel, to the Swiss Alps where he "went in for long rambles, generally alone, and was very fond of climbing into dizzy places where no sound could overtake him and there, stretched at his length on the never-trodden moss, of pulling his hat over his eyes and lounging away the hours in perfect immobility" (*RH,* p. 472). He dies appropriately by falling from a high cliff during a storm.

Two reasons can be postulated for James's choosing the landscape vista as the main setting in this novel. Recalling the New Testament presentation of Satan tempting Christ from the mountaintop, James could appropriately accept the view of the landscape as a symbolization of unwarranted hopes and false expectations. The landscape entices Roderick Hudson. It is a semblance of that world which offers him success and glory in his art; it passes before him like the vision of Christina Light, the woman he loves; but when he reaches for success or love, they become only a void and a darkness. The second reason for the use of the landscape is that James conceived this novel under the aegis of Byronism. The imperatives actuating the character of Roderick are genius and passion, imperatives that are portrayed as powerful, instinctual forces that Roderick senses but cannot control. His impulses drive him to reach out for the aura of freedom and escape found in these settings. Like Manfred's, his egoism impels him to seek these solitary elevations that complement his sense of his own psychological loneliness and exaltation.

In his second important novel, *The American,* James neglected the landscape in favor of the search for the figure in the shrine. As the story of an American who tries to marry the daughter of an old aristocratic French family, this novel of necessity is a study of Christopher Newman's attempt to penetrate into that family. The penetration is, in part, Newman's effort to understand the Bellegardes and secure their good will, but in just as large measure it is Newman's actual physical penetration into the milieu of this family whose very name signifies their opposition to his attempt. The Bellegardes live in the Rue de l'Université, one of "those grey and silent streets of the Faubourg Saint Germain whose houses present to the outer world a face as impassive and as suggestive of the concentration of privacy within as the blank walls of Eastern seraglios" (*TA,* p. 59). Their *hôtel* is characterized as "stoutly guarded" (*TA,* p. 113), as vast, dim, cold, ancient, ornamented with "elaborate and ponderous mouldings" (*TA,* p. 181) and "long-faded gilding" (*TA,* p. 164), and hung with carefully mended tapestries. It is a house of unexpected turnings, of panels that appear to be doors, of mysterious corners and secreted chambers. Newman's task is to penetrate into this hostile environment; his obligation is to understand finally the significance of Valentin de Bellegarde's confession:

> My mother's strange, my brother's strange, and I verily believe I'm stranger than either. You'll even find my sister a little strange. Old trees have crooked branches, old houses have queer cracks, old races have odd secrets. (*TA,* p. 162)

Newman finally does penetrate to the Bellegarde's secret—a cold, vicious murder. This secret is, in one sense, the figure in the shrine, objectified as it is for Christopher as a piece of yellowed paper long hidden from view. In another sense, however, the figure Newman finally discerns is the nature of a closed society. For Newman this discovery entails frustration because it leads him, who otherwise "looks straight over ever so many high walls" (*TA,* p. 137), figuratively to a blank wall constructed not so much by the Bellegardes as by their source of social acceptance, the Duchess d'Outreville, who appears to Newman as "a very fair likeness to a revered effigy in some idolatrous shrine" (*TA,* p. 319).

In its final sense, though, the figure in the shrine is Claire de Cintré herself, her fine, pale slenderness set off by her white costumes, Claire who in her final desperation muffles her beauty in "ascetic rags" (*TA,* p. 419) and entombs herself in the Carmelite nunnery. After he had lost her, Newman

> mused a great deal on Madame de Cintré—sometimes with a dull despair that might have seemed a near neighbour to detachment. He lived over again the happiest hours he had known—that silver chain of numbered days in which his afternoon visits, strained so sensibly to the ideal end, had come to figure for him a flight of firm marble steps where the ascent from one to the other was a momentous and distinct occasion, giving a nearer view of the chamber of confidence at the top, a white tower that flushed more and more as with a light of dawn. (*TA,* p. 524)

Instead, at the end of the novel he is left staring from outside her refuge at the "dull, plain edifice with a blank, high-shouldered defence all round. . . . The pale, dead, discoloured wall stretched beneath it far down the empty side street—a vista without a human figure" (*TA,* p. 532). Despairingly, he concluded: "I measured the wall. I looked at it a long time. But it's too high—it's beyond me" (*TA,* p. 536).

James's use in this novel of the quest for the figure in the shrine developed naturally from the exigencies of his story. Its conclusion, however, seems oddly askew from the natural potentialities inherent in the figure-in-the-shrine motif. Newman obtains a glimpse of the figure only to have it snatched from him. Whatever Newman learns from his experience comes primarily from the figure's alienness or inaccessibility. But then enshrined figures are to be seen, not touched, or at least James understood this to be so, and the result is an illustration of a favorite Jamesian theme, renunciation. If we seek for an analogy in the travel sketches, we find there that James as a tourist relied only on observation, not acquisition. He looked at pictures; he did not buy them. So it was enough if one understood what he saw; he did not need to possess it.

The quest persists in varied forms in later novels. The structure of *Portrait of a Lady* develops logically from the two crucial prospect scenes, the first introducing Gardencourt and the Touchett family in England, the second presenting the Florentine villa of Gilbert Osmond in Italy. The values that Isabel Archer discovers are meaningful at Gardencourt betray her into a false estimate of the values commensurate to what appears to be the equally beautiful world of Gilbert Osmond. Without Isabel's first acquiescence, her second would have been impossible. *The Princess Casamassima* is constructed on the opposing moral commitments of Hyacinth Robinson, the first to the anarchists, made hastily in the warmth of social rapport; the second to the past and its heritage of beauty, accepted only after a slow, painful quest that leads Hyacinth from a theater box to a London mansion, then to Medley, the country estate, and from there to Paris and finally to Venice. In *The Ambassadors* the Lambinet scene, that picture within a picture, sits at the center of the novel's equivocal message, and *The Golden Bowl* has—besides the bowl secreted in a London shop to which most of the characters make their pilgrimage—another central image, the pagoda, to which Maggie Verver is placed in meaningful perspective, first outside, trying to seek an entrance, and then later, in possession inside. To this pattern James adds, as complication, shifting perspectives of depth and height that help him to illustrate Maggie's growing moral ascendancy.

All these examples are useful in illustrating James's use of the quest and its possible conclusions. An example more nearly perfect remains, *The Wings of the Dove*. This novel begins for the heroine, Milly Theale, as she is introduced to Europe high in the Swiss Alps. There, while stopping at a wayside inn, she discovers "a 'view' pure and simple, a view of great extent and beauty, but thrown forward and vertiginous" (*TWOTD*, 1: 123). The point of the scene is soon made clear: "She was looking down on the kingdoms of the earth, and though indeed that of itself might well go to the brain, it wouldn't be with a view of renouncing them" (*TWOTD*, 1:124).[8] Milly's opportunity and her motivation are thus made clear; she has access to the best Europe can offer and she intends to grasp it. The suggestion of danger in the prospect she prefers to ignore, at least for the moment. The remainder of the novel, portraying her quest for acceptance, for health, and for love, leads in each instance to a figure in the shrine that demonstrates with increasing clarity the ironic falseness of the view from the Alpine cliff.

This series of three enshrined figures begins with the Bronzino portrait. Invited to a gathering at Matcham, one of those magnificent English temples to the social graces which James so frequently uses as settings, Milly was told that she must see this portrait whose subject resembles her greatly. Her progress through the house to it was "not of the straightest; it was an advance, without haste, through innumerable natural pauses and soft concussions" (*TWOTD*, 1: 217), for the Bronzino painting was "deep within, and the long afternoon light lingered for them on patches of old colour and waylaid them, as they went, in nooks and opening vistas" (*TWOTD*, 1: 219). When Milly stood before the portrait, "things melted together—the beauty and the history and the facility and the

---

8. In an essay "A Note on the Symbolic Pattern in *The Wings of the Dove*" (*College Language Association Journal* [March 1967], pp. 256–62), published a year after my essay appeared, John Hagan explores more fully than I have done here the use James makes of the vista or prospect in this novel.

splendid midsummer glow" (*TWOTD*, 1: 220), and she found herself "looking at the mysterious portrait through tears" (*TWOTD*, 1: 220). Sensing that this perfect afternoon was a fulfillment of the promise the view in the Swiss Alps had seemed to offer, she tried to express her sense of the moment to her companion, Lord Mark. But instead of a clear acclamation, her remark was cryptic: "I shall never be better than this" (*TWOTD*, 1: 221), a remark capable of including her realization that the subject of the portrait was "dead, dead, dead" (*TWOTD*, 1: 221). There, at the moment of her greatest social achievement, "in the great gilded historic chamber and the presence of the pale personage on the wall, whose eyes all the while seemed engaged with her own" (*TWOTD*, 1: 225), Milly sensed the equivocality of life and something of its import as she puzzled over the intentions of the man she loved, Merton Densher, and the ambiguities of her own health.

The second figure in the shrine is Sir Luke Strett, "the greatest of medical lights" (*TWOTD*, 1: 226), to whom Milly appealed for some certitude, even though the answer may be that "she was in some way doomed" (*TWOTD*, 1: 236). And so she sought him out, in his

commodious "handsome" room, far back in the fine old house, soundless from position, somewhat sallow with years of celebrity, somewhat sombre even at midsummer—the very place put on for her a look of custom and use, squared itself solidly round her as with promises and certainties. She had come forth to see the world, and this then was to be the world's light, the rich dusk of a London "back," these the world's walls, those the world's curtains and carpet. (*TWOTD*, 1: 237)

This doctor's chamber became Milly's "brown old temple of truth" (*TWOTD*, 1: 241), where she learned that her health was uncertain and that to improve it she should seek a more salubrious climate.

She chose Venice, a city where "the pictureque fact has best mastered the pious secret of how to wait for us,"[9] and over all is "the pervasive mystery of Style" (*TWOTD*, 2: 203). She selected as the setting of her waning life the Palazzo Leporelli, holding "its history still in its great lap, even like a painted idol" (*TWOTD*, 2: 135). This palace became her refuge: "The romance for her, yet once more, would be to sit there for ever, through all her time as in a fortress; and the idea became an image of never going down, of remaining aloft in the divine dustless air . . . (*TWOTD*, 2: 147). Here, enclosed in her "great gilded shell" (*TWOTD*, 2: 152), her "temple to taste" (*TWOTD*, 2: 146), she "moved slowly to and fro as a priestess of the worship" (*TWOTD*, 2: 135), until she, Milly Theale, "the heiress of all the ages" (*TWOTD*, 1: 109), "the princess, the angel, the star" (*TWOTD*, 2: 174), gradually was transfigured into the final image in the shrine, secluded in "that glorious great *salone*, in the [wonderful white] dress she always wears, [in] her inveterate corner of her sofa" (*TWOTD*, 2: 328). Her devotees, through whose eyes alone we now see her, must approach her, as one did the Bronzino portrait, through opening vistas: first gliding across the water to the sweeping flight of water-steps, then up the steps to the great high doors that open onto the basement chamber,

9. Henry James, *Italian Hours* (Boston and New York: Houghton, Mifflin, 1909), p. 45.

tall and dim, and dominated by a "trememdous old staircase" (*TWOTD*, 2: 147) that rises to

> high florid rooms, palatial chambers where hard cool pavements took re-
> flections in their lifelong polish, and where the sun on the stirred sea-water,
> flickering up through open windows, played over the painted "subjects" in
> the splendid ceilings. (*TWOTD*, 2: 132)

This is Milly's sanctuary, where everyone is under the "spell of a general, a kind of beatific mildness" (*TWOTD*, 2: 213). Here Milly, as the image in the shrine, activates Merton's final realization that he and Kate would never be as they once were.

Milly Theale's quest leads her from the expansive optimism of Nature seen from the Swiss Alps to the great Babylon of London, teeming, pushing, brilliant and brutal, intensely competitive and vitally alive, and then finally to Venice, the city of art and history, of romance and death, a nostalgic memorial to humanity, a museum. The Alps offered a promise that London half granted, half denied; London offered a truth that Venice fulfilled. As an emotional experience Milly's quest begins with enthusiasm and high hopes, and moves through the fluctuations of disquieting revelation to a final resignation and quiescent benefi-cence. Intellectually her quest begins in the shimmer of deluding expectations and moves to a final calm clarity that has seen human greed and betrayal and then has forgiven them. In this quest landscape and shrine are juxtaposed as opposites of appearance and reality, of falsehood and truth.

As a fictive device the quest works. In part its viability comes from its source in the experience of James. If the Bronzino portrait or the Lambinet landscape, or London or Venice, had not been vital experiences for him, then they would no doubt have deteriorated into clichés in his fiction. But that they become vital fictive experiences also lies, in good part, not only in the experience but in James himself. Given his physical aptitude for visual rather than auditory or kinesthetic impressions, given his sense of a vocation and of devotion to a valuable cause, given his tendency to make the observed fact burgeon with signifi-cance, and given his sense of life as ritual, then these experiences can become components in some such meaningful pattern as the quest.

Perhaps the answer to why James would have accepted the landscape and the figure in the shrine as the ends, the ultimates, of the quest lies in his peculiar transitional position between the Romantics and the Moderns. The landscape that to the Transcendentalists had been a source of truth and moral beneficence no longer appears so to James. As a gesture of obeisance he would still present the landscape, but no longer could he accept its significance as quite that conceived by his forefathers. He goes back, instead, to what in Christian terms is a more conventional interpretation. In contrast, what appears to be his primary interest, the figure in the shrine, anticipates modern tendencies to explore and analyze, to penetrate into the heart of darkness, the heart of the matter, closely allied as that figure is to our interest in mythical symbols and psychological inquiry. This propensity for penetration also correlates with the modern author's more obsessive absorption in himself as well as with his intenser sense of artistic seriousness. James's good fortune let him be born at that moment which not only allowed him to use both past and future interests but also permitted him to participate in a cultural experience, the tour, the mysteries and distinctions of which not only photography but all of modern technology would soon break down, mysteries and distinctions that to James were vital to its significance.

James, then, has made from some of the idiosyncrasies of his personal predilections and his time a pattern energized and fruitful enough to carry forward the weight of the fictive intent assigned to it. It is not a new pattern, certainly, but James has refashioned it of materials different enough to suggest newness and to support conclusions at variance from the expected. Drawn as it is from personal experiences vital to the author but hardly within the purview of more conventional fictional interests, the quest, as James uses it, helps the reader appreciate and accept his evaluation of what is significant in experience: his ideals of dedication, perceptive awareness, and achievement through renunciation. What began as the *jeu d'esprit* and musings of the tourist became a structural pattern that helps give vitality and meaning to the novels built upon it.

Déjà Vu and the Effect of Timelessness in Faulkner's *Absalom, Absalom!*

JOHN HAGAN

State University of New York, Binghamton

COMMENT BY THE AUTHOR

Since the publication of my essay, of course much has been published on Absalom, Absalom! *that has illuminated that novel from a variety of angles, and I have been glad to profit from these insights. I should like to believe, however, that my original conclusions still retain their validity.*

Few readers will come away from Faulkner's *Absalom, Absalom!* without experiencing the hallucinatory intensity of its hold upon the senses and emotions; from beginning to end its medium is the haunting one of dream, nightmare, or vision, wherein we sense, as in reading Proust, that something has been rescued from the vortex of time and lifted into the realm of the timeless and enduring. I am not referring only to the great central episode of Henry's shooting of Bon at the gates, to which all the narrators finally return and which hovers magically over the whole novel—a single moment of permanent moral significance retrieved from a dark and stormy passage of history and raised—fragile, but serene, lucent, and eternal—above the wreckage and dust of human existence. I am referring also to the Sutpen story as a whole, for *Absalom* strives throughout with desperate urgency and exaltation to render the tragic drama of a whole epoch not chronologically as a continuous, causally connected series of events, but all at

First published: 11, no. 2 (1963): 31–52. The essay has been slightly revised for this collection.

once as a single event—a sombre instant, changeless, fathomless, and still, as it might be known to us under the aspect of eternity. Opposed to the impotent stasis of Thomas Sutpen's own career is the luminous stasis, wherein time is suspended and motion frozen, conferred by the visionary author.

This profoundly moving effect is achieved, of course, in several ways. The narrative method, by continually blurring our ordinary temporal distinctions, tends to reduce all "periods" of time to one; all the past becomes mysteriously single and merges with the present. Faulkner also relies heavily upon imagery that points explicitly to conditions of stasis and suspension. But he achieves his effect by constructing elaborate parallels and complexly intertwining motifs and images of other kinds as well. It goes without saying that parallelism and recurrent motif are ubiquitous in modern fiction; but, as their functions in works as different as *A la recherche du temps perdu, Der Tod in Venedig,* and "The Dead" reveal, they can be put to a variety of uses.

To understand a vital way in which Faulkner has used them in *Absalom,* we need first to examine the structure. This may be looked at in more than one way, but whereas most critics have chosen to define it on the basis of narrative frame rather than on that of the Sutpen story itself, a shift of our attention to the latter discloses a clear three-part division that is perhaps the most fundamental one of all. The first of these three divisions covers chapters 1–6 and presents the whole of the Jefferson phase of the saga from start to finish—from Sutpen's arrival in the town in June 1833, through the building of his mansion, his marriage to Ellen Coldfield, the birth of Henry and Judith, the debacle caused by the arrival of Charles Bon, the War years and their terrible aftermath, and the tragic story of the life and death of Bon's son, Charles Etienne. By the end of chapter 6 the once lordly mansion is nothing but a rotting shell, the graves themselves of Sutpen, Ellen, Charles, Charles Etienne, and Judith are falling into ruin, and the only member of the family to have survived (Clytie and Henry having perished in the burning house, as we learn later) is Sutpen's great-grandson, the idiot Negro, Jim Bond. We have witnessed the arc of Sutpen's dynasty both rise and fall—we have witnessed, in short, nearly all of the tragic *effects* of his grandiose design. In chapters 7–8, therefore, Faulkner passes to the three principal *causes* of those effects. Bringing them forward in an order calculated to produce maximum surprise and climax, he tells us in chapter 7 about the genesis and nature of the design itself (pp. 220–38)[1]—the First Cause, so to speak, of the entire story; next he reveals the first of the two crucial facts about Bon that enable us, in retrospect, to make the drama of the first six chapters intelligible, namely, that he was Sutpen's son by his first wife (p. 265); and finally, in chapter 8, he discloses the second crucial fact about Bon, that he was part Negro (p. 355). With this disclosure the whole drama falls at last, with overwhelming effect, into perspective. There remains only chapter 9 to complete the requirements of the form by revealing the hidden existence of the authority (Henry Sutpen) from whom Quentin presumably came to know these two vital facts about Bon (pp. 372–73),[2]

---

1. All page references are to the Modern Library edition (New York: Random House, 1951).
2. On Bon's paternity and race and the source of Quentin's knowledge of these, see my "Fact and Fancy in *Absalom, Absalom!*," College English 24 (December 1962): 215–18; and Cleanth Brooks, *William Faulkner: The Yoknapatawpha Country* (New Haven and London: Yale University Press, 1963), pp. 436–40.

and by rounding off the family tragedy with a dramatization of the deaths of Henry and Clytie, which had taken place in the time between chapters 5 and 6.

This structural pattern (this movement of the narrative from effect to cause, rather than, more conventionally, from cause to effect), combined with an elaborate development of parallels and recurrent imagery, works to produce a deeply moving effect of timeless stasis. As we read the crucial revelations of chapters 7 and 8, we have not only the satisfying intellectual experience of seeing the preceding parts of the novel pulled into coherence, but in a less conscious area of our minds the uncanny sense of somehow having heard or known all these things before; they are both strikingly new and vaguely familiar. In the same way, returning to the first six chapters themselves, we feel in them both a strange reembodiment of what lies dead in the remote fictional past and, at the same time, because this past is not to be described until chapters 7 and 8, a prophecy of what has yet to be revealed.

The impression produced is comparable to that familiar psychological experience known as the illusion of false recognition or *déjà vu,* one of the best descriptions of which has been given by Bergson.

> Some one may be attending to what is going on or taking part in a conversation, when suddenly the conviction will come over him that he has already seen what he is now seeing, heard what he is now hearing, uttered the sentence he is uttering—that he has already been here in this very place in which he now is, in the same circumstances, feeling, perceiving, thinking, and willing the same things, and, in fact, that he is living again, down to the minutest details, some moments of his past life. The illusion is sometimes so complete that at every moment whilst it lasts he thinks he is on the point of predicting what is going to happen; how should he not know it already, since he feels that he is about to have known it? It is by no means rare for the person under this illusion to perceive the external world under a peculiar aspect, as in a dream.[3]

The point is not that this sensation is felt in *Absalom* by any of the characters (as it is felt, for example, by Marcel in *A la recherche du temps perdu* or by Hans Castorp in the chapter entitled "Snow" in *The Magic Mountain*), but that it is one that can be strongly experienced by the reader himself. Because Faulkner has carefully prefigured his crucial revelations in chapters 7 and 8 by developing elaborate parallels and clusters of related motifs and images, the reader experiences the curious sensation of learning truths of which the lineaments are already adumbrated in his consciousness. And this effect, in turn, contributes in an almost unanalyzable way to his sense of the whole drama as a timeless instant, for each detail seems suddenly and inexplicably gathered into, absorbed by, every other one—crystallized into a oneness. "Identity of meaning serves to bind together happenings widely separated in time; it makes them into repetitions of one and the same happening, which thus loses its 'past' character and becomes a perennial possibility." These words written by Fritz Kaufmann about one of the techniques of Thomas Mann[4] may also be applied to *Absalom,* wherein repetitions and correspondences work to produce an uncanny effect of simultaneity.

---

3. "Le Souvenir du présent et la fausse reconnaissance," *Revue Philosophique* (December 1908), pp. 561–62; quoted in Karl A. Menninger, *The Human Mind* (New York: Knopf, 1945), p. 229.

4. *Thomas Mann: The World as Will and Representation* (Boston: Beacon, 1957), p. 263.

I should like to examine a number of these patterns in close detail, restricting the discussion to those which acquire their full relevance only in the light of the disclosures about Sutpen and Bon made in chapters 7 and 8. For convenience the analysis may be divided into three parts, the first considering the relation of certain motifs in the first six chapters to the disclosures made in chapter 7 about Sutpen; the second, the relation of other motifs in these chapters to the disclosures made in chapters 7 and 8 about Charles Bon; and the third, the relation of the story of Charles Etienne Bon in chapter 6 to the disclosures in chapters 7 and 8 about *both* Sutpen and Bon.

I

The aspect of Faulkner's method I have in mind becomes apparent early in chapter 7 when we see for the first time the vision of the ideal life that had burst upon Sutpen during his boyhood on the Tidewater plantation.

> And the man was there who owned all the land and the niggers and apparently the white man who superintended the work, and who lived in the biggest house he [Sutpen] had ever seen and who spent most of the afternoon . . . in a barrel stave hammock between two trees, with his shoes off, and a nigger who wore every day better clothes than he or his father and sisters had ever owned and ever expected to, who did nothing else but fan him and bring him drinks. (Pp. 227–28)

The attentive reader will sense the presence of another image very similar to this hovering in the background and, returning to chapter 6, will discover it in Quentin's reconstruction of Sutpen's behavior in the days of his highest prosperity—

> *the old days, the old dead Sunday afternoons of monotonous peace which they* [Sutpen and Wash Jones] *spent beneath the scuppernong arbor in the back yard, the demon lying in the hammock while Jones squatted against a post, rising from time to time to pour for the demon from the demijohn and the bucket of spring water which he had fetched from the spring more than a mile away then squatting again, chortling and chuckling and saying "Sho, Mister Tawm"* each time the demon paused. (P. 183)

The irony resulting from our recognition of the parallel between the two scenes is devastating. Each undercuts the other by revealing that the climax of fulfillment toward which Sutpen was to push the energy of his manhood was destined to become nothing but a grotesque looking-glass version—terrible, pathetic, and ridiculous all at the same time—of a child's-eye view of reality. To put this another way, the parallelism works to fuse the two periods of Stupen's life into one—to telescope time so that we can see the man already latent in the boy. As the boy lay hidden all afternoon, watching the plantation owner, his life had still to unfold itself, but in a vital sense it was already completed, the stasis of its tragic futility decreed. The same effect is produced when Sutpen's wild carriage rides to church on Sunday mornings—one of which was for the young Rosa Coldfield

> a glimpse like the forefront of a tornado, of the carriage and Ellen's high white face within it and the two replicas of his face in miniature flanking her, and

on the front seat the face and teeth of the wild negro who was driving, and
he . . . all in a thunder and fury of wildeyed horses and of galloping and of dust
(P. 23)

are ultimately revealed as the man's bizarre duplication of another of the boy's
experiences on the plantation:

> He remembered one afternoon when he and his sister were walking along the
> road and he heard the carriage coming up behind them and stepped off the
> road and then realized that his sister was not going to give way to it, that
> she still walked in the middle of the road with a sort of sullen implacability
> in the very angle of her head and he shouted at it: and then it was all dust
> and rearing horses and glinting harness buckles and wheel spokes; he saw
> two parasols in the carriage and the nigger coachman in a plug hat shouting:
> 'Hoo dar, gal! Get outen de way dar!' and then it was over, gone: the carriage
> and the dust, the two faces beneath the parasols glaring down at his sister:
> then he was throwing vain clods of dirt after the dust as it spun on. (P. 231)

Sutpen's early days in Virginia are subtly adumbrated by other characters too.
When Henry (according to Mr. Compson's version of the story) accompanied Bon
to New Orleans in the winter of 1860–61, he experienced in that strange, exotic
city as acute a shock to his moral nature as had his father in being suddenly
transported to the Tidewater from the mountains (cf. pp. 110 and 225–26).
And both his assiduous aping (postulated by Mr. Compson) of the dress and
manners and attitudes of the "splendid" Bon (pp. 95, 96, 102, 110) and Wash
Jones's fanatical hero-worshiping of the "Kernel" *"who once galloped on the
black thorough-bred about that domain two boundaries of which the eye could
not see from any point"* (p. 184) are nothing less than versions of Sutpen's own
intense boyhood dream of aping the romantic life of the great plantation owner.
Henry's subsequent flight from Sutpen's Hundred to New Orleans, with the
man of whom he was already a caricature (p. 102) and whom he aspired to
resemble still more, may even be interpreted as a distorted mirroring of Sutpen's
flight from Virginia to Haiti.

That flight and the fairy-tale dream that gave impetus to it were brought into
being, we finally learn, on a day when the young Sutpen stood at the door of the
plantation house with a message from his father and was abruptly turned away
by a Negro servant. Here the relevant parallel is again with Wash Jones. For
Jones was not only a poor, "white trash" settler on a lordly domain as the "Kernel"
had been before him, but it is repeatedly emphasized that, as long as his master
was around, the door of the Jefferson mansion remained as effectually closed to
him as the door of the Virginia mansion had been to Sutpen himself: "Until
Sutpen went way, [Jones] had never approached nearer than the scuppernong
arbor behind the kitchen" (p. 125; cf. pp. 134, 183). Moreover, the one who
barred his way into the house, the one *"who would forbid him to pass the kitchen
door with what he brought"* (p. 183; cf. p. 281), was, exactly as in Sutpen's case,
a Negro (Clytie). The past seems to repeat itself with hallucinatory strangeness.

Indeed, once chapter 7 has alerted us to the central importance of the closed
door episode in Sutpen's history, the earlier chapters reveal numerous prefigur-
ations of it. The fact that as a girl Miss Rosa *"lurked, unapprehended as though
. . . [she] displaced no air, gave off no betraying sound, from one closed forbidden*

door to the next" (p. 145) takes on entirely new relevance. As Sutpen's life was warped in childhood, so too was hers, because she had to spend it in "a Cassandralike listening beyond closed doors" (p. 60; cf. p. 73). Years later, on the afternoon of Bon's murder when, as an adolescent, she hungered like the young Sutpen for recognition, respect, and love, a closed door barred her way once more as she hurried into the mansion and up the stairs only to be *"stopped in running's midstride"* by *"Judith standing before the closed door"* (p. 142; cf. pp. 149–50). Thus in evaluating the significance of Bon's death in the perspective of her whole life, she tells Quentin that the sound of the fatal shot *"was merely the sharp and fatal clap-to of a door between us* [Rosa, Judith, and Clytie] *and all that was, all that might have been"* (p. 158). Bon's world—the world of youth, gallantry, romance—was the world the girl could not enter, as the world of the luxurious plantation house was that forbidden to the youthful Sutpen; and this deprivation left its wound as deep in her psyche as had the analogous trauma of the boy. A door image also dominates Mr. Compson's description of the home of Bon's mistress in New Orleans, before which in some uncanny fashion it appears in retrospect to be not Henry waiting for it to open but a reincarnation of his father:

> now would come the instant for which Bon had builded—a wall, unscalable, *a gate ponderously locked, the sober and thoughtful country youth just waiting, looking, not yet asking why? or what?* the gate of solid beams in place of the lacelike iron grilling and they passing on, Bon knocking at a small adjacent doorway from which *a swarthy man resembling a creature out of an old woodcut of the French Revolution erupts, concerned, even a little aghast, looking first at the daylight and then at Henry.* (P. 112; my italics)

Parallels extend even to the narrative frame itself: as Sutpen, Jones, Rosa, and Henry were halted by closed doors, so too is Quentin because of his obsessive interest in the trio of doomed youths, Henry, Bon, and Judith.

> But Quentin was not listening [to Miss Rosa], because there was also something which he too could not pass—that door [of Judith's room], the running feet on the stairs beyond it almost a continuation of the faint shot, the two women [Judith and Clytie] . . . looking at the door . . . as the door crashed in and the brother stood there. (P. 172)

> he had not been listening [to his father], since he had something which he still was unable to pass: that door. (P. 174)

This development of imagery of the closed door enables Faulkner to produce the haunting effect of *déjà vu* by anticipating his disclosure in chapter 7 of the critical moment in Sutpen's childhood to which all his subsequent behavior was traceable. But by means of other patterns of imagery developed concurrently and contributing to the same impression, Faulkner also prefigures what we are to discover were for Sutpen the crucial psychic *consequences* of that moment. Reading chapter 7, we learn that Sutpen's chief failure was a failure to grow—to achieve a capacity for adult moral response, to evolve an effectual conscience, to transcend a pre-moral level of awareness. In his case, the child was father of the man in a sinister and tragic sense. The compulsive resolution that the country boy made on that day when he was stopped short at the door was the resolution that gave direction to the whole of his life. His was not conscious malevolence, not the deliberate willing of evil, but simply a terrible naiveté, as if the moral faculty in him had never come into being, or, at the very least, had been permanently anaesthetized. Throughout his life Sutpen remained aware only of his boyhood shame and the obsessive ambition that sprang from it; others existed for him only as means, instruments, tools for the fulfillment of his grandiose design. This imprisonment in a rigidified, mechanical habit of ruthless exploitation is memorably revealed in chapter 7 on the occasion of his autobiographical conversation with Grandfather, which took place in 1833 at the site of the mansion during interludes in the merciless hunting-down of the French architect whom Sutpen had not paid for his work and who was trying to escape. The structure of the chapter at this point (pp. 217–58) may seem perverse because Sutpen's account of the genesis and nature of his design is being continually interrupted by details of the manhunt. But this counterpointing of the story of one pursuit against that of another crystallizes our impression of how thoroughly conditioned to his boyhood's mode of response Sutpen really was. At the very moment he was telling Grandfather of the outrageous way in which he felt he had been affronted by the "monkey nigger" at the door, he himself was hunting down his own architect as coldbloodedly as if the latter were a wild beast—treating him as ruthlessly as he felt he himself had been treated, and yet remaining completely oblivious to the parallel, compulsively fulfilling the requirements of his design because he had developed in all the intervening years no more moral awareness than the youth who had calmly crushed the Haitian uprising (p. 254).

These crucial revelations about Sutpen's impregnable "innocence" are made for the first time in chapter 7, and yet, as we encounter them, we sense that we have been strangely familiar with them all along. The conscienceless reduction of a human being to the level of an animal, the compulsiveness and obsession, the inflexibly conditioned response, the arrested development are not only characteristics of Sutpen's own behavior but themes that have been implied with varying degrees of subtlety throughout the novel by a number of deeply suggestive images and motifs. It is no accident that there is a striking similarity between the description in chapter 7 of the ill-fated architect's "embroidered vest and Fauntleroy tie" (p. 219) and the earlier description of Bon's "slightly Frenchified cloak and hat" (p. 95) and of the "expensive esoteric Fauntleroy clothing" (p. 194) worn by Charles Etienne. For the story of Sutpen's relentless pursuit of the architect through the miasmal swamp is actually a brilliant nightmare reenactment of the rejections of Bon and his son narrated previously. The point to be made here, however, is that all three of these acts are symptomatic of a dehumanizing habit of thought and behavior that is pervasive in this novel; characters are prone to regard each other not as human beings to be valued for their intrinsic worth but as animals or impersonal objects that lend themselves to the grossest forms of manipulation. This dehumanization of feeling, albeit most conspicuous in Sutpen (see, e.g., pp. 16, 29, 36, 40, 42, 58, 61, 85, 158, 167, 168, 180, 185, and 286) was nothing less than a disease infecting the whole society in which he lived— a society that tried to sustain itself on the great moral evil of slavery.

Thus Mr. Compson imagines Bon as having recalled that in the ante bellum South it was customary for a black concubine to be sold "body and soul for life to him who could have used her with more impunity than he would dare to use an animal, heifer or mare" (p. 116). Indeed, Bon's own son, Charles Etienne, was in the almost identical situation of being the "complete chattel of him who, begetting him, owned him body and soul to sell . . . like a calf or puppy or sheep" (p. 114); nor did his condition improve in adulthood, for he was treated by Clytie as if he were "some delicate talonless and fangless wild beast crouched in its cage in some hopeless and desperate similitude of ferocity look[ing] upon the human creature who feeds it" (p. 198); and Judith, on the occasion when she summoned him to her room after his marriage to the Negress, looked upon him *"as if he were some wild bird or beast which might take flight at the expansion and contraction of her nostrils or the movement of her breast"* (p. 208). In the light of this, it is no small irony that he himself is thought by Mr. Compson to have regarded his wife in much the same way: to have taken her "to the ruined cabin which he had chosen to repair and installed her, *kenneled* her with a gesture perhaps, and returned to the house" (p. 206; my italics).

To reduce human beings to the status of animals, however, is only one way of dehumanizing them; they may also be reduced to mere lifeless objects, completely impersonal pawns. In effect, this is the sin of which Miss Rosa is guilty in that "demonizing" which Faulkner explicitly compares at one point (p. 280) to "Sutpen's morality." Sutpen has become for her not a man whose motives are to be sought and understood, but an "ogre," a "demon," a mere thing that she can accommodate to her own obsessive design of venting upon the past her cold, implacable hatred and frustration. She is as ruthless with respect to this design as Sutpen was with respect to his; the real Sutpen has been refashioned by her into a creature of mere dream or hallucination.[5] Her counterpart is her

---

5. At first there may seem to be something comparable to this in the often fanciful speculations of Quentin and Shreve, who, in their eagerness to give the Sutpen legend coherence, do not hesitate to create, "out of the rag-tag and bob-ends of old tales and talking, people who perhaps had never existed at all anywhere" (p. 303), and to conserve "what seemed true, or fit the preconceived" (pp. 316, 335). But Quentin and Shreve go about this task in a spirit entirely different from Rosa's. The coldness and tomblike quality of their room symbolize what they might have been but for a time successfully escape: men examining the past in an impersonal spirit of scientific detachment akin to the destructive logic and morality of Sutpen himself. Faulkner makes this explicit when he sardonically describes the icy college room as "dedicated to that best of ratiocination which after all was a good deal like Sutpen's morality and Miss Coldfield's demonizing" (p. 280). That Quentin and Shreve resist this temptation to indulge in mere "ratiocination" is represented by Shreve's putting on his bathrobe (p. 265) and overcoat (p. 293) and Quentin's sitting "hunched in his chair, his hands thrust into his pockets as if he were trying to hug himself warm between his arms" (pp. 294, 324, 346). By means of this resistance they achieve what neither Rosa nor Mr. Compson could achieve—something close to the full truth. On the one hand the closed, tomblike house associated with Rosa symbolizes the same excessive and sterile involvement in the past that stultified Sutpen—the stifling heat without light of their manias; on the other hand, the cold, the snow, and the tomblike room in Cambridge symbolize the equally sterile intellectual impersonality that characterized both Mr. Compson's narrative and Sutpen's ruthless design. Between these polarities there is the saving way of Quentin and Shreve—the way of poetic insight through the moral imagination. At the end of the novel, it is true, Quentin seems to renounce his liberating vision and allow the closed room of the past to imprison him again. But it is precisely because of what he does momentarily achieve that his final defection can be measured. By means of the moral imagination he rescues something from the ruins of time as Sutpen, in spite of all his struggle to found a dynasty, could never do. By means of this he holds alive forever that moment of a quiet afternoon in 1865 when Bon and Henry rode up to the gates for the last time—that very moment when in the closed room of *his* purblind effort to transcend time by violence, Sutpen denied the moral imagination most and thus condemned himself and his house and all but this moment itself to oblivion.

sister Ellen, who, "corrupted" by Sutpen in his heyday (p. 72), hungered for Bon to become Judith's husband

> as if he were three inanimate objects in one, or perhaps one inanimate object for which she and her family would find three concordant uses: a garment which Judith might wear as she would a riding habit or a ball gown, a piece of furniture which would complement and complete the furnishing of her house and position, and a mentor and example to correct Henry's provincial manners and speech and clothing. (P. 75)

For Ellen he was no more than "the esoteric, the almost baroque, the almost epicene objet d'art which with childlike voracity she essayed to include in the furnishing and decoration of her house" (p. 101)—no more than *"some esoteric piece of furniture—vase or chair or desk"* (p. 149; cf. p. 320). The courtship, in her eyes, was something merely to be "engineered" (pp. 103–4), planned, arranged down to the last detail, as if one were moving about lifeless pieces on a chessboard or reenacting "the campaigns of dead generals in the textbooks" (p. 321)—or, one is compelled to add, reenacting the live Sutpen's brutal use of his soldiers to transport his pompous tombstones (pp. 189–90).

Attitudes like these link the motif of dehumanization with that of arrested development. The adjective *childlike* above is carefully considered; for Ellen's conception of Bon is of a piece with her treatment of the merchants in Memphis, which is "not contemptuous, not even patronizing exactly," but "a bland and even *childlike* imposition" (p. 73; my italics)—a milder version, different in degree but not in kind, of Sutpen's equivocal "innocence." It springs from an analogous absorption in a child's private dream-world—in her case "a fairy tale written for and acted by a fashionable ladies' club" (p. 76), "a bland region peopled by dolls" where she can live in "a perennial bright vacuum of arrested sun" (p. 70). Similarly, as in a real sense the clock stopped for Sutpen on the day he was turned away from the door, so it stopped for Rosa on the day Sutpen made his brutal proposition after their engagement. This shock to her moral and sexual sensibilities, by reinforcing the effects of the conditioning she had received in childhood from her rigidly Puritan and genteel home, the fanatical attitudes of her sex-starved maiden aunt, and the frustration she experienced when Henry shot Bon, left her "embattled for forty-three years in the old insult, the old unforgiving," out of which emerges her fairytale demonizing (p. 14). Not only is her appearance still that of a child (pp. 7–8, 65, 176), but her manner of narration, like Sutpen's, is childlike in a certain respect too: as he, in telling the story of his early life to Grandfather in chapter 7, disgards causal connections and "logical sequence and continuity" (p. 247; see, e.g., pp. 239, 246, 247, 249, 254), so, with an equally childlike disregard, Rosa re-creates for Quentin in chapter 1 the scene of Sutpen's arrival in Jefferson—"Out of quiet thunderclap he would abrupt (man-horse-demon) upon a scene peaceful and decorous as a schoolprize watercolor" (p. 8)—and later his return from the War:

> *That was how we lived for seven months. And then one afternoon in January Thomas Sutpen came home; someone looked up where we were preparing the garden for another year's food and saw him riding up the drive. And then one evening I became engaged to marry him.* (P. 158)

For the salient fact about both Sutpen and Rosa is that their actions are ineluctably defined by patterns laid down in childhood and early youth. Each is a kind of automaton. Rosa calls the room in which she and Quentin sit "the office because her father had called it that," and keeps the blinds closed and fastened "because when she was a girl someone had believed that light and moving air carried heat and that dark was always cooler" (p. 7; cf. pp. 66, 88, 175). The subtlest link between her and Sutpen in this regard is the way in which each compulsively continues to respond to a single peculiar stimulus with which his past history is crucially associated—the smell of wistaria in Rosa's case and the smell and taste of sugar in Sutpen's. At that point in the narrative to Grandfather in chapter 7 where Sutpen is describing the native uprising in Haiti, he speaks of the sugar fields and barns catching fire, and goes on to tell

> how you could smell it, you could smell nothing else, the rank sweet rich smell as if the hatred and the implacability, the thousand secret dark years which had created the hatred and implacability, had intensified the smell of the sugar: and Grandfather said how he remembered then that he had seen Sutpen each time decline sugar for his coffee and so he (Grandfather) knew why now but he asked anyway to be sure and Sutpen told him it was true; that he had not been afraid until after the fields and barns were all burned and they had even forgot about the smell of the burning sugar, but that he had never been able to bear sugar since. (P. 249)

We may be troubled at this point by the seeming inconsequence of this detail about Sutpen's psychology, but may also feel that we encountered something analogous to it earlier. It will be recalled that at the very beginning of the novel, when Quentin paid his visit to Rosa and sat talking with his father afterwards, repeated emphasis was placed upon the pervasive scent of wistaria (pp. 7, 8, 31, 89); it was the wistaria too that formed an important part of Quentin's memory of the scene four months later when he was sitting in his room at Harvard (pp. 173, 181). At first such passages seem merely "atmospheric," until we discover in chapter 5 that the summer of 1860 when Rosa fell in love at a distance with Bon was *"a summer of wistaria"* too (*"It was a pervading everywhere of wistaria [I was fourteen then] as though of all springs yet to capitulate condensed into one spring, one summer..."* [pp. 143–44]). It was precisely because of this correspondence between the September of 1909 and the summer of 1860 that Rosa's memory was so powerfully activated, that she poured out to Quentin her torrent of reminiscence, and, we must infer, that she finally decided to go out with him to the decaying mansion. *"That is the substance of remembering—sense, sight, smell,"* she says: *"the muscles with which we see and hear and feel—not mind, not thought ... the brain recalls just what the muscles grope for: no more, no less..."* (p. 143). For her, memory, like Sutpen's aversion to sugar, is mindless compulsiveness; both are conditioned responses to critical experiences of early life; and both render the arrested development of their characters in metaphorical epitome.

But an equally prominent metaphor for this psychic condition is the image or action that suggests rigidity. If, as we read the revelations about Sutpen in chapter 7, we continue to experience the peculiar *déjà vu* sensation, it is to an important extent because Sutpen has already been mirrored in caricatured form not only by Rosa but by her father, a character who on first reading seems super-fluous. The latter's miserliness—that "tedious and unremitting husbandry" (p. 50) which made him feel that it would have been "incumbent on him to supply his granddaughter with clothes if she were indecently clad or if she were ragged and cold, but not to marry in" (p. 77)—was the manifestation of as rigid a "conscience," as inflexible a calculation of profit and loss, as governed Sutpen's applications of his "old impotent logic and morality." Coldfield's consuming desire to lay up in heaven a store of grace was *his* unyielding design, the "Puritan" counterpart of Sutpen's purely secular drive to establish a lasting dynasty on earth (p. 84); and as the latter identified morality with the "logic" dictated by his design, Coldfield identified grace with his hoard of money. Like Sutpen, too, he sacrificed to the rigid dictates of his design not only all humane feeling but even, in the end, his own life. When he and Rosa used to make their annual visits to Sutpen's Hundred, "they would get into the buggy and depart, Mr. Coldfield first docking the two negroes for the noon meal which they would not have to prepare and (so the town believed) charging them for the crude one of leftovers which they would have to eat" (p. 66; cf. p. 84). Again, what he objected to in the War, according to Grandfather, was "not so much . . . the idea of pouring out human blood and life, but . . . the idea of waste: of wearing out and eating up and shooting away material in any cause whatever" (p. 83). His conduct was as fanatical, as mechanically "logical" as Sutpen's own—and he left behind precisely what Sutpen was to leave behind, a rotting building and the lasting hatred of his contemporaries: "The store was just a shell, the deserted building vacated even by rats and containing nothing, not even good will since he had irrevocably estranged himself from neighbors, town, and embattled land, all three by his behavior" (p. 84).

Finally, with Coldfield Faulkner also establishes a link between the theme of rigidity and recurrent imagery of claustrophobic entrapment. The attic, in which the miser imprisoned himself, reappears in the story of Bon's thwarted son, Charles Etienne, whose Negro blood ultimately condemns him at Sutpen's Hundred to the solitude of a "garret room" (p. 199), which is only a harsher version of that "silken prison lighted by perpetual shaded candles" (p. 139) he had known in boyhood. The mansion Sutpen lived in before its completion was a "house the size of a courthouse . . . *without a window or door* or bedstead in it" (p. 16; my italics), a "Spartan shell . . . *without any feminized softness of window pane or door* or mattress" (pp. 39–40; my italics); and when at the end of the novel Henry returns to this house, it is to die in a "bare stale room whose shutters were closed" (p. 373). The meaning of this imagery becomes clear in chapter 7 as soon as we discover as the key to Sutpen's behavior his imprisonment in a predetermined mode of response; the image of the closed room then takes on as much significance as that of the closed door. That the latter represents the cause of Sutpen's fixity and the former the fixity itself is also established unmistakably by a pattern worked out in the first six chapters with great consistency: at one time or another several characters become prisoners, literally or figuratively, in closed rooms, and in each case, as in Sutpen's own, this results from some kind of paralyzing shock or frustration. In addition to the examples of Coldfield and Charles Etienne, there is that of Judith who, when her attempt to drive her father's crazy carriage to church was thwarted, was put to bed in a "quiet darkened room with the blinds closed" (p. 26), an image both of her frustration and of the dark and narrow world of her compulsions. At later periods her mother, the victim of another thwarted obsession (to have Judith marry Bon), retired to "a darkened room which she was not to quit until she died two years later" (p. 79); and Bon's mistress, visiting Sutpen's Hundred after his death, passed the week of her stay "in bed . . . [in a] room airless and shuttered" (p. 194). Part of the same imagistic pattern is that "household like an overpopulated mausoleum" (p. 176), where Rosa had grown up in "a grim mausoleum air of Puritan righteousness and outraged female vindictiveness" (p. 60). Visiting this house at the beginning of the novel, Quentin found himself enclosed in "the airless gloom of a dead house" (p. 14); the room in which he sat was "dim hot airless" (p. 7), pervaded by a "dim coffin-smelling gloom sweet and oversweet" (p. 8); and to get into it he had to pass through "the gloom of the shuttered hallways whose air was even hotter than outside, as if there were prisoned in it like in a tomb all the suspiration of slow heat-laden time which had recurred during the fifty-five years. . ." (pp. 10–11).

II

The first six chapters of *Absalom* thus prefigure the disclosures made in chapter 7 about Sutpen in such a way that we are moved by the curious sensation of having been dimly aware of them all along—a sensation that I have compared to the familiar psychological experience known as false recognition or *déjà vu,* and that contributes in a vital, albeit elusive, way to the dreamlike atmosphere of the novel and the powerful illusion it creates of holding a whole period of history in a kind of luminous and timeless suspension—of completely presenting the entire story at any given moment. But this sensation is present to us with equal force when we examine both chapter 7 and chapter 8 from the point of view of the revelations that are made in each about Sutpen's son, Charles Bon.

Everyone will be struck by the very close resemblance between what Quentin and Shreve in chapter 8 imagine Bon's childhood to have been and what we learned earlier had been Rosa's (see pp. 299–300, 305–6). Especially notable is a parallel between the child Rosa staring at Sutpen "across the table with still and curious and profound intensity" (p. 66) only to receive no recognition, and Bon yearningly gazing at his father years later only to find "no sign, no more sign at parting than when he had seen it first, in that face where he might (he would believe) have seen for himself the truth and so would have needed no sign, if it hadn't been for the beard; no sign in the eyes which could see his face because there was no beard to hide it, could have seen the truth if it were there: yet no flicker in them" (p. 321).

But this picture of Bon is, after all, only a creation by Shreve; the resemblances it bears to what we know about Rosa are readily accounted for on the supposition that Shreve's imagination was influenced by what he came to learn from his conversation with Quentin. More securely grounded in objective fact are a number of details that parallel the revelation that comes to be made about Bon's paternity. This skeleton in Sutpen's past is subtly prefigured by the one in Coldfield's—the shady deal by which the latter helped Sutpen acquire some of his first possessions in Jefferson. And the annual trips Coldfield made out to Sutpen's Hundred during Rosa's childhood, because he "wanted to see his grandchildren regarding whom he was in a steadily increasing unease of that day *when their father would tell the son at least of that old business between them"* (p. 64; my italics), foreshadow Sutpen's final disclosure of the truth about Bon to Henry. Similarly, with a few slight changes, Rosa's remark about not remembering having seen Ellen before one of those Sundays in her girlhood when Sutpen would ride wildly to church ("It was as though the sister whom I had never laid eyes on, who before I was born had vanished into the strong hold of an ogre or a djinn, was now to return through a dispensation of one day only, to the world which she had quitted" [p. 23]) could later have been said about their half-brother by both Henry and Judith. Even more prophetically, albeit unwittingly, Mr. Compson describes Bon on one occasion as "some effluvium of Sutpen blood and character" (p. 104).

Bon's was more than Sutpen blood, however, and this fact permits the most ironic parallels of all—those dependent upon the climactic revelation in chapter 8 that Bon was part Negro. In the light of what we eventually learn of the threat posed by Bon's blood to Sutpen's design, reminders in the first two chapters of Sutpen's reliance upon his wild Negro retainers ("the only men on whom he could depend" for protection against the town at the time of his second wedding [p. 55]) become strokes of boldly sardonic humor. And when at last we realize that the success of Sutpen's design in his own eyes depended upon the complete suppression of a man who was part Negro, a richly equivocal meaning gathers around all those early references to "the black foundation on which it [his house] had been erected" (p. 78), "the wild stock with which he had created Sutpen's Hundred" (p. 124), and, bitterest of all, to those townspeople at the time of Sutpen's greatest prosperity "who believed even yet that there was a nigger in the woodpile somewhere" (p. 72). Faulkner takes us still closer to the truth in passages suggesting a relationship between Sutpen blood and Negro blood either explicitly, as in references to Clytie's "Sutpen coffee-colored face" (p. 136; cf. 30), or metaphorically, as when Sutpen is said by Miss Rosa to have resembled the driver of his carriage, "his face exactly like the negro's save for the teeth (this because of his beard doubtless)" (p. 23). The parenthetical remark here, seemingly so pointless, acquires startling relevance much later in chapter 8 when, in a passage I quoted a moment ago in another connection, Shreve supposes that it was this very beard that Bon may have come to regard as a mask deliberately worn to conceal the face that was otherwise so "exactly like" the part Negro son's (p. 321).

Faulkner also goes so far as to adumbrate specifically the cause of Sutpen's repudiation of his first wife and son by having Mr. Compson speculate in chapter 4 upon Bon's alleged unwillingness to repudiate his octoroon concubine (pp. 117–18). The irony here is not limited to the fact that this repudiation of the part-Negro wife in exchange for a white one was possibly not true of Bon but was certainly true of Sutpen; it also resides, terribly, in the fact that the words with which Mr. Compson re-creates the hypothetical scene in which Bon justifies his repudiation to Henry echo words that (we learn in chapters 7 and 8) were to be spoken to Grandfather and Henry when Sutpen was contemplating *his* repudiation of Bon himself (cf. pp. 118, 274, 354–55). Indeed, the duel between Sutpen and Bon is suggested even in the references in chapters 5 and 6 to the contests of Clytie with Wash Jones and Rosa: as the latter are the white people turned away from Sutpen's house by its Negro mistress, so Bon was the part

Negro turned away from the same house by its white master. Or, looked at in another way, Rosa and Wash stopped by Sutpen's Negro daughter may remind us of Sutpen himself stopped by his part-Negro son. Even more powerful is the way in which the brutal outcome of that conflict is adumbrated as early as chapter 1 in a scene whose total significance can be grasped only much later: the scene of Sutpen's ferocious wrestling matches with his Negro retainers—matches after which he was once found "standing there naked and panting and bloody to the waist, *and the negro just fallen evidently, lying at his feet and bloody, too . . .*" (p. 29; my italics).

III

I have reserved for the final place in this discussion the story of Bon's part-Negro son, Charles Etienne, not only because it is one of the most deeply moving single sequences in the whole novel, but because it has crucial links with what we come to know in chapters 7 and 8 about *both* Sutpen and Bon, and thus, in effect, it fuses the stories of those two earlier generations into something like timeless oneness that I have pointed to as one of the final impressions of the novel as a whole. So masterful is Faulkner's organization of his vast material that the story of Charles Etienne is made to function in two different ways. It brings the narrative of the Sutpen family to the threshold of its final collapse (after it only the deaths of Henry and Clytie remain to be dramatized), and, occurring as it does at the very end of the section (chaps. 1–6) dealing with Sutpen's actions and immediately before the section (chaps. 7–8) dealing with their causes, it anticipates those causes with brilliant irony: as the novel approaches its decisive revelations, the story of the third-generation Sutpen becomes, in modified form, the story of his first- and second-generation progenitors. Charles Etienne emerges as both the young and incredulous Sutpen turned away from the door of the Virginia plantation and the part-Negro Bon turned away from Sutpen's Hundred—as if the patterns assumed by the lives of the older men were broken up and the pieces scrambled into a new order.

Most obviously, of course, Charles Etienne is a replica of his father: we recognize at once the parallel between the former's "Fauntleroy suits" (p. 195), "the delicate garments of his pagehood" (p. 196), "his silk and broadcloth" (p. 204) and the feminized clothing—the "flowered, almost feminized gown" (p. 95), "the outlandish and almost feminine garments of his sybaritic privacy" (p. 96)—which Mr. Compson imagined had been worn by Bon at the University. But what becomes apparent only in retrospect is that Charles Etienne and Bon were alike in a more fundamental way as well: the tragic fate that descended upon the former because he was the part-Negro son of an octoroon mother was the key, had we but known it, to the tragic fate that had befallen his father. For the tragedy of the Sutpen house does not end with the frustration and death of Sutpen himself: one of the most terrible results of his evil is that his descendants are compelled to reproduce it. After reading the disclosures in chapter 8 we cannot fail to look back upon the story of Charles Etienne at Sutpen's Hundred as essentially a repetition by Judith of her father's treatment of Bon. Again, "the young man with a young man's potence" who was still a "lonely child" (p. 204; cf. what Quentin and Shreve imagine had been the father-starved Bon's reiterated reflections upon his youth: pp. 320, 321, 333, 347) comes from New Orleans to Jefferson; again, he is taken into the mansion, crossing "that strange threshold, that irrevocable demarcation" (p. 197); and again, his Negro blood condemns him, driving him finally to invite those bloody beatings and maulings, those "blows and slashes" from Negroes and whites alike (p. 202), that reproduce as in the bizarre distortions of a fever-dream the very doom that befell his father.

But Charles Etienne's career also mirrors some of the very first phases of his grandfather's. Upon rereading that after his mother's disappearance the bewildered young boy was suddenly swept back to Jefferson, after having been "hunted down" (pp. 195–96) in New Orleans by the indomitable Clytie, and that he "could have only suspected, surmised, where she was taking him, could have known nothing certainly except that all he had ever been familiar with was vanishing about him like smoke" (p. 197), we experience the dreamlike impression, the *déjà vu* effect, not only of following again the course of Bon, his father, but also of being back with the young Sutpen himself on that long-ago journey from the mountains of West Virginia to the Tidewater (p. 223–25). Even "that harsh and shapeless denim cut to an iron pattern and sold by millions—that burlesque uniform and regalia of the tragic burlesque of the sons of Ham" (p. 196; cf. p. 204) which Clytie and Judith substitute for Charles's "Fauntleroy suits" are a nightmare duplication of the boy Sutpen's "garments his father had got from the plantation commissary and had worn out and which one of his sisters had patched and cut down to fit him" (p. 229). And as the young Sutpen later found himself in Haiti able to speak English but not French (p. 248), so Charles Etienne finds himself in Jefferson able to speak French but not English (pp. 195, 196).

Still more significantly, Sutpen's marriage to the octoroon is brutally, surrealistically caricatured by Charles's marriage to that haunting projection of all the hidden fears and guilt of Sutpen and his kind, the "coal black and ape-like" Negress (p. 205). And when it is imagined by Quentin that Judith, sitting alone one night in a quiet lamplit room of the old house (p. 207) summons Charles into her presence and tells him that he might *"put aside"* his marriage to *"one who is inescapably negro"* and go North (p. 208), we are not only witnessing a grotesque duplication of the fatal interview between Sutpen and Henry in the bivouac in 1865, when the former asked the latter to repudiate his Negro half-brother and intimate friend (pp. 352–55), but we are hearing again Sutpen's very words to Grandfather in 1833, when he told him "how he had put his first wife [Charles Etienne's grandmother] aside like eleventh- and twelfth-century kings did" because "she was not and could never be . . . adjunctive or incremental to the design" (p. 240). Indeed, Grandfather himself, anticipating Judith's advice by telling Charles that "he must go away, disappear" (p. 204), echoes the very thoughts that must have been in Sutpen's own mind when, having "put aside" his wife, he left Haiti and came to Jefferson: "Whatever you are, once you are among strangers, people who don't know you, you can be whatever you will" (p. 204). Thus, as Charles, years later, appears suddenly in Jefferson, "with a face not old but without age, as if he had had no childhood . . . as if he had not been human born but instead created without agency of man or agony of woman and orphaned by no human being" (p. 196), so too had Sutpen himself, "apparently complete, without background or past or childhood" (p. 93), he and his horse "looking as though they had been created out of thin air and set down in the bright summer sabbath sunshine in the middle of a tired foxtrot" (p. 32).

With our retrospective view of the novel from the vantage points of chapters 7 and 8, then, Faulkner's remarkable artistry and the final irony of Charles Etienne's story strike us with shattering impact: the grandson is both a tragic victim of the design and a mirror of its origin; it was his fantastic destiny to coalesce past and present—to reenact in the pattern of his life the dark origins of his own doom. "The schoolmen of the Middle Ages," Thomas Mann has said, "would have it that time is an illusion; that its flow in sequence and causality is only the result of a sensory device, and the real existence of things is an abiding present" (*The Magic Mountain,* chap. 7).

As I Lay Dying as an Existential Novel

ROBERT M. SLABEY

University of Notre Dame

COMMENT BY THE AUTHOR

The essay below, an early discussion of existential issues in Faulkner's fictional world, offered one way of seeing As I Lay Dying *as a whole. With over sixty important interpretations now in print, Faulkner's self-acknowledged tour de force still remains elusive—a multifaceted, technically brilliant, and discontinuous sequence of implausible philosophical meditations by a group of poor, uneducated hill folk. That the novel's complex form and tone have been described, variously, as naturalism, romance, comedy, tragedy, epic, apocalypse, allegory, myth, ritual, fable, farce, tall tale, black comedy, and parody suggests the impossibility of capturing it in any single critical category. But a significant number of commentators have settled on the word* existential *to describe a book whose center is dying and death and that probes aloneness, being, existence, and reality, many of its monologues specifically focusing on what it means to be in the face of nonbeing.*

Among the best ontological or absurdist readings are essays by James M. Mellard ("Faulkner's Philosophical Novel: Ontological Themes in As I Lay Dying," *The Personalist* 48 {1967}: 509–23); *Calvin Bedient ("Pride and Nakedness:* As I Lay Dying," *Modern Language Quarterly* 29 {1968}: 61–76); *and Robert Hemenway ("Enigmas of Being in* As I Lay Dying," *Modern Fiction Studies* 16 {1970}: 133–46). *Edmond L. Volpe, who finds that in the novel "the meaninglessness of existence is viewed as a macabre joke"* (A Reader's Guide to Wiliam Faulkner {New York: Noonday, 1964}, p. 127), *overemphasizes the absurd comedy, while other critics stress the Bundren's "heroism" and "humanity." Melvin Backman, for example, sees Faulkner suggesting an answer to alienation in a comedy rooted in*

First published: 11, no. 4 (1963): 12–23. Slightly revised.

the earth and in countryfolk and lighted by a faith in humanity (Faulkner: The
Major Years *{Bloomington, Ind.: Indiana University Press, 1966}, pp. 50–66).
And Cleanth Brooks defines the novel's complexity of tone this way: "The
surface of the Bundren life shows squalor, crassness, selfishness, and stupidity,
but beneath the surface there are depths of passion and poetry that are terrifying
in their power"* (William Faulkner: The Yoknapatawpha Country *{New Haven
and London: Yale University Press, 1963}, p. 165). Joseph Gold's recent " 'Sin,
Salvation and Bananas': As I Lay Dying"* (Mosaic 7, no. 1 *{Fall 1973}: 55–73)
presents a religious interpretation; in a struggle of viewpoints Faulkner is seen
siding with those who "endure" (Cash, Anse, Dewey Dell, Vardaman, Tull,
Samson, and Rachel). The fullest treatment must be André Bleikasten's book*
Faulkner's As I Lay Dying *(trans. Roger Little {Bloomington, Ind.: Indiana University Press, 1973}), an analysis of the genesis, style, technique, and themes (death
and madness) and apocalyptic atmosphere, with a useful annotated checklist of
criticism appended. Bleikasten insists that the book may be read in more than
one way.*

As I now see it, the crux of As I Lay Dying, *its totality, remains ambiguous
because the whole is a montage of fragments with a vision both absurd and
meaningful. Faulkner's strategy, a simple plot and a complex technique, indirect
and centripetal, provides grist for numerous possible readings. Many of the
"existential" interpretations (my own included) have underestimated affirmation
within the action. An absurdist view is, undoubtedly, in the reflective monologues;
the affirmation is in the external acts of courage and endurance. While nihilism
is assuaged, the heroism is undercut. The Bundrens' actions, physically heroic,
are metaphysically absurd. There is, moreover, triumph of mediocrity and a defeat of imagination and passion. Darl recognizes the absurdity of existence, and
Addie has enormous physical and spiritual vitality, but these two extraordinary
consciousnesses are destructive of others as well as of themselves. Pragmatically
the Bundrens are better off without them, but existentially they will now never
know that they do not know whether they exist or not. The parasitic Anse
"endures," renewing himself with new teeth and a new "Mrs. Bundren." Cash
impresses the reader as more humane: he is conscientious but unimaginative,
naive but not callous. What Cash says of Darl could be applied to Addie as well:
"This world is not his world; this life not his." Darl's reflections (the most compelling and comprehensive in the novel) encompass the comic, the tragic, the
ironic; finally, with eight hysterical "yeses," he accepts insanity as his family
returns to normalcy. "This world" belongs to the least conscious, to Anse and
Cash, to the reckless Jewel and the visceral Dewey Dell.*

As I Lay Dying *is an "existential necromance," the ambiguous victory of the
comic and the superficial over the tragic and the profound, the endurance of
primitive life-styles (a variation on the conclusions of* The Sound and the Fury
and Light in August), *but here positive impulses do not so much master negative
ones as merely survive them. The final words on the conundrum of existence—of
death in life, isolation in community, sanity in madness, stasis in flux—and on
the metamorphosis of being and nothingness in Yoknapatawpha should be by the
"sole owner and proprietor." In describing his ability to make the world anew
and to move his people around in time, Faulkner said that reality exists exclusively*

in the present tense: "There is no such thing as was—*only* is. *If* was *existed, there would be no such thing as grief or sorrow."*

Whenever Jean-Paul Sarte has looked at Faulkner's work, he has not liked what he found there. He did not like *Sartoris* because it is made up of "gestures"; he did not like *The Sound and the Fury* because (to put it quite bluntly) Quentin Compson is not an existentialist.[1] Sartre's discussions of Faulkner are intelligent but impressionistic. On the whole his conclusions are puzzling, somewhat eccentric, and difficult to understand. But in spite of Sarte's objections, an examination of Faulkner's work will reveal that he is on the side of the existentialists. My purpose in this essay is to define tentatively the "existential" aspect of a work of art and to present an analysis of *As I Lay Dying.*

I

In *The Sound and the Fury* Dilsey "endured" because she had the "courage to be"; this courage made her superior to the whole Compson family. The "courage to be" is thus revealed as the fundamental requirement for human existence. Those who have it are alive; those who do not, though they may breathe and sweat and suffer, are not truly alive. Quentin Compson's speculations about human existence *("Non fui. Sum. Fui. Non sum . . .* I was. I am not") did not qualify him for the school of Sartre any more than they prepared him for life in the real world. Donald Mahon of *Soldiers' Pay,* Bayard Sartoris of *Sartoris,* and Quentin were death-directed, but their motivation was not consonant with Martin Heidegger's view of existence as basically "Being-toward-Death" *("Sein zum Tode").*

"To be, or not to be—that is the question." Hamlet was not an existentialist, but he did contemplate the ultimate fact of the human predicament. To be is to discover that one can *not* be. Man suffers anxiety because he is constantly threatened by death. And the only way he can cope with this anxiety it to have the "courage to be," to accept this ultimate threat and to affirm life and the self in the face of nonbeing.[2] The results of failing to accept the essential facts of the human condition are stagnation, isolation, sterility, and disintegration. Although acceptance does involve a struggle, may require pain and suffering and even a stage of negation, it ultimately produces renewal, wholeness, vitality, and order. Authentic humanity requires the acquisition of knowledge, the performance of meaningful actions, and the establishment of a vital relationship with life in all its fullness.

Many works of literature are concerned with existential themes—death, despair, anguish, dread; man's need for decision, commitment, involvement; man's freedom, solitude, contingency, and estrangement. But in what manner can they be meaningfully discussed as "existential"? An *existentialist* novel is one in which the themes

---

1. Jean-Paul Sartre, "Sartoris," *Literary and Philosophical Essays,* trans. Annette Michelson (London: Rider, 1955), pp. 73–78; "Time in Faulkner: *The Sound and the Fury,*" trans. Martine Darmon, in *William Faulkner: Two Decades of Criticism,* ed. Frederick J. Hoffman and Olga W. Vickery (East Lansing, Mich.: Michigan State College Press, 1951), pp. 180–88.

2. See Paul Tillich, *The Courage to Be* (New Haven: Yale University Press, 1952).

are deliberately related by the author to philosophical existentialism. Sartre's novels clearly and directly belong in this category. Other novels, however, record existential experiences but are unrelated to a specific philosophical system; these works might be called *existential*[3] or *pre-existentialist*: "fiction that comes to the [existential] view independently, as a discovery in the novelist's craft, rather than formally, pushing a wheelbarrowful of speculative thought."[4] A prominent place is given to existential themes, but the writer presents neither a metaphysics nor the concrete embodiments of philosophical ideas. He presents a vision of the human situation, using symbolic techniques to reveal man's existence, his finitude, and his aspirations.

II

Several critics[5] have called attention to the existential aspect of *As I Lay Dying*, but their comments need to be qualified and expanded. Addie Bundren's death, funeral journey, and burial are the major events of the novel. But many of the interior monologues are concerned with more basic and universal human problems. Addie's problem is isolation; she is described as "a lonely woman, lonely with her pride, trying to make folks believe different, hiding the fact that they just suffered her" (p. 353). When she discovered that she was pregnant for the first time, she concluded that life was terrible and that the words of her father were all too true: "The reason for living [is] to get ready to stay dead a long time." Her whole life was a search for identity. Before her marriage, as a teacher, she hated her pupils because their blood was strange to hers; she looked forward to occasions when she could whip them because only through violence, "only through the blows of the switch could [her] blood and their blood flow as one stream" (p. 463). Like the protagonist of Sartre's *No Exit* she makes the discovery that "Hell is other people." She could find neither real human existence in, nor identity with, her husband Anse, who to her did not represent living, vigorous action, but dead, hollow words. When she realized that Anse was "dead," that his words were not deeds, she took revenge in a violation of her marriage vows: "I would be I; I would let him be the shape and echo of his word." With the minister Whitfield, she could consummate this urge without words in a natural setting close to the dark land with "the red bitter flood boiling" through it. For Addie, the problem of becoming "unalone" involved blood, sex, and the earth.

Addie's futile search for identity is an example of what Sartre calls the basic contradictory desire to be an "in-self-for-self." An object, as "in-self'" just is; being there now, fully and completely, it has an advantage over the hollow living individual, fleeing from the present and trying to become the nonexistent future.

3. This useful distinction between *existentialist* and *existential* novels is made by Robert Champigny, "Existentialism and the Modern French Novel," *Thought* 31 (1956): 365–84.

4. Stanley Edgar Hyman, "Some Trends in the Novel," *College English* 20 (1958): 6.

5. Olga W. Vickery, *The Novels of William Faulkner* (Baton Rouge, La.: Louisiana State University Press, 1959), pp. 50–65; William Van O'Connor, *The Tangled Fire of William Faulkner* (Minneapolis, Minn.: University of Minnesota Press, 1954), pp. 45–54; Edward Wasiolek, *"As I Lay Dying:* Distortion in the Slow Eddy of Current Opinion," *Critique* 3 (1959): 15–23; Maurice Le Breton, "Le Thème de la vie et de la mort dans *As I Lay Dying,"* *Le Revue des Lettres Modernes* 5 (1959): 292–308. All page references are to the Modern Library edition of *As I Lay Dying* (New York, 1946).

A subject, a "for-self," conscious of himself and so divided against himself, envies the simple, individual presence and impermeability of the object, and the one supreme object is the past. The only full identification that man can make is that of his dead body with the earth—for Addie, the cemetery at Jefferson where her people are buried. Because of his basic, impossible desire, Sartre calls man "a useless passion."

Anse, inaction incarnate, is forced by his promise to Addie to direct and perform an act in the face of nearly impossible obstacles. This makes the central event of the novel, the journey, an ironic one because for the first time Anse's words are transformed into deeds. Unlike his father, Cash, the oldest son, is inarticulate and constantly fumbles for his words. During the journey he suffers the most, and when he becomes spokesman for the family, he is revealed as a sympathetic and sane person. Problems of existence do not perplex Anse or Cash, but do touch Darl, Dewey Dell, and Vardaman.

All the neighbors think that Darl is strange, different, queer; Tull suggests that the trouble with Darl is that "he just thinks by himself too much." Darl is the only Bundren whose experiences reach outside of the family: he had been "in the war." Occasionally his stream of consciousness contains images of the mystery of existence:

> In a strange room you must empty yourself for sleep. And before you are emptied for sleep, what are you. And when you are emptied for sleep, you are not. And when you are filled with sleep, you never were. I don't know what I am. I don't know if I am or not. Jewel knows he is, because he does not know that he does not know whether he is or not. He cannot empty himself for sleep because he is not what he is and he is what he is not. Beyond the unlamped wall I can hear the rain shaping the wagon that is ours, the load that is no longer theirs that felled and sawed it nor yet theirs that bought it and which is not ours either, lie on our wagon though it does, since only the wind and the rain shape it only to Jewel and me, that are not asleep. And since sleep is is-not and rain and wind are *was,* it is not. Yet the wagon *is,* because when the wagon is *was,* Addie Bundren will not be. And Jewel *is,* so Addie Bundren must be. And then I must be, or I could not empty my self for sleep in a strange room. And so if I am not emptied yet, I am *is.*
>
> How often have I lain beneath rain on a strange roof, thinking of home. (P. 396)

In this passage it appears that the problem is one of existence in time and space under the conditions of finitude and estrangement. Beyond the *cogito* lies the problem of the nature of the *sum.* (The phenomenologists and existentialists reverse the Cartesian formula.) Roquentin, in Sarte's *Nausea,* describes his awareness of his existence in a similar way: "I am, I exist, I think, therefore I am; I am because I think. . . . I am because I think that I don't want to be."

Darl expresses his desire for the dreamless sleep of nothingness: "It would be nice if you could just ravel out into time. . . . ravel out into the no-wind, no-sound, the weary gestures wearily recapitulant: echoes of old compulsions with no-hand on no-strings: in sunset we fall into furious attitudes, dead gestures of dolls" (pp. 492, 491). In his final monologue Darl, on the train to Jackson, speaks of himself in the third person. The section concludes with a vision of the living death he is going to. Having become a "pure consciousness," he can maintain a complete detachment from all material contingencies, including his own body. Roquentin also expressed a romantic desire for liberation from all "existing" things and from his body in particular, which he had found *"de trop,"* gratuitous, absurd. But mind divorced from matter is out of touch with reality, and, therefore, insane.

Darl's most unusual quality is his ability to *see* and to *know* things. His descriptions of Addie's death and the completion of the coffin are the two most striking examples of his narration of events at which he is not present, but many other details are included in his sections which he could not have witnessed: for example, Peabody's arrival, Jewel with his horse in the barn, and the family in the wagon eating bananas. He knows Addie's secret and he knows that Dewey Dell is pregnant. He is able to communicate with Dewey Dell telepathically. Darl's attitude is one of "involvement," in contrast to a merely theoretical or detached attitude. It is "existential" in the sense that it is participation in a situation, especially a cognitive situation, with the whole of one's existence; and this includes temporal, spatial, psychological, and biological conditions. It is a participation in another self, an existential breakthrough into the center of another being.

In his monologues, Darl, Addie's unwanted child, focuses his attention on Jewel, her "love" child. For Darl, activity and expression are intellectual, but for Jewel, expression must take the form of action and violence. He shares Cash's inarticulateness, but his furious rebellion is expressed by curses. He always expresses his emotions violently; reveals his fierce love for his mother by the vehement manner in which he carries her coffin down the hill and by the fearless acts in which he rescues it from the river and from the burning barn. His ambivalent nature is revealed symbolically by the manner in which he treats his horse—with "obscene caresses." Jewel's furious desire to be independent of every one, including Addie, is represented by his horse. Although he shares the loneliness of the other members of the family, his devotion to Addie makes him unique among them. He expresses his desire for peace and privacy: "It would just be me and her [Addie] on a high hill and me rolling the rocks down the hill at their faces, picking them up and throwing them down the hill, faces and teeth and all by God until she was quiet" (pp. 347–48).

For Dewey Dell, the problem of existence is much the same as it was for Addie. Like her mother, she finds pregnancy painful: "the process of coming unalone is terrible" (p. 382). Her motive in seeking an abortion is partly to keep everyone from knowing about her sin, but more important it is a passionate desire to remain unattached, free from responsibility and involvement. Although he is only a child, Vardaman shares the perplexity about the meaning of life that confronts Addie and Darl. Witnessing his mother's death has a terrible effect on him; everything suddenly becomes strange and unintelligible; and in his childish grief he becomes temporarily insane. He associates the fish he caught and cut up with his mother's death; ceasing to be a living person, she becomes a dead fish:

> It was not her because it [the fish] was lying right yonder in the dirt. And now it's all chopped up. I chopped it up. It's laying in the kitchen in the

bleeding pan, waiting to be cooked and et. Then it wasn't and she was, and now it is and she wasn't. And tomorrow it will be cooked and et and she will be him and pa and Cash and Dewey Dell and there won't be anything in the box so she can breathe. It was laying right yonder on the ground. I can get Vernon. He was there and he seen it, and with both of us it will be and then it will not be. (P. 386)

Addie, Darl, Dewey Dell, and Vardaman are faced with "the ontological mystery"—metaphysical problems of being and nonbeing, existence and essence. For Cash and Jewel, nearly everything is met and solved on the physical level alone, with action, and in the case of Jewel, with violence. Anse is content with the "logical" or purely verbal approach; everything can be reduced to words. While Cash and Jewel do things, Anse says things: Cash makes Addie's coffin, and Jewel saves it from the fire and the flood; but to Anse, the journey is only words, his promise to Addie. Darl's existence is both metaphysical and epistemological: he considers the relationship between reality and the mind in both directions—reality to the mind (the problem of existence), and the mind to reality (the problem of knowledge). Darl, who knows things, is ultimately defeated by knowing—when Vardaman finds out Darl's secret and tells Dewey Dell. Darl, as an absurdist, perceives that life is meaningless; and he is able to laugh at the journey, realizing its grotesqueness and futility. The only actions that he performs are selfish and negative: setting fire to Gillespie's barn, abandoning the wagon in the flood, and emerging with his hands *"empty out of the water emptying the water emptying away."*

Each member of the family responds in his own way when called upon to make a contribution toward the new mules needed to complete the trip to Jefferson: Jewel and Cash respond physically, Jewel with his horse, Cash with the money he had been saving for a "graphophone"; Anse responds with another promise, a mortgage on his cultivator and seeder; Darl again stands empty-handed; Vardaman has nothing to contribute; and Dewey Dell cannot give her ten dollars because then she would become "unalone."

III

Many of the recurrent images in *As I Lay Dying* reinforce the basic problems and clarify the meaning of the novel. A dichotomy is established between words and actions. Addie preferred doing to saying; she was suspicious of words because they confused appearances with reality, and any one who relied upon mere words for communication with others was doomed to remain alone:

And when I knew that I had Cash, I knew . . . that words are no good; that words don't ever fit even what they are trying to say at. When he was born I knew that motherhood was invented by someone who had to have a word for it because the ones that had the children didn't care whether there was a word for it or not. I knew that fear was invented by someone that had never had the fear; pride, who never had the pride. I knew that it had been, not that they [her pupils] had dirty noses, but that we had to use one another by words like spiders dangling by their mouths from a beam, swinging and twisting and never touching. (P. 463)

Like Roquentin, Addie saw language and the world helplessly divided from each other; language became an absurd structure of sounds, an attempt to conceal the formless heaving mass of human consciousness. She believed that Anse's use of hollow and empty words was like "a significant shape profoundly without life like an empty door frame." Whitfield could bifurcate his words from his actions; he could preach in church one day and go the next to meet Addie in the woods. At Addie's funeral Tull commented on Whitfield's sermon: "It's like they are not the same. It's like he is one, and his voice is one, swimming on two horses side by side across the ford and coming into the house, the mud-splashed one and the one that never even got wet, triumphant and sad" (p. 404).

The vertical-horizontal image is used to develop the disparity between saying and doing. Words "go straight up in a thin line, quick and harmless," while "doing goes along the earth, clinging to it, so that after a while the two lines are too far apart for the same person to straddle from one to the other" (p. 465). The imagery connected with Addie is always moving and horizontal: the journey, the coffin, Jewel's horse, Vardaman's fish, the flowing images; but the images associated with Anse are inert and perpendicular. His house is on the top of a bluff, and he is always standing with his feet planted firmly on the ground. Dr. Peabody notices this and thinks, "Too bad the Lord made the mistake of giving trees roots and giving the Anse Bundrens He makes feet and legs. If He'd just swapped them, there wouldn't ever be a worry about this country being deforested some day. Or any other country" (p. 367). Anse believed in staying in one place: "When [the Lord] aims for something to be always a-moving, He makes it long ways, like a road or a horse or a wagon, but when He aims for something to stay put, He makes it up-and-down ways, like a tree or a man. . . . Because if He'd a aimed for man to be always a-moving and going somewheres else, wouldn't He a put him longways on his belly, like a snake?" (p. 362).

A distinction is also made between town and country, Jefferson and French-man's Bend (the Bundrens' neighborhood), civilization and nature. All the things associated with town are lifeless and mechanical: the cemetery, Anse's store teeth, Cash's gramophone, Vardaman's (later Darl's) train, and Dewey Dell's abortion. The Bundrens' arrival in town is marked by an angry exchange between the "natural" man, Jewel, and a "town fellow." The second Mrs. Bundren, with her "hard-looking pop eyes like she was daring ere a man to say nothing" (p. 531) and her phonograph with its mechanical voice, is from town. Although Addie had been identified with nature, living, with "the terrible blood, the red bitter blood boiling through the land" (p. 446) and dying, with "a bundle of rotten sticks" (p. 369), her family had been town folks. The kindly Dr. Peabody can work in both town and country, but as a "pussel-gutted" town man, it is impossible for him to climb the "durn mountain" that separates the Bundrens from the world. And ironically, the Bundrens' hilltop house (nature, up-and-down) stands for nonlife, while the road to town (civilization, "longways") is the means for the life journey to death.

Integrated into the total structure of the novel, the images suggest a basic contrast or valuative division between appearances and reality, death and life, non-being and being, negation and affirmation, pseudo-existence and authentic existence, emptiness and fulfillment, the prose of moral tags and the poetry of action.

The imagery reinforces man's predicament as it is portrayed in the book: man is a lonely anguished being in an ambiguous world.

IV

The center of *As I Lay Dying* is in the journey to Jefferson with Addie's body; it is a grotesque and ludicrous situation. Tull, commenting on the macabre determination of the Bundrens, says, "They would risk the fire and the earth and the water and all just to eat a sack of bananas" (p. 438). Traditionally the journey motif has been symbolic of the life journey. But "life" for the Bundrens is dark, empty, joyless, and futile. And what does the future offer for them? Anse is in debt to Snopes; Cash will not be able to work for a year; Darl has gone to Jackson which is *"further away than crazy";* Jewel is badly burned and deprived of his beloved horse; the new "duck-shaped" Mrs. Bundren will preside over the house; and in a short time Dewey Dell's secret will become apparent to all—*"by the womb of time: the agony and the despair of spreading bones, the hard girdle in which lie the outraged entrails of events."* The journey of the Bundrens is not the Christian journey to eternity because it ends at the cemetery where Addie, now only a material object, "a bundle of rotten sticks," can become identified with the dust of those who bore her: "the reason for living was to get ready to stay dead a long time."

The flowing images in the novel suggest the continual process of becoming. Death is given importance as a part of the life cycle because every day man dies a little bit; he is (as Unamuno said) "The man of flesh and bone; the man who is born, suffers, and dies—above all, who dies." But death is not presented as a release from the temporal into the infinite. Life supposedly is preceded by nothing and is followed by nothing. Dr. Peabody speculates on death: "The nihilists say it is the end; the fundamentalists, the beginning; when in reality it is no more than a single tenant or family moving out of a tenement or a town" (p. 368). The Bundrens lack traditional values; and the only religious sentiments, those of Whitfield and Cora, are selfish, hollow, and insincere.

The situation in *As I Lay Dying* is similar to the one presented by Tolstoy in "The Death of Ivan Ilych": the significance of life is recognized only as one lies dying; for at the hour of death, or at the moment when one realizes the uncertainty of his every action and the immediate possibility of his own death, the actuality of life in all its superficiality and hypocrisy stands exposed, stripped of all its futile and worthless shams and adornments. When the dying person realizes that death is the only certainty in, the only reality of, and the principal reason for human existence, the horror and dread of death disappear. This is the realization of Addie Bundren, whose existence became death-directed, revealed generally in her resignation to the perpetual imminence of her inevitable death and specifically in her deathbed supervision of the building of her coffin. The "phenomenology of death" in the novel resembles Martin Heidegger's concept of human existence as essentially "Being-toward-death."

Addie's dead and decomposing body becomes a cohesive force holding the family together in the journey; the fact of death overshadows and sublimates their own petty selfishnesses and dissensions; they can endure as a unit only until the moment when the last spadeful of sod has covered her coffin. With death ceasing to be an immediate and inescapable reality for them, Jewel can turn on Darl, Cash can go to the doctor, Dewey Dell can get her "pills," Anse, his teeth, and Vardaman, his bananas.

The symbolism of the novel suggests a separation between those who exist and those who do not. Addie has the "courage to be," but Anse does not. Cash is practical but pathetically simple-minded. Dewey Dell lacks the courage to face the future, and Vardaman is bewildered by his excursion into the adult world. The only Bundrens who make the journey without selfish motives, Darl and Jewel, are incomplete human beings. Jewel is a "committed" man, but (to quote Darl) he "does not know whether he is or not" (p. 396). In these two brothers there is a Cartesian split between the self as matter and the self as thought, accentuated in Darl's estrangement from his own body. Jewel is a "doer"—he acts but does not think (his single monologue is filled with "thoughts" of action). Darl is a thinker (or a "seer")—he thinks but does not act (his only actions are negative). Not one of the Bundrens seems capable of love. Addie's liaison with Whitfield is destructive; she used him as an instrument of revenge, not as a person. The relationship between Addie and Jewel is violent and ambiguous, with suggestions of repressed incestuous desires. Darl probes ultimate questions of ontological existence, but he never translates thoughts into actions or considers ethical responsibility. He tries to stand outside his body and to use his material self as a tool. All the Bundrens treat other people as *objects*, not as *subjects*. The Bundren way is a vitiation of human existence. Cora's opinions are not usually worth much, but one of her observations is truer than she could realize: "A Bundren through and through, loving nobody, caring for nothing except how to get something with the least amount of work" (p. 352).

As I Lay Dying does not conclude with a cry of despair; nor is there hope that the sun will rise again. Although the novel is both humorous and sad, the theme is neither the comedy of human frailty nor the tragedy of human endeavor; it is the absurdity of human existence. This should make it evident why the French translation was received enthusiastically by the Parisian existentialists; they could agree with the picture of life in the novel, especially the emphasis on existence, the treatment of a scene by one "engaged" in it, the antichronology of events, the utter nullity of nonexistence, the loneliness and anguish of man, and the emptiness and futility of life.

But a picture of meaninglessness need not be meaningless. The novelist, omniscient in his imaginary world, can express meaning through the form in which he casts his story. The shifting chronology and different points of view in *As I Lay Dying* give a richer, multi-sided impression, but, more important, they represent an attempt to reveal tensions below the surface. A reaffirmation of life is found not in the plot but in Faulkner's creative and critical awareness and interpretation of the situation, communicated through the total structure of the work. Behind the consciousness and unconsciousness of the characters there is the superior mind of the artist, who has seen the meaninglessness of their existence and has had the courage to face it and to express it. Although the materials of the novel are nihilistic, the form is dynamic. *As I Lay Dying* presents a powerful and original picture of the moral predicament of the twentieth century. And the meaning of the book is clarified and its significance increased when it is examined in the context of existentialism. The present analysis should help the reader understand Faulkner's profound image of man and appreciate his artistic achievement. In *As I Lay Dying* Faulkner has written an existential novel of depth and merit.

Faulkner's "Golden Book":
The Reivers as Romantic Comedy

JAMES M. MELLARD
Northern Illinois University

The Reivers lacks the technical and stylistic grandeur of William Faulkner's best four or five novels, yet it provides the perspectives and themes that finally complete the picture of the world of Yoknapatawpha. Without equal in American fiction, Faulkner's mythopoeic vision is many-sided, but until the last novel, character emphases have often been on the weak and defeated, while themes and structures have usually been tragic or ironic. In *The Reivers,* however, Faulkner gives us the "upper norm" against which the other levels of his world may be judged; and he has presented this norm in a fictional form that, from him, seems quite unexpected. In his greatest novels Faulkner experiments with a variety of forms and techniques, but his basic methods are those of "modal counterpoint" and what Susan Sontag calls "radical juxtaposition." *The Sound and the Fury* offers the best examples of both methods. In the four original sections of the novel Faulkner creates four separate narrative modes—Benjy's is a type of romance, Quentin's is tragedy, Jason's is irony-satire, and Dilsey's is comedy. These narrative modes are counterpointed rather than blended, however. Likewise, in the same four sections Faulkner employs four distinct techniques—or what Northrop Frye calls "radicals of presentation": Benjy's narrative is presented dramatically, Quentin's lyrically, Jason's as oral narration, and Dilsey's pictorially.[1] These

---

First published: 13, no. 3 (1965): 19–31. The essay has been expanded in its introductory paragraph, slightly altered here and there throughout, and brought up to date in its bibliographical notes.

1. For a more detailed discussion of some of these matters, see my essays, "Caliban as Prospero: Benjy and *The Sound and the Fury,*" *Novel* 3 (Spring 1970): 233–48; "*The Sound and the Fury*: Quentin Compson and Faulkner's 'Tragedy of Passion,'" *Studies in the Novel* 2 (Spring 1970): 61–75; "Jason Compson: Humor, Hostility, and the Rhetoric of Aggression," *Southern Humanities Review* 3 (Summer 1969): 259–67; and "Faulkner's Jason and the Tradition of Oral Narrative," *Journal of Popular Culture* 2 (Fall 1968): 195–210.

radicals of presentation, like the narrative modes, are juxtaposed, but they are not blended. Though one would never claim that Faulkner's novel ultimately fails at achieving a synthesis, the point to be made is that his techniques and forms follow this pattern rather consistently, for we can see either or both modal counterpoint and radical juxtaposition in *As I Lay Dying, Light in August, Absalom, Absalom!, The Unvanquished, The Wild Palms,* and *Go Down, Moses*— all the major works of the major phase, in short. The distinction that *The Reivers* has lies in its melding disparate, contrasting, or competing modes into a unified, nondisjunctive form, one more traditional and conventional than might be expected from such a dedicated experimentalist.

The Reivers is neither a comic satire on "boy's adventure stories" nor a romantically nostalgic reminiscence, as several critics have suggested, though elements of both comedy and romance must certainly be recognized. As Cleanth Brooks writes in his *William Faulkner: The Yoknapatawpha Country* (New Haven and London: Yale University Press, 1963), the novel "is consistently comic in spirit" (p. 350), but its version of Yoknapatawpha "takes on something of the attraction of a country in romance" (p. 351). Yet such observations do not place the novel very exactly. Hence, the following analysis, in order to set the novel in a particular formal tradition, will show that characters, structure, and themes belong, first, to the mode of comedy generally and, second, to the form of romantic comedy specifically.

Before a discussion of structure and theme, we turn briefly to characterization. Reviewers have noted, of course, Lucius Priest's affinities to several youthful heroes in Faulkner and to such other figures in American fiction as Huck Finn, Tom Sawyer, Henry Fleming, and Holden Caulfield. What may need discussion, therefore, are other characters in *The Reivers* who also belong to long-established archetypal patterns. Northrop Frye, in *Anatomy of Criticism* (Princeton, N.J.: Princeton University Press, 1957) tells us that in comedy there are four major character types: *eirons* or sympathetic characters, *alazons* or blocking characters, *bomolochoi* or buffoons, and *agroikos* or churlish and rustic characters (pp. 171–77). All four major types, as well as several subtypes, are found in *The Reivers*.

Buffoons, the characters who set the comic mood or atmosphere, are found among Boon Hogganbeck, Miss Reba and Mr. Binford, Minnie of the gold tooth, Sam Caldwell and the "mud farmer." Boon is the major representative, although at times he threatens to be taken seriously as protagonist rather than buffoon. His function in maintaining the humorous atmosphere may be seen from the outset, where his magnificent ineptitude with a gun is comically demonstrated, through the end, where he battles Butch, the deputy, not for sleeping wth Boon's girl friend, but for calling her a "whore." Most of the novel's humor is based upon one or another of these comic characters, yet they serve other plot purposes by either causing or eliminating complications. Their major importance, however, is in keeping the situations in the novel from becoming either tragic or ironic. Mr. Binford's comments about Lucius's staying in a bawdy house, for example, underplays the boy's moral plight, while Miss Reba's remarks about Corrie's succumbing to Butch keeps that event in the perspective of comedy. And, of course, Boon's potentially serious conflict with Butch can never be taken too seriously as long as Boon stays in character.

Butch Lovemaiden, the corrupt deputy, is the only real antagonist for the reivers, for the other conflicts are either psychological (between Lucius and his conscience) or "artificial" (between the two sides in the horse races). As the archetypal figure of the blocking character in comedy, Butch is both the embodiment of a cruel law and a physical rival to the romantic desires of the protagonists, principally Boon Hogganbeck. In function, Butch is a conventionally comic *alazon*, though in personality he is more melodramatically villainous than humorous. But as a type Butch is a variation of the *miles gloriosus*, a blustering, braggart, cowardly nonentity who is easily routed when the institutional props are kicked out by his opposite, Mr. Poleymus, the tough but kindly Parsham lawman.

Just as romance characterization is usually dialectical, the characterization of romantic comedy often shows sets of counterparts. Noted in *The Reivers*, for example, are the amorous contrasts between Boon and Butch and the institutional contrast between Butch and Mr. Poleymus—the corrupt law and the benevolent law. A contrast that is essentially parallel to Boon's and Butch's, because it is centered on Miss Corrie, is that between Lucius and Otis, the physically and morally deformed fifteen-year-old. Whereas Otis exploits Corrie and attempts to make money by surreptitiously charging others to see her work during her business hours, Lucius raises her to a higher moral and social level by "converting" her from her life of sin to the life of redeeming motherhood through his own innocent belief in her goodness. Thus, Otis is the *agroikos* or churl who stands opposite the sympathetic protagonist, Lucius. He becomes a blocking character, in the same general category with Butch, by attacking the hero's innocent view of life; Lucius, on the other hand, becomes the central *eiron* in *The Reivers* and, by withstanding Otis and transforming Miss Corrie, may be seen as the agent of salvation or redemption—as his names ("light" and "priest") suggest—who is usually present in romances. But Lucius, a moral catalyst rather than a reagent, plays another major role, for he provides the innocent, unworldly point of view from which the reivers' adventures can be judged as meaningful rather than only juvenile and absurd.

In addition to Lucius and Boon, who may be grouped with the *eirons* despite his buffoonery, three other characters belong to this type: Miss Corrie, Grandfather Priest, and Ned McCaslin. Miss Corrie, despite her profession, has most of the characteristics of the heroine of comedy. She is a representative of the rebirth suggested in most comedy, and she helps to bring about the comic resolution; moreover, as heroine she is at once a mother figure (to Lucius), the goal of a quest that is essentially sexual (for Boon), and the figure, after her conversion, around whom a recrystallized, reintegrated society forms.

Grandfather Priest, the "benevolent-father figure," and Ned McCaslin, the "tricky servant," are characters who are important because of special structural requirements. The first, Grandfather Priest, serves two conventional functions: he withdraws, at the beginning, so that the major events of the plot may occur (the reivers' taking the automobile, going to Memphis and the bawdy house, and then on to Parsham and the races) and he returns, at the end, to conclude the action. Ned McCaslin also serves conventional purposes. An extremely "tricky servant," he is required because of the limitations of his cohorts. Neither Lucius nor Boon is capable of bringing off the comic actions, so to the youth of one Ned brings maturity, and to the simplicity of the other he brings intelligence. Admittedly, without Ned, Lucius and Boon would never have got into so many escapades, but without him they might never have emerged triumphant at all. Certainly without Ned, who seems both the novel's comic spirit and the author's agent for a happy ending, *The Reivers* would be a much less interesting work.

The Reivers is an initiation story, as most reviewers and critics have observed. But it is really quite different from most of the stories it is linked to, primarily because of such characters as Ned and Grandfather Priest, who manage to avoid either tragic or ironic conclusions to Lucius Priest's initiatory ritual. Moreover, because of these characters, as well as the plethora of strictly comic figures, and the structure they give the novel's plot, the basic themes of *The Reivers* suggest no real loss of innocence nor do they insist that the world as we know it is any less desirable than our imagined dream worlds. Consequently, *The Reivers* illustrates "the archetypal function of literature in visualizing the world of desire, not as an escape from 'reality,' but as the genuine form of the world that human life tries to imitate" (Frye, p. 184), a function that few of our more famous initiation stories execute. And *The Reivers* can suggest such attitudes primarily because its structure and themes are characteristic of romantic comedy rather than a less idealized form such as that illustrated by stories of initiation, such as Joyce's "Araby," Anderson's "I'm a Fool," and "I Want To Know Why," or even Faulkner's own "Barn Burning," "The Bear," and *Absalom, Absalom!*

Northrop Frye tells us that the structure of comedy generally represents the movement from disorganization and social alienation to unity and social integration, a movement often symbolized by the pairing-off of male and female characters in the final scene, while the basic structure of romance is the quest. Combining elements of both comedy and romance, the structure of romantic comedy usually represents the movement from the normal world to a world of desire and back to the normal world (cf. Frye, pp. 181–84). And as a phase of comedy that has very close affinities to a corresponding phase of romance, romantic comedy is thus organized around a rhythmical pattern of departure, adventure-initiation, and return. Similar in structure to the sequence of "rites of passage" suggested by anthropologists and clearly (even if almost a parody) related to the mythological pattern of the "adventure of the hero" noted by Joseph Campbell, this cycle is represented in *The Reivers* by Boon's, Ned's and Lucius's leaving Jefferson, going to the Memphis "underworld" where they begin a series of fantastic adventures, and returning finally to Jefferson where Lucius, at least, learns the full meaning of the journey.

The individual episodes of *The Reivers* are grouped around the three points of cyclical movement expected in romantic comedy; thus the narrative structure of the novel includes episodes of departure from the normal world and travel to the desired world (chaps. 1–4), episodes of adventure and initiation in the world of fantasy and desire (chaps. 5–12), and episodes concluding the journey and returning the adventurers to the normal world (chap. 13).

The episodes concerned with getting the reivers out of Jefferson and on their way to Memphis take up most of the first third of the novel. In these chapters, Boon and Lucius make the decisions, precautions, and acquisitions necessary to accomplish the trip. After Lucius's family and Grandfather Priest, the owner of the requisite automobile, are called away to a funeral, Lucius and Boon decide to "borrow" the car; then they tell the people with whom Lucius is supposed to be staying that he is going to remain in town with his cousin Ike McCaslin instead. Finally, thinking they have covered their tracks completely, Boon and Lucius depart for Memphis, but not before Ned McCaslin stows away under a tarpaulin in the back of the automobile, to reveal himself only after much of the difficult trip is accomplished.

The novel's next few crises center on the trip to Memphis, which involves a series of obstacles increasing in difficulty and significance. The first objective is simply to get out of Jefferson and past the fork in the road that goes back to Aunt Callie's, where Lucius is expected to stay; but, Lucius says, "the fork, the last frail impotent hand reached down to save me, flew up and passed and fled, was gone, irrevocable," and looking forward to Memphis, he exults, "All right then. Here I come."[2] The next obstacle is Hurricane Creek, four miles from town, but Boon and Lucius, with a mighty effort, are able to push, pull, and virtually carry the auto through the quagmire that guards each side of the creek's wooden bridge. After spending the night at the legendary Ballenbaugh's, the site of the Iron Bridge and a milestone itself, the intrepid trio, for Ned finally rather gauchely reveals his presence, reach Hell Creek bottom, the final and greatest obstacle in their path. Hell Creek is almost too much for the runaway group, however, for they become seemingly inextricably stuck in the mud of the creek bottom. But ambivalent fortune approaches the reivers in the form of a backwoods "farmer" who offers to use his team of mules to tow the car from the mud. Boon accepts the offer, although reluctantly, and the "mud farmer," a "Charon-surrogate figure"[3] who keeps the road plowed so travelers will get stuck, pulls them out and charges Boon outrageously for the service. Once across Hell Creek, however, there is no turning back for the three reivers:

> Because the die was indeed cast now; we looked not back to remorse or regret or might-have-been; if we crossed Rubicon when we crossed the Iron Bridge into another county, when we conquered Hell Creek we locked the portcullis and set the bridge on fire. (P. 93)

Past Hell Creek, the symbolic barrier between two worlds, the three adventurers move out of their normal, "real" world into a new world of dreams come true. "The very land itself seemed to have changed," Lucius says. "The farms were bigger, more prosperous, with tighter fences and painted houses and even barns; the very air was urban" (p. 94). For Lucius, this brave new world is his fantasy land because it is, he thinks, the apotheosis of all that is urban, sophisticated, and exciting, but for Boon and Ned it is a realm of desire because of their anticipations of sexual and bacchanalian revels. For all, however, the episodes begin here that will dispel their illusions. The first episodes, providing some of the better if rather reminiscent humor of the novel, are centered on the innocent rustics' effects on life in a bawdy house. The romantic encounters here between Lucius's innocence and Memphis's degradation are climaxed by Miss Corrie's "conversion," which leads to yet another romantic plot, the conflict between Boon and Butch.

---

2. William Faulkner, *The Reivers* (New York: Random House, 1962), p. 68. Subsequent references to this novel are cited in parentheses in the text.

3. Peter Swiggart, *The Art of Faulkner's Novels* (Austin: University of Texas Press, 1962), p. 209.

Also begun at this time are the comic episodes relating to the stolen racehorse for which Ned had traded the "borrowed" automobile. These plots and subplots,

> camouflaging and masquerading Lightning at midnight through the Memphis tenderloin to get him to the depot; ruthlessly using a combination of uxoriousness and nepotism to disrupt a whole boxcar from the railroad system to get him to Parsham; . . . having to cope with Butch, Minnie's tooth, invading and outraging Uncle Parsham's home and sleeplessness and . . . homesickness and . . . not even a change of underclothes (P. 229),

all come to a climax at the end of the third race, when the boy "looked down from Lightning . . . and saw Grandfather and passed to him . . ." (pp. 303–4).

The events of the third stage in the cyclical movement of the narrative structure are essentially undramatic, but Faulkner manages to make this section important and interesting, for in it he reveals the methods by which the several comic and romantic resolutions have been accomplished. We learn, for example, that Minnie's gold tooth, stolen by the wizened Otis, has been restored by Ned McCaslin, that Miss Corrie has given herself to the villainous Butch in order to get Ned and Boon out of jail so that they can run the second and third heats in the horserace, that Ned has used his knowledge of Lightning's love of sardines to cause him to win the third race, and that Boon, upon being let out of jail, has fought and whipped Butch, "pistol and all," for calling Corrie a "whore." Finally, Faulkner devotes the last few pages to clarifications of motives and themes and the revelations that Ned has bet against Lightning in a special fourth race and has won a large sum of money as a result of his *not* using the miraculous sardines on the horse again, that Lucius is reconciled with his family and accepts his responsibilities, and that Boon Hogganbeck and Miss Corrie eventually get married, have a child, and name it after Lucius Priest.

The thematic development of *The Reivers* parallels the development of narrative, for the novel's themes are also from both romance and comedy. The major themes of romance suggest the triumph of the world of life, love, fertility, innocence, over the world of death, lust, sterility, experience; the major theme of comedy is the integration of the family and society (cf. Frye, pp. 186–95, 163–71). The novel's romance theme, the maintenance of the world of innocence against the assaults of the world of experience, is suggested in the first part of the narrative, in which the reivers make the decision to leave Jefferson to go to Memphis, symbolically the decision to leave the normal, real world for the fantasy world of desire. In this section, Lucius is concerned about his virtue and innocence, his ignorance and lack of power to act, and his use of free will. But because he has determined to go even before Boon tries to "seduce" him, Lucius obviates his claims to either innocence or ignorance. Faulkner writes, for example, that the child is neither innocent nor ignorant, that there is not a crime an eleven-year-old has not thought of: "His only innocence is, he may not yet be old enough to desire the fruits of it, which is not innocence but appetite; his ignorance is, he does not know how to commit it, which is not ignorance but size" (p. 46). Thus only lacking in size and power of action, Lucius is more a seducer of Boon than the reverse, for he becomes Boon's intellectual guide, a fact that Lucius, Faust-like, recognizes and revels in saying, "I was the leader, I was the boss, the master" (p. 53).

Having discovered that "the goddess in charge of virtue seems to be the same one in charge of luck, if not of folly also" (p. 51), Lucius reaches some interesting conclusions. He decides that in the battle between virtue and non-virtue, virtue has little chance of success, although in a moment of weakness he almost gives up his plans for adventure: he says, "suddenly I wanted my mother; I wanted no more of this, no more of free will; I wanted to return, to relinquish, be secure, safe from the sort of decisions and deciding whose foster twin was this having to steal an automobile" (p. 66). But, as Lucius realizes, it is too late: "I had already chosen, elected; if I had sold my soul to Satan for a mess of pottage, at least I would damn well collect the pottage and eat it too . . ." (p. 66). Although confident that he will resist all temptation to relinquish his decision, Lucius nevertheless has moments of doubt as he leaves behind both the psychological and physical barriers, the crossroads going back to Aunt Callie's, the Iron Bridge, Hurricane Creek, and Hell Creek. But finally he and the others emerge on the other side, in what they think of as their dream worlds, feeling that "it did seem as though we had won to reprieve as a reward for invincible determination, or refusal to recognize defeat when we faced it or it faced us"; feeling also, and thematically more importantly, that "maybe it was just Virtue who had given up, relinquished us to Non-virtue to cherish and nurture and coddle in the style whose right we had won with the now irrevocable barter of our souls" (pp. 93–94). So now the three adventurers, but particularly Lucius, are no longer of the world of virtue, but neither are they of the world of "un-virtue." They are in a kind of moral and ethical never-never-land in which they must eventually make meaningful choices.

The second phase of thematic development reveals an essential fact concerning Lucius's conclusions about virtue and nonvirtue and his (and Boon's and Ned's, in fact) conception of a dream world: they were all wrong. Lucius had lost neither his virtue nor his innocence, but had decided only to test them, and his conception of a dream world was actually only an illusion. That he had not lost his youthful innocence is suggested in a number of his actions and statements. In his encounters with Otis and "pugnuckling," for example, Lucius shows an almost unaccountable lack of worldly knowledge, and he manifests a rather knightly devotion to virtue and decency when he attacks Otis for having debased the privacy of Corrie in "her defenseless and undefended and unavenged degradation" (p. 157). Similarly, because of the Boon-Corrie-Butch triangle, Lucius reveals a strong sense of idealism and outraged innocence in a momentary hatred for all those who suffer, as well as those who cause human suffering: he cannot help

hating all of [them] for being the poor frail victims of being alive, having to be alive—hating Everbe for being the vulnerable helpless lodestar victim; and Boon for being the vulnerable and helpless victimised; and Uncle Parsham and Lycurgus for being where they had to, couldn't help but watch white people behaving exactly as white people bragged that only Negroes behaved—just as [he] had hated Otis for telling [him] about Everbe in Arkansas and hated Everbe for being that helpless lodestar for human debasement which he had told [him] about and hated [himself] for listening, having to hear about it, learn about it, know about it; hating that such not only was, but must be, had to be if living was to continue and mankind be a part of it. (P. 174)

The knowledge of self and the world revealed in this passage suggests a progress toward disillusionment and loss of innocence. Lucius even says a moment later that "innocence and childhood were forever lost, forever gone from me" (p. 175). But to stress too much Lucius's initiation into a world of unredeemed evil is to more or less contradict the meaning of subsequent passages. After the first heat of the race, for example, Lucius reverts to his innocent, childlike ways and bawls "like a baby . . . against Uncle Parsham's shirt" (p. 246) as they ride peacefully along in a mule-drawn wagon. Similarly, he wishes for home and his mother after he gets back to Uncle Parsham's and still has to wait for Ned and Boon to get out of jail. Moreover, he manifests his continuing innocence and idealism when he fails to believe that Corrie had yielded her reconstituted virtue to the villainous Butch; and the same faith is indicated, in a rather different way, when he accepts her reasons for compromising and evidently accepts the ultimate durability of her "conversion." And at the novel's conclusion Lucius is himself aware that very little had outwardly changed since he, Boon, and Ned had left Jefferson less than a week before, despite his having learned a great deal more about himself, other people, and the world.

What had actually changed was Lucius's attitude toward his own world, for he replaces the illusion with the vision of reality. Now he realizes that not Memphis with its spurious charms is the ideal, but that it is the firm, earthly, and gentlemanly haven of Jefferson and Parsham. Lucius's realization of the value of his own way of life comes in chapter 11; there he suffers a kind of dark night of the soul and finds solace and peace through confession and communion with Uncle Parsham, the old Negro who temporarily takes the place of Grandfather Priest. Although the initial realization comes here, Lucius's actually replacing as an ideal the old Memphian fantasy-world with his own way of life and his sense of belonging in it come in the final chapter.

In the theme of integration and social unity, symbolized by Corrie's conversion, her marriage, and Lucius's reconcilation, we find our clearest indication of the basic theme of comedy. Though Lucius's knowledge of the real world reveals the falsity of his illusions and pushes him toward an acceptance of an ordinary existence, the most meaningful change is that the normal existence itself then becomes the ideal. This turn in the thematic development represents the greatest difference between a story like, say, "The Bear" and *The Reivers*. In "The Bear" Ike's disillusionment is with the real world, which he all along had idealized; thus what Ike rejects is that which Lucius wholeheartedly embraces at the novel's conclusion. Clearly, however, such a distinction is not always obvious (perhaps because of Faulkner's inability to handle the theme) and critics can read the novel in two rather contradictory ways: at first Cleanth Brooks, for example, writes, "In the experience of the last four days Lucius had stepped across the boundary from boyhood to manhood . . ." (p. 351), but later he says, Lucius "can now throw off his responsibility . . . and be a child again" (p. 365). Actually, the contradictions can be minimized and virtually eliminated if one recognizes the structures and themes of romantic comedy in the novel. Lucius is not so much initiated into manhood as he is integrated into the society to which he truly belongs.

Although such passages as those showing Lucius at Uncle Parsham's contribute to his awareness of the value of his own everyday mode of living, the youthful Lucius's idealization of the normal world occurs in the third stage of the narrative and thematic structure. In the final chapter an early suggestion of Lucius's changed attitude comes in his expression of admiration for the home of Mr. Van Tosch, a representative of Lucius's own social class. But the best indication of the change in Lucius's value system is the development of what Brooks calls the theme of the gentleman. Prepared for earlier by Uncle Parsham's comments on the "gentleman" mule and Lucius's admiration for Mr. Poleymus, it is given its fullest treatment in the final chapter in comments from major characters. For example, when Lucius breaks into tears because of the strain of his ordeal, his grandfather tells him, "a gentleman cries too, but he always washes his face" (p. 303). Similarly, Lucius himself says, "a gentleman always sticks to his lie whether he told it or not" (p. 304). Ned, too, implies some ideal code when he talks about the ethics of his and the grandfather's gambling. Lucius's grandfather makes perhaps the most important statement about the "normal" but rather idealized code that both he and, now, Lucius represent; he tells the youth that he will live over the recent adventures because

> "a gentleman always does. A gentleman can live through anything. He faces anything. A gentleman accepts the responsibility of his actions and bears the burden of their consequences, even when he did not himself instigate them but only acquiesced to them, didn't say no though he knew he should." (P. 302)

Through the theme of the gentleman, then, *The Reivers* emphasizes responsibility and freedom of the will, themes treated often in other Faulkner novels, but here the treatment is romantic and comic, not ironic and tragic.

In an interview with Jean Stein, Faulkner said that his last novel would be the Doomsday Book, the Golden Book, of Yoknapatawpha.[4] The first term sounds rather ominous, but, coupling it as he did with the other, Faulkner could only have meant that the last Yoknapatawpha novel would complete his mythic vision: as it stood in the works up to *The Reivers*, Faulkner's *Weltansicht* seems to be dominated by the tragic view and the forces of experience—lust, sterility, frustration, and death. But implicit in many of the "darker" works, particularly *Light in August* and *Go Down, Moses,* is a view, the comic, that is radically different,

---

4. "William Faulkner: An Interview," in *William Faulkner: Three Decades of Criticism,* ed. Frederick J. Hoffman and Olga Vickery (East Lansing, Mich.: Michigan State University Press, 1960), p. 82. For a different approach to the novel as "Golden Book," see the essay by Elizabeth M. Kerr, "*The Reivers:* The Golden Book of Yoknapatawpha County," *Modern Fiction Studies* 13 (Spring 1967): 95–113. My conclusions can be augmented by William Rossky, "*The Reivers:* Faulkner's 'Tempest,'" *The Mississippi Quarterly* 18 (Spring 1965): 82–93, and by the late Olga Vickery's excellent chapter on *The Reivers* in her revised edition of *The Novels of William Faulkner* (Baton Rouge: Louisiana State University Press, 1964), pp. 228–39.

emphasizing as it does the contrary forces of innocence—love, fertility, fulfillment, and life. Because *The Reivers* contains the themes and employs the structure of romantic comedy, it becomes Faulkner's "Golden Book" in which he presents his most clearly comic vision. But there are other suggestions of the novel's "naive" assumptions. A technical indication, in addition to the romantic-comedy structure, is the novel's point of view. Narrated by Lucius Priest, the aged grandfather, rather than the eleven-year-old protagonist, it is told, apparently, to a group of children (the novel begins: "Grandfather said:") a situation that implies that the story is in fact the kind one might expect in a child's "Golden Book." Moreover, this convention suggests the novel's affinity to an even more romantic literary phase than romantic comedy itself: this phase, which Frye calls the *penseroso* stage of romance, is found, in popular literature, in "what might be called cuddle fiction: the romance that is physically associated with comfortable beds or chairs around fireplaces and cosy spots generally" (Frye, p. 202). Of course, this is barely implied in *The Reivers,* but another "characteristic feature of this phase is the tale in quotation marks" (*ibid.*), which *The Reivers* actually presents, though Faulkner avoids the inconvenience of that punctuation. As a "Golden Book" for children, the novel is a bit gamey at times, but as one for adults it certainly may be palatable, and it is not surprising that the movie version—excellently casting Burgess Meredith as the narrator and Will Geer as Grandfather—is colored over with the golden hues of an almost Disney-like period piece. Neither "fairy tale" nor pure romance, the two forms that allow the greatest freedom in the comic direction, *The Reivers* is as near to either as Faulkner could come and still remain within the literary canons of realism.

It is only appropriate that Faulkner should conclude this way, not simply because he predicted it but because his "world" is thus made complete. Faulkner's earlier novels show the consequences of man's exercising his will and responsibility, but the outcome is almost invariably somber. In *The Reivers,* Faulkner implies that man is most human in exercising his free will, but he also suggests that he has the distinct possibility of achieving a happy end, an end that is desired because the world itself is desirable and because innocence, like Lucius's, for example, is able to withstand the assault of experience and never necessarily loses the battle. Thus, the world of innocence, seen earlier but never so clearly, is pictured as both attractive and powerful in *The Reivers.* Where in the past its forces had fallen to the powers of darkness, here they resist and, in fact, vanquish their enemy in a triumph represented by the new life that enters with the Hogganbeck's child, named, significantly enough, after Lucius Priest, the novel's bringer of light. And we feel, at the novel's conclusion, whether we agree with him or not, that we have at last seen what Faulkner considers the best of his world, a world in which man not only endures but can also prevail.

Jay Gatsby and Dr. Diver: Fitzgerald's Songs of Innocence and Experience

CLINTON S. BURHANS, JR.

Michigan State University

I

Coupling Fitzgerald with Blake would seem at first glance to be little more than a fruitless exercise in academic ingenuity. Blake's reality is as far removed from that of Fitzgerald as are the manner and the materials in which he expresses it. A God who made both lamb and tiger; who lives as immediate presence in the pure soul of the young boy, joyous in nature; and who remains implicit and judging behind the urban world's tarnishing of that soul—all of this has very little to do with the Jazz Age and the Côte d'Azur. Clearly, one had better be wary about stretching any connection too far.

Still, Blake's poems make an interesting and revealing context for experiencing Fitzgerald's major novels. Five years elapsed between Blake's two groups of songs; nine years separate Fitzgerald's two stories. Despite the obvious differences between the writers and their art, the contrast between Fitzgerald's novels constitutes a qualitative change similar in nature to that between Blake's works and exceeding it in extent. Most important, the vast differences between Blake's sense of reality and Fitzgerald's indicate the essential terms for understanding the change from Jay Gatsby to Dick Diver, from innocence to experience as Fitzgerald here perceives them.

Fitzgerald's reality is entirely secular and humane and is most clearly reflected in the theme around which most of his writing centers: dream and disillusion.[1]

This is the first publication of the essay.

1. I have stressed this theme before in "Structure and Theme in *This Side of Paradise*," *Journal of English and Germanic Philology* 68, no. 4 (October 1969): 605–24; and in " 'Magnificently Attune to Life': The Value of 'Winter Dreams,' " *Studies in Short Fiction* 6, no. 4 (Summer 1969): 401–12. In addition, Michael Steinberg of Michigan State University's Department of American Thought and Language is currently completing under my direction a dissertation on this theme in Fitzgerald's thought and art.

From Amory Blain to Monroe Stahr, in serious writing or in pot-boilers, Fitzgerald plays variations on man's ineluctable capacity for demanding the heart's desire in terms that contain their own disillusion, whether the dream be lost or out of reach or won and found wanting, and on the worse disillusion following the inability or the loss of the power to dream. It is a serious theme, a noble and even a tragic one, a theme that transmutes Fitzgerald's individual experience into national and universally human significance.

Both *The Great Gatsby* and *Tender is the Night* derive their dynamics and their magnitude from this theme at all three levels of its significance, though in obviously different terms. More specifically, the differences between Jay Gatsby and Dr. Diver make a study in contrasts between a kind of innocence and a kind of experience, but in meanings far removed in most respects from Blake's. Consciously or subconsciously, Fitzgerald senses that innocence and experience for modern man have little to do with questions of sex or of a conflict between nature and civilization and nothing whatever to do with religious or metaphysical absolutes. At least by implication, Fitzgerald locates the qualities of innocence and experience entirely in human consciousness, in psychological and emotional imperatives that bring man into conflict with his existential realities. In Gatsby and Diver he suggests that innocence and experience are involved in problems of omnipotence and limitation, in Gatsby's unshakable conviction that he can do whatever he wants, even to turning back the clock and re-creating the past, and in Dr. Diver's gradual awareness of unbreakable bonds. And nowhere more than in this, perhaps, does Fitzgerald speak more meaningfully to our time, for he is also highlighting the tragedy of American history and life and the central problem in contemporary man's struggle for survival.

II

After the party that Daisy attends at Gatsby's house, Nick realizes that Gatsby wants everything to be exactly as it once was, "just as if it were five years ago." When Nick tells him "you can't repeat the past," Gatsby is astounded: "'Can't repeat the past?' he cried incredulously. 'Why of course you can!'" (p. 111).[2] Here is Gatsby's true song of innocence, the burden of that "romantic readiness' (p. 2) which so impresses Nick Carraway. To understand this innocence, its sources and implications, we must, of course, turn to Nick, the Yale humanist through whose consciousness we see this singer of a song whose nature denies him the awareness of singing it.

Nick's account of Gatsby's dreams occurs just past midpoint in the novel, very much *in medias res*. Born Jimmy Gatz on a poor North Dakota farm, Gatsby had become his own progenitor: "his parents were shiftless and unsuccessful farm people—his imagination had never really accepted them as his parents at all. The truth was that Jay Gatsby of West Egg, Long Island, sprang from his Platonic conception of himself." The phrase is Nick's, of course—Gatsby could not conceivably think in such terms—and it is crucial to an understanding of Gatsby and his dreams. These dreams are ultimately unanchored, supernal. Unlike

---

2. Page references in parentheses after quotations are to the Scribner's Student's edition (New York, 1953).

Dexter Green of "Winter Dreams," who "wanted not association with glittering things and glittering people—he wanted the glittering things themselves,"[3] Gatsby's dreams express his inescapable and overwhelming sense of unlimited wonder, of unconditioned beauty and greatness. They "hint of the unreality of reality, a promise that the rock of the world was founded securely on a fairy's wing."

Here is Gatsby's magnificence, that "heightened sensitivity to the promises of life" which Nick so deeply appreciates (p. 2); but here, too, is Gatsby's tragedy. Whatever it may be founded on, the rock of the world is where he must pursue his dreams; and the dust of its conditions and experiences must inevitably give those limitless and supernal dreams a limited and material form that will doom them. This, too, Nick understands: Gatsby, he says, "was a son of God—a phrase which, if it means anything, means just that—and he must be about His Father's business, the service of a vast, vulgar, and meretricious beauty." What else could be in the mind of a Jimmy Gatz, bursting with youthful energy and dreams on a bleak and failing North Dakota farm, to give those dreams some meaningful shape? "His heart was in a constant, turbulent riot," Nick adds. "The most grotesque and fantastic conceits haunted him in his bed at night. A universe of ineffable gaudiness spun itself out in his brain while the clock ticked on the washstand and the moon soaked with wet light his tangled clothes upon the floor. Each night he added to the pattern of his fancies until drowsiness closed down upon some vivid scene with an oblivious embrace" (pp. 98–100).

A brain exploding with dreams beside a ticking clock, moonlight soaking tangled clothes—no wonder Dan Cody's yacht and the opportunity implicit in saving it come as an epiphany to Jimmy Gatz, giving immediate and tangible form to the ineffable gaudiness of his dreams and turning him into Jay Gatsby. And if his dreams, thus materialized and limited, are thereby doomed, they nevertheless protect him by their very nature from realizing it and from the dust floating in their wake.

Dan Cody and his yacht, then, and all they represent of wealth and power, give Jimmy Gatz's immortal longings a local habitation and a name; they give him a "singularly appropriate education; the vague contour of Jay Gatsby had filled out to the substantiality of a man" (p. 102). Not surprisingly, he finds in Daisy the complete embodiment of his dreams; all his yearnings and their "vulgar and meretricious" expression in his experience with Dan Cody fuse in her mystery and excitment and beauty. As an Army officer, he is able for the first time to move freely on her social level; "she was the first 'nice' girl he had ever known." Her house has "a ripe mystery" for him; it hints "of bedrooms upstairs more beautiful and cool than other bedrooms . . . of romances that were not musty and laid away already in lavender, but fresh and breathing and redolent of this year's shining motor-cars and of dances whose flowers were scarcely withered" (p. 148). Her voice is full of a mysterious excitement; even Nick is so impressed by it that he recalls at least a dozen times "her low, thrilling voice. It was the kind of voice that the ear follows up and down, as if each speech is an arrangement of notes that will never be played again . . . there was an excitement in her voice that men who had cared for her found difficult to forget: a singing

---

3. F. Scott Fitzgerald, *Babylon Revisited and Other Stories* (New York: Scribner's Sons, 1960), p. 118.

compulsion, a whispered 'Listen,' a promise that she had done gay, exciting things just a while since and that there were gay, exciting things hovering in the next hour"(pp. 9–10).

If Daisy's mystery and excitement give her for Gatsby the quality of his dreams, she is even more what life with Dan Cody had taught him to seek in pursuit of those dreams. He finds her "excitingly desirable" (p. 148); she is beautiful, popular, well-born, and rich. "Her voice is full of money," he later tells Nick; and Nick agrees. "That was it. I'd never understood before. It was full of money—that was the inexhaustible charm that rose and fell in it, the jingle of it, the cymbal's song of it . . . High in a white palace the king's daughter, the golden girl . . ." (p. 120).

Aware that his uniform is only a temporary passport into Daisy's world, Gatsby at first "intended, probably, to take what he could and go"; but he is caught in the current of his dreams. Sitting on her porch two days after they first make love, a porch "bright with the bought luxury of star-shine," he becomes "overwhelmingly aware of the youth and mystery that wealth imprisons and preserves, of the freshness of many clothes, and of Daisy, gleaming like silver, safe and proud above the hot struggles of the poor." The embodiment of Gatsby's dreams has flowered into love, and "now he found that he had committed himself to the following of a grail" (pp. 149–50). When he loses this grail to Tom Buchanan because of time and distance and Daisy's inconstancy, Gatsby makes a melancholy pilgrimage to the places he and Daisy had shared. Leaving in the hot and empty evening, his uniform gone, and penniless, "he stretched out his hand desperately as if to snatch only a wisp of air, to save a fragment of the spot that she had made lovely for him . . . he knew that he had lost that part of it, the freshest and the best, forever" (p. 153).

Nevertheless, some four years later, Gatsby stands on his lawn in West Egg, rich and powerful, yearning toward the green light across the bay on Daisy's dock, convinced that he can turn the clock back to that lost moment. And here, I think, is the crucial problem in understanding Gatsby's innocence. Nothing in Nick's description of Gatsby's sad departure from Louisville suggests that he has any idea whatever of trying to win Daisy back; yet his later yearning toward her across the bay implies that he has thought of little else. Probably because Gatsby was mostly silent about it, Nick does nothing to bridge this gap; we are left with a tantalizing lacuna. But somewhere in the weeks and months after leaving Louisville, he must have focused his dreams again on all that had first made Daisy shine for him: money, clothes, houses, position, all the things whose "vast, vulgar, and meretricious beauty" had always given form and substance to the "ineffable gaudiness" of those dreams. And slowly, as increasing success brought him these things in abundance, the image of Daisy must have begun again to dominate his imagination as their exemplar. With money flowing in and his power growing, he must have become convinced almost to the point of obsession that he could do anything, that he could even regain Daisy, rescue from her "terrible mistake" (p. 131) the lovely girl whose voice was full of money. And so this strange knight, arrayed in the white flannel armor of his pure dreams and the silver shirt and gold tie (pp. 84–85) of their inevitable incarnation, set off to seek the lost grail.

Here, too, insofar as it can be discerned and inferred, Gatsby's imaginative process in the course of his quest is as crucial as it is complex. In the beginning, of course, he must have wanted to regain Daisy simply for herself, the best and most beautiful of all his dreams and all the more desirable for being lost. But as the months and years rolled by, his desire must have become of endlessly deepening intensity; and his image of Daisy, separated longer and longer from its real source, must have taken on the limitless expansion of his supernal dreams. More important, this image must have grown subtly for Gatsby into more than just a dream, however beatific: it preserves his capacity for dreaming amid the dust and dirt and disorder of the activities bringing him the means to regain her. Certainly, when he and Daisy are reunited at last in Nick's house, Gatsby is a seething turbulence of dreams and desires beyond any secular and mortal fulfillment.

Gatsby doesn't know this, of course, and never does; this is precisely his innocence. But he cannot entirely escape a puzzling sense of clouds passing across the sun. After telling Daisy about seeing the green light at the end of her dock, "he seemed absorbed in what he had just said. Possibly it had occurred to him that the colossal significance of that light had now vanished forever. Compared to the great distance that had separated him from Daisy it had seemed very near to her, almost touching her. It had seemed as close as a star to the moon. Now it was again a green light on a dock. His count of enchanted objects had diminished by one" (p. 94).

So it is too with Daisy. Ecstatic as it is for him to be with her again at last, he finds, at least momentarily, an unaccountable gap between his dreams of her and their reality. Nick recalls that "the expression of bewilderment had come back into Gatsby's face, as though a faint doubt had occurred to him as to the quality of his present happiness. . . . There must have been moments even that afternoon when Daisy tumbled short of his dreams—not through her own fault, but because of the colossal vitality of his illusion. It had gone beyond her, beyond everything. He had thrown himself into it with a creative passion, adding to it all the time, decking it out with every bright feather that drifted his way. No amount of fire or freshness can challenge what a man will store up in his ghostly heart" (p. 97).

Unlike nearly all of Fitzgerald's other dreamers, however, Gatsby's doubts and bewilderment never fester into disillusion or loss. They pale into insignificance against the blaze of what his dream of Daisy has become, before the brilliance of its second and infinitely deeper dimension. For Gatsby no longer seeks Daisy as an end in the realizable present; his dream has truly "gone beyond her, beyond everything." In saving his capacity for dreaming, her image has become the means in his desperate pursuit of his own lost self, the self he has come to sense went astray in that moment when he had made her the apotheosis of all his dreams. In the years since then, he has begun to feel, though never sufficiently to bring realization or changed behavior, the vast disparity between the nature of his dreams and their materialization. The Daisy he seeks to regain is therefore neither the real woman he meets in Nick's house nor her inexpressible idealization; she is the young girl in whom he had first incarnated his dreams, the girl who has thus become for him the beginning of that long and puzzling process in which everything has gone subtly wrong by grossly succeeding. "He wanted to recover something," Nick explains, "some idea of himself perhaps, that had gone into loving Daisy. His life had been confused and disordered since then, but if he could once return to a certain starting place and go over it all slowly, he could find out what the thing was" (pp. 111–12).

This "starting place," Gatsby tells Nick, is the moment when he first kissed Daisy; and Nick interprets his "appalling sentimentality" by relating it implicitly to what he had earlier described as Gatsby's "Platonic conception of himself":

> One autumn night, five years before, they had been walking down the street when the leaves were falling, and they came to a place where there were no trees and the sidewalk was white with moonlight. . . . The quiet lights in the houses were humming out into the darkness and there was a stir and bustle among the stars. Out of the corner of his eye Gatsby saw that the blocks of the sidewalks really formed a ladder and mounted to a secret place above the trees— he could climb to it, if he climbed alone, and once there he could suck on the pap of life, gulp down the incomparable milk of wonder.
>
> His heart beat faster and faster as Daisy's white face came up to his own. He knew that when he kissed this girl, and forever wed his unutterable visions to her perishable breath, his mind would never romp again like the mind of God. So he waited, listening for a moment longer to the tuning-fork that had been struck upon a star. Then he kissed her. At his lips' touch she blossomed for him like a flower and the incarnation was complete. (P. 112)

The incarnation is complete; and the pattern, the tragic pattern, is established. Gatsby lost Daisy not when she married but when he kissed her, and he senses now that he had lost his own best self at the same time. No wonder he wants to repeat and re-create the past and is unquestioningly convinced that he can. What he does not know—indeed, cannot know—is that he can neither avoid such incarnations nor alter their essential consequences. To know this would be to die as Gatsby, and it is to preserve Gatsby, after all, that he sets out to repeat the past. "I'm going to fix everything the way it was before," he promises Nick. "She'll see" (p. 111). To know that he must repeat the past is to know that he can: in the dreamer of limitless dreams, necessity breeds the conviction of omnipotence and armors it in an incorruptible innocence.

And in this innocence, Gatsby goes unwaveringly to his death. It is proof against what Nick calls "the foul dust" that "floated in the wake of his dreams" (p. 2): it is even proof against the incredible weakness and vulgarity and corruption of Daisy and her world. He looks upon this wasteland with the eyes of Dr. T. J. Eckleburg, blind to ashes, and dies, I am certain, with his innocence unchipped, still convinced that only he can rescue the king's daughter from her sad mistakes and with her return to the beautiful land of his supernal dreams.

In all of this, in Gatsby's dreams and what they inevitably bring him to, Fitzgerald makes him metaphoric, microcosmic. Looking out over the Sound after Gatsby's death, Nick sees the full significance of him and his monstrous house in this place, in this time:

> Most of the big shore places were closed now and there were hardly any lights except the shadowy, moving glow of a ferryboat across the Sound. And as the moon rose higher the inessential houses began to melt away until gradually I became aware of the old island here that flowered once for Dutch sailors' eyes—a fresh, green breast of the new world. Its vanished trees, the trees that had made way for Gatsby's house, had once pandered in whispers to the last and greatest of all human dreams; for a transitory enchanted moment man must have held his breath in the presence of this continent, compelled into an esthetic contemplation he neither understood nor desired, face to face for

the last time in history with something commensurate to his capacity for wonder. (P. 182)

In general situation, in many details, and in several images, Nick's thinking about the Dutch sailors parallels his thoughts about the moment when Gatsby first kissed Daisy. Both scenes are connected with moonlight. Gatsby looks at Daisy, and the Dutch sailors look at Long Island through the agency of limitless dreams; for both, the object they gaze on is subtly threatening but irresistibly tempting. Both pause for a moment, filled with a sense of wonder; and each inevitably proceeds to materialize his ineffable dream. So it is also with imagery. Gatsby looks into "Daisy's white face"; the Dutch sailors are "face to face" with the American continent. Gatsby "could suck on the pap of life, gulp down the incomparable milk of wonder"; the sailors face "a fresh green breast of the new world," something equal to their "capacity for wonder." And when Gatsby kisses Daisy, "she blossomed for him like a flower"; the island "flowered once for Dutch sailors' eyes."

The correspondences here are too close to be accidental; clearly, Fitzgerald means us to see in Gatsby an analogy with the Dutch sailors and in Gatsby's dreams and their working out an analogy with the American experience. Like Gatsby, America has always been partly a "Platonic conception"; from the beginning, American history has been characterized by the limitless promise of the American dream. Like Gatsby, too, the American dream has bred its concomitant in American innocence, in the conviction that American resources and endeavor are boundless, that Americans can do anything. And, again like Gatsby, the American dream has all too often materialized in "a vast, vulgar, and meretricious beauty," has left in its wake the same "foul dust" of every other human activity. Both in Gatsby and in the American experience the process would seem to be inevitable: the "vanished trees" of the new world must always make "way for Gatsby's house."

For, at the deepest level, the tragedy of Gatsby and of the American dream is the tragedy of man. He is, Fitzgerald suggests, a creature who can dream a perfection he can never realize, a perfection whose fulfillment must always deny the dream of it. He lives between the "unutterable vision" and the "perishable breath," innocent in the conviction that somewhere, somehow, he can discover or create the ineffable beauty of his dream but doomed to find only its mutable materialization. The world is lethal to innocence like Gatsby's; death comes to him, after all, as a friend.

III

The story of Dr. Dick Diver sings a different song, a melody more intricate and somber, a song of experience with lyrics of limitation. In many respects, Diver is Gatsby inverted. Both men know dreams and desires, but Gatsby is dominated by dreams that originate in an intangible realm of ineffable visions; Diver's dreams are limited, diffuse, and secular. Both center their dreams in a girl, a process dramatized in a first kiss nearly at midpoint in each book: Gatsby's dream is preserved when he loses the girl; Diver's is doomed to attrition when he marries her. Both are concerned with the past and time: Gatsby is convinced that he can repeat and re-create the past and conquer time; Diver grows increasingly aware of a vanished and irredeemable past and hears time trickling away. In short, Gatsby is unique and redeemed by it; Diver is, in the end, like everyone else and doomed by it.

Like nearly everything else about him, Dr. Diver's origins vary substantially from Gatsby's. He was born in 1891 in Buffalo, New York, after the death of two young sisters; his father was an obscure but comfortable clergyman, a man "of tired stock" (p. 203)[4] who nevertheless found the strength to become the boy's moral guide. "His father had been sure of what he was, with a deep pride of the two proud widows who had raised him to believe that nothing could be superior to 'good instincts,' honor, courtesy, and courage" (p. 204). Later, Dick often "referred judgments to what his father would probably have thought or done" (p. 203). He studied at Yale, was a Rhodes Scholar at Oxford, took his degree in psychology at Johns Hopkins, studied and wrote in Vienna, and took a degree in psychiatry in Zurich. He then served for a year as an administrative officer in an Army medical unit, spending most of his time preparing for publication his first book, *A Psychology for Psychiatrists*. Before leaving to join his Army unit he had visited Franz Gregorovious, his friend and a clinician at the Dohmler Clinic in Zurich; there he had met Nicole Warren, a beautiful young American in therapy. They had corresponded while in the Army; and after his discharge in 1919, he returned to the Clinic to see her, interested in her, with ominous foreshadowing, both as a person and also as a patient.

Dr. Diver's dreams and desires differ as profoundly from Gatsby's as do his origins and background. From the beginning, his dreams take the forms, though not the specific content, into which Gatsby's quite different dreams are inevitably forced; that is, Diver dreams of tangible objects, secular goals, and particular human qualities. Money and wealth are never central dreams or even principal concerns for him; still, they lurk always in the background. "Watching his father's struggles in poor parishes had wedded a desire for money to an essentially unacquisitive nature" (p. 201). Far more characteristically, he dreams of greatness in a particular career: he wants "to be a good psychologist," he tells Franz, "maybe to be the greatest one that ever lived" (p. 132). Franz considers this a peculiarly American attitude and gently suggests some of the limitations life imposes on such dreams, but he also believes in Dick's brilliance and promise. Dick had been a bright and totally dedicated student, and his first book is recognized in his profession as the precocious first fruits of greatness.

In addition, Dick dreams of love. Until he meets and becomes involved with Nicole, he knows love only at two extremes: either "the young maidens he had known at New Haven in 1914" who "kissed men, saying 'There!,' hands at the man's chest to push him away" or "hot-cheeked girls in hot secret rooms" (p. 136). But Dick wants more than this; "he wanted to be loved, too, if he could fit it in" (p. 133). Moreover, he dreams of being a certain kind of man, romantic dreams of greatness through difficulty and suffering, of becoming what Hemingway describes as being stronger at the broken places. "Lucky Dick can't be one of these clever men," he thinks; "he must be less intact, even faintly

---

4. Page references in parentheses after quotations are to the Scribner Library edition (New York, 1962).

destroyed. If life won't do it for him it's not a substitute to get a disease, or a broken heart, or an inferiority complex, though it'd be nice to build out some broken side till it was better than the original structure" (p. 116). He feels guilty and even a bit regretful that a lucky mistake had brought him election to a Yale club he would not otherwise have got into: "it would have served me right if I'd swallowed my pin in the shower and set up a conflict." He wants life to bring him "a little misfortune"; he thinks that "the price of his intactness was incompleteness" (p. 117).

There is a Chinese proverb to the effect that we must be careful what we want because we might get it, and so it is with Dr. Diver. All his dreams come true, but not in the form in which he dreamed them or with the results he imagined; instead of being stronger at the broken places, he finds himself increasingly shackled with limitations, both in himself and in the nature of things. This can be seen best and most clearly in his relationship with Nicole, which is, of course, the heart of his story.

When Dick goes to see Nicole after leaving the Army, he enters a relationship with her characterized by an almost total lack of choice. His background and most of his dreams conspire to give Nicole a multifaceted attraction irresistible to him. As a psychologist and psychiatrist, he is interested in her as a patient; but he is fully aware of the dangers he is courting. He knows that "obviously the logic of his life tended away from the girl" (p. 137), and Franz reminds him of the high odds against the dual role marriage to her would impose on him (p. 140). He even agrees to leave (p. 141), but his growing love for her is bound up in some measure with a sense that he does help her. "He tried honestly to divorce her from any obsession that he had stitched her together—glad to see her build up happiness and confidence apart from him; the difficulty was that, eventually, Nicole brought everything to his feet, gifts of sacrificial ambrosia, of worshipping myrtle" (p. 137).

Most of all, it is this growing love, this new and tidal emotion, that limits Dick's choice and binds him to Nicole. For both of them, it is first love in all its force: Nicole has been incapable of love before; and for Dick, she is neither a flirt like the girls of his Yale days nor one of the "hot-cheeked girls in hot secret rooms." She is a "scarcely saved waif of disaster bringing him the essence of a continent" (p. 136). Conscious of the profound and intricate danger in loving her, he finds no help in the advice of others: "he had little faith that Dohmler would throw much light on the matter; he himself was the incalculable element involved. By no conscious volition of his own, the thing had drifted into his hands" (p. 139). He realizes "how far his emotions were involved" (p. 146) and tries to extricate himself, but he cannot. "It occurred to Dick suddenly, as it might occur to a dying man that he had forgotten to tell where his will was, that Nicole had been 're-educated' by Dohmler and the ghostly generations behind him; it occurred to him also that there would be so much she would have to be told. But having recorded this wisdom within himself, he yielded to the insistent face-value of the situation" (pp. 153–54). And when Nicole's sister questions his motives, "she did not know that twice Dick had come close to flinging the marriage in her face. All that saved it this time was Nicole finding their table and glowing away, white and fresh and new in the September afternoon" (p. 159).

As Fitzgerald describes them, then, love and in some degree his profession function as limitations that drive Dick against all sense and reason into a marriage doomed thereby to develop in terms of such limitations. Moreover, Fitzgerald suggests that these bonds on Dick's choice are reinforced by others at both conscious and subconscious levels. His somewhat masochistic need to suffer, supported by his feelings of guilt for getting what he wants too easily, must surely be involved in his curious inability to resist more strongly a relationship whose problems and dangers he more than most people knows thoroughly. No less influential are the values he derives from his clergyman father: Dick dreams of being kind and wise and good and, most especially, of being loved (p. 133). Back in his hotel once, after being with Nicole, he finds himself "without a memory of the intervening ten minutes, only a sort of drunken flush pierced with voices, unimportant voices that did not know how much he was loved" (p. 150). Added to Nicole's need for his professional abilities and the force of first love she stirs in him, these other dreams and desires bind him to her inexorably from the moment he first meets her.

As it does for Gatsby, there comes a moment for Dr. Diver when he accepts the embodiment of all his dreams and desires in the kiss of the girl he loves. "He felt the young lips, her body sighing in relief against the arm growing stronger to hold her. There were now no more plans than if Dick had arbitrarily made some indissoluble mixture, with atoms joined and inseparable; you could throw it all out but never again could they fit back into atomic scale. As he held her and tasted her . . . he was thankful to have an existence at all, if only as a reflection in her wet eyes" (p. 155). When he leaves her at the door of the sanitarium the next day and "she turned and looked at him he knew her problem was one they had together for good now" (p. 157).

The situation in which both Gatsby and Diver embody their dreams may be roughly similar, but Fitzgerald treats the two scenes in notably and significantly different terms. Gatsby's moment, at least as Nick Carraway describes it, centers on the qualities of his dream and ends with the kiss; Diver's begins with the kiss and focuses on the problems and limitations it implies. And thereafter, the story of Dr. Diver is a song of experience, a discord of encroaching limitation. Money, for example, played no part in Nicole's attraction for Dick, and after their marriage, he tries to ignore her wealth and pay his own way; but it soon becomes a golden shackle. "Again and again it was necessary to decide together as to the uses to which Nicole's money should be put. Naturally, Nicole, wanting to own him, wanting him to stand still forever, encouraged any slackness on his part, and in multiplying ways he was constantly inundated by a trickling of goods and money" (p. 170). He is upset by "a discrepancy between the growing luxury in which the Divers lived, and the need for display which apparently went along with it" (p. 165). Moreover, he becomes increasingly sensitive to the attitude toward him of Nicole's family. "We own you," he senses them thinking, "and you'll admit it sooner or later. It is absurd to keep up the pretense of independence" (p. 177).

Far more galling, however, are the limitations that grow constantly clearer and stronger in his impossibly dual relationship to Nicole. From the beginning, he loses not only his financial independence but also his separate self; Dick and Nicole become "Dicole" (p. 103). "The fact of the Divers together is more important to their friends than many of them realize" (p. 43). Rosemary thinks of "the person whom she still referred to in her mind as 'the Divers'" (p. 51), and she tells Dick that "I'm in love with you and Nicole . . . I love you and Nicole—I do." He understands: "so many times he had heard this," he thinks, "even the formula was the same" (p. 63).

Dicole reflects a shining aura of insouciant freedom and beauty, but this brilliant and glamorous façade masks desperate efforts required to preserve it against the incessant pressures of its inevitable limitations (pp. 21, 99). "Dick tried to think what to do. The dualism in his views of her—that of the husband, that of the psychiatrist—was increasingly paralyzing his faculties" (p. 188). He finds it impossible to be a subjective psychiatrist: "his work became confused with Nicole's problems; in addition, her income had increased so fast of late that it seemed to belittle his work" (p. 170). Breaking up his partnership with Franz, he is "relieved. Not without desperation he had long felt the ethics of his profession dissolving into a lifeless mass" (p. 256). Nor is he any more able to be an objective husband: "many times he had tried unsuccessfully to let go his hold on" Nicole (p. 180); but, "somehow Dick and Nicole had become one and equal, not apposite and complementary; she was Dick too, the drought in the marrow of his bones. He could not watch her disintegrations without participating in them" (pp. 190–91). Marriage to Nicole, then, binds Dick in limitations with double locks, shackles for which he can find no key because there is none. "One writes of scars healed," Fitzgerald remarks, "a loose parallel to the pathology of the skin, but there is no such thing in the life of an individual. There are open wounds, shrunk sometimes to the size of a pin-prick but wounds still. The marks of suffering are more comparable to the loss of a finger, or of the sight of an eye. We may not miss them, either, for one minute in a year, but if we should there is nothing to be done about it" (pp. 168–69).

Not surprisingly, therefore, Dick sees in Rosemary a second chance, a way to regain some part of the self he had lost in marrying Nicole. "He had lost himself—he could not tell the hour when, or the day or the week, the month or the year. Once he had cut through things, solving the most complicated equations as the simplest problems of his simplest patients. Between the time he found Nicole flowering under a stone on the Zürichsee and the moment of his meeting with Rosemary the spear had been blunted" (p. 201). A beautiful young girl, simple and uncomplicated, who loves him from the moment she first sees him, Rosemary represents for Dick all the dreams and desires that have gone so awry in marrying Nicole; and he can no more resist seeking them anew in Rosemary than he had been able to turn away from Nicole. "Dignified in his fine clothes, with their fine accessories, he was yet swayed and driven as an animal. Dignity could come only with an overthrowing of his past, of the effort of the last six years. . . . Dick's necessity of behaving as he did was a projection of some submerged reality . . . Dick was paying some tribute to things unforgotten, unshriven, unexpurgated" (p. 91).

In effect, then, his relationship to Rosemary is characterized by the same limitation of choice as his relationship to Nicole, and experience soon makes this even more obvious. His infatuation evokes the banal and superficial jealousy of a schoolboy (pp. 88–89), but he is unable to respond when Rosemary wants him to be her first lover. "There'd be so much to teach you," he thinks; and he tells her that "things aren't arranged so that this could be as you want." When she cries, he is "suddenly confused, not about the ethics of the matter, for the impossibility of it was sheerly indicated from all angles, but simply confused" (p. 65). The real Rosemary sometimes fails to correspond with his visions of her: at times, he views her "with an inevitable sense of disappointment" (p. 104). Moreover, if Dick is limited by the internal dynamics of their relationship, he is even more limited by the external fact that, after all, he really does love Nicole. What he feels for Rosemary has nothing to do with the "wild submergence of soul, a dipping of all colors into an obscuring dye, such as his love for Nicole had been. Certain thoughts about Nicole, that she should die, sink into mental darkness, love another man, made him physically sick" (p. 217). Rosemary becomes only a further experience of limitation for Dick: "the beauty of Nicole had been to the beauty of Rosemary as the beauty of Leonardo's girl was to that of the girl of an illustrator. Dick moved on through the rain, demoniac and frightened, the passions of many men inside him and nothing simple that he could see" (p. 104).

Underscoring the central significance of Nicole and Rosemary, Fitzgerald provides additional lyrics of limitation for Dick's song of experience. His dream of being the greatest psychologist in the world, for example, is a polar opposite of Gatsby's "Platonic conception of himself." Dick has doubts "as to the quality of his mental processes" (p. 116), and he pokes fun at his own dream. "I was only talking big," he tells Franz (p. 132); and later he remarks that "I got to be a psychiatrist because there was a girl at St. Hilda's in Oxford that went to the same lectures" (p. 138). His efforts to write other books after the success of his first one bring him a powerful sense of limitation: "like so many men he had found that he had only one or two ideas—that his little collection of pamphlets now in its fiftieth German edition contained the germ of all he would ever think or know" (p. 165). Planning an amplification of this first book, he feels that "when a man with his energy was pursued for a year by increasing doubts, it indicated some fault in the plan" (p. 166).

Dick's clinical experience points equally to limitation. "Doctor Diver's profession of sorting the broken shells of another sort of egg had given him a dread of breakage" (p. 177), and he finds many people he cannot help. Chief among these is the beautiful woman whose body is covered with an eczema in which she lies "as imprisoned as in the Iron Maiden." Her condition defies medical tests and explanation; it is apparently the psychosomatic result of wounds sustained in long and lonely spiritual battles. Only Dick can comfort her, perhaps because she senses an affinity with him. "I am here as a symbol of something," she tells him. "I thought perhaps you would know what it was." But he can do nothing to save her; and the abyss between the platitude, which is all he can offer, and her suffering, which is beyond imagination, fills him with an existential horror:

Yet in the awful majesty of her pain he went out to her unreservedly, almost sexually. He wanted to gather her up in his arms, as he so often had Nicole, and cherish even her mistakes, so deeply were they part of her. The orange light through the drawn blind, the sarcophagus of her figure on the bed, the spot of face, the voice searching the vacuity of her illness and finding only remote abstractions.

As he arose the tears fled lava-like into her bandages.

"That is for something," she whispered. "Something must come out of it."
He stooped and kissed her forehead.
"We must all try to be good," he said. (P. 185)

This is, quite simply, a remarkable scene, a short set piece of poetic symbolism
unlike anything else in Fitzgerald and rare in any fiction. Its concrete mystery
is unforgettable and defies explication; but whatever it *means,* it evokes unlimited obstacles of infinite limitation.

For Dick, there are still other limitations, many of them qualities of his
own personality and character. His charm, his desire to be useful, his command
of any situation, all the qualities that make him so magnetically attractive to
Rosemary and that surround him with friends and followers are more mask than
reality, and experience slowly raises the mask. As a young student, "he had no
idea that he was charming, that the affection he gave and inspired was anything
unusual among healthy people" (p. 116). He soon loses this innocence, however;
and when he visits Franz after leaving the Army, "he made Kaethe Gregorovious
feel charming, meanwhile becoming restless at the all-pervading cauliflower—
simultaneously hating himself too for this incipience of he knew not what
superficiality" (p. 133). When Rosemary observes that he likes to help everybody,
he replies that "I only pretend to" (p. 84), and he tells her mother that "my
politeness is a trick of the heart" (p. 164). To Nicole's sister he insists that
his social finesse is "a trick" (p. 216). Dick's grace and charm, his social
command, are a role imposed on his personality by experience:

> Nicole saw . . . the excitement that swept everyone up into it and was inevitably
> followed by his own form of melancholy, which he never displayed but at
> which she guessed. . . . Save among a few of the tough-minded and perennially
> suspicious, he had the power of arousing a fascinated and uncritical love. The
> reaction came when he realized the waste and extravagance involved. He some-
> times looked back with awe at the carnivals of affection he had given, as a
> general might gaze upon a massacre he had ordered to satisfy an impersonal
> blood lust.
> But to be included in Dick Diver's world for a while was a remarkable
> experience: people believed he made special reservations about them,
> recognizing the proud uniqueness of their destinies, buried under the com-
> promises of how many years. . . . So long as they subscribed to it completely,
> their happiness was his preoccupation, but at the first flicker of doubt as to
> its all-inclusiveness he evaporated before their eyes, leaving little communicable
> memory of what he had said or done. (Pp. 27–28)

A related source of conflict and limitation in Dick are the values by which
he wants to live, the values of his clergyman father and of an earlier world that
Dick feels has vanished forever. Back in Zurich after leaving the Army, he faces
this conflict directly: "the truth was that for some months he had been going
through that partitioning of the things of youth wherein it is decided whether or
not to die for what one no longer believes. In the dead white hours in Zurich
staring into a stranger's pantry across the upshine of a street-lamp, he used to
think that he wanted to be kind, he wanted to be brave and wise, but it was all
pretty difficult. He wanted to be loved, too, if he could fit it in" (p. 133). Later,

waiting to return to America for his father's funeral, he stands thinking, "remembering so many things . . . and wishing he had always been as good as he had intended to be" (p. 204).

Most of all, of course, Dick is trapped in his need to be loved, the need that imposes so many of the bonds in his relationship to Nicole and Rosemary. There is "a pleasingness about him that simply had to be used—those who possessed that pleasingness had to keep their hands in, and go along attaching people that they had no use to make of" (p. 87). Dick is aware that "you never knew exactly how much space you occupied in people's lives" (p. 207), but he cannot resist their need for him. In the end, just after Nicole has at last cut the cord between them, he rouses himself at Mary North's call for help to make still another tilt at the same old windmill:

> He got up and, as he absorbed the situation, his self-knowledge assured him that he would undertake to deal with it—the old fatal pleasingness, the old forceful charm, swept back with its cry of "Use me!" He would have to go fix this thing that he didn't care a damn about, because it had early become a habit to be loved, perhaps from the moment when he had realized that he was the last hope of a decaying clan. On an almost parallel occasion, back in Dohmler's clinic on the Zürichsee, realizing this power, he had made his choice, chosen Ophelia, chosen the sweet poison and drunk it. Wanting above all to be brave and kind, he had wanted, even more than that, to be loved. So it had been. So it would ever be. (P. 302)

Experience also confronts Dick with external bonds, subtle limitations but profound in their effects. He is often disturbed by feelings that the order of things rides insecurely on a bottomless sea of confusion and chaos. Standing in the tram station after Nicole has been unable to meet him, he is frightened by a feeling that "the station, the hospital, was hovering between being centripetal and centrifugal" (p. 144). When he kisses Nicole and embodies his dreams in her, a thunderstorm suddenly crashes around them: "mountains and lake disappeared—the hotel crouched amid tumult, chaos and darkness" (p. 156). And when Dick tells the tortured lady imprisoned in eczema that what she was looking for was only "a greater sickness," he "heard himself lying, but here and now the vastness of the subject could only be compressed into a lie. 'Outside of that there's only confusion and chaos'" (p. 185).

More important, Dick is subtly fettered by the past. "A part of Dick's mind was made up of the tawdry souvenirs of his boyhood. Yet in that somewhat littered Five-and-Ten, he had managed to keep alive the low painful fire of intelligence" (p. 196). When he goes to Zurich to study during the war, he goes "on less Achilles' heels than would be required to equip a centipede, but with plenty—the illusions of eternal strength and health, and of the essential goodness of people; illusions of a nation, the lies of generations of frontier mothers who had to croon falsely, that there were no wolves outside the cabin door" (p. 117). Dick soon loses all such illusions, but never the need for them. Lunching one day with Nicole and Rosemary, he sees a group of Gold-Star mothers; and "in their happy faces, the dignity that surrounded and pervaded the party, he perceived all the maturity of an older America. For a while the sobered women who had come to mourn for their dead, for something they could not repair, made the room beautiful. Momentarily, he sat again on his father's knee, riding with Moseby while the old loyalties and devotions fought on around him. Almost with an effort he turned back to his two women at the table and faced the whole new world in which he believed" (pp. 100–101).

Unlike Gatsby, Dr. Diver has no conviction that he can repeat or re-create the past; he knows it is gone beyond recall, and he is often nostalgic for it. Touring a World War I battlefield, he argues that its trench warfare "couldn't be done again, not for a long time. . . . This took religion and years of plenty and tremendous sureties and the exact relation that existed between the classes. . . . You had to have a whole-souled sentimental equipment going back further than you could remember. . . . Why, this was a love battle—there was a century of middle-class love spent here. This was the last love battle. . . . All my beautiful safe world blew itself up here with a great gust of high explosive love" (p. 57). He pretends somtimes "that the world was all put together again by the gray-haired men of the golden nineties who shouted old glees at the piano" (p. 174). After Abe North's death, he wakes one morning "to a slow mournful march passing his window. It was a long column of men in uniform, wearing the familiar helmet of 1914, thick men in frock coats and silk hats, burghers, aristocrats, plain men. It was a society of veterans going to lay wreaths on the tombs of the dead. The column marched slowly with a sort of swagger for a lost magnificence, a past effort, a forgotten sorrow. The faces were only formally sad but Dick's lungs burst for a moment with regret for Abe's death, and his own youth of ten years ago" (p. 200). And at his father's funeral, "he knelt on the hard soil. These dead, he knew them all, their weather-beaten faces with blue flashing eyes, the spare violent bodies, the souls made of new earth in the forest-heavy darkness of the seventeenth century. 'Goodbye, my father—good-bye, all my fathers'" (pp. 204–5).

Similarly, Dick becomes increasingly aware of time and of its inescapable penalties. He is disturbed by "irritating accusations of waning vitality" (p. 197), worried by "a lesion of enthusiasm" (p. 208), and aware of "a distinct lesion of his own vitality" (p. 222). In a scene few middle-aged men can read without a chill of embarrassed identification, he fails awkwardly in attempting before Rosemary and some young people an aquaplane stunt he had once performed with ease and grace (pp. 282–85). There are occasions now when he sits for "a long time listening to the buzz of the electric clock, listening to time" (p. 171).

In the end, the circles of limitation close and lock him in, imprisoned in a different way but just as tightly as the scabbed lady he could help no more than he can help himself. "The change," he tells Rosemary, "came a long way back— but at first it didn't show. The manner remains intact for some time after the morale cracks" (p. 285). In a process foreshadowed in the sad long decline of Abe North, Dick's manner flickers out, too: he drinks too much and gets in ugly brawls, grows bitter and cynical, and makes people with him miserable. "I guess I'm the Black Death," he admits to Rosemary. "I don't seem to bring people happiness any more" (p. 219). As Nicole grows toward health and Tommy Barban, and as Dick can find no way to regain his lost self, his old mask of charm and control falls apart (pp. 260, 267, 275, 283). When Nicole achieves her independence, he is left in ironic liberty, free at last to confront alone and undistracted the problem he has really faced from the moment he met her: "I'm trying," he tells her, "to save myself" (p. 301).

In a different context, of course, this is Gatsby's real quest, too; but his death is a tragedy of innocence, a death with his sense of omnipotence unshattered. Dick's end is a tragedy of experience, a long winding down of living in the full knowledge and amid the debris of limitation. After a drunken papal blessing above the beach he had created and ruled, he disappears to wander in the wasteland of rural New York: "his latest note was post-marked from Hornell, New York, which is some distance from Geneva and a very small town; in any case he is almost certainly in that section of the country, in one town or another" (p. 315).

Like Gatsby, too, though less explicitly, the significance of Dr. Diver extends beyond his own story to American and universal experience. Dick's nostalgia for an older America and his wanderings in all that is left of it shed a somber light on what became of the Dutch sailors' dream; the Warrens and the world they reflect are Gatsby's house writ large. So it is, too, with Dick's whole song of experience: its burden of limitation suggests something of the sense of constricting horizons and of the pall of despair that clouded much of America in the 1930s after the collapse of the apparently limitless promise of the 1920s. Moreover, Dr. Diver's tragedy is the tragedy of every man. Few of us die with either our dreams or our caapcity for dreaming intact; all of us must sooner or later confront our inevitable limitations and live on in the midst of what they make of us. " 'God, am I like the rest after all?' [Dick] used to think starting awake at night—'Am I like the rest?'" (p. 133). The answer, of course, is Yes; and his story makes it abundantly clear. Dr. Diver's song of experience is one that, ultimately, in this key or that, we all must sing.

IV

Blake's *Songs of Innocence* and *Songs of Experience* thus make a useful double frame in which to place the figures of Jay Gatsby and Dr. Diver. Seen side by side in this way, they become sharper in outline and clearer in detail; and they illuminate each other by reflection. Looking at them together also helps to explain Fitzgerald's problems with the structure and point of view of *Tender is the Night*. Both novels begin *in medias res* and arouse the reader's interest in a fascinating and mysterious man by presenting him through the eyes of another character. Both underscore this fascination and mystery by holding back on biographical information until roughly midway through the book. These similarities, coupled with those between Gatsby and Diver, argue that Fitzgerald, wanting desperately to repeat the success of *The Great Gatsby,* made it the model for his structure and to a limited degree, at least in Book One, for his point of view in *Tender is the Night.*

He was wrong, of course, and he must have sensed it as strongly even in the beginning as he came to know it when he began to revise the later novel just before his death. Unlike the consistent and flawless first-person point of view in *The Great Gatsby,* for example, the story of Dr. Diver is told by a third-person narrator who seems unsure of what he is doing. In Book One, he presents the Divers and their retinue through the wide-eyed innocence of Rosemary; but he breaks in to comment whenever he wants to make an observation or an interpretation obviously beyond her knowledge or ability. Almost with a sigh of relief, he takes over entirely in Book Two and thereafter; but then he is forced to zig-zag back and forth in a confusion of times.

Fitzgerald's mistake came in overlooking the differences between Gatsby and Dr. Diver that make their stories almost reverse images of each other, thereby invalidating analogy. The essence of Gatsby's story is the ultimate mystery of his dreams and his unquenchable innocence despite what becomes of them, and these qualities can be evoked most convincingly by a structure that establishes them before illuminating their sources. And they could hardly be more effectively preserved than by an involved narrator who can understand both the dream and also its inevitable consequences without either explaining away the one or blaming the dreamer for the other. Neither this structure nor this point of view seems well adapted to the story of Dr. Diver. The essence of his story is the growing agony of the inevitable and endless process in which both dreamer and dreams reveal their limitations, a process probably best reflected in the inexorable movement of a chronological structure and in the analytical and interpretive fullness and the shifting focus open to a third-person, omniscient narrator. Fitzgerald's failure to see this clearly, perhaps because of the tempting but false analogy of *The Great Gatsby,* may explain some of the later novel's technical flaws and indecisiveness.

In another way, too, Blake's *Songs* make a valuable framework for understanding Gatsby and Dr. Diver and the relationship between them. The different meanings that innocence and experience have for Fitzgerald and the vastly different reality they reflect highlight the almost unbridgeable distance that separates modern man and his world from even their recent past. The world that drags Gatsby down and destroys him is the world in which Dr. Diver must live. It is a world without supernatural or transcendental reference and without significance beyond itself, a world in which man's consciousness is the locus of his reality and is at once his greatest glory and his tragic doom. Gatsby points back to an earlier America, to a time before dream became materialization; Dr. Diver points forward to what we are and have become. Gatsby embodies the tragic consciousness of man; Dr. Diver suggests man forced at last to confront fully and directly the limitations of his life on this fragile earth. In Jay Gatsby and Dr. Diver, then, Fitzgerald has written, like Blake, songs of innocence and experience particularly and poignantly of his own and of our time; and the music they make seems increasingly haunting.

Alain Robbe-Grillet: Scientific Humanist

H. A. WYLIE
University of Texas

A return to stylistic experimentation sets Robbe-Grillet and the *nouveau roman* apart from their predecessors, the existentialists.[1] Early criticism preoccupied itself with these technical innovations, with Robbe-Grillet's visual images and his striking use of language and vocabulary. This analysis seemingly considered subject matter of lesser importance or irrelevant. The truth is probably that early critics were unable to find a connecting link between Robbe-Grillet's themes and his literary technique. My description of the novelist as a "scientific humanist" is an attempt to provide this link.

By *humanist* I mean to describe any writer who concerns himself primarily with man and with those basic, unchanging problems which traditionally have been the province of literature, themes such as faith and despair, love, madness and war, freedom and creativity. The term *humanist* seems to have been first applied to various Renaissance scholars and philologists (Petrarch, Boccaccio, Erasmus, Luther, Montaigne) who sought to arrive at a comprehension of man through intensive analysis of language and elucidation of the basic texts of their civilization: the Bible and the "Classics." These and later attempts to define man's essence by scholarly efforts unaided by recourse to revelation and dogma have

First published: 15, no. 2 (1967): 1–9. The author has made substantial additions to his orginal essay.

1. The "New Novel" in France has been largely defined, in practice and in theory, by Robbe-Grillet. His two shorter novels, *Le Voyeur* and *La Jalousie* are accessible to the reader wishing a general introduction. *Les Gommes* and *Dans le labyrinthe* are denser, more complex, perhaps Robbe-Grillet's most serious, most "humanistic" work. Both the published scenario (in French or English) and the film *L'Année dernière à Marienbad* (*Last Year at Marienbad*) are important for an understanding of the author. Robbe-Grillet's critical essays have been collected in *Pour un nouveau roman.*

Two other important practitioners of the *nouveau roman* and their key works are Michel Butor, *La Modification, L'Emploi du temps;* and Nathalie Sarraute, *Le Planétarium* and *Portrait d'un inconnu.*

given the term *humanist* the further implication of secular thought, of independence from any preconceived religious or political system.

By *science* I mean not only a certain attitude toward truth and knowledge but also a particuar vision of reality and nature, even an emotional set toward matter and energy, toward the correspondence between mental and physical phenomena. Science as science is marked, usually, by a materialistic bias, by the implicit belief that man's frame of reference is the biophysical world of matter and motion. Science may also be defined through its detachment and objectivity, by its desire to know through systematic and sustained observation, while humanism suggests a pursuit of human values and goals.

Since first publication of this essay, the traditional concept of science, the "classical" conception based on a thoroughgoing and rigorous objectivity, has been openly questioned, both inside and outside the scientific community. Both R. D. Laing and Carlos Castaneda stand as important figures in a rapidly evolving cultural landscape, in which science is being asked to reveal consciously its bias, its "commitment," its implicit values and assumptions. Science and the humanities have openly confronted each other on the battlefield of the social sciences.

Trained as a plant pathologist and having spent several years in the patient study of the diseases of banana trees in the tropics, Robbe-Grillet as writer manifests both attitudes and approaches. He may be added to the company of notable figures to whom the label *scientific humanist* has been applied: Alfred North Whitehead, C. P. Snow, Teilhard de Chardin. He shares with them the belief characteristic of the scientific humanist that the hidden mainsprings of the material world are of critical importance to the understanding of our human condition, and that the relation of physical reality to our mental processes—perception and thought—is the key to knowledge and truth.

What then are the primary manifestations of this humanistic concern? It must be made clear at the outset that Robbe-Grillet's continuing interest in the natural sciences is an integral part of this humanism. For Robbe-Grillet the ultimate metaphysical problems are those of epistemology and ontology, of how can we have true knowledge of ourselves and our world. Robbe-Grillet has said that science is an essential instrument of our comprehension and has implied that the arts should make use of the latest scientific discoveries and techniques. Quantum theory, which demonstrates the dependence of physical phenomena on their observer, seems to interest the author particularly.[2] Its definition of science is inclusive and fluid, allowing a vital communication between science and the arts. But the intellectual detachment of the scientist and his quest for objectivity are responsible for that stylistic precision and sharpness which set Robbe-Grillet apart from much that is shoddy in twentieth-century thought. Perhaps it would be fair to say that like Théophile Gautier and the Parnassians, Robbe-Grillet has bothered to master the technical problems of his craft and hence has attained the impersonal validity of the scientist. He prefers to remain silent rather than voice a half-truth or a provisionary truism.

2. Few critics have tried to describe the relation between Robbe-Grillet's scientific work and his writing; one of the brief treatments of this link may be found in an interview reported in the *New Yorker,* January 9, 1954, pp. 24–25.

The first problem attacked was the fundamental one of the nature of existence: the existence of man in his surroundings. This ontological problem was found to be inseparable from the problem of knowledge: how can man know his fellows and his environment? Thus in *Les Gommes* Robbe-Grillet studies one man's attempt to penetrate misleading appearances and circumstances in order to arrive at a true understanding of a relatively simple situation. With irony the author depicts the two hermetic realms of material reality and the related mental processes that twist the exterior reality into a new entity. Especially important in this study of the nature of the mind and its dependence or independence of the material world is the typical "object"; in *Les Gommes* this is often a *clue*. Robbe-Grillet is fascinated with clues, and probably for this reason cast his first novel, *Le Voyeur,* as a detective story. A material clue is for Robbe-Grillet closely related to the surrealist object as defined by Maurice Nadeau: "tout objet dépaysé" or "sorti de son cadre habituel."[3] A clue is no longer a mere gum eraser or piece of chalk but takes on a heightened existence, an immediacy, a human relevance. It serves as a link between man and the inert surroundings, as a *correspondance* in the Baudelairean sense. Perhaps this humanizing factor explains some of the continued popularity of Simenon, Ellery Queen, and Agatha Christie.

Critics have realized the importance of these clues but have been at a loss to explain their value, since in the light of Robbe-Grillet's critical writings they have been hesitant to view them as symbols. The eraser, the famous quarter of tomato, the draw-bridge serve to focus our awareness, to channel our psychic energy. A repeated image in Robbe-Grillet's works is that of a man rapt in meditation before a poster, a painting, or a statue. It would seem that the individual is attempting to penetrate to ultimate reality through complete comprehension of even one banal, everyday object.

The natural scientist was soon forced to admit that both the problem of being and that of knowing were essentially psychological. In the Surrealist sense, in the sense proclaimed by Rimbaud, man's mind creates the universe around it, particularly the modern technological cityscape. So Robbe-Grillet broadened his perspective to take in the area of human creativity, especially as expressed in the labyrinthian architecture of modern life. Bruce Morrissette has noted that in *Dans le labyrinthe* it is the narrator and not the author who is the creator of this involved, convolute fiction: "le narrateur est occupé à l'élaboration d'une fiction destinée à composer une harmonie en soi, une sorte de 'roman pur.' "[4] We might say that Robbe-Grillet has given us an unusual illustration of existential man in the act of self-creation.

Now turning outward again we can see that the typical protagonist of Robbe-Grillet creates his own environment by his observation, his response to and interaction with it. This is most apparent at the beginning of *Dans le labyrinthe,* where, as James Lethcoe has remarked, the conflicting detail and the hesitancy in choice of tense represent either the narrator's fumbling attempts at imagining his tale or his difficulty in recounting a previous event.[5] The mutual interaction and interdependence of man and his surroundings are also responsible for the baffling

3. *Histoire du surréalisme* (Paris: Editions du Seuil, 1945), p. 212.
4. *Les Romans de Robbe-Grillet* (Paris: Editions de Minuit, 1963), p. 160.
5. "The Structure of Robbe-Grillet's Labyrinth," *French Review* 38 (1964): 499–507.

"false scenes" of which Robbe-Grillet is so fond. Perhaps *Les Gommes* provides the best example; here the variant passages are most characteristically the detective's projections of various possible solutions to the "givens" furnished by the clues.

Robbe-Grillet has insisted that his novels are not nonhuman and has pointed to the central presence of a perceiving, thinking protagonist in each of his works. This human presence is responsible not only for its own being and for the particular existence of its surroundings, as we have seen, but also for the action that ensues and for the evaluation of both the present situation and the future outcome. Time for Robbe-Grillet, as for Proust, is a living, changing thing; even the past is not fixed, dead. But increasingly Robbe-Grillet has turned toward the future. As we shall see, hope has become an important element in the author's outlook.

Many of Robbe-Grillet's critics have refused to treat thematic or "philosophic" content in his works. Is it true, as Robbe-Grillet once seemed to say, that we can make no generalization about the discrete entities that surround us? Recurring images and themes, ideas repeated by his characters and key statements of his own in *Pour un nouveau roman* would indicate that certain objects, certain modes of action and perception, certain ideas are "privileged" in the Proustian sense or have an aura that detaches them from the purely meaningless. I have already noted the themes of contemplation and of creation, both involving the problem of comprehension. I might now briefly enumerate two other themes.

Foremost among those subjects which are given sustained treatment are love and sexual passion. Since Baudelaire and Proust, few writers have presented such a polyvalent description of human affection and desire or have probed so deeply into their related motives and thoughts. Always the "realist" seeking a true understanding of a human phenomenon, Robbe-Grillet has not falsified what his observation has told him, has not evoked a sentimental or romantic picture of love. Instead, he gives us without comment descriptions of passion, with all the bewildering complexity and demonic intensity of the emotion of Racine's Phèdre or Baudelaire's madonna. This love is often tormented or twisted, as in *Le Voyeur* and *La Jalousie;* but *L'Année dernière à Marienbad* is more full of hope in its suggestion that through the Surrealist linking of love and revolt the lovers can win through to freedom.

The erotic has welled up in the later works to the point of overflowing, of seeping into all areas of Robbe-Grillet's creation. The sadomasochistic imagery of *Trans-Europ Express, La Maison de rendez-vous, L'Homme qui ment* and *Projet pour une révolution à New York* may be seen as the projection of personal obsessions. In any case, this proliferation has clearly overwhelmed the restraint of the earlier works and weakened the later ones.

The sustained analysis of love, transforming scientific case history into the archetypal patterns of art, reveals several humanistic implications. Love, for Robbe-Grillet, is often illusory or obsessive, the result of Freudian displacement of psychic energies caused by free association. Robbe-Grillet condemns self-deceit and hypocrisy in our efforts to picture romantic love. But he also seems to suggest—in the lovers of *Marienbad* and the spontaneous relation between the soldier and the boy of *Dans le labyrinthe*—that authentic affection is possible and worth striving for.

As a psychological observer of human behavior, Robbe-Grillet knows that "love is blind," that the lover really is in love with an image that he creates by interpreting the other, that "love" is that magical aura which imagination and hope add to the banal reality of another person. The loved one is taken out of everyday life and set in a mythic, timeless context. Eros is the motivating force, the principle of attraction that makes lovers gravitate to each other for a while, like the insects around the lamp in *La Jalousie;* love is the mythic product, the value created; invention or illusion is the mechanism. Love is thus seen as an alternative form of creativity or narration, a particularly complex one in that eros and thanatos, creation, aggression, and destruction mingle in a hothouse atmosphere. Love is one of those realities *pour soi* whose existence *en soi* is problematical.

A second major object of attention is the technological landscape with which man has surrounded himself. The traditional humanist has tended to look upon the modern with a biased eye, yearning to return to a simpler, sweeter, mythical past. Robbe-Grillet was one of the first writers to believe with Lewis Mumford that ever-increasing technological complexity would ultimately produce a new simplicity or harmony. The "Neo-Technic" technology Mumford described in *Technics and Civilization* is now more rapidly clearing away the debris, the vestiges of the monstrously inhuman technology of the Industrial Revolution, as the world becomes a tribal village through extension of electronic nerves and as ecological concerns lead us to view our planet as a living organism.

Perhaps a new humanism, in harmony with neotechnic science, engineering, and art, is evolving to bring new order and meaning into our lives and our environment.

One example will illustrate both Robbe-Grillet's handling of the imagery of the neotechnic world and his characteristic "technological" lyricism:

> Un groupe, immobile, tout en bas du long escalier gris-fer, dont les marches l'une après l'autre affleurent, au niveau de la plate-forme d'arrivée, et disparaissent une à une dans un bruit de machinerie bien huilée, avec une régularité pourtant pesante et saccadée en même temps, qui donne l'impression d'assez grande vitesse à cet endroit où les marches disparaissent l'une après l'autre sous la surface horizontale, mais qui semble au contraire d'une lenteur extrême.[6]

This evocation of the *métro* escalator is followed by the description of a corridor and a man:

> En dépit de la taille énorme du dessin et du peu de détails dont il s'orne, la tête du spectateur se penche en avant, comme pour mieux voir. Les passants doivent s'écarter un instant de leur trajectoire rectiligne afin de contourner cet obstacle inattendu.[7]

In dispassionate understatement the author muses on the perversity and freedom of man. Only one of these scurrying Dantesque voyagers of the underworld has stopped to reflect, to contemplate the modern Beatrice; but who knows? If Brunetto Latini, whom the poet Dante acknowledged as master, could sing in Hell,

---

6. "Dans les couloirs du métropolitain," *Instantanés* (Paris: Editions de Minuit, 1962), pp. 77–78.
7. *Ibid.*, p. 88.

this solitary figure, disrupting the flow of harried souls, may resist even the subway.

The attempt, not to pigeonhole the author but rather to put him in the context of his age in relation to his predecessors, is difficult but important. The comparisons with Camus, the Surrealists, and Sartre are particularly rewarding. Robbe-Grillet states that Camus's anthropomorphic metaphors, coming at key moments in the stylist's carefully worked prose, falsely humanize nature; Camus's famed *absurde* becomes a form of tragic humanism. Robbe-Grillet rejects, like André Breton, this acquiescence in a tragic view of man, this seeming conquest of the absurd by a new linking of man and nature through this *solidarité douloureuse*. For Robbe-Grillet the cosmos is neither absurd nor tragic; it simply *is*. With the Surrealists, Robbe-Grillet looks toward the future and hopes for an ultimate harmony with nature.

Thus it is up to man to impose both order and meaning on his surroundings. Although some of Robbe-Grillet's protagonists may seem passive, the most important—Wallas in *Les Gommes*, the hunted soldier of *Dans le labyrinthe*, and X, the lover in *Marienbad*—are persistent in their efforts to uncover or to create a moral and human truth. To Camus, who felt at home in a primitive and underdeveloped Algeria, man's state is fixed and unchanging, whereas to Robbe-Grillet man is constantly modifying the essence of his life through technological and cultural evolution. For Robbe-Grillet history is neither cyclical nor static.

The boldest and most sustained effort mounted in our own century to know ourselves and nature through art is that of the Surrealists: Guillaume Apollinaire, André Breton, Paul Eluard, Max Ernst, Joan Miró, Alberto Giacometti, Picasso. In rejecting traditional definitions and limitations of reality, they strove, in varying ways, to find new freedom, new strength for man in liberating the subconscious and creating a new mental and intellectual "super-reality." This would be accomplished by reconciling the subconscious and conscious mind with our inanimate, indifferent world. Breton states in the *Manifesto of Surrealism* that the channel and form for this new harmony would be a fusion of art and science.

Robbe-Grillet is close to the Surrealists in his interest in artistic form and technique; he too is a literary technician and experimenter, a *magicien ès lettres*. His formal innovations lend a haunting musicality to his prose, the product of a characteristic density and texture closely related to those of the atonal serial music he describes in *Marienbad*. This musicality, however, is far from that of Verlaine. Here the *volupté* is that of the gnarled and twisted tree: sharp and hard consonants replace the rather gooey vowels of Verlaine. The words are precise, objective, scientific, and have a cerebral sensuality; typical are *scrutigère, centimètre, rectiligne, périphérique, homogène, imperceptiblement*.

Robbe-Grillet is close to the Surrealists too in his interest in Freud, in the subconscious, and in dreams. Several critics have pointed out the presence of multiple layers of consciousness and the important roles played by the subconscious in both the observation and description of objects and in the cross-relations among them. It is really the subconscious that provides the missing links between scenes in a work by Robbe-Grillet. Kafka is one of the non-French writers to whom Robbe-Grillet turned for inspiration; the latter's work shows the influence of the fantastic, non-Aristotelian logic of his precursor. The dream atmosphere of a Robbe-Grillet novel has been often noticed, particularly in *Marienbad*. There is always an aura of mystery, of strangeness, awakened by the immanence of obsessive images and by incantatory language. The Surrealist force of the quarter tomato of *Les Gommes* derives perhaps from the synthesis of these elements, whose essence is represented by the *gelée verdâtre*.

The last major bond between Robbe-Grillet and the Surrealists is their common rebellion against all forms of servitude and their quest for total freedom. For Robbe-Grillet the labyrinth is a recurring image of man's imprisonment; but the possibility of escape exists, and at times Robbe-Grillet suggests that his characters do or will escape from the enclosure of the room, the hotel, or the maze of city streets. Especially at the end of *Marienbad* is the hope of a definitive departure strong. Robbe-Grillet refuses any resignation and often returns to the potentiality of man's finally breaking out of those restraints and frontiers which bind him. The true life will be fluid, an eternal flux, a life always looking forward: "vous étiez maintenant déjà en train de vous perdre, pour toujours, dans la nuit tranquille, seule avec moi."[8]

The passage of time has revealed how much Robbe-Grillet owes to our twentieth-century literary titan Jean-Paul Sartre. A number of critics have seen that Sartre's distinction between the existence of an object (*en soi*) and the existence of a person, a free agent possessing imagination (*pour soi*) gives us the key to much that had been enigmatic in this new novelistic world. Lucien Goldmann concluded his study on Robbe-Grillet by noting the parallel courses of the two writers:

> Pour le sociologue et l'historien, le fait que l'évolution de la société contemporaine ait amené deux écrivains aussi différents et même opposés à la même impasse ou, pour être plus exact, à deux impasses aussi proches apparaît au plus haut point significatif.[9]

In his article "Mind and Reality in Robbe-Grillet and Proust," Jack Murray devoted attention to the contact between Robbe-Grillet and Sartre. Murray sees the two as sharing a basic exploratory realism that makes them pathfinders:

> Robbe-Grillet shares Jean-Paul Sartre's curiosity as to what that other domain, the world outside, is really like—i. e., before it has been domesticated by man and converted into a mere accessory of his own existence.[10]

And in an intriguing article, "Sartre, Robbe-Grillet and the Psychotic Hero," Dennis Porter states that the madman is a hero in the modern world, that the "schizophrenic's experience of the world is indissolubly confused with the intellectual's speculative thought."[11] He concludes:

> If Sartre's fiction undermines the norms of psychiatry by setting up an ironic contrast between health and mental sickness, such bourgeois norms disappear altogether from the fiction of Robbe-Grillet. Their very existence in the world is denied by their omission in the fiction. The conclusion is an existentialist one. We have been tutored from birth to believe in the objective

---

8. *L'Année dernière à Marienbad* (Paris: Editions de Minuit, 1961), p. 172.
9. *Pour une sociologie du roman* (Paris: Gallimard, 1964), p. 217.
10. *Wisconsin Studies in Contemporary Literature* 8 (Summer 1967): 416.
11. *Modern Fiction Studies* 16 (Spring 1970): 18.

validity of a man-made model of the universe, to believe in that universe's order, stability and predictability and in our own capacity to know and control it. What both Sartre and Robbe-Grillet assert is that such confidence is wholly unwarranted.[12]

From one angle we may view Robbe-Grillet as the ultimate phenomenologist, surpassing Sartre in stripping away interpretive elements from the raw phenomena of existence, in objectivizing even more of the human, psychological, and emotional frames. The freedom of the imagination, of the potential, is more radically contrasted with the determinism and the fullness of that which is, as Jean Alter has so well demonstrated in his *Vision du monde d'Alain Robbe-Grillet*.[13] Robbe-Grillet's characters, like Mallarmé's Igitur, are haunted by their own imperfection when confronted with the physical object that is perfectly what it is. Robbe-Grillet may be more pessimistic than the author of *Being and Nothingness* in putting less faith in the dialectical process whereby I define myself in interaction with the other. Robbe-Grillet's "Eros" is more objective, physical, mechanical than Sartre's. In a Sartrean world Eros is active, dynamic, building social organisms of many cells, open to the "polymorphous perverse," or better, to the polymorphous erotic. Sartre leads on to *Eros and Civilization* and *Love's Body*.

The open world of Robbe-Grillet is infinitely complex, a plenitude in which the reader can plumb the depths, can lose himself in the labyrinthian passages of this watery timeless realm. There is an addictive quality to these works; one runs the same danger of being engulfed here as in Proust's *Combray*. But like Theseus, we will emerge from the maze with new understanding and increased vigor.

---

12. *Ibid.*, p. 25.
13. The most penetrating description of this confrontation is in his chapter "L'Homme." (Geneva: Droz, 1966), p. 101.

Nathalie Sarraute:
Alienated or Alienator?

MADELEINE WRIGHT
University of Wisconsin Center System—Madison

The premise on which this paper rests is that narrative fictions that reject characters, plot, stylistic effects, and art for art's sake point to a literature that also rejects society: in works of literature, stylistic research, psychology, and plot all postulate that the elaboration of a single work involves more than a single consciousness.

If by "character" we mean that element of the narrative to which actions and attributes refer, the syntactic subject of a narrative clause somehow constitutes the "character" of that clause. The subject or subjects of Nathalie Sarraute's narratives are mainly personal pronouns; and, since personal pronouns are deictic terms; since, furthermore, the referent of a deictic term can be identified only in relationship to the other participants, a discourse in which all the participants are deictic terms has no distinct and precise referents. As a result, the function of these subject pronouns in Sarraute's narrative is not, cannot be that assumed by proper names in the traditional novel, in which proper names stand for individualized persons.

Thus, the "he" of *Entre la vie et la mort,* for instance, continually changes identity; his multiple aspects cast him in a wide variety of roles, but these roles are nevertheless linked through the very lack of stable referents: a new syntactic approach creates a new meaning. Sarraute's characters no longer exist in relationship to other characters, but they exist in relationship to the different level that they may observe within their own consciousness. They are their own referents.

Thus a Sarraute text presents, on the one hand, as many predicates as the

This is the first publication of the essay.

number of roles a single consciousness can assume, and on the other, a variety of syntactic subjects completely devoid of semantic content: between these two parts of speech, nothing suggests the relationships of coincidence and continuity without which the "individual person" cannot emerge. Consequently, Sarraute's vast but undifferentiated human cosmos includes none of the psychological "laws" that have seemed to guide the development of the character in the traditional novel: nothing between predicates and subjects permits the balance of similitudes and opposites through which edifices of character can be built; consciousness, in Sarraute's novels, remains global because no paradigmatic process of association through resemblances or contrasts divides it into distinct characters. Instead of "psychology," Sarraute therefore evolves a "psychologism" in which an infinity of possibles replaces selective constructs of character. By upsetting syntactic interpropositional relationships, she upsets the reader's traditional vision of the world. Indeed, Sarraute contends that each of us contains the seeds—possibly even more than the seeds—of all possible behavioral patterns; according to her, there is, for instance, a murderer in each of us.

The traditional plot brings into the novel a world that is alien to the novel and to the novelist but that enables the novel to transcend its boundaries and reach into the world of the reader. In Sarraute's novels, the action is centered upon what she calls "tropisms" (movements that, in her own terms, "glide quickly round the border of our consciousness and compose the small, rapid, and sometimes very complex dramas concealed beneath our actions, our gestures, the words we speak, our avowed and clear feelings").[1] Tropisms are inner manifestations that precede the classifications to which characters and organized plots must be sacrificed; these classifications are selective and exclusive; they breed the unity of action that remains one of the criteria of success of the traditional novel. Tropisms, however, are irreducible to such classifications; in a world in which all actions are possible, no specific pattern has priority over any other. In addition, an action that takes place at the level of inarticulate tropisms within a single consciousness automatically eliminates the possibility of that consciousness communicating with another: it takes words to communicate; Sarraute's novels being in the main the translation of the preverbal into language, any interaction between two or more "persons" would have to take place *after* the writing of the work! In other words, our traditional concept of a "plot" is bound to disappear because there can be no conflict between the tropisms of one consciousness and those of another consciousness. This does not mean that Sarraute's novels offer no action; but their action is movement, the movement of tropisms that continually try to exteriorize themselves; and the elements of these conflicts result from the attempts of the preverbal to permeate linguistic, conscious forms.

Stylistic effects are dictated by a set of conventions that constitute a repertory of universal—or quasi-universal—prescriptions. These prescriptions reflect a social, or collective, consciousness. The collective consciousness delegates to words

1. Nathalie Sarraute, "New Movements in French Literature: Nathalie Sarraute Explains Tropisms," *The Listener,* 9 March 1961, p. 428.

the function of expressing its full scope and weight. Words are communicable symbols, interchangeable commodities. Tropisms, on the other hand, are preverbal and do not yield easily to naming: "Cela ne porte aucun nom."[2] Their animal or vegetal characteristics are more easily perceived through the senses. Collective consciousness rejects the senses as a mode of communication, possibly because they are inner, subjective, and therefore exclusive realities. Tropisms are irreducible to the decrees of collective consciousness, and, therefore, of stylistic conventions. Tropisms are as crude, as disorganized, as jarring, and as unbalanced as the psyche of the individual in whom they form. Stylistic purists, however, cannot tolerate the vague reporting of a vague feeling, nor the realistic rendering of a distasteful reality, nor the jerky progression of dislocated emotional states. Nathalie Sarraute does not belong to that school of thought which claims that styles are imbedded in the language, built-in consequences of its structure.[3] Rather, she evolves a style in order to reproduce as closely as possible the circumvolutions, nuances, and depths of her own psyche. All her efforts tend to subordinate language to those inner states which she proposes to transcribe on paper as accurately and as realistically albeit incoherently as she possibly can, and without the slightest regard for the ultimate refinements of an elegant prose.

Stylistic effects, when they are merely structural properties, belie the inner reality that is the object of Sarraute's investigation; they tend to separate form from content, thereby actually proclaiming the supremacy of content over form: content no longer needs an appropriate, matching form to come through clearly; whatever the author's intentions, a preestablished form stands ready to receive his message, be it emotive or symbolic,[4] poetical or argumentative. These recognized stylistic effects help a text to meet the reader's preconceived criteria of literary excellence, independently of the kind of rhetoric specifically required by the particular work he is reading.

Paradoxically enough, art for art's sake, which proclaims the supremacy of form over content, would also belie the particular inner reality of concern to Sarraute. Art for art's sake suggests a form of beauty accessible to all; but the highly subjective and therefore unique type of phenomenon represented by the tropism is, by definition, the very opposite of uniformity. Tropisms are movement, eternal beauty is static; and the capture of Beauty (with a capital B) is not the object of Sarraute's quest: what she pursues, rather, is a certain form of authenticity—an authenticity that relies on integrity, on the exact reproduction of realities experienced, witnessed by the author herself. Viewed from this angle, Sarraute belongs to the school of realism; one might even suggest that she spearheads

---

2. Nathalie Sarraute, *Entre la vie et la mort* (Paris: Gallimard, 1968), p. 102.

3. See, e.g., Oswald Ducrot and Tzvetan Todorov, "Les styles sont dans la langue, et non dans la psyché des utilisateurs, le style reste une propriété structurale, non fonctionnelle," in *Dictionnaire encyclopédique des sciences du langage* (Paris: Editions du Seuil, 1972), p. 384.

4. In a study of the influence of language upon thought, C. K. Ogden and I. A. Richards oppose emotive words to symbolic ones as follows: "The symbolic use of words is *statement;* the recording, the support, the organization and the communication of references. The emotive use of words is a more simple matter; it is the use of words to express or excite feelings and attitudes. It is probably more primitive" (*The Meaning of Meaning* [New York: Harcourt, Brace & World, 1946], p. 149).

a new naturalistic movement. By rejecting content as nonessential, art for art's sake delegates inspiration to what should remain, for Sarraute, a mere vehicle: language and its components, words; and language is never the object of Sarraute's narrative. Her intention, therefore, seems to be to rule out—not arbitrarily but necessarily—most of the technical props that traditionally helped bridge the gap between the world of the writer and the world of the reader. The goal she has set herself not only is extraneous to those props, but is contrary to them. In two cases, nevertheless, modified versions of the traditional props reappear in Sarraute's novels. Her quest for reality leads her to demystify those fictions which conceal the real. The plot is no longer for her the indispensable ingredient of a fictive work, and the adventures of the tropisms she projects constitute an action that takes place within a single consciousness, but on two distinct levels: the tropisms either confront one another, or, when they are caught in the nets of verbal consciousness, they confront the external, social, and collective world.

Sarraute's modified versions of fiction and action, however, exclude all concern other than what is required by her initial goal: to intercept inner reality. The game is therefore played between the writer and his double, not between the writer and his public. She is engaged in a creative act that goes far beyond the definition of literature as a universally recognizable art form. Literature for Nathalie Sarraute becomes a strictly personal pursuit, a quest for indentity that revolves entirely around the subject's psyche. From inspiration through form to the author's ultimate reincarnation, a loop is looped.

Nathalie Sarraute sets up for herself two very stringent criteria of success: the work must come alive, and some kind of contact must be made.[5] But two questions immediately arise: for whom should the work come alive? and with whom is the contact made? The life of the work is subordinated to tropisms that must remain intact throughout their verbal translation. Tropisms are transferred from the subconscious to the conscious with the help of language. This means that any man for whom an articulate awareness of his deeper self is vital engages in a literary quest of his own. This literary pursuit then becomes a matter of "life or death" for the writer, the life or death of the work being equivalent to the life or death of his own psyche. But in itself the content of a psyche has no meaning for another psyche. It is too shapeless and too erratic; it offers no essential point of reference, no basis for analysis and interpretation. As a result, the more accurate, the more faithful, the more literal even, its verbal or literary translation happens to be, the more opaque that translation becomes to a consciousness other than the subject's. The very qualities of a literary technique aiming at the linguistic expression of a preverbal state consequently become directly responsible for the probable hermetism of the finished product. A second argument reinforces the first: only the author can evaluate the life of a work that sets out to reproduce an experience known to the author alone. Only Sarraute possesses the frame of

---

5. The first of these criteria is clearly stated by the narrator of *Entre la vie et la mort*: "Mais entre nous deux mots suffisent. Aussi grossiers que ceux-là: c'est mort. C'est vivant" (p. 99). The second criterion was voiced by Nathalie Sarraute herself in the course of an interview granted to me on June 13, 1972.

reference against which the life of her novels can be measured: the initial tropisms that are her models and her inspiration, the personal impulse that gave birth to the literary form. As a result, no one but Nathalie Sarraute can fully evaluate the life-or-death status of her production.

Contact is established mainly between the writer and her work for very similar reasons. Such contact can come about only within a very closed circuit. The literary form best capable of capturing tropisms does not include universal frames of reference and does not yield to universal recognition and understanding. For Sarraute, tropisms are privileged means of communication, not with the outside world, but with her double, with her many doubles. The consciousness at work in Sarraute's novels is that of a character looking for an author. The contact takes place and the work comes alive when there is a fusion between both.

This does not necessarily mean that contact between work and reader is totally out of the question. But the nature of tropisms makes any subjective form of interpretation hazardous, if not preposterous. A look at Sarraute's imagery will help to verify the accuracy of this statement. Like Gaston Bachelard, she seems to differentiate sharply between metaphors, which offer rational frames of reference accessible to all, and images, which function like Proust's involuntary memory, skipping a number of echelons in the process. Such images can be apprehended only through personal efforts of interpretation and re-creation; they do not yield to the intellectual process; they cannot be discussed. Sarraute entrusts the translation into words of tropisms almost exclusively to images; but Bachelard's intense faith in the communicative power of images[6] is of no avail in Sarraute's case: her brand of "rêverie" does not purport to transcend reality, but rather to grasp and possess it in its entirety. In other words, the deeper the reality she tries to express, the more subjective the form she adopts in order to do so. The decoding of such images may be rich in possibilities for the outsider, but there can be no guarantee whatsoever that the result will coincide with the reality behind the image itself. The opacity of Sarraute's images is the by-product of a self-contained psyche that must block out all outside interferences in order to communicate with itself.

For the critic, therefore, only one avenue of investigation perhaps remains open: the linguistic, semantic, and formal analysis of the work. The reader confronts what is, in fact, an individual language within a code language. The code language consists of very common words, about which Sarraute herself wrote: "I had to create . . . an unreal dialogue made up of usual words to express what it not ordinarily spoken about. The most ordinary words are used, but what is said is not what is being talked about. . . ."[7] This code language, which is immediately accessible to the reader, does not reveal the writer's inner truth; on the contrary, it constitutes the fictive portion of the work. It relies largely on humor, which Sarraute manipulates in order to denounce the collective myths—mostly verbal— that blur our vision of reality. The techniques that preside over the writing at

---

6. Gaston Bachelard, in his *Poétique de la rêverie* (Paris: Presses Universitaires de France, 1960), strongly suggests that images can indeed be transmitted: the writer who indulges in his "rêverie" communicates with an ego on a higher level than his original self; and the reader who recognizes the increased value of the writer's new ego is eager to improve his own self through the intermediary of the writer's image.

7. *Le Monde,* January 18, 1967.

this level can be analyzed systematically, but such an elucidation leads only to the negative aspect of the work: a void is created, which tropisms will fill once the clichés have been swept away. In contrast, Sarraute's language, which is immediately accessible to her, is not immediately accessible to the reader, and its deciphering is an exercise in hermeneutics. Sarraute's literary techniques seem to rest on the double postulate that the usual semantic content of words is deeply misleading, and that reality is best expressed through whatever escapes the linguistic conventions of symbolic meaning.

In conclusion, I should like to suggest that Nathalie Sarraute, as a writer, is not alienated from herself, since the very theme of the work is the pursuit and capture of those inner realities which constitute her true, authentic self. She is a writer very largely reconciled with herself. True, her quest for identity is not a continuous success; she admits willingly the perilous moments of her literary journey, the fragile, evanescent quality of the matter she pursues, the frequent failures, the occasional discouragement. But the creative act, for her, is the polar opposite of self-alienation: she starts from a reality within herself, expresses it through the media of her choice, and considers the endeavor a success if and when her writings bring her back to the reality she started from. The reader, however, is forced to accomplish the itinerary backwards. He must start from the text in the hope of capturing a reality that is not his, and the narrative techniques at work make no attempt at bridging the gap between his world and the author's. The traditional novel goes at least halfway in presenting the public with an assortment of common denominators, apparently bridging the gap between the real and the fictional; the new novel does not. Paradoxically enough, the more of these common denominators a novel can boast, the more fictive the result. Sarraute's novels come closer to the truths she wishes to express as their form breaks sharply away from accepted formal codes. There is a definite progression in her literary production, a progression that goes from her relatively accessible works like *Tropismes* and *Le Planetarium* to her latest (and more obscure) novels, *Entre la vie et la mort* and *Vous les entendez?* The earlier works include, if not characters, at least occasional proper names and the embryo of a story; but the expression of tropisms in these novels remains somewhat ambiguous; it owes too much to psychology, to introspection, to the form of introspection that reasons, argues, discusses—that is, analyzes. It stems from the writer's intellect. The role of the intellect, in her latest works, is much more strictly delineated: as a professional writer, she uses it to choose her techniques and control the structure of her works; she is definitely highly conscious of her goals, of her efforts, and of the results obtained. But she no longer allows her intellect to tamper with the raw material she starts from. It is quite possible that the closer she gets to her goal, the greater will be the distance between novel and reader. The reader approaches the novel through the formal deciphering of a work that rejects formalism; a certain discrepancy seems unavoidable. Yet, formalism may well be the most valid approach for the reader or critic anxious to break through the deceptive layer of her code language in order to reach the inner core of her private world. Her work, which sets itself over and beyond style, is nevertheless at the mercy of stylistic analyses. The public is likely to feel somewhat alienated from novels written, not only *by*, but mostly *for* the author herself.

Nabokov's *Pnin*: Floating and Singing

DABNEY STUART

Washington and Lee University

I. THE NOVEL AS BIOGRAPHY

It is possible to consider all of Nabokov's novels as, to some degree, revealing the fiction of biography, and at least one of them, *Ada,* as a biography of Fiction. *The Real Life of Sebastian Knight* has been written about from the former perspective,[1] and I think it is rewarding to think of *Pnin,* Nabokov's twelfth novel and his fourth in English, in the same way.

The general implications of the novel, read from this angle, are similar to those of most of Nabokov's work. As in other cases, three of which I have considered elsewhere,[2] one moves finally into the shifting ambience of parody, and what is parodied turns out to be not so much a literary form used by other writers, as more basic assumptions about perception and its relationship to so-called factual reality, that term which Nabokov has said should always be surrounded by quotation marks. In this instance, however, the particular form that is used to intensify those marks is more intimately associated with *facts* than is, for instance, the cinema, or the play. One picks up a biography expecting automatically not to encounter fiction, but to be presented with an objective account of a life, and I suspect that even when one has read two or three biographies of the same person, that is to say, two or three versions of a "reality," he still has trouble relinquishing his illusion that there is a factual base, which he can piece together, underlying the various ornamentations of it. That piecing together would, of course, be nothing more than another version, another biography; such a process of interlocking and superimposing versions has, in fact, been

---

This is the first publication of the essay.

1. By Susan Fromberg, convincingly, in her "The Unwritten Chapters in *The Real Life of Sebastian Knight," Modern Fiction Studies* 13, (Winter 1967–68) : 427–42.

2. See my "Angles of Perception," *Modern Language Quarterly* 29, no. 3 (1968) : 312–38; "All the Mind's a Stage," *University of Windsor Review* 4, no. 2 (1969) :1–24; and "The Dimensions of Parody," *Tri-Quarterly,* no. 17 (1970), pp. 72–95.

at the core of *The Real Life of Sebastian Knight,* and recurs, more subtly and with another purpose, in *Pnin.*

Unlike the earlier novel, *Pnin* is structured so that very few signals of its parodic nature occur; one has to wait until the last chapter of the novel to be sure that his illusions have been monkeyed with, for it is not until then that the suspicious relationship of the narrator with his subject surfaces, becomes explicit. There is in *Pnin* no acknowledgment of the process of accumulating data—nobody is visiting the friends of a dead person, trying to organize the bits and pieces he picks up into a unified whole. We are presented the whole to begin with, or so it appears, and our tendency to settle comfortably into the easy chair of reportage is encouraged. It takes a while for the needle in the cushion to work its way into our flesh.

The methods of encouragement are familiar to biography—an emphasis on names, places, dates. Almost all of the characters who appear in *Pnin,* no matter how minor they seem, are given names: the students who enroll in Pnin's Russian language classes, the expatriates who gather in the summers at Al Cook's, even Judith Clyde at Cremona College and Grigoriy Belochkin, who may or may not have turned over a glass of pear *kvas* at a famous resort on the Baltic coast. The only important character who goes nameless is, strikingly, the narrator, but it is possible, as I will argue later, that the whole novel is in the process of naming him.

Places are handled with the same care, giving the same impression of local identity. Waindellville is, in effect, on a map, after a chapter or so, a map we are partly familiar with, for it includes Albany, New York, and is clearly of an upstate New York and New England area. Victor's trip to visit Pnin is presented in such a way as to underline this, giving us another "real" city, Boston (to which Framingham is adjacent), by which we can orient ourselves. This is carried to something of a finite extreme by the narrator's aerial perspective on Pnin's highway and dirtway vicissitudes on his way to Cook's.

And the novel abounds with dates as well: Pnin's series of "heart attacks," beginning on July 4, 1920; his birthdays, two of which are central events in the novel, the recurrent reminders of how long he has been at Waindell, the temporal exactness of occurrences from his past. Overriding these specific instances is the concern with chronology, beginning first with the specification of the year, and eventually of the seasons within the year, and the time of day.

Name, place, date, the chronology of events. It is no wonder that we believe we are reading the true story of Timofey Pnin, presented objectively, if with sympathy, by someone who has the inside information, who is trustworthy, and who has no stake in what he is writing, no axe to grind.

But even without chapter 7, it would be surprising if a reader of this novel could get very far with that belief, for we are given hints that the case is other-wise—given them gently, and with reserve, but tellingly nonetheless. To begin, for instance, where the novel begins—with the narrative perspective, not with Pnin—one sees the gentlest of these suggestions right away. After Pnin's appearance has been described in the novel's first two paragraphs, the narrator remarks, "Thus he might have appeared to a fellow passenger; but except for a soldier asleep at one end and the two women absorbed in a baby at the other, Pnin had the coach to himself."[3] The conditional is suggestive—he *might* have

---

3. *Pnin* (New York: Atheneum, 1964), p. 8. All subsequent quotations are from this edition, and are followed by page numbers in parentheses.

appeared thus to someone else, but then again he might not—but what is more interesting is the question of who is seeing Pnin if no one on the train has paid him any attention. This is followed immediately by the narrator's imparting of the "secret," known to no one in the coach, including Pnin himself, that Pnin is on the wrong train. The only person who can be both observing and knowing is the narrator; as soon as the novel begins, Nabokov is, as always, making his preparations carefully. Further, it is no slip on the author's part that the narrator speaks of the distance between Waindell and Cremona in terms of *versts* instead of miles. In this same chapter we learn that the narrator had assisted Pnin in writing a letter to the *New York Times* in 1945; he begins to show as well his habit of referring to Pnin as "my friend," which we learn later is something of a liberty.

This process of suggestion, designed to undermine the reader's belief in the detachment of the narrator and therefore in the appearance of a factual account of Pnin's life, continues, becoming a little more obvious with each, of the next five chapters, and becoming, predictably, more complex in its implications. The narrator's involvement in Pnin's past shows more sharply, for instance, when we learn that a relative of his helped with Pnin's emigration from Europe in 1939, and we begin to wonder what he is holding back when he refers to Pnin's love letter to Liza, in which Pnin proposed, as "now safe in a private collection" (p. 45). His reference to the "littérateur" with whom Liza had an affair, as a result of which she attempted suicide, has the same effect. His pronunciation of "Tsentral Park and Reeverside" (p. 62), which are echoes of Pnin's pronunciation, intensify one's sense that he is Russian himself. Once the novel reaches the way-station of Al Cook's rambling country house one is certain; the narrator more or less completely sheds the appearance of emotional distance he has more or less been trying to sustain, as his comments on Cook's childless marriage illustrate.

Moreover, in these chapters (2 through 6) the narrator continues to "report" Pnin's activities so as to extend the suggestiveness of his opening observations. He goes where Pnin goes, and because of Pnin is never alone, even when he dreams.[4] Two particular passages may be to the point of the general technique here. The first is the closing paragraph of chapter 4.

> Presently all were asleep again. It was a pity nobody saw the display in the empty street, where the auroral breeze wrinkled a large luminous puddle, making of the telephone wires reflected in it illegible lines of black zigzags. (P. 110)

Somebody *does* see it, however, and gives it to the reader as though it were a perception no different from the other perceptions in the book. A more extensive example occurs in the opening five pages of chapter 5. The narrator presents Pnin's search for Cook's house from the perspective of a fire tower overlooking the countryside. His observation is set in the same negative mode as the opening description of Pnin on the train, and the sight of the puddle I have just referred to. It is *as if* no one was there to see.

---

4. Just in case it is necessary, I should say that this is more than the simple, limited, omniscient point of view. That perspective is being used, obviously, but *used* for purposes that make it more than a minimal necessity of telling a story. And as soon as the narrator arrives for his guest lecture at Waindell, which "causes" Pnin's departure, the point of view changes.

[Pnin's] various indecisions and gropings took those bizarre visual forms that an observer might have followed with a compassionate eye; but there was no living creature in that forlorn and listless upper region except for an ant who had his own troubles, having, after hours of inept perseverance, somehow reached the upper platform and the balustrade. (P. 115)

But, again, it is seen; the narrator, in fact, follows that ant to the "right beam leading to the roof of the tower," and lets us know the names visitors have penciled on the balustrade of the tower. The details of each of these scenes are given and taken away at the same time, but nonetheless they are *seen,* and the basic effect of the *way* they are seen is to make us aware that the narrative intelligence of the novel is working in a mode fundamentally different from the usual mode the biographer assumes. If one becomes aware of the imaginative nature of such scenes, he should begin to question the nature of other details that are not apparently surrounded by an aura of invention.

To the narrator's involvement in Pnin's past, the indication that he is with-holding information, and his ability to see and know things that no one else, including Pnin, sees or knows, Nabokov adds another dimension that serves to alert his reader to the fictional nature of this apparent biography. He has the narrator at least twice comment on the narration, a tactic that is familiar in his novels and is used more sparingly here than elsewhere. In chapter 1 he notes,

> Some people—and I am one of them—hate happy ends. We feel cheated. Harm is the norm. Doom should not jam. The avalanche stopping in its tracks a few feet above the cowering village behaves not only unnaturally but unethically. Had I been reading about this mild old man instead of writing about him, I would have preferred him to discover, upon his arrival to Cremona, that his lecture was not this Friday but the next. (Pp. 25–26)

And in chapter 2, after the Waindell bells have been modulated into the ringing telephone in the Clements's house, he says,

> Technically speaking, the narrator's art of integrating telephone conversations still lags far behind that of rendering dialogues conducted from room to room, or from window to window across some narrow blue alley in an ancient town with water so precious, and the misery of donkeys, and rugs for sale, and minarets, and foreigners and melons, and the vibrant morning echoes. (P. 31)

In themselves these passages should at least alert the reader that he is in the presence of fiction, as well as the presence of the intelligence creating it. But it should do a little more. The details used—the avalanche, the windows and the alley, the donkey, rugs, and minarets—should, by the inappropriateness of their appearance in the context of the novel, suggest, through their own romantic and fantastic (to an American reader) qualities, that perhaps, *mutatis mutandis,* basically everything that surrounds them is just as inappropriate in the larger arena of apparent factual reality. The kind of extrapolation these details suggest is similar to the one carried a bit further in *The Murder of Gonzago* in *Hamlet*: here is a play presented by traveling players, here are other players—Gertrude, Hamlet, and so on—watching the play, here are other people (the audience, or also players?) watching the players watching the players. And who is watching them? It is not simply a matter of noticing consciously that we're reading fiction, but that its deceptive appearance as reported fact is not limited to this book, or even to the act of reading.

As I have said, all this is merely suggestive until chapter 7. At that point a good deal becomes explicit and the pattern of earlier hint and evocation is fulfilled. The narrator openly acknowledges his relationship with Pnin, from its beginning in 1911 when he had a mote removed from his eye by Pnin's father.[5] He recounts later meetings with Pnin, in Paris and New York, and reveals much of what he had teasingly (to the reader) withheld previously. The "private collection" in which Pnin's letter of proposal to Liza resides is the narrator's (p. 182), and he quotes the letter. The "littérateur" with whom Liza had the nearly fatal affair is the narrator, of course (pp. 180–82); it is he, finally, who is the "fascinating lecturer" who takes Pnin's place at Waindell. The reference made in chapter 5 to Mira and "amateur theatricals" (p. 133) is expanded in more detail (pp. 177–79), as is the role of the Baltic resort in Pnin's adolescence. It is even possible that Victor's art teacher, Lake, who has "studied in Paris" (p. 95) and whose decision to "bury himself" (pp. 95–96) in an anonymous New England boys' school puzzles those who recognize his genius, has also had an affair with Victor's mother, for in the letter of proposal Pnin refers to "the celebrated painter who made your portrait last year [who] is now . . . drinking himself to death . . . in the wilds of Massachusetts" (p. 183).

This much, I think, is easy, and could be set aside, a little game played with the reader's expectations that gives in the end a pleasure similar to the kind that solving a puzzle affords, and as easily forgotten. But, as is the case elsewhere in his novels, what seems in Nabokov to be an answer, or a solution, is rather the grounds for a more illuminating mystery. He conceals the keys of his patterns so that one considers him kin to the designer whom Pnin's narrator refers to as "the destroyer of minds, the friend of fever" (p. 23).

In chapter 7 we are led beyond the clarifications we receive. The narrator's language, first of all, is revealing in places. For example:

> Perhaps because on my visits to schoolmates I had seen other middle-class apartments, I *unconsciously* retained a picture of the Pnin flat that *probably* corresponds to reality. I can *report* therefore that *as likely as not* it consisted of two rows of rooms divided by a long corridor; on one side was the waiting room, the doctor's office, *presumably* a dining room and a drawing room further on. (P. 176, my italics)

The clarification of details from Pnin's (and the narrator's) life in this chapter may, after all, simply confirm the reader's sense that all is well, that the little game of coy obfuscation still results in the reporting of facts. But a passage such as this makes that conclusion impossible; one wonders how much else that has been "reported" is presumption and probability. Moreover, that this is so is intensified by Pnin's denial of the narrator's presentation of some details of his past.

---

5. This rather fatuously implies that the narrator is to be compared with Tolstoy at least, and possibly Dostoevski. See the references to these two writers, and Dr. Pavel Pnin, pp. 21, 26 of the novel.

I tried not only to remind Pnin of former meetings, but also to amuse him and other people around us with the unusual lucidity and strength of my memory. However, he denied everything. He said he vaguely recalled my grandaunt but had never met me. He said that his marks in algebra had always been poor and that, anyway, his father had never displayed him to his patients. . . . He repeated that we had never seen each other before. (P. 180)

With that we should be sure that what we have been reading is invention, an imaginative construction, a fiction partly disguised as fact; if we wish in spite of this to cling to the factual appearance, then we must take sides arbitrarily with Pnin or the narrator, and the façade must again crumble. But again I think one could live with this comfortably, by putting it aside as part of a book, intriguing but merely literary. The final dimension toward which this process moves, and in which it is left to reside, is, however, much more disturbing, and though it can be spoken of as though it is understood, it remains impossible to explain away.

The novel stops, but does not conclude, with this passage:

Cockerell, brown-robed and sandaled, let in the cocker and led me kitchenward, to a British breakfast of depressing kidney and fish.

"And now," he said, "I am going to tell you the story of Pnin rising to address the Cremona Women's Club and discovering he had brought the wrong lecture."

The novel has opened with an account of Pnin's trip to deliver a lecture to the Cremona Women's Club, but in that account he has forestalled getting caught with the wrong lecture by intricate precautions, and eventually by getting off a bus and recovering the "right" lecture at the bus station where he had left it. The final passage of the novel seems to take us back to its beginning, as in a circle, though in reality it takes us back to a point analogous to the beginning but not identical with it. The figure of a spiral would perhaps be a more accurate metaphor for the movement involved.—Back to the lecture and the trip, but with a different emphasis, or in a different version. We have seen this event once; if Mr. Cockerell, who lets in his cocker were to deliver his account, we would see it again, but changed.[6]

Cockerell has, in fact, used up the narrator's evening and early morning before breakfast with an exhausting series of imitations of Pnin, done so well that the narrator is forced to wonder "if by some poetical vengeance this Pnin business had not become with Cockerell the kind of fatal obsession which substitutes its own victim for that of the initial ridicule" (p. 189). The particular events that Cockerell has recounted during his imitations have, with only a few exceptions, already been presented to us by the narrator during the course of his book-length imitation of Pnin: "Pnin teaching, Pnin eating, Pnin ogling a coed. . . . We got Pnin in the Stacks, and Pnin on the Campus Lake. We heard Pnin criticize the various rooms he had successively rented" (p. 187). It is not stretching things to imagine the evening with Cockerell as another novel called *Pnin,* presented

---

6. Cockerell's version, with its unhappy ending, would please the narrator.

via synopsis, created by a man with an obsession who has "acquired an un-mistakable resemblance to the man he had now been mimicking for almost ten years" (p. 187).

The last two sections of the novel, then, open, suddenly, questions of a queasy sort, it you happen to be a person to whom facts, and the assumption that there are such things, are important. Who is Pnin? The one we have been accepting for 180 pages or so has gradually been revealed as the narrator's invention. We are given still another invention by Cockerell. There seems, indeed, to have been a walking, talking, teaching, eating, ogling person called "Pnin" whom characters other than the narrator and Cockerell have seen and talked with and consoled and manipulated, but is he possibly only a convenience? Does he have any identity beyond the imitations we have been asked to accept as the man be-hind them? Is he an occasion by means of which others can identify themselves? Is he perhaps, as the pronunciation of his name suggests, a pun with an echo?

In the midst of such questions one might notice the degree to which twins are important in the novel. There is a set, Igor and Olga Poroshin, who appear, to disappear, at Cook's. The gas station attendant who gives Pnin directions is called "false Hagen," and Laurence Clements and Dr. Eric Wind briefly merge in Pnin's mind during his party. Pnin takes a book back to the library for the person who has requested it, who turns out to be himself, something more than absent-mindedness. There is the long diversion on Tristram Thomas and Thomas Wynn, Twinn and Winn, Tvin and Vin, that is carried through Pnin's inviting one while he thinks he is inviting the other to his party. Such twinning is said to be, by the narrator, common in academic communities, and he adds, "I know, indeed, of triplets at a comparatively small college where, according to its sharp-eyed president, Frank Reade, the radix of the troika was, absurdly, myself" (p. 148). Not, assuredly, Waindell College, whose president is named Poore—assuredly, until we think of Timofey, Cockerell, and the narrator. But of course Pnin and the narrator have not been at Waindell College at the same time. Or have they? The shadowy play of twinning on the surface of the novel is taken into the same dimension the last passages lead us toward when Clements says to Thomas, "He probably mistook you for somebody else, and for all I know you *may* be somebody else" (p. 165). This is reminiscent of the conclusion of *Sebastian Knight,* but it is not conclusive in the same way here.

There are no explicit conclusions in *Pnin* to compare with Sebastian's half-brother's ability to say "I am Sebastian Knight, or Sebastian is I, or perhaps we both are someone whom neither of us knows." The narrator of *Pnin* may be no less ambiguous than "V," but he is less explicit, and I believe the novel itself is less explicit, too. For the time being I will leave the possibilities that the questions I have raised adumbrate, and return to them in Part III. Suffice it at this point to say that the presence of these possibilities makes it impossible to cling to the rock of fact, the illusion of biography; the book moves where all perception moves, in the imagination, where composition of realities takes place, and beyond which one puts reality in question marks. The nature of the composition can be approached (as I have been approaching it) as focusing on the relationship between form and perception, but it can also be approached from another direction.

II. RECURRENCE: EXILE

During the later stages of Pnin's party we are allowed to ovehear a segment of Joan Clements's hawing conversation:

"But don't you think—haw—that what he is trying to do—haw—practically in all his novels—haw—is—haw—to express the fantastic recurrence of certain situations?" (P. 159)

The immediate reaction of anyone acquainted with Nabokov's work is to take him to be the antecedent of Mrs. Clements's pronouns, but one does not have to trust that acquaintance because immediately following her comment one of those recurrences takes place. It is a simple one, not very fantastic, but it is set where it is to key the relevance of Joan's statement to the novel in which it appears. Laurence Clements tells an off-color joke, to which Pnin responds, "I have heard quite the same anecdote thirty-five years ago in Odessa, and then I could not understand what is comical in it" (p. 160).

What is suggested briefly turns out to be threaded into the fabric of the whole novel, most noticeably in Pnin's unpredictable (or predictable) recollections of his own past.[7] A number of these occur, and are handled so that they seem to be not simply recollections but instances of the recurrence of events and people from a supposedly dead time. Nabokov's method seems, in fact, to be similar to Proust's use of the uneven flagstones, the napkin, the knocking pipe, and the madeleine.

Just before he begins to deliver his lecture to the Cremona Women's Club Pnin's audience is transformed:

In the middle of the front row of seats he saw one of his Baltic aunts . . . Next to her, shyly smiling, sleek dark head inclined, gentle brown gaze shining up at Pnin from under velvet eyebrows, sat a dead sweetheart of his . . . Vanya Bednyashkin, shot by the Reds in 1919 in Odessa . . . was gaily signalling to his former schoolmate. And in an inconspicuous situation Dr. Pavel Pnin and his anxious wife, both a little blurred but on the whole wonderfully recovered from their obscure dissolution, looked at their son with the same life-consuming passion and pride that they had looked at him that night in 1912 when, at a school festival, commemorating Napoleon's defeat, he had recited . . . a poem by Pushkin. (Pp. 27–28)

Similar recollections occur again, though the contexts affording the impetus for them change, in each chapter of the novel except the last. Sometimes the recurrence is treated, as here, in some detail: his transformation of Cook's summer house and its guests, for example, in which his father plays chess with Dr. Belochkin, and he meets Mira for the last time (pp. 132–36). On other occasions it is briefly presented: while he is leafing through a Russian-language periodical

7. During the following discussion I will, most of the time, accept the convenience of Pnin as a character who in some way has an existence of his own, apart from the narrator's imitation of him. That convenience is, as I have tried to suggest, *part* of the identity named "Pnin"; it is a manner of speaking. The novel is, of course, finally the narrator's embroilment, and to him the convenience of Pnin as a man apart from himself is of crucial importance. I will return to this focus in my conclusion.

in the library he sees, "for no special reason," his father and mother relaxing in a drawing room in St. Petersburg in 1913 (pp. 75–76); on his way home from the Starr's "Russian evening," and as he drifts off to sleep, he walks a Russian countryside, along a road that emerges into "the romantic, free, beloved radiance of a great field unmowed by time" (p. 82); at the gas station on the way to Cook's he becomes a Petrograd freshman again (p. 114) and recalls that instance a bit later (p. 124); his own rooms in the first *house* he rents remind him of Russian country houses (p. 146). The most significant constant in these instances is the time period that recurs: in each case it is *before* the 1918–19 revolution. I will come back to this in the context of Pnin's "illnesses" and his research.

Perhaps memory, even when it is treated in such a way as to shade it toward the past's recurrence, it not quite fantastic enough a mode, however, since we have invented psychological tools by means of which we think the fantasy can be removed. I don't think so, but perhaps. In view of the perhaps, it becomes somewhat important to me that Nabokov has used more than one means to make recurrence part of the experience of the book. The usual label for the following instances is "coincidence," a good term both because it explains nothing and because its primary meaning is in keeping with the purport of the novel. Chapter 4, which deals wholly with the second excruciatingly poignant visit Pnin has from a loved one, this time Victor, opens and closes suggestively. Victor dreams of his father as a king in the midst of a revolution that threatens his throne and his life. He envisions the king as responding decisively to the situation, choosing to escape by water. Victor never brings his vision to a conclusion, however, never gets the king his father to the beach and into the delivering motor-boat, because "the very act of postponing that thrilling and soothing episode, the very protraction of its lure, coming as it did on top of the repetitive fancy, formed the main mechanism of its soporofic effect" (p. 86). The closing scene involves Pnin's dream as he sleeps at the end of the evening he has spent with Victor: "Pnin saw himself fantastically cloaked, fleeing through great pools of ink under a cloud-barred moon from a chimerical palace, and then pacing a desolate strand with his dead friend Polyanski as they waited for some mysterious deliverance to arrive in a throbbing boat from beyond the hopeless sea" (pp. 109–10).

The dreams of "father" and "son" coincide, one completes the other, and the footprints that approach Pnin, and cause him to wake up, may belong to the friend of fever. This is difficult to see as anything but fantastic, and the agent of the fantasy signals his presence.

This instance of recurrence, or coincidence involves Pnin and Victor, exiles from home and from each other; as such it is resonant with the recollections I have discussed. But people other than Pnin and his immediate "family" are included in the pattern. The "Russian revelers" whom Entwhistle fooled into thinking he was a compatriot (p. 36), for example, may have been the group at the champagne party cooked up to bribe "an influential critic . . . to devote his next *feuilleton* in one of the Russian-language newspapers to an appreciation of Liza's muse" (p. 45). Both incidents take (or took) place at the Ougolok ("little corner") café in Paris. Or consider Jan van Eyck's "ample-jowled, fluff-haloed Canon van der Paele," to whom Laurence Clements bears a striking resemblance, as the narrator observes (p. 154). At the point of the observation Clements is holding an

English-Russian, Russian-English dictionary in his hand, a book he puts aside later in favor of a volume entitled *Flemish Masterpieces,* in which he finds himself, or rather Canon van der Paele. The unusual situation is more resonant still: the volume of reproductions has been given to Victor by his mother, and in turn left by its owner with Pnin; Victor is a budding artistic genius whose pursuits are spoken of this way:

> If Degas could immortalize a *calèche,* why could not Victor Wind do the same to a motor car?

> One way to do it might be by making the scenery penetrate the automobile. A polished black sedan was a good subject. . . . Break the body of the car into separate curves and panels; then put it together in terms of reflections. . . . In the chrome plating, in the glass of a sun-rimmed headlamp, he would see a view of the street and himself comparable to the microcosmic version of a room (with a dorsal view of diminutive people) in that very special and very magical small convex mirror that, half a millennium ago, van Eyck and Petrus Christus and Memling used to paint into their detailed interiors. (P. 97–98)

Again there is coincidence; this time the artistic locus is explicit, and the detail of the mirror serves to intensify the reflection of one experience in another. Finally, note that two pairs of characters who appear briefly have names that are nearly interchangable: Christopher and Louise Starr, colleagues of Pnin's at Waindell, and Christine and Louis Stern, psychologists who test Victor. This connection is compounded later when we learn a few details of Liza's attempted suicide in the early twenties. Who saved her life? Why those two obliging English neighbors of hers, Chris and Lew.[8]

I think, further, that the instances of twinning that I have discussed in another context also bear on the theme of fantastic recurrence. Clements's statement to Thomas, "And for all I know you *may* be somebody else," may be considered in conjunction with a comment the narrator makes about Pnin, some thirty pages earlier, immediately after the longest single instance of recollection in the novel:

> The sky was dying. He did not believe in an autocratic God. He did believe, dimly, in a democracy of ghosts. The souls of the dead, perhaps, formed committees, and these, in continuous session, attended to the destinies of the quick. (P. 136)

The most important details, however, and the most complexly associative, that have to do with the imaginative composition of realities in the novel are the occasions of Pnin's "attacks," and his research, which are basically connected in the figure of the squirrel.

Timofey has two "attacks" in the novel. Even if the narrator, his "physician for the nonce," did not register his doubt that the seizures are heart attacks, their presentation would lead us to the doubt by themselves. No doctor has

---

8. Another such instance involves Robert Karlovich Horn, a steward of the narrator's aunt's estate (1916), who "recurs" as Bob Horn, the bus station attendant who assists Pnin on his way to Cremona (1950).

been able to understand them in the past; Pnin has had four prior to the first one in the novel, which occurs just after he has left the bus in Whitchurch. This one defies medical explanation, too. It is characterized by a sense of the divestment of the flesh, which is death, by a "tingle of unreality," and by a sense of becoming one with one's surroundings. It is both frightening and attractive, as occurrences that approach the miraculous tend to be: "It may be wonderful to mix with the landscape, but to do so is the end of the tender ego" (p. 20). Yet the end of the tender ego we know may be the beginning of a tougher, more enduring one. The effect of this experience in Whitchurch on Pnin is to dislocate his ego from time: during the course of it he is both seated on the stone bench in the strange park in 1950 and lying in his bed with a fever in his home in St. Petersburg in 1910. There appear in the park rhododendrons and oaks; the same vegetation is pictured on the wallpaper of his room. On the polished wood screen near his bed are a path, an old man hunched on a bench, and a squirrel; he has walked down a path to the stone bench he is now (now?) hunched on, and when he comes out of his seizure his first sight is a squirrel on the ground before him.

He is, moreover, referred to as "a poor cocooned pupa" in the context of his childhood illness, but the context of the seizure makes that situation merge with the present so that the image applies to him on the bench as well. A cocooned pupa is in a stage of transformation, as we know; in that condition Pnin looks at the wallpaper of his room (and the landscape of the park) and thinks that "if the evil designer—the destroyer of minds, the friend of fever—had concealed the key of the pattern with such monstrous care, that key must be as precious as life itself and, when found, would regain for Timofey Pnin his everyday health, his everyday world" (p. 24). The passage, and the experience of which it is a part, are magnificent. In the dual temporal focus we see the dual significance of the illnesses: in 1910 Timofey recovered from his fever and regained his everyday world, and yet 1910 is inseparable from 1950: the Timofey of one time is also the Timofey of the other: he is still "ill" and still looking for that key. His everyday health and world are what he is exiled from: prerevolutionary Russia, the self that took that time and place as home and still retains it, fragmented and elusive, in the imagination. The self named Pnin has been composed narratively as fluid, as having versions, because that self, though it appears in particular places at specified times, is finally both placeless and timeless, a floating possibility that has nowhere to rest—except, perhaps, in some dimension we have no terms to realize, a dimension suggested by the image of the cocooned pupa, and to which we make ourselves available through continuous imaginative composition, keeping alive and touching what seems to have been irrevocably lost.[9]

9. The manner in which Pnin's exit is handled in the next-to-last paragraph of the novel, and Lake's color theory, seem to me to be other ways in which such a dimension is suggested. As Timofey passes the beer truck and disappears into the distance, the narrator ventures, "There was simply no saying what miracle might happen" (p. 191). And "among the many exhilarating things Lake taught was that the order of the solar spectrum is not a closed circle but a spiral of tints from cadmium red and oranges through a strontium yellow and a pale paradisal green to cobalt blues and violets, at which point the sequence does not grade into red again but passes into another spiral, which starts with a kind of lavender gray and goes on to Cinderella shades transcending human perception" (p. 96). Because of passages such as these I have used the spiral, Pnin's most constant resting place, as a figure for the form of the narration itself.

Note how this circles about within the book. Pnin discusses his "condition" with his old friend Chateau prior to his swim at Cook's. Chateau reveals that he must have an operation in the near future, to which Pnin responds, "laughing, that every time *he* was X-rayed, doctors vainly tried to puzzle out what they termed 'a shadow behind the heart'" (p. 126). A bit later Chateau cautions Pnin that he will someday lose the Greek Catholic cross he wears on a chain about his neck.

> "Perhaps I would not mind losing it," said Pnin. "As you well know, I wear it merely from sentimental reasons. And the sentiment is becoming burdensome. After all, there is too much of the physical about this attempt to keep a particle of one's childhood in contact with one's breastbone." (P. 128)

The breastbone, the heart, the shadow behind, one's childhood—the combination of details extends the suggestions implicit in the first seizure.

Further, Pnin goes swimming immediately after these exchanges, which perhaps is a reminder that he has been characterized as Victor's "water father" by Eric Wind. Water is almost always associated with emigration in the novel, the "actual" one across the Atlantic by the whole "family" being the central instance. The vision that Victor conjures to make him sleep, which is completed in Pnin's dream, bears upon this theme, too, for there the mode of escape from death at the hands of the revolutionaries is water. As I have suggested, this is a more complex kind of recurrence; later I will return from another point on the circle to both the water imagery and Pnin's sense of burdensomeness.

The second "attack" he experiences in the novel occurs at Al Cook's. Its symptoms are the same as those of the first: "It was not pain or palpitation, but rather an awful feeling of sinking and melting into one's surroundings" (p. 131). As in the previous occurrence, the details of his surroundings in the year of the seizure, 1954, are reflections of those of a past period, 1916 (or 1917): Cook's country house and the people visiting it coincide with the country house rented by Dr. Pavel Pnin's chess opponent, Yakov Belochkin, and the other people visiting there. The two scenes merge, as did the two scenes (and times) of the first seizure, this time accompanied by comment that makes the basic implications of Pnin's physical condition even clearer.

> Pnin, with hallucinatory sharpness, imagined Mira slipping out there into the garden and coming toward him among tall tobacco flowers whose dull white mingled in the dark with that of her frock. *This feeling coincided somehow with the sense of diffusion and dilation within his chest.* (P. 133, my italics)

An additional focus appears, however, in the closing long passage of this attack. Mira died in a Nazi concentration camp, Buchenwald; the precise way she died is unknown, which means for Pnin that she continues to die in his imagination, over and over:

> Mira kept dying a great number of deaths in one's mind, and undergoing a great number of resurrections, only to die again and again, led away by a trained nurse, inoculated with filth, tetanus bacilli, broken glass, gassed in

a sham shower bath with prussic acid, burned alive in a pit on a gasoline-soaked pile of beechwood. (P. 135)

This should be intolerable to a human being, and for the most part Pnin exists by not thinking about it. It is only during his seizures that he is able even to begin to cope with it.

> Only in the detachment of an incurable complaint, in the sanity of near death, could one cope with this for a moment. In order to exist rationally, Pnin had taught himself, during the last ten years, never to remember Mira Belochkin—not because, in itself, the evocation of a youthful love affair, banal and brief, threatened his peace of mind (alas, recollections of his marriage to Liza were imperious enough to crowd out any former romance), but because, if one were quite sincere with oneself, no conscience, and hence no consciousness, could be expected to subsist in a world where such things as Mira's death were possible. (Pp. 134–35)

Thus, Pnin's spatial and temporal exile involves something more than the loss of his country where home was defined; it involves the world of supposedly human beings who not only allow such things as Mira's death to occur but participate in them. It is not the truncated love *affair* that is painful to face, it is the destruction of the assumption that human beings are loving creatures. This is a more profound exile.

In this condition of exile Pnin goes about the charade of quotidian existence, but of the many activities with which he occupies himself only one seems to be of any real importance to him, his research. It is the one activity that one might venture to call "normal" that touches the possibility of a whole self, or perhaps more accurately, fuses the disparate selves he is composed of in the way that memory and his seizures do.

Fittingly, his subject is a history of Russian culture, but a particular kind of history:

> A *Petite Histoire* . . . in which a choice of Russian curiosities, Customs, and Literary Anecdotes, and so forth would be presented in such a way as to reflect in miniature *la Grande Histoire*—Major Concatenations of Events. (P. 76)

His sense of his subject is itself a reflection of the way the novel is composed—a focus on the concatenations of small events, obliquely and peripherally presented—and it echoes as well in the phrase *reflects in miniature,* Victor's approach to his art, which has been associated with van Eyck's convex mirrors.

The relationship between what he reads and thinks about as he conducts his research in the carrel, and the scenes from the past he is able to keep alive through memory, is evident. There are, however, more complicated connections that Nabokov knits into the fabric. I have mentioned the association of water with exile in another context; that association can be approached through Pnin's research as well. As he reads the passage about the pagan rites of Green Week in Kostromskoy's volume on Russian myths, he is struck not simply by the description of peasant maidens making wreaths and singing and garlanding the willows, but also by a "curious verbal association" that he cannot specify. After looking up the correct pronunciation of "interested" in Webster, he suddenly clarifies the association:

> . . . plila i pela, pela, i plila . . .
> . . . she floated and she sang, she sang and floated . . .

Of course! Ophelia's death! *Hamlet!* (P. 79)

He notes the similarities between the scenes of Ophelia's suicide and of the peasant maidens' activities, and thus explains to himself why the association occurred in his mind. But the pattern is wider than he is aware. When he was having trouble making the association conscious, the narrator dropped in a suggestive adjective: "he could not catch it by its *mermaid* tail" (p. 77, my italics). The word is fitting, of course, since the maidens are floating among the loosed garlands, and Ophelia is in a like situation, weeded, though dead. But it is intended to lead us, if not Pnin, to recall Joan Clements's attempt, after Liza's visit, to cheer Pnin by means of a cartoon in a magazine.

> "this is a desert island with a lone palm, and this is a bit of broken raft, and this is a shipwrecked mariner, and this is the ship's cat he saved . . . and this is a rather wistful mermaid hanging around." (P. 60)

Pnin is implicitly in such a situation himself, without the mermaid, and we are again in the presence of his islanded life, "floating and singing." His direct response to the cartoon is in terms of literature—he starts to comment on two poems by Lermontov—which may be said to lead us back to his library carrel; his reponse to the whole experience of which Joan's effort is the last stage is to say, sobbing, "I haf nofing left, nofing, nofing" (P. 61). The short association between the peasant girls and the scene from *Hamlet* is apparently superficial and transient for Pnin, but it serves a more complicated purpose for the novel, revealing again that nothing is disconnected from the bereft condition named Pnin.

Pnin's sense of the burdensomeness of "keeping a particle of one's childhood in contact with one's breastbone," which I have commented on in another context, is similarly handled from the vantage of his research. We are told in the only other passage that goes into any detail about his studies, that "this research had long entered the charmed stage when the quest overrides the goal, and a new organism is formed, the parasite so to speak of the ripening fruit" (p. 143). Recall that, in the context of his first seizure, Pnin had been spoken of as regarding his heart "with a queasy dread, a nervous repulsion, a sick hate, as if it were some strong slimy untouchable monster that one had to be parasitized with, alas" (p. 20). Without freezing the connection into a mathematical equation, one becomes aware of the double-edged nature of what is at the source of Pnin's possible identity: the demand, the necessity, of keeping the possibility of an integral self open by keeping the past alive affords the only way out of exile, and yet becomes a profound burden, dramatizing emotionally the quality of exile itself—unnatural, and causing one to employ unnatural methods of living with it. To attempt to live creatively within a situation that is intolerable means continuously to be aware of the situation itself. All one's ruses become reminders.

The *form* of the novel, as I have been trying to suggest, communicates this without let-up. No matter where one enters it he is led to central foci; with respect to the particular entrance I am presently in the midst of—Pnin's research—there is another detail that affords similar connections perhaps more obviously than either the "mermaid" association or the quest of the heart as parasitic. I am referring to the squirrel, which keeps popping up throughout the book.

In the first passage devoted to his studies Pnin is described as if he is observed by other people, students, in the library.

> Many good young people considered it a treat and an honor to see Pnin pull out a catalogue drawer from the comprehensive bosom of a card cabinet and take it, _like a big nut,_ to a secluded corner and there make a quiet mental meal of it. (P. 76, my italics)

By itself this would be little more than a simile suggesting the pleasure of mental digestion, but it doesn't occur by itself. It may be seen as an explicit center of many suggestions radiating through the novel.

We first notice the squirrel in the context of Timofey's first seizure: it is pictured on the wooden screen of his room in St. Petersburg. In his fever he becomes worried to figure out what the "reddish object" it holds in its front paws could be, a "dreary riddle" that is modulated into the riddle posed by the wallpaper, the solution of which, Timofey thinks, would mean his restoration. As he emerges from the seizure the first thing he sees is "a gray squirrel on comfortable haunches on the ground before him . . . sampling a peach stone" (p. 24).

The squirrel's second appearance occurs after Liza's visit, near the close of Pnin's day, not long before the incident of the cartoon. Pnin is as close to open despair as he comes in the novel.

> He seemed to be quite unexpectedly . . . on the verge of a simple solution of the universe but was interrupted by an urgent request. A squirrel under a tree had seen Pnin on the path. (P. 58)

It jumps up on the water fountain Pnin is walking by, and in all but words requests a drink. Pnin obliges, pressing the foot pedal that controls the flow of water. And then, "the water father continued upon his way"(p. 58).

Pnin is on campus again when the animal makes its third appearance. On his way to the library for an afternoon with his history, Pnin watches a squirrel, escaping the rocks of "delinquents," dash across a patch of sunlight and hide itself in a tree. It is Pnin's birthday—he is 55[10]—and he slips on the icy pavement;

---

10. There are many places at which this note could occur; I have chosen to put it here for convenience only. The chapter in which this event occurs, chapter 3, is wholly controlled by the importance of the date: February 15 (Georgian calendar, or "disguise" as the narrator calls it), 1953. The narrator makes a little game of hiding while revealing that it is Pnin's birthday ("O Careless Reader!" [p. 75]), calling attention to the fact, of course, as though it is important. And it is, for each segment of the chapter points to aspects of Pnin's exile, gently but poignantly. In his class he quotes Pushkin's poem, the lines of which recur to him after he watches the squirrel climb the tree; he goes to the library and eats his big nut and discovers his mermaid association; he goes to the Starr's Russian evening and sees movies of his homeland, and returns to the Clements's weeping; finally, he even loses his room because Isabel, her marriage broken, returns. Each occurrence shimmers with loss—of his childhood, his homeland, his wife, his current residence—so that the word _birthday_ becomes resonant in a way it rarely is.

immediately after regaining his balance he thinks, as he has had occasion to do already in the morning, of the lines from a poem in which Pushkin wonders about the precise moment and place of his death.

All three of these occurrences precede the image of Pnin munching the "big nut" of the index card, and each one focuses suggestions that reveal the implications of that comparison. In the first one the squirrel appears in the context of Pnin's "illness," the mode through which both time and place are suspended for Pnin, and the concomitant suspension of the identity that bears his name dramatized. In the second the context is Liza's disappointing visit and departure, the concatenation of themes involving Pnin's loss of his wife, his erstwhile son, and his identification as "water father," exiled and isolate. In both these instances, moreover, the squirrel is associated with Pnin's awareness of the need to find some key to the riddle of his life and the universe. In the third instance, the associations include the personal quality of his teaching, and his consideration, through the prism of Pushkin's poem, of his own death. The complexity of these accumulated associations is intended to be evoked, I think, when Pnin is observed with that index card. His research is directed toward his own condition, into the dimensions of his exile, his isolation, his loss, his fragmentation, the major concatenations that his own *petite histoire* adumbrates.

I do not wish to labor this since it seems, if only because of the frequent recurrence of the squirrel, to be the most noticeable aspect of the novel's patterns. Nevertheless, it might be noted that the associations built around this detail extend, finally, beyond Pnin. Victor mails him a postcard with a picture of a gray squirrel on it, and the color of the bowl he sends to Pnin is discussed (at the party, especially p. 158) in terms that return to the squirrel, terms that add the story of Cinderella and her magic slipper to the earlier suggestions that the little animal brings into focus.[11] Victor, then, would seem to be involved in a situation similar to that of his "water father," himself exiled and deprived. From that perspective his art assumes an importance analogous to Pnin's research. There is in fact, something uncannily prophetic about the whole coincidental series, for, chronologically in Pnin's life (though placed near the novel's end), the first appearance of the squirrel is on a shelf in his boyhood room (p. 177).

III. THE NARRATOR

Pnin is an imaginative construction of the terms by which exile can be confronted, an engagement of possibilities in a world where only possibilities can be engaged. This is also true of Pnin. The sources of identity are lost—that is the given in which the composition resides; yet there is also the given necessity that they not be lost irrevocably. The composition is thus formed to give the illusion of biography as though that illusion is a mirror image of a basic need, an identity that can be believed, and believed in.

The illusion, then, is purposeful, as all illusions are. It is, primarily, the narrator's illusion, and the basic need it mirrors is his own. He must create a "Pnin" who can be believed in as an object of biography, a person who can be *spoken of as if* he has an independent existence. Why? Because "Pnin" is a name

---

11. And through the addition swings us back to the terms of Lake's color theory.

for a particular identity that is not only *formed by* a condition of exile, but *is* a condition of exile as well. As such it is a possible identity *for the narrator,* who is an émigré exile himself. "Pnin" must be confronted, known, ejected, and replaced so that the narrator may be free of the possibility he embodies.

More simply, though the language smacks a bit too much of the psychological for me, the narrator consciously objectifies part of himself in Pnin in order to exorcise it. Pnin is a fabrication, but he is real; he is lovable, kindly, poignant, dedicated, and because of these qualities he is dangerous, since they make the condition of exile he presents attractive. For he is, basically, a victim of his losses, meshed in patterns of endless recurrence, and the moral value of the experience of the novel lies in the narrator's choice of refusing to play that role himself.

In this light, the narrator's replacement of Pnin at Waindell becomes a fulfillment, metaphorically, of the threat he poses to Pnin from the novel's beginning. As Pnin's creator he may also be Pnin's disposer. Thus Pnin's hostility toward him; thus the narrator's ability to afford the attitudes of tenderness and amusement toward Pnin. However I think that these latter attitudes are more than a function of condescension: the narrator is, after all, deciding against possibilities he finds within himself, and he is sympathetic toward them. If he weren't, there would be no need for the novel.

To return to the considerations I suggested at the close of the first part of this essay, I hope I have shown that Pnin is a convenience of considerable importance. He must seem as true a biographical figure as possible because *he is a life,* a life the narrator envisions and, eventually, supplants. But, simultaneously, he is an imaginative invention, and the reader must be as continually aware of that as he is of the biographical design. In the phrase *biographical illusion,* both terms are indispensable.

The illusion gets the accent, however, because the context is finally, and always, a book. The narrator's need cannot be fulfilled except through the creation of Pnin, which is to say through composition. Perhaps this is analogous to the author's relationship to *Pnin.* Who knows? At any rate, the novel realizes a simultaneous defeat and victory, out of which perhaps emerges a dignity and a hope, but not in such high terms as these. Pnin passes that beer truck, and perhaps shares somehow in the victory (as the narrator shares in defeat), for "there was simply no saying what miracle might happen" (p. 191). As the narrator has exorcised Pnin, so Pnin is free of the narrator.

The Romantic Self and
Henderson the Rain King

DANIEL MAJDIAK

University of Illinois

Men are ungrateful to others only when they have ceased to look back on
their former selves with joy and tenderness. They exist in fragments. Anni-
hilated as to the past, they are dead to the future, or seek for the proofs of
it everywhere, only not (where alone it can be found) in themselves.

—Coleridge, *The Friend*

The fate of the Romantic self in modern life is the main idea in question in
Henderson the Rain King. The place of the self in modern mass society is the
essential theme of *Seize the Day, Henderson, Herzog,* and Bellow's most recent
novel, *Mr. Sammler's Planet,* but in *Henderson* he works out this theme in terms
of the decline and fall of the concept of self bequeathed to us by Romanticism. This
concept determines the mode and the key metaphors of the work as well as
its theme,[1] and we cannot properly comprehend Bellow's meaning in it without

First published: 19, no. 2 (1971): 125–46. The author's recent comment is his added
paragraph to footnote 1.

1. The subject of Romanticism in Henderson is touched on by Irvin Stock in "The Novels
of Saul Bellow," *The Southern Review,* no. 3 (1967), pp. 13–42, and by Jeff H. Campbell in
"Bellow's Intimations of Immortality: *Henderson the Rain King,*" *Studies in the Novel,*
no. 1 (1969), pp. 323–33. However, neither treats it in terms of the broader question of
the fate of the self and neither analyzes Bellow's use of Romantic elements in *Henderson* in
proper depth. The most thorough treatment of Blakean ideas in *Herzog* is in Max Schulz's
Radical Sophistication (Athens: Ohio University Press, 1969), pp. 126–44.

For a different view of Bellow's picture of the fate of the self see Helen Weinberg, *The
New Novel* (Ithaca, N. Y.: Cornell University Press, 1970), pp. 85–102. The author forcefully
argues that Bellow's portrayal should be linked to the views and strategies of Kafka. And
for a masterful overview of the concept of the self and its fate in European literature from
the seventeenth century to the present see Lionel Trilling, *Sincerity and Authenticity*
(Cambridge, Mass.: Harvard University Press, 1972). Especially apposite to the argument
of this essay are the analyses of self and sincerity, of the differences between the English and
American novels of the nineteenth century, of Conrad's *Heart of Darkness,* and the brief
but cogent commentary on Bellow's stance vis-à-vis literary nihilism.

this perspective. When we look at it in this way we find that of his four major novels it provides the most comprehensive rationale for his opposition to the nihilistic tendencies of modern literature.

At the outset, one needs to be clear on Bellow's view of the place of the individual in modern mass society. Bellow grants the common premise that the Romantic concept of the glorified personality on which the humanists founded their ideal of society would be obsolete in a true society of the masses, but he is not willing to accept the idea, as so many have, that such a society already exists.[2] Were selfhood thus extinct, Bellow argues, the possibility for moral significance would cease, and clearly the belief that it has not ceased is at the basis of his art. What worries him is the fact that so many of our thinkers seem to accept "the loss of the self," for such acceptance can only accelerate the undeniable drift toward mass society. Bellow agrees that in the main the Romanic self is an erroneous image of man, but abhors the reaction to that image which produces, as he has Herzog put it, "the commonplaces of the Wasteland outlook, the cheap mental stimulants of Alienation, the cant and rant of pipsqueaks about Inauthenticity and Forlornness."[3] The Romantic view of the self is no longer acceptable, but, as Herzog argues, it "guarded . . . the most generous ideas of mankind during . . . the most accelerated phase of the modern . . . technical transformation" (pp. 204–5). Furthermore, Bellow believes that the most characteristic aspect of the Romantic concept of self is essential to an adequate picture of man. He believes, as did all the Romantics, that the source of power in the self is the creative imagination. It is a kind of "primitive prompter or commentator advising us, telling us what the real world is."[4] Our great problem is that the system within which we live "loves abstractions . . . and is not friendly to the imagination; it prefers preparedness to impulse, . . . it resists new forms of reality."[5] Within this system the Romantic concept of self is no longer tenable, but, as "we have barely begun to comprehend what a human being is, we must do all we can to foster our imagination."[6] Bellow wonders if such mental growth will be possible for much longer; there are so many distractions that one cannot be certain "whether there will ever be enough tranquillity under modern circumstances to allow a contemporary Wordsworth to recollect anything."[7] As we shall see, this problem of distraction is especially relevant to Henderson's dilemma.

The only hope for man in this situation lies in what the Romantics called the "sympathetic" powers of the imagination which, in turn, they evoked in defining their concept of love. Again, Bellow is in agreement with them: love brings us to attention, it enables us to believe in the existence of others as unique individuals. This idea is truly central to Bellow's art, for he holds that "novels are about others.

2. *Recent American Fiction* (Washington: Library of Congress, 1963), p. 12. That Bellow continues to hold this view is evident in his defense of traditional values in *Mr. Sammler's Planet*.

3. *Herzog* (New York: Fawcett, 1965), p. 96. All other citations are given by page number in the text. Other editions used are *Henderson the Rain King* (New York: Fawcett, 1969) and *Mr. Sammler's Planet* (New York: Viking, 1969).

4. Gordon Lloyd Harper, "Saul Bellow: An Interview," *Paris Review*, no. 36 (Winter 1965), p. 57.

5. "The Writer and the Audience," *Perspectives USA*, no. 9 (Autumn 1954), p. 101.

6. "Where Do We Go From Here: The Future of Fiction," in *Saul Bellow and the Critics*, ed. Irving Malin (New York: New York University Press, 1967), p. 219.

7. Harper, p. 66.

They lack everything if they lack this sympathetic devotion to the life of someone else."[8] A work of fiction consists of a series of moments during which we are willingly engrossed in the experience of others."[9] Echoes of Coleridge may be discerned here, but more important to *Henderson* is the parallel to Wordsworth's concept of "spots of time" in art. Bellow's essential agreement with this concept can be seen more clearly in his speculation that art is an "achievement of stillness in the midst of chaos . . . , an arrest of attention in the midst of distraction."[10] I shall come back to this in analyzing *Henderson,* but before I do I must more fully outline what Bellow believes about the self.

Modern society makes possible a rich private life for unprecedented numbers of persons, yet the individual is limited, the self lacks power because it is disoriented by distractions. The real purpose of these distractions, Bellow speculates, is the destruction of individual being. " 'Let it be obliterated,' is the secret message. And many in their hearts answer, 'Yea, so be it.' "[11] "Almost nothing of a spiritual, ennobling character is brought into the internal life of a modern American by his social institutions";[12] so he must trust to his luck as an explorer (as does Henderson) and turn to himself to find value and order. But he finds, as did many of the Romantics, that there are distractions within as well. He finds, like Henderson, Herzog, Sammler, that private life can also be an affliction, "the imprisonment of the individual in a shameful and impotent privacy."[13] As Herzog points out, this leads the individual to yearn for collectivity, and since he returns to the masses "in a frenzy of failure" he adds to the growing reservoir of hate for individuality (p. 218). Sammler provides a unique perspective on this hatred. He survived the attempt of the Nazis to exterminate the Jews and has spent the many years since trying to put that experience into a general picture of mankind. He comes to the conclusion that the Nazi murders, especially in the numbers and manner in which they were committed, are an extraordinarily clear example of the general attack on the "clumsy pretensions, towards the bad joke of the self which we all feel" (p. 235).

Yet, for all his pessimism, Bellow refuses to join the trend of modern literature to nihilism. He feels that there must be more positive ways to resist the control of the masses, realistically to value the self. As Herzog puts it, the self "has millions of secret resources" (p. 202), and while the Romantic ideal of the whole, independent self seems impossible to attain, those resources can be drawn on to create a desirable self. But where are these resources, one must ask. Sammler, even after his horrifying experiences, supplies what seems to be Bellow's basic reply: "That depends. It depends in part on the will of the questioner to see merit. It depends on his talent and his disinterestedness. It is right that we should dislike contrived individuality, bad pastiche, banality, the rest. It is repulsive. But individualism is of no interest whatever if it does not extend truth" (p. 238). Henderson's individualism does extend truth, I believe, and it does so by reaffirming

---

8. Nina A. Steers, " 'Successor' to Faulkner?" *Show* (Sept. 1964), p. 37.

9. "The Sealed Treasure," *Times Literary Supplement,* July 1, 1960, p. 414.

10. Harper, pp. 65–66.

11. "Distractions of a Fiction Writer," in *The Living Novel,* ed. Granville Hicks (New York: Macmillan, 1957), p. 12.

12. "Where Do We Go From Here," p. 215.

13. Harper, p. 69.

the still valid insights into the self that the Romantics discovered while exploring their individualism. Like Wordsworth, especially in the terms given in the "Ode: Intimations of Immortality," Henderson draws on his past to renew himself; and with the aid of insights very similar to Blake's, he finds a way to break out of the imprisonment of a solipsistic private life. But while Bellow reaffirms these Romantic conceptions of the self he also qualifies them through his characteristic comic irony. The picture of the individual presented in *Henderson* shows him "somewhere between a false greatness and a false insignificance."[14] While he reaffirms the Romantic assertion that spiritual growth is the end of existence, he shows that in modern life it manifests itself in strange and unexpected forms.

Bellow chooses to treat the growth of the spirit comically, perhaps because at present that is the only way to treat it realistically and yet affirmatively. As he points out, modern comedy "has to do with the disintegrating outline of the worthy and humane self,"[15] but it differs from the other forms of modern literature by refusing to give in to despair and alienation. Thus the comic spirit is "the spirit of reason opposing the popular orgy of wretchedness in modern literature."[16] The same motives may be adduced for Bellow's choice of romance as the mode for *Henderson*. Historically romance has been associated with idealism, and indeed it is for that very reason that the romance plot became central to Romanticism. But the Romantics altered the traditional pattern of the quest in two highly significant ways: the poet himself became the quester, and his goal became the discovery of his identity. The theme of this kind of romance, therefore, is the achievement of expanded consciousness and this is precisely the theme of *Henderson*. "I am really kind of on a quest" (p. 58) he explains to the prince of the Arnewi, and the words that come to him as he meets his first test as quester (the wrestling match with Itelo) are ones that Shelley used to describe his first experience of mind expansion: "I do remember well the hour which burst my spirit's sleep" (p. 60).[17] So Bellow chooses the Romantic quest for *Henderson* because it exactly suits his ideas, but his use of it is also dictated by his opposition to the predominant trend in modern literature. Realism's tendency, he points out, "is to challenge the human significance of things."[18] Obviously, Bellow does not want to encourage this tendency, and his use of the romance mode is in part tied to his attempt to continue the affirmation of human significance in literature.

Like all narrators of the Romantic quest, Henderson feels impelled to describe his experiences because "living proof of something of the highest importance has been presented" in them (p. 22). But as he begins, the problems besetting the modern self inhibit communication. The distractions cause a "disorderly rush" of memories and associations, which result in the wonderfully comic false starts of the first four chapters. In the digressions and evasions of those opening chapters the facts of Henderson's private life emerge and it is vividly clear how anguishing the imprisonment of the individual can be: "my parents, my wives, my girls, my children, my farm, my animals, my habits, my money, my music lessons, my drunkenness, my prejudices, my brutality, my teeth, my face, my soul!" (p. 7).

---

14. "The Sealed Treasure," p. 414, col. 4.
15. *Recent American Fiction*, p. 10.
16. "Literature," *The Great Ideas Today* (New York: Encyclopedia Britannica 1963), p. 171.
17. The line is taken from the third stanza of the Dedication to *The Revolt of Islam*.
18. Harper, p. 63.

As narrator, Henderson must make order out of this chaos to validate his claim of having extended truth. But if his claim is valid, why is his task so difficult?

He has been plagued, he explains, by a ceaseless inner voice that cries "I want, I want" (p. 14). This is the voice of distraction and it relentlessly drives. him from one unsatisfying pursuit to another—home-improvement, violin lessons, pig farming. And among these there is an erratic search through his father's library (he was an eminent scholar) "to see whether [he] could find some helpful words, and one day . . . read, 'The Forgiveness of sins is perpetual and righteousness first is not required' " (p. 7). In his reading habits Henderson is as eccentric as in anything else he does: "I am a nervous and emotional reader. I hold a book up to my face and it takes only one good sentence to turn my brain into a volcano" (p. 205). (A particularly striking example of such excitement is his description of his first wife as being "like Shelley's moon, wandering companionless" [p. 8]. The allusion is to a fragmentary poem of Shelley's "To the Moon," hardly read by anyone, much less remembered.) And he experienced a mental explosion when he read the saying about forgiveness; though he could never again locate the book in which he read it he goes around repeating it to himself over and over. A statement in Blake's introduction to *Jerusalem* is very similar:[19] "The Spirit of Jesus is continual forgiveness: he who waits to be righteous before he enters into the Savior's kingdom . . . will never enter there." Further, the phrase incessantly repeated by the voice of distraction is from Blake's *The Gates of Paradise,* where it forms the caption to the ninth plate. Also, the opening lines of this work are reminiscent of the lines from *Jerusalem*: "Mutual forgiveness of each Vice/ Such are The Gates of Paradise." These lines from Blake cause Henderson's mental lava to flow for two reasons. First, Blake's concept of "mutual forgiveness" is part of a cure for the diseased self. Forgiveness must be "mutual" in the sense that we forgive ourselves as well as others. But self-forgiveness matters most, for individuality can be nothing but imprisonment without it. And the forgiveness must be for failures as well as for vices. Now Henderson's feeling of failure is at the heart of his problems, and this feeling arises from his belief that he can never become a proper heir to the family name and fortune (all of his mad behavior is a result of this belief). He emphasizes this at the beginning of his narrative: "I was one of three children and the only survivor. It took all my father's charity to forgive me and I don't think he ever quite made it altogether" (p. 8). This conviction is the reason his catalogue of woes begins with "my parents." In Blakean terms the forgiveness must be given by both the authority figure and the individual he accuses; in Henderson's case neither forgives. The plate in *The Gates of Paradise* for which "I want, I want" forms the caption is especially relevant in this connection. It shows a diminutive figure standing at the bottom of a steep ladder that reaches away in the direction of the moon. Blake's symbolism illustrates the endlessness of man's desire *and* the impossibility of complete satisfaction. Further, the impossibility is not recognized because mankind is caught up in what Blake calls the Orc cycle. Orc is a symbolic figure who represents the recurrence of desire in the form of destructive rebellion, and in the version of the Orc cycle given in *The Gates of Paradise*

---

19. Stock is the only commentator on *Henderson* who has pointed this out, but he does not do more than note the allusion. See "The Novels of Saul Bellow," p. 33.

the rebellion occurs because of failure of love (mutual forgiveness) in exactly the form experienced by Henderson. In plate eight of Blake's work an old man is shown collapsed in a thronelike seat, his head down, his sword used as a support. Passing in front is a youth holding a spear aimed at the old man. The caption reads "My Son! My Son!" There is no mutual forgiveness in this relationship; rather, we see the Orc cycle in its bitterest form, the Oedipal conflict. The worst part about the cycle in this form is the ironical transformation of the young rebel into an aged authority figure at the end of his life, for this change assures the recurrence of the cycle in exactly the same terms. Henderson's conflict with his son Edward reflects the same process. When his son tries to assert his individuality and marry a woman of his choice, Henderson's reaction is the same as his father's: "I look at this significant son, Edward, with his crew-cut hair, his hipless trunk, his button-down collar and Princeton tie, his white shoes— his practically faceless face. 'Gods!' I think. 'Can this be the son of my loins? What the hell goes on around here?'" (p. 108). The son cannot forgive the father and the father cannot forgive the son; the self is dominated by guilt. In Romantic terms this situation is hopeless because guilt stifles the imagination, and only the imagination can envision a way to end the cycle. As Dahfu puts it, "this cannot be what the thing is for, over and over. . . . There is no issue from that cycle for a man who do not take things into his hands" (p. 249). To be free of his father Henderson must become a proper father himself.

The specific factors of Henderson's case emerge gradually as he struggles to bring order and meaning to his narrative. At first he cannot tell the story of his father: "He was a well-known man. He had a beard and played the violin, and he . . . No, not that" (p. 22). In fact, not until his quest is nearly over can he face the truths of his relationship with his father: "I suppose my dad wished, I *know* he wished, that I had gotten drowned instead of my brother" (p. 267). In his reaction to this rejection Henderson's behavior is a classic example of the pattern Freud outlined in his essay "Mourning and Melancholia."[20] Feeling cut off from the loved object he begins to harbor murderous feelings toward it (probably toward both his brother and his father), but when these feelings threaten to become conscious his guilt over them leads him to direct these feelings toward himself. And as they are very intense, death seems to be the only possible atonement for such evil. Indeed, Bellow has said that anxiety over death is what really motivates Henderson,[21] and his brooding and obsessive speculations about his own death dramatize his unconscious defense against secret aggressive and murderous thoughts and impulses. Everywhere Henderson goes he seems to encounter death. "Why is it always near me—why? Why can't I get away from it for a while! Why, Why?" (p. 212). Obviously, he cannot answer this question until he sees the cause of his death anxiety and, as both Blake and Freud would have it, forgive himself. Only in this way can he escape the belief that his brother was "the rightful one" and that he himself is merely a displaced person (a feeling many Bellow characters share).

In the theme of displacement Bellow draws his parallel between Henderson's neurosis and fate of the self from the Romantic period down to our own. Before

20. *Collected Papers*, ed. Ernest Jones (London: Hogarth Press, 1956–57), 4: 152–170.
21. Steers, p. 38.

his experiences in Africa, Henderson was disposed to think like those who argue that the society of the masses is already established. "Nobody truly occupies a station in life any more. There are mostly people who feel that they occupy the place that belongs to another by rights. There are displaced persons everywhere" (p. 32). In an earlier version of a chapter of *Henderson,* published in *Botteghe Oscure,* this line of thinking is even more evident. Here, the arrival of mass man is placed back in the era of Henderson's father and Bellow gives him many of Henderson's traits: "He was a man of large capacity, *Magnus.* But he had no chance to make proper use of his capacity, and so became mad. One hundred million Americans were against him. He condemned business, he preached liberty and poetry. . . . But he only wanted to be obedient to a proper purpose."[22] And as he goes on with his analysis of his father's problems and those he inherited from him Henderson's ideas sound strikingly like those in *One-Dimensional Man:* "A single man is afraid of the weight of the many, and their anger, and what-ever he does is apt to be a peril to him. Why couldn't I do as others at home do. To escape my father's fate, I have made myself coarse and ignorant in order to achieve normalcy." All of this is the result, he says, of the fact that "somebody else is active for us. Government is active for us, it commits crimes for us by murdering millions. . . . But why do my small offenses seem so wrong? Because I have tried to muscle in on the state monopoly, in order to bring a little interest into my life. . . . A few people in Washington, New York, and Hollywood, have taken all the initiative. They do and we watch. We are at best spectators and at worst trophies."[23]

The reasons Bellow has for putting the entire problem of being displaced on Henderson's shoulders in the revised version of the novel are not hard to find. This change makes the fate of the self more dramatic and, more important still, it allows for Henderson's recovery. If mass society had in fact already been dominant in the lifetime of Henderson's faher, the Oedipal struggle, in which Henderson fights to become a self in a contest with his father, would be funda-mentallly altered. For as Herbert Marcuse argues in his provocative essay "The Obsolescence of the Freudian Concept of Man," in a mass society in which power is shifted from the father to technical and political "administration," the self is methodically indoctrinated and manipulated, and "the direct management of the nascent ego through the mass media, school, . . . gangs, etc. . . . shrinks [it] to such an extent that it seems no longer capable of sustaining itself, as a self."[24] The sovereign self of the Romantics, the decent self of the Victorians, even the minimal stoic self of the Hemingway type (which Henderson parodies in part) all disappear. But Bellow will not accept this analysis. Henderson can still look back to a time when the father was authority, a self of strength and dignity to whom he still has ties, however ambivalent and painful. Because of these ties there is still a strong desire to be a proper son and a proper father and so there is still a strong desire to be an individual and not a member of the masses. Para-doxically, in Bellow's ironic comedy Henderson's greatest problem is that he is *not* one-dimensional. He may feel unworthy of his heritage, but he persists in

---

22. "Henderson in Africa," *Botteghe Oscure,* no. 21 (1968), p. 222.

23. *Ibid.,* p. 223.

24. *Five Lectures,* trans. Jeremy J. Shapiro and Shierry M. Weber (Boston: Beacon, 1970), p. 47.

the belief that "the eternal is bonded onto us. It calls out for its share. This is why guys can't bear to be so cheap" (p. 267).

The event that actually sends Henderson on his African journey is directly involved with Bellow's analysis of our historical situation. On the day in question, one of his stormy rages causes his old housekeeper to have a fatal heart attack. In confusion, he leaves her body and wanders over to her cottage where he finds a scene that symbolizes the whole death-oriented existence of his world:

> Bottles, lamps, old butter dishes, and chandeliers were on the floor, shopping bags filled with string and rags, and pronged bottle openers . . . ; and bushel baskets full of buttons and china knobs. And on the walls, calendars and pennants and ancient photographs.
> And I thought, "Oh, shame, shame! Oh, crying shame! How can we? Why do we allow ourselves? what are we doing? The last little room of dirt is waiting. . . . So for God's sake make a move, Henderson, put forth effort. You too will die of this pestilence. Death will annihilate you and nothing will remain, and there will be nothing but junk. Because nothing will have been." (P. 37)

So he begins his journey, and the many mythic parallels that critics have noted appear. The one that is relevant to the fate of the Romantic self is the one into which all the others—fertility rituals, dying god figures, et cetera—merge, the myth of renewal or resurrection. This is a recurrent myth in Bellow's work; it is important to *Seize the Day, Herzog,* and *Mr. Sammler's Planet,* but in *Henderson* he treats it in specifically Romantic terms, most noticeably those worked out by Wordsworth in the "Ode." In these terms the power for renewal is asserted to be within the self, a self strong enough to recognize great loss and yet be confident of future gain. This power resides in the imagination, which enables us to see what we were and are and where we are going. The possession of the imagination assures us, as Herzog puts it, that the inspired condition "is not reserved for gods, kings, poets, priests, shrines, but belongs to mankind and to all existence" (p. 205). The mythic parallels reemphasize this belief, which Bellow holds no less fervently than the Romantics.

Still another way in which Bellow expresses this belief is in his refutation of the nihilistic Romanticism so common at the end of the nineteenth century. Here again the mythic parallels are important, but even more so are the many allusions to and parodies of the literature of Romantic nihilism,[25] in particular *Heart of Darkness.* Conrad's theme is a perfect contrast for Bellow. In Kurtz's boundless will, in his attempt to subsume all reality in the self, Conrad dramatizes the darkness of man's will to power and its utter futility. In drawing a parallel between Henderson's journey and Marlow's, Bellow tries to demonstrate that reality is not all darkness and that man can see the light. However, he does not try to maintain a consistent parallel between Henderson and Marlow or Kurtz and Dahfu; indeed at times he gives Henderson attributes disturbingly like those of "the emissary of light," but in the end they always demonstrate that all is not dark in Henderson's heart. For example, the catalogue of woes quoted earlier

---

25. Robert Alter, "The Stature of Saul Bellow," *Midstream* 10, no. 4 (Dec. 1964), makes the point that *"Henderson* is a composite parody of all the memorable 20th-century novels of personal or mythic quest into dark regions."

is very like the ravings of Kurtz's mad soul: "My intended, my ivory, my station, my river, my—."[26] But Henderson recognizes that this subjectivity is mental imprisonment, and his journey is an attempt to escape. Likewise, though he echoes Marlow's frustration at trying to communicate the experience—"not the least of the difficulties is that it happened as a dream" (p. 22)—he will not concur in Marlow's pessimistic belief that the attempt is "vain . . . , because no relation of a dream can convey the dream sensation" (p. 40). In contrast to this Romantic pessimism, Henderson's narrative is much more like Wordsworth's achievement in the "Ode," where the expression of the loss of "the glory and the freshness of a dream" is also its recapture. Marlow relates one of his "inconclusive experiences" out of the gloom of depression, whereas Henderson responds to an obligation to communicate "living proof of something of the highest importance" (p. 22). Among other things, he has found proof that there is more to human freedom than just a choice of nightmares. He does in fact see the kinds of abominations among the Wariri that Marlow found among Kurtz's followers, but in the Wariri king, Dahfu, he finds a very different alter ego. Each narrator remains faithful to the man he meets in darkest Africa to the end "and even beyond"; each is left with a memory of a voice which, as Henderson puts it, "once heard will never stop resounding in your head" (p. 131). But the truths they articulate are entirely different: "the horror" is the message Marlow hears, but Henderson is told that "the noble will have its turn in the world" (p. 182).

However, before he meets Dahfu, Henderson comes upon the Arnewi (who are a kind of comic African version of Blake's children of innocence), and it is among them that he has his initial experience of spiritual growth. The first society Henderson observes in "the ancient bed of mankind" seems to him the childhood of the race. His encounter with them is unnerving: "The kids were unanimously silent, they only looked, and I looked at them. That's what they call reality's dark dream?" (p. 45). The phrase Henderson takes from Coleridge's "Dejection: An Ode" to sum up the situation is certainly apt. It is apparently another of those "single sentences" that turn his mind into a volcano, and it is not hard to see why. Henderson is preeminently a man of dejection (the bit from the 25th Air of Handel's *Messiah,* "And Who shall Abide the Day of His Coming," stays in his thoughts for the same reason), and he has come to Africa trying to find reasons to rejoice in himself. The silent reception of the Arnewi children makes Henderson think they view his coming with foreboding, but in reality their somber mood is caused by a plague of frogs which, because of their taboos, is preventing them from watering their sacred cattle. When he learns of this taboo Henderson thinks the whole thing very propitious for him since he can play the role of savior and thus, for the first time in his life, become an accepted and even honored member of the community. And the event that most convinces him that his arrival among the Arnewi is propitious is his interview with their queen, Willitale. Everything about her seems right. She is considered both mother and father of her tribe, which would seemingly preclude any possibility of Oedipal conflict. And since her vision is not obscured by the failure of mutual forgiveness, she should be able to tell Henderson the solution to his problems. In a comical gesture of return to the womb, Henderson performs the ritual of kissing Willitale's

---

26. *Heart of Darkness* (New York: Washington Square Press, 1967), p. 76.

navel and then asks her for the answer to the riddle of existence. The first thing she tells him is that the world is strange to a child. Henderson immediately applies this to himself and it gives him a major insight. It shows him that, like the children in the "Ode," he has "never been at home in life" (p. 73). Again, this is a persistent theme in Bellow's writing. Herzog puts it best: "The children of the race, by a never-failing miracle, opened their eyes on one strange world after another, age after age, . . . eagerly loving what they found" (p. 174). However, as Henderson points out (as does Wordsworth in the "Ode"), "there's strangeness and strangeness. One kind of strangeness may be a gift, and another kind a punishment" (p. 238). The gift, Wordsworth says, is "a sense of the indomitableness of spirit" and "that dreamlike vividness and splendour which invests objects of sight in childhood." And the punishment, as he says in the "Ode," is indeed the darkness—the Romantics had envisioned it long before Conrad—in "which we are toiling all our lives . . . ,/ in darkness lost, the darkness of the grave." Henderson's whole adult life dramatizes the effects of this death-orientation, and he begins to see this in his encounter with Willitale. "The world may be strange to a child, but he does not fear it the way a man fears. He marvels at it. But the grown man dreads it. And why? Because of death. So he arranges to have himself abducted like a child. So what happens will not be his fault" (p. 74).

The queen also tells Henderson "Grun-tu-molani," "Man want to live" (p. 74). Henderson agrees and adds, "not only I molani for myself, but for everybody." He is on the side of life, true, but that is not enough. As Bellow says apropos of Herzog, "he wants to live? What of it! . . . Simple *aviditas vitae.* Does a man deserve any credit for this?"[27] No. Henderson must learn *how* to live, how to accept himself and his failures in mutual forgiveness and recapture something of his birthright, not just as a Henderson but as a human being.

The first stage of his renewal comes in a scene just before he ruins the Arnewi cistern in his attempt to blow up the frogs. It is at sunrise (recalling the sun imagery in the "Ode" where the progress of the sun from east to west parallels the journey of the child into life), and Henderson is struck by the quality of the light:

> I felt the world sway under me. . . . Some powerful magnificence not human, . . . seemed under me. And it was the same pink color . . . that did it. At once I recognized the importance of this, as throughout my life I had known these moments when the dumb begins to speak, when I hear the voices of objects and colors; then the physical universe starts to wrinkle and smooth. . . . Thus on this white wall with its prickles, like the gooseflesh of matter, was the pink light. . . . It must have been at least fifty years since I had encountered such a color, and I thought I could remember waking as a tiny boy, alone in a double bed, . . . and looking at the ceiling where there was a big oval of plaster in the old style, with pears, fiddles, sheaves of wheat, and angel faces; and outside, a white shutter, twelve feet long and covered with the same pink color. (P. 87)

And this memory leads immediately to another, the focus of which is the image of his father, who "would carry Dick and me into the mill pond and stand with

---

27. Harper, p. 70.

us under the waterfall, one on each arm. With the beard he looked like Triton; with his clear muscles and the smiling beard" (p. 87).

Both memories are remarkable examples of the vividness of childhood vision, and Henderson, like Wordsworth in the "Ode," evokes them with remarkable power even while sorrowing over the loss of this existence. However, he is not yet able to take advantage of these memories because his destructive impulses still dominate; the pink light fades and Henderson vents his aggression on the frogs. Likewise, his insights into the noumenal fail to help him for the same reason. What Henderson normally experiences in the presence of nature is a typically modern alienation. He shows how he usually relates to it in his description of an average day on his estate:

> I see a large pine tree on my property, and in the green darkness underneath, which somehow the pigs never got into, red tuberous begonias grow. . . . The sun is like a great roller and flattens the grass. . . . When the air moves the brilliant flowers move too in the dark beneath the trees. . . . I am there and am looking for trouble. The crimson begonias, and the dark green and the radiant green and the spice that pierces and the sweet gold . . . , the brushing of the flowers on my undersurface are just a misery to me. . . . To somebody these things may have been given, but that somebody is not me. (Pp. 28–29)

Again, Henderson in his typical existence is more like the Coleridge of "Dejection: An Ode" than like Wordsworth. He can see the beauty of nature but not feel it, except as it causes him misery. And this, again, is because he cannot rejoice in himself. He must try to answer dejection as Wordsworth does and look to those spots of time which assure him that the self can be desirable. He may wish his days to be bound each to each by natural piety, but there are too many distractions. He must first literally remember himself, see himself in a life-giving relation to his father—as in the marvelous mythic image in the mill pond—before he can accept the painful paradox that the child is father to the man. Even before he meets Dahfu, Henderson intuits something of this, hence his energetical rejection of the view of man given by Eliot in *Burnt Norton*. He expresses this rejection immediately after his experience of the pink light. "There is that poem about the nightingale singing that humankind cannot stand too much reality. But how much unreality can it stand? . . . I fired that question right back at the nightingale. So what if reality may be terrible? It's better than what we've got" (p. 91). Eliot's poem is about lost potentiality never fulfilled, but Henderson will not accept the view that this potentiality is irrevocably lost, and he goes on to show that one can heed the bird's call and find his past self. Like Wordsworth he learns to use memory to renovate himself and create a self-image for the future.

Illumination comes to Henderson with increasing frequency and ever greater clarity once he meets Dahfu. Though he leaves the Arnewi in despair, he finds in the king of the Wariri a person of such nobility and depth of thought that he is inspired by him to one last grand effort at renewal. And the effort is successful because for the first time Henderson finds a person with traits he loved and admired in his father and brother who, in turn, respects Henderson's qualities. However much failure Dahfu recognizes in Henderson, he still puts his faith in him and so moves Henderson to be worthy of that faith. Indeed, though he is the younger man, Dahfu soon takes on the role of an older brother; whereas Marlow found his dark alter ego in Kurtz, Henderson finds his admired lost brother. Further, in a crucial way his quest is the same as Dahfu's. In order to gain his identity of the king of the Wariri Dahfu must capture a male lion believed to incarnate the soul of his dead father. Thus they are both on a quest for the father in whom they will find their own proper selves. And just as Henderson can never be the self his father was, Dahfu, however much strength and nobility he has, must fail also. His concept of the self and of what a man may do are too out of line with those of the superstitious people of his tribe (the mass men of primitive society) and they insure his destruction, but not before he has helped Henderson to find the way to renewal.

Dahfu believes that evolution is still in process (an idea frequently voiced by Bellow characters). Further, he believes evolution to higher forms of existence is made possible by the imagination. But he sees, as Blake tried to show in his myth of the fall and the subsequent development of neurotic mankind, that there can be a kind of regressive evolution as well, and that this kind of evolution in fact prevails. In Henderson he finds a glaring example of noble character deformed, a comic, bound promethean. In his plan for reversing this process he apparently takes literally Blake's sardonic maxim that "the tigers of wrath are wiser than the horses of instruction" (p. 219). He believes, like Mr. Sammler, that the imagination cannot create new images for the self out of whole cloth, that it must have proper models, and his model is the lion. He tries to learn from lions the proper way to experience life, and he wants Henderson to try to learn also. Because of this love for Dahfu Henderson does try—"nothing could have been more painful than to lose my connection with him" (p. 218)—and in some of the best comic scenes of the novel we see him roaring out his soul in agony. But it is no good, he realizes: "But then what good could an animal do for me? . . . A beast of prey? Even supposing that an animal enjoys a natural blessing? We had our share of this creature blessing until infancy ended. But now aren't we required to complete something else, . . . the second blessing?" (p. 242). In this insight he grasps the concept of evolution Wordsworth developed in the Intimations "Ode," an evolution not of the body, which must age and die, but of the spirit, which provides the vision to look through death. And indeed Henderson must see a way to do this because he no sooner finds his lost brother than he loses him again to death. The mutual respect and, it turns out, the mutual forgiveness between Dahfu and Henderson give him the means to come to terms with this loss.

In the long journal letter to his wife written just before the king's death, his interjected comments to himself show how far he has come to solving his problems. When he asks "how did I get so lost," and "how do I get back," his memory immediately provides him with a picture of his lost self and in so doing revives in him his potential for growth and renewal: "It is very early in life, and I am out in the grass. The sun flames and swells; the heat it emits is its love, too. I have this self-same vividness in my heart. There are dandelions. I try to gather up this green. I put my love-swollen cheek to the yellow of the dandelions. I try to enter the green." The sense of relation through love is the insight Henderson takes from this memory and Dahfu's teachings jibe with this: ". . . he tells me I should move from the states that I myself make into the states which are of themselves. Like if I stopped making such a noise all the time I might hear something nice. I might hear a bird" (p. 239). His acceptance of these ideas leads him to see that in order to grow into something worthy of our beginnings we must recognize the futility of the Orc cycle: "I don't think the struggles of desire can ever be won" (p. 240). The essential truth is, "love makes reality reality. The opposite the opposite" (p. 241).

Even during the intense strain of the hunt for the lion supposed to be Dahfu's father Henderson can now respond to reality with love and give it the proper attention to know it in and of itself. "The small blossoms of the cactus in the ravine, if they were blossoms and not berries, foamed red, and the spines pierced me. Things seemed to speak to me. I inquired in silence about the safety of the king who had a crazy idea that he must capture lions. But I got no reply. This was not the purpose of their speech. They only declared themselves, each according to its law, declaring what it was" (p. 257). But the real test of Henderson's capacity for love and mutual forgiveness comes at the king's death when he finds out that, as rain king, he has been picked by Dahfu as his successor. This means that he must live under all the dangers and demands Dahfu did; he must be husband to a demanding harem (the service ideal with a vengeance!) or face certain death, and he must capture and tame the lion containing Dahfu's soul. He feels betrayed, for Dahfu's only answer to his question about Dahfu's motives for doing this is "it was done to me" (p. 262). But in pondering this answer Henderson comes to realize that "love may be like this, too" (p. 267). In choosing him as successor Dahfu had actually given Henderson the greatest proof of his faith in his ability to renew himself; he had, that is, really expressed mutual forgiveness. "He believed that I was royal material, and that I might make good use of a chance to start life anew" (p. 265). This is what Henderson needed to burst the spirit's sleep and come to himself, to accept the rhythms of existence, including "the worst rhythm there is. The repetition of a man's bad self" (p. 276). In accepting this rhythm Henderson opens the gates of memory wide, and he is granted recollections that make possible his new outlook on life.

On his flight home he remembers the day of his brother's funeral when he ran away from home because his father made him feel the "family line ended with Dick." But instead of avoiding the fact he now faces it and forgives him: "An old man, disappointed, of failing strength, may try to reinvigorate himself by means of anger. Now I understand it" (p. 282). And he is able to see the family house, a symbol of the self for both father and brother, in terms of present realities: "the joint isn't modern. It's not like the rest of life at all, and therefore it's misleading" (p. 282). It is, as in the memory of the pink light, "that imperial palace whence he came," but he cannot re-create life there as it once was and there is no need to punish himself because he cannot. And other memories of later experiences are of great value as well, notably that of his first journey away from home. This memory concerns his manner of supporting himself when he ran away; the situation is typical of Bellow's wonderfully creative humor. Henderson found a job in a circus, and one of his duties was to ride in a roller coaster with an old brown bear called Smolak. The memory is especially important to him because he finds in it conclusive proof that he "didn't come to the pigs as a tabula rasa" (p. 284). Like the Romantics refuting Locke's denial of innate ideas, Henderson dismisses the notion that he was always unworthy. And, also, the memory provides a spot of time that vividly demonstrates for him that "whatever gains [were] ever made were always due to love and nothing else. And as Smolak . . . and I rode together . . . we hugged each other . . . with something greater than terror. . . . I shut my eyes in his wretched, time-abused fur. He held me in his arms and gave me comfort. And the great thing is he didn't blame me. He had seen too much of life, and somewhere in his huge head he had worked it out that for creatures there is nothing that ever runs unmingled" (p. 284). In this great comic-grotesque image of mutual forgiveness Henderson finds his symbol of renewal. He has recollected a desirable image of the self, and, though greatly diminished from the sovereign self of the Romantics, it still allows him to assert, with Bellow, "that truth is not always so punitive" as most modern literature would have it, that "there may be truths on the side of life."[28] So at the end of his narrative, as he looks at an orphan boy he has befriended on the plane, he again affirms the conception of the human spirit that Wordsworth presents in the "Ode" as an answer to dejection: "As for this kid resting against me, bound for Nevada with nothing but a Persian vocabulary—why, he was still trailing his cloud of glory. God knows, I dragged mine on as long as I could till it got dingy, mere tatters of gray fog. However, I always knew what it was" (p. 285). In exactly the same metaphor that Wordsworth uses, Henderson's mental travel takes him eastward back to himself when his relation to life was whole and perfect and then forward again to see the connection between that self and the present man; thus assured that his days are bound each to each, he can accept the loss, rejoice in his spiritual growth, and continue his westward journey in peace. And, in facing the dread of discontinuity, in affirming the existence of the self, however diminished, in shaping the chaos of his life into the order of his narrative, he has shown, as Wordsworth showed in the "Ode," "that chaos doesn't run the whole show. That this is not a sick and hasty ride, helpless, through a dream into oblivion. No, Sir! It can be arrested by a thing or two. By art, for instance. The speed is checked, the time is redivided" (p. 149).

---

28. Harper, p. 73.

Giles Goat-Boy:
Satire Given Tragic Depth

JOHN W. TILTON

Bucknell University

COMMENT BY THE AUTHOR

In addition to Robert Scholes (see my footnote 2), only Raymond Olderman ("The Grail Knight Goes to College," in Beyond the Waste Land, *pp. 72–93) has attempted an exegesis comparable to mine. Olderman's approach to* Giles, *like mine, concentrates on the mythical, but it is less comprehensive, since it focuses on the Grail myth of the Waste Land.*

On occasional points the work of both Scholes and Olderman overlaps mine. But the overlaps are minor, since neither critic has attempted as comprehensive a study of the mythography of the novel as I have. In short, their studies complement mine rather than supplant it.

A brilliant comic novel *Giles Goat-Boy* certainly is. Yet it is a great deal more than just a hilarious and witty romp through the vagaries of herohood and the insanity of modern life. Any reader of *Giles* who has followed Barth from *The Floating Opera* through *End of the Road* and into *The Sot-Weed Factor* senses, even if he cannot articulate his perceptions, that in *Giles* Barth has taken a giant's step forward in the direction that the earlier novels have moved, toward a definition of man, his universe, and his plight. I believe that with this step he has arrived at that definition.

Giles is a true culmination in the sense that it coherently fuses a great many of Barth's ideas about the nature of man that in the three earlier novels gave a

---

First published: 18, no. 1 (1970) : 92–119. The essay is slightly revised for this collection.

philosophical substance and an emotional depth of great power. In *Giles* Barth has synthesized and, as it were, realized those ideas to produce a consistent and comprehensive insight into the condition of man in an absurdly meaningless universe. And for *Giles,* Barth has found or created the form needed for the organic development of this integrated vision of man's fate. Or it may be that the form served as the means of integration: the myth of the hero that Barth adopted as his framework may have revealed to him the possibility of so inter-relating the conditions of men in all ages and cultures that the plight of modern man could be given a profound and universally valid interpretation. The precise relation between the form and content of *Giles* is a difficult subject to essay, and the attempt is almost impossible without first establishing an interpretive base from which one can sally out to explore the vast reaches of Barth's archi-tectonic imagination.

As a means of orientation, it may be best to begin with an account of the basic narrative structure of the novel. When reduced to its fundamental plot line, *Giles* is not much different from *The Sot-Weed Factor.* As J. B. of the "Cover-Letter to the Editors and Publisher" remarks, "One novel ago I'd hatched a plot as mattersome as any in the books, and drove a hundred characters through eight times that many pages of it."[1] This mattersome plot is, however, relatively simple in outline, like that of *Giles.* Each is a novel of initiation or education as conceived in the satiric tradition of Swift and Voltaire. By convention somewhat episodic, this plot sends the young and naive hero into a world where varied adven-tures and encounters constitute an educational process relieving him of his naiveté and producing a maturity of sorts. For purposes dictated by his parody of the hero myth that serves as the structural matrix of *Giles,* Barth has created a *naïf* who is not so much naive as ignorant of human affairs, a boy raised as a goat far from the world of men. And George the Ag Hill goat-boy is no passive pupil in the school of the world; as a self-styled hero, savior, and great teacher, he actively seeks and reaches an understanding of the world and man through experiencing the nearly catastrophic effects of his attempts to be a mover and shaper of human affairs.

This much may be clear to the casual reader, but *Giles* does not yield its true form and content to the casual reader. To understand the complex variations Barth has played upon this basic plot and to grasp their thematic implications, even the most assiduous and perceptive reader is hard put unless he has at his command a far-ranging knowledge of the mythology upon which the novel is built. For ease of exposition, the three basic mythological components of the novel will be explicated separately. Concurrently with this exegesis I shall attempt to isolate and describe the major structural principles of the novel and to draw inferences about its meaning and relevance. This process should reveal some of the subtle and complex interdependencies among its distinctive formal con-figuration, its satirical perspectives, and its commentary on the plight of man.

---

1. *Giles Goat-Boy* (Garden City, N. Y.: Doubleday and Company, 1966), p. **xx/*xxiv.*** Further references to *Giles* will be made in the text by citing in parentheses the page number of the 1966 edition, followed in italics, as above, by the corresponding page number in the paperback edition (Greenwich, Conn.: Fawcett Publications, n.d.), since it may be more readily available.

The three components are: first, the Hero Myth, centering on Giles, Bray, and Anastasia as the major figures in Barth's thorough, intricately patterned parody of the myth of the hero; second, the Founder's Hill Myth, embracing Stoker and Lucius Rexford and exploring the myth of the devil; and, third, the Boundary Dispute Myth, involving the rivalry between East and West and Barth's mythopoeic interpretation of that conflict.[2]

I

Barth's parody of the hero myth is both the basic structural principle of the novel and its matrix of meaning. Although the parody becomes quite explicit at times, particularly when Max Spielman and Giles discuss herohood, innumerable details and several of its large symbolic elements are left to the discovery of the reader. To trace the parody in detail or even to outline it briefly is a task for WESCAC. I must be content here to suggest how extensively Barth has manipulated the myth.

As embodied in the mythology of nations and tribes around the world, the story of the hero begins with virgin birth. The mother of the hero is a royal virgin, his father a king or god, and the circumstances of his conception unusual. At his birth, his father or maternal grandfather attempts to kill him, often because of a prophecy of the hero's eventual displacement of the father. Abandoned in the wilds or set afloat in a basket or box to die, the infant hero often has his leg injured in some way before he is discovered, spirited away, and raised by foster parents in a far country. Consider the birth of Giles. His mother is in name and fact a virgin, Virginia Hector, the unwed daughter of the Chancellor of New Tammany College at the time, Reginald Hector. "Seduced" by the lustful automatic computer WESCAC, she is impregnated by osmosis, as it were, without so much as a kiss. The maternal grandfather is fearful of Giles's Prenatal-Aptitude-Test phrase "Pass All Fail All" and abandons him to die in WESCAC's tape lift, where, in that box- and basketlike cage, his leg is "bunged up" by the tape cans, resulting in a permanent gimp. A Negro assistant librarian discovers the infant hero there, rescues him, and carries him to Max Spielman at the goat barns, where he is raised as a goat.

As here grossly outlined, almost devoid of comic detail and presented in a strict chronological order that Barth restructures into intricate and suspenseful plotting, the birth of the hero is the first of the three rites of passage—birth, initiation, and death—that together form the whole myth. The second stage, that of initiation, begins with the hero's coming to manhood, when he receives the call to adventure and returns to the scene of his birth to fulfill his destiny; continues through a period of trial (tests, tasks, battles) and his victory over

---

2. Perhaps I have done just what Robert Scholes warned against in *The Fabulators* (New York: Oxford University Press, 1967), p. 170: "to take the mythography of *Giles Goat-Boy* in too heavy a way would do the story violence." Since my study was completed in essentially its present form in 1966 during four sabbatical months following the publication of *Giles,* the warning came too late. I remain convinced that the mythography must be taken "heavily." See Scholes's excellent chapter on *Giles,* pp. 135–73: I find his approach a valuable complement to my own.

his enemies; and culminates in his marriage to the princess (the Queen Goddess of the World) and atonement with his father. Death, the third rite of passage, soon ensues. The hero loses favor with the gods or his subjects, is driven from the city, and on the top of a hill meets a mysterious death, usually by burning or being struck by lightning.

Barth has exploited the full spiritual implications of the hero myth: he has conceived of Giles as a cultural hero whose quest has profound significance for the welfare of humanity. The major spiritual dimensions of the myth can be briefly sketched. At a moment of spiritual and social crisis a hero arises whose destiny it is to bring about a rejuvenation. His quest—to seek the boon that will restore the world—is at once a search for the father-creator, for self-identity, and for the truth. In his way stands his greatest enemy, the dragon, who represents the old generation. As keeper of the past with a vested interest in maintaining the status quo, the dragon is a tyrant holding man in bondage and preventing rejuvenation. Having slain the dragon, the hero is qualified to face the supreme ordeal: the meeting with the Queen Goddess, world creatrix, *magna mater,* the source of life. In his marriage to the Queen Goddess, the hero replaces the Father; and in the love experience itself, he has an illumination of the truth and is reborn. Having supplanted the Father, he realizes that he and the Father and the truth he had sought were within himself all along.

Barth's hero, Billy Bocksfuss ("goat-foot," like Oedipus), takes the human name of George once he becomes aware of his humanity and later assumes the more meaningful name *Giles* (probably derived from St. Giles, patron saint of cripples and beggars, an Athenian of the seventh century called then Aegidius, "wearer of the aegis [goatskin]," an apt name for Barth's goatskin-clad, crippled hero) but the name has a deeper significance in the meaning of the acronym GILES: "Grand-Tutorial Ideal: Laboratory Eugenical Specimen." Since the semen constituting the GILES was "taken from all New Tammany males between puberty and senility" (p. 321/361), Giles's true father is not WESCAC, merely the instrument of impregnation, but collective man, with whose seed WESCAC infused Virginia Hector. Almost literally, then, "Giles" means "son of man."

And in an almost literal sense, the quest of this naive, would-be hero is to discover what it means to be the son of man. Under the mistaken impression that WESCAC is his father and that the current international tension between East and West is the crisis he is destined to resolve, Giles rushes in headlong and, Quixote-like, nearly causes disaster before he comes to understand his true mission. The *naïf* undergoes a process of maturation and self-realization culminating in his grasp of the realities of life and in a revelation that the true crisis is a spiritual one inherent in the nature of man. This process of self-realization entails his overcoming Bray, who represents the dragon forces holding man back from full awareness of life and from acceptance of human nature and man's fate, and his symbolic marriage to Anastasia, who represents the Earth Goddess in union with whom Giles experiences the creative force of human love that brings him to full understanding of the nature of man.

The hero myth calls for a protective figure who provides the hero with amulets against the dragon forces and acts as mentor and guide. This is the role of Maximilian Spielman (whose surname probably links him to the *Spielman* of ritual drama, whose role is to lead the hero into the action eventuating in his death). Max's sounding of the blasts upon the *shophār* or ramshorn he fashioned from the horn of Freddie is the hero's call to adventure, which in the higher mythology is a call to respond to a spiritual crisis. In the Rosh Hashanah service, the three blasts of the ramshorn—*Teruah, Tekiah, Shebarim*—call upon Israel to rally to its God and exhort it to a spirit of self-analysis. These calls and their symbolic significance go unheeded, however, and Giles responds instead to the sounding of the EAT whistle—to a political crisis, which Giles must learn the hard way is merely a symptom of a spiritual crisis soluble only when man heeds the true call of the *shophār* to rigorous self-analysis.

In addition to his parodic role as the hero's mentor, Max has two other roles, both in what may be called the allegory of modern life, the tenor of all of Barth's mythological vehicle. Max represents the humanitarian scientific community of the atomic age and the psychoanalytic community of Freudian psychiatry. He is portrayed as a German-Jewish scientist whose hatred for Nazi genocide is complicated by his self-hatred for having been instrumental in the nuclear annihilation of the Japanese. Discharged and banished on the grounds of questionable loyalty during the administration of Reginald Hector (Eisenhower, the McCarthy Era), Max retires to the goat barns, where his misanthropy flourishes.

In banishment, Max makes great advances in proctology, the satirical equivalent of Freudian psychoanalysis with its emphasis on anal-eroticism. His Maxim, "Der goats is humaner than der men, and der man is goatisher than der goats" (p. 7/44), may not be a direct parody of Freudianism, but along with another of his maxims, *"Self-knowledge is always bad news"* (p. 84/121), it pretty well indicates the depths of misanthropy to which "plumbing the bottom of man's nature" may lead. With its echoes of the Oedipus tragedy, the latter maxim sums up a prevailing attitude that modern man shares with ancient man, an attitude that Max and his scientific and Freudian counterparts must somehow temper if they are to gain a balanced, sane perspective on the nature of man and thus to face life on realistic terms. The way in which Max's misanthropy is gradually transformed into a love of mankind without loss of his awareness of man's goatishness, a transformation implying Barth's comment on all the misanthropes among us, is too complex to detail here. Suffice it to assert that his experiences lead him to heed the call of the *shophār* to self-analysis and self-awareness, and that he comes to love mankind the more he understands his own nature. His death by crucifixion is a martyrdom he gladly welcomes as an expression of his love for mankind and an affirmation of his love of life.

Significantly, Max's martyrdom and Giles's final rout of Harold Bray occur almost simultaneously. Clearly, since Max has achieved self-realization and dies in confirmation of his newly gained awareness of himself and of the nature of humanity, the rout of Bray signifies Giles's final achievement of his own self-realization. The last obstacle to the fulfillment of the hero's quest has been overcome.

While Bray's parodic role in the hero myth as the dragon figure, the archenemy of the hero, is not in doubt, just what he represents allegorically and thus exactly what obstacle Giles has overcome is a difficult question. Since Barth seems to operate from the existential premise that God is dead, it stands to reason that the archenemy of a modern hero striving for identity and self-awareness would be organized religion and the established church, the agents propagating the illusory transcendentalism that exploits man's propensity to seek his identity and essence outside of the self. This interpretation of the role of Bray seems reasonable both in the light of internal evidence and in view of the meaning that the name *Bray* is likely to have for Barth.

The surname of this enigmatic figure is very probably that of Thomas Bray, an Anglican clergyman credited with the establishment of the Church of England in Maryland. Thomas Bray's extensive missionary activity in that colony, coinciding precisely with the historical setting of *The Sot-Weed Factor,* must certainly have become known to Barth during his research in Maryland's colonial history. For Barth to have associated Bray's name with personification of the church in the present allegory is understandable: Bray is the founder of the Society for Promoting Christian Knowledge and the Society for the Propagation of the Gospel. Another society, the Associates of Dr. Bray, was formed to assist him in administering a legacy devoted to use in pursuing the conversion of Negroes and Indians. That the name appears as *Harold* instead of *Thomas* Bray may be accounted for by Barth's desire to avoid literal duplication and by the aptness of the name *Harold* itself: meaning literally "hereweald" ("army power") or "powerful general," it well suggests the power and militancy of the church.

That this is Bray's allegorical role is also suggested by some details of Barth's parody of the New Testament. Bray is patently portrayed as John the Baptist (a proph-prof, like "John the Bursar," pp. 510–11/563) and as the Antichrist ("antigiles"): Giles, the new Christ, calls him "my adversary" (p. 703/759). Like Paul's conception of Christ's adversary, Bray is that satanically inspired human being who, demanding worship of himself, establishes himself in the temple and pretends to divinity. As Paul envisions Christ's annihilation of the Antichrist, so Giles routs Bray.

These two parodic roles coalesce and have their relevance in Bray's allegorical function as a personification of institutionalized religion, particularly the dominant religion of the West, Christianity. In every speech and action, Bray can be seen as an embodiment of ecclesiastical authority. Having announced at his first appearance "I'll show all of you who believe me the way to Commencement Gate! I'm the way myself, believe me!" (p. 314/354), Bray proceeds to certify everyone, nearly every time quoting an appropriate passage of the Founder's Scroll (Bible). In effect, he deludes all by indiscriminately promising passage (salvation) to all. Having declared "Tragedy's *out;* mystery's *in!*" Bray satisfies the people's desire for mystery and for miracles as signs of a supernatural agency beyond their world. Having announced "I'm your Grand Tutor!" Bray establishes himself as an authoritarian figure and father image to whom the people rush to commit themselves, desperately flocking to him seeking promise of Commencement (rebirth into everlasting life). Like the church, Bray upholds the conventional morality on which continuance of the accepted social structure and way of life depends: in conjunction with WESCAC, which embodies the principle of Differentiation, Bray approves when Giles advises the absolute separation of good and evil (the Christian duality of God and Satan) and damns Giles when he advocates rejection of all distinction between the two. And like the church, Bray forms an alliance with the government and is granted recognition, powers, and privileges on the tacit assumption that he will in no way disturb or contravene established domestic or international policies; and to him, like the church, is committed the supervision not only of religious services but of the educational system as well. Bray's power over New Tammany College is an apt representation of ecclesiastical power.[3]

Since the allegory fuses the mythological dragon and the biblical Antichrist into the one role of the established church as the enemy of Giles, Giles's rout of Bray is in a sense the fulfillment of Voltaire's imperative, "Ecrasez l'infame!" The infamy of the church is its opposition to the fully realized life; it is an obstacle to man's understanding of himself and acceptance of his fate. Encouraging man's preoccupation with death and fostering his futile, desperate search for transcendental reasons for his existence, the church creates illusions that blind man to his true existence. It inhibits man's self-realization when it supports the illusion of a moral duality, portraying good and evil as universal, opposed principles or forces, whereas man must perceive good and evil as polarities of his own psyche, as inseparable elements of his own nature. It falsifies the terms of man's existence on earth by promising an eternity of life hereafter and deludes man by gratifying his desperate longing for an extraterrestial paradise that is no part of man's fate. If life is to be understood and lived on its own terms, not on imagined terms, the illusory tenets of the church must be rejected; one must defeat the tendency in oneself to transfer to suprahuman authority the responsibility for the guidance and direction of one's own life. Giles personally manages to defeat Bray; but Giles knows that, years after the rout, people still believe in Bray and await his reappearance: the Bray in man dies hard, probably never will die. If Bray did not exist, most people would have to invent him, for few will ever face the truth about themselves.

The import of Giles's rout of Bray seems clear: he has overthrown the illusions fostered by the church; he has faced the truth about himself. In the allegory of contemporary life, Giles is modern man, for whom heroism is a complete acceptance of his humanity and acquiescence in man's fate. Portrayed in Giles as he describes himself in the "Posttape" is a sobered and subdued man who has cast off illusion and rejected the vain pretense of the reformer and the vain ambition of the idealist, who has learned to accept both in himself and in others "the ineluctable shortcomings of mortal studenthood" (p. 700/756), and who is sustained not by dreams but by the possession of self-knowledge. Since *"Self-knowledge is always bad news,"* since man can be defined as a potential for both good and evil, learning to accept oneself may not be pleasant; but the truth can give satisfaction and serve as a guide for the sensible conduct of one's life. To accept oneself, one must, as Giles overcame Bray, reject the established church because it exploits man's propensity to hide from the bad news, to escape reality.

Essentially, Giles's learning to accept himself is a process of humanization. Conceived in mythological terms, it is a process of rebirth; and in this process Anastasia figures prominently. The name *Anastasia* is Greek for "resurrection," an apt characterization of her function in the parody of the hero myth as the

---

3. This Church-State dimension of Bray's role calls to mind the anonymous eighteenth-century poem "The Vicar of Bray" as a possible source of the name *Bray*. Barth has Ebenezer Cooke use the Vicar of Bray as a metaphor in *The Sot-Weed Factor*. The speaker of the poem, the Vicar, recounts the opportunistic shifting of allegiances he indulged in to gain preferment from whatever monarch ascended the throne.

Earth Goddess in union with whom the hero is reborn. In the hero myth, the Earth Goddess is the world creatrix, *magna mater,* source of life; and the hero's meeting with the Goddess is a test of his ability to win the boon of love, *amor fati* or love of life itself. Their sacred marriage represents the hero's total mastery of life: it is a union of opposites signifying the attainment of wholeness and completion and constituting regeneration and rebirth.

In the Belly of WESCAC Anastasia fulfills her functions actively and consummately (pp. *672–73/730–31*); earlier she serves as the passive agent of Giles's partial illumination and "delivery" (p. *651/709*). Called by Leonid "a Commencèd martyr" and by Peter Greene "a flunkèd floozy" because she has given of herself so freely, Anastasia is both, Giles suddenly realizes. He understands in a flash of illumination that like all the other fundamental contradictions of passage and failure, the contradictory judgments of Anastasia's character are equally true. He is released, "delivered" from the mind-forged manacles, one of which is the conventional morality that constrains man to view woman in the exercise of her sexual function as either blessed or damned. His delivery is an abandonment of the search for *the* Answer and an embracement of life in all its contradictory, inexplicable variety.

This flash of illumination, this "delivery," is in itself a partial rebirth, an intellectual enlightenment that goes a long way toward making Giles a new man by freeing him from the trammels of old modes of thought. It will be worthwhile to pause here to trace the stages of Giles's intellectual development toward this enlightenment, even at the risk of displacing Anastasia momentarily; for the significance of Giles's total rebirth in the arms of Anastasia will be lost if one does not fully grasp the import of this partial rebirth. Through Giles, Barth is commenting upon the potential rebirth of modern man, and in Giles's intellectual development Barth traces the progress of mankind toward an enlightened outlook on life. In this commentary Barth's satirical assessment penetrates deep into the reasons for man's benighted condition.

Giles's progress toward the truth is best seen by analyzing the changes in his tutoring. The three distinct phases of Giles's tutoring correspond to stages in the moral history of Western man: the past, the present, and a future that Giles sees little hope of coming to pass. The first is the period when Giles advises according to the principle of Differentiation (Passage is Passage, Failure is Failure), a period representing the moral absolutism of the past fostered predominantly by the Christian Church, whose conception of the duality of good and evil embodied in God and Satan is equivalent to Giles's insistence upon absolute separation of the passèd and flunkèd. The second period represents the present, the age of moral anarchy and rejection of absolutes. During this period Giles advises all to "acknowledge, embrace, and assert" their natural inclinations and to abjure all discipline and distinction: passage and failure are the same, he argues, indistinguishable and equally unreal.

Both of these positions are stages in Giles's progress toward the truth. Each emanates from Giles himself in response to the problem of human conduct. The error that Giles makes as his tutoring proceeds is to assure himself that each position arrived at is *the only* Answer, or the whole truth: he recapitulates Western man's error of assuming that the then-current value system and ethical code are the only truth.

The third and final stage is near at hand when Giles conceives of the separate validity of the two preceding answers or truths: "Passage *was* Failure, and Failure Passage; yet Passage was Passage, Failure, Failure! Equally true, none was the Answer . . . " (p. 650/708–9). The final Answer that comes to him at the moment of "delivery" is not only that they are different, nor only that they are the same, but that both their sameness and difference are simultaneously true. Passage and Failure, good and evil, are different, just as, to use theological terms, God and Satan are different, yet they are the same: Satan is an accessory to God and an embodiment of the Tigerness of God, who is Tiger-Lamb. They are not strict opposites but polarities, together forming a unity in the harmony of opposites. Giles realizes that man is a microcosmic unity of Tiger-Lamb, of evil and good.

This discovery of unity in polarity Barth renders symbolically by incorporating ancient mythology in the design of the PAT device that Giles finally understands at the moment of delivery. One can grasp the structure and meaning of this device if one removes the Prenatal-Aptitude-Test phrase "Pass All Fail All" to reveal the

quadrated circle , ancient symbol of cosmic unity. The circle alone,

sometimes called the Supreme Ultimate, is that which contains all, symbolizing wholeness or completeness. The halving of the circle represents the division of the primal chaos into apparently opposite forces, which are polarities harmoniously interacting to form a unity.

The multiplication of polarities in a complex system is symbolized in the quadrated circle, which also represents the universe, with its center (the *axis mundi* or world navel) marked by the intersection of lines drawn from the four cardinal directions.

In the first stage Giles conceived of Passage and Failure as opposites, different

and separable, like white and black In the second stage, by rejecting all

distinction and asserting that Passage and Failure are the same, he set the circle in motion, as it were, making it spin so rapidly that white and black fuse to gray, which, neither white nor black, is a blurring of their real distinction. Finally he grasps the significance of the PAT device, "beginningless, endless, infinite equivalence" (p. 650/708). His "delivery" is a recognition of the white, of the black, and of the white-black, which though they "spin" never merge into gray. Passage and Failure are two poles of a unity.

Though one can diagram this truth in oversimplified form, one does not easily assimilate it into his being. As Giles realizes, it is a truth that cannot be taught; it can be grasped and assimilated only by a sort of mystical insight and only by the individual who plunges into life with all of his faculties alert and says, like Giles, "I must wrest my answers like Swede roots by main strength from their holes" (p. 409/455).

Barth offers little hope that many of us will try to or can earn the feel of this truth upon our pulses, but Giles does make it a part of his being. Its effect upon him is to bring instantaneous illumination, freedom, intellectual rebirth. But fully to comprehend the truth of his own nature and thus to find his identity as a human being—to be totally reborn—Giles must come to understand and integrate the emotional component of man. It is the function of Anastasia to bring about this ultimate comprehension, to complete the process of humanization. For Giles, Anastasia's repeated profession of love is the final mystery; "that final shadow" (p. 671/730) is his inability to understand the human need to love and to be loved. Her mysterious but unquestionably sincere professions of love lure Giles, draw him out of the shadow until the light of love finally wipes out the shadow. At last he understands what it means to be human.

The consecrative act confirming this understanding, the union of Giles and Anastasia in creative love, takes place in the Belly of WESCAC, the very spot where Giles was conceived. To enter the Belly, Giles and Anastasia ride down in the tapelift, symbolically for Giles a return to infancy and an approach to rebirth since he had been abandoned in the tapelift as a newly born infant. There is further symbolism in the position they assume in the tapelift: in its narrow confines, crowded "Knees to chin and arsy-turvy," they resemble not only twins in the womb but also "that East-Campus sign of which her navel had reminded"

Giles earlier (p. 671/729). That sign is the *Tao* 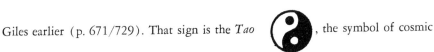 , the symbol of cosmic

order sometimes called the *yin-yang* because of the union it represents of the masculine principle *yang* and the feminine *yin*. Incidentally, they are also in position 69, and the ribald comic tone of this tapelift scene is soon intensified when Giles and Anastasia form what may be the most hilarious copulation in literature: twined round Giles and impaled upon his member, Anastasia wears the mask of Bray; and Giles wears over his head a bag drawstringed around his neck. Masked and bagged, they tumble together through the port and slide down into the Belly.

In the Belly, scene of two premature abortive attempts at rebirth, Giles is reborn when he grasps the meaning of the unity that he and Anastasia now demonstrate coupled together in love: like *yin-yang,* they are male and female made one in the act of love, and Giles understands the macrocosmic implication of their microcosmic union—the universe is one. He experiences that expansion of consciousness which allows him to embrace all of the contradictions, the antagonisms and oppositions, the differences of all men and all nations as manifestations of a single life force. He embraces life.

The scene concludes with Giles and Anastasia in orgasmic rapture, he now fully illumined, fully realized as a human being, fully in grasp of the mystery of life. He imbibes his divinity, which is humanity, from the "nipple inexhaustible" of the goddess; he then feeds himself himself; and together they cry "Oh wonderful!"

(p. 673/731), chanting as one a "mystical rapture of the knower of universal unity" from the *Taittiriya Upanishad* (3.10.5–6):

> Oh, wonderful! Oh, wonderful! Oh, wonderful!
> I am food! I am food! I am food!
>
> .   .   .   .
>
> I am the first-born of the world-order,
> Earlier than the gods, in the navel of immortality!
>
> .   .   .   .
>
> I, who am food, eat the eater of food!
> I have overcome the whole world!

Anastasia, experiencing an orgasm for the first time in innumerable loveless copulations, receives the seed of humanity and, in love, conceives a child.

Giles now is assured that he is indeed the Grand Tutor, yet ironically he can no longer tutor. He cannot teach because the illumination he experienced in the arms of Anastasia cannot be conceptualized, cannot be taught. But others mistakenly assume that Giles's Answer can be codified and transmitted. Gilesianism is made out to be teachable doctrine, and a new religion is created. Giles explicitly disowns Gilesianism, speaking of it as Anastasia's "term, for her invention" (p. 700/756). But she and Peter Greene style themselves disciples of the New Christ and devote their lives to the spreading of "Giles' word."

But even they, who knew Giles intimately, disagree about just what Gilesianism is. Already, strong signs of factionalism, schism, and eventual strife herald for *The Revised New Syllabus* a fate like that of the Bible. It may be that Gilesianism will become, like Christianity, a battleground of contention because its disciples are guilty of oversimplification, prejudiced interpretation, or self-aggrandizement. Greene's formulation of Gilesianism, for example, seems to be based on his own life history: he says of his own attempt at rejuvenation, "I'm going to start from scratch, what I mean *understandingwise*" (p. 652/710), words translatable into the doctrine "Become as a kindergartner." Thus formulated, the doctrine is a fair approximation of the experience Giles has undergone and of the gist of his illumination. It does suggest regeneration and rebirth in the recovery of lost or hidden dimensions of one's nature. And it suggests further the return to innocence accomplished by regaining the fully integrated personality that existed before the self was fragmented in its many attachments to the external world. But how does one teach people to become as little children? Giles knows that, like Buddha's Enlightenment, his Answer or truth is not communicable: it must be experienced, and only a few will ever have the illumination granted to him. Greene and Anastasia attempt to teach the unteachable.

Like other great teachers who intuitively grasped the need to reenter the microcosm of the self—the Grand Tutors Buddha, Socrates, Christ—Giles can leave behind him as his doctrine only the embodiment of the Truth, his life as recorded in *The Revised New Syllabus*. The essence of true Gilesianism must be distilled from the story of Giles, just as the exemplary lives of the Grand Tutors both reveal and conceal the essence of their teaching. *The Revised New Syllabus* will be a further contribution to the body of wisdom available as a guide for humanity. It will join "such root pedagogical documents as the Moishianic Code, the Founder's Scroll, the *Colloquiums* of Enos Enoch, the *Footnotes to Sakhyan* [that came] from individual students who had matured and Graduated over the semesters [and are] the best Answers that studentdom had devised . . . " (p. 255/301). But Giles knows well that few will profit from this wisdom: the world will go on as it has for centuries.

In the Founder's Hill Myth that examines and defines the "diabolical" in human nature, Barth embodies the cosmic insights that underlie the satirical perspective conveyed through Giles's awareness that nothing will change.

II

The hill bearing the Founder's Shaft and containing Stoker's Powerhouse located over a raging subterranean volcano is the parodic counterpart of the world navel or Primeval Hill of ancient mythology. A metaphysical point set at the axial center of the world (*axis mundi*), the world navel was established in ancient ritual as the source of creative energy, and there mysteries were performed celebrating the generation of life and the creation of the cosmos. It was ritualistically conceived as the connecting link among the three planes of existence, the sky world or Heaven, the Earth, and the Underworld. In Sumerian culture, the Primeval Hill, the fountainhead of emerging life, was given symbolic form in the ziggurat, the Mountain of the Gods connecting Heaven (the male principle) with Earth (the female principle) and with the Waters of the Abyss, the water of life. In the Garden of God on the Mountain was the World Tree, the tree of life, at whose annual waning the ritual king adminstered the food and water of life. In the "Posttape," Giles envisions a place much like this garden as the scene of his "turning off": "on the highest rise of Founder's Hill," where stands one oak and runs a spring, his end will come in flashes of lightning (p. 708/764).

But the Underworld is of greater significance than the summit of the hill. In Stoker's Living Room, where Earth and the Underworld meet, Giles joins Stoker's Spring Carnival Party and participates in a rite of renewal similar to the mystery celebrated at the world navel. The cycle of death and birth is celebrated in the literal cremation of the dead G. Herrold and in the homeopathic act of procreation as Giles "services" Anastasia in drunken animal abandon. Both of these mockeries prefigure real acts of fulfillment that occur, significantly, nine months later: Max is then cremated on Founder's Shaft in the same flame that consumed G. Herrold, but his death is a sacrifical crucifixion on behalf of mankind, and thereby a consecration of love and life; and Giles and Anastasia then unite in an act of love that constitutes the rebirth of Giles.

Stoker's Powerhouse, the cap on the volcano as he describes it (p. 178/220), is on the same level as the Living Room and appropriately so; for Stoker's role in the Living Room as master of the revels in the orgiastic celebration of life is one manifestation of his larger role as director and controller of the elemental power of the volcano, the source of creative energy, the life force. Literally, Stoker's Powerhouse supplies the power that lights the Light House, operates WESCAC and EASCAC, and in general runs the University; on a deeper level of meaning, Stoker controls the elemental energy that feeds life to the world. He is the embodiment of the life force that animates all men: without his power, there is only stagnation and death.

So fearful have Christian moralists been of the life force that they have called it evil, personified it in the devil, and then reviled it as the enemy of the good. To make Stoker recognizable as a force commonly thought diabolical,

Barth has provided a few unmistakable signs: his surname seems to derive from his role as the devil who stokes the fires of hell, and, of course, he wears a "sharp beard, like a black spade" and has hornlike ridges of black hair "from the front of either temple up to his hairline" (p. 151/192).

But Stoker is not the Satan of Christian mythology. He is more like the god of the underworld of Greek mythology, terrible but just and not the enemy of man. Pluto-like, Stoker was stricken with a desperate love or need for the Earth Goddess Anastasia, who like Persephone satisfies his need of alignment with the feminine creative force of nature. And as director of the Powerhouse, he serves a Pluto-like function as a god of the fertility of the earth, controlling the flow of the life force to the world of men.

In the parody of the Bible, Stoker as Dean o'Flunks is satanic only in that he functions like the Satan of the Book of Job: he serves good by testing and tempting the righteous. Only in the eyes of the conventional moralists is he seen as the archenemy of the good: with his native insight, Giles senses immediately that "there was something *right* in Stoker's attitude" (p. 211/253). Right indeed, for Stoker is a personification of evil as interpreted by the most profound mythologies, particularly the Oriental, which conceive of evil as a pole of the good: evil and good together form the divine. But since in Barth's world the only divinity is man, Stoker is an embodiment of the evil emanating from *human* nature: *man's* inherent urge to live unfettered and unhampered by reason, codes of conduct, or any authority. He is the flunkèd in all of us, our urge for disorder, our spirit of rebelliousness against order and authority. Ranging from mere obstreperousness, through calculated opposition, to a potentially violent destructive impulse, all of our inclinations to evil as manifested in Stoker can be seen as an irrepressible life spirit chafing at any form of restriction or containment. But the unrestrained life force is disruptive and chaotic; restriction and containment are necessary if society is to flourish. For good reason Stoker's authority is limited to the Powerhouse and Main Detention.

On the literal level of the narrative, the person who enforces this restriction of Stoker's authority is the Chancellor of New Tammany College, Lucius Rexford. *Rexford* seems to be a combination of Latin roots for "strong king," befitting his character and his position. In the allegory Chancellor Rexford represents, in particular, former President Kennedy and, in general, the world leader at a time of international crisis. Rexford's description of "the typical Graduate" (p. 368/411–12) fits Rexford himself and John F. Kennedy point for point; and numerous details about Rexford, including his physical appearance (unmanageable forelock of bright, fair hair), demeanor (grace, wit, and gusto) and thought (for example, his stress on physical fitness and intellectual development), confirm that Kennedy is the model for the largely favorable portrayal of Rexford.

But the contemporary political allusion to Kennedy seems almost incidental except insofar as it helps to establish *Giles Goat-Boy* as a commentary on contemporary life. Rexford is an allegorical modern leader upon whom rests the awesome responsibility of power; but he is first a man who must come to a realization of his own potentialities before he can function effectively as a leader and carry out policies designed to help mankind realize its potentialities.

This theme is conveyed through Barth's utilization of the mythological notion of the rivalry of two brothers: Rexford's first name, *Lucius,* meaning "light," corresponds to the first name of Stoker (Maurice, "dark") to suggest the mythological role of Rexford and Stoker as the brothers whose rivalry represents the opposition between light and darkness. In mythology this rivalry symbolizes an ultimate cosmic unity: the brothers, apparently opposite like day and night, are rather polarities; and their interaction is a harmony and balance like the life cycle of day-night.

Rexford has to learn to accept Stoker as his brother or other half without affirming the kinship; he can neither fight against him nor yield to his power. When, under the influence of Giles's erroneous first tutoring, Rexford denies his kinship with Stoker and kills Stoker's spirit by enforcing puritanical laws, the college stagnates and dies. Conversely, when Giles's second tutoring, also erroneous, persuades Rexford to embrace Stoker, openly avow kinship, and live like him, chaos results: the unrestrained life urge or evil runs rampant, threatening destruction of the college. The proper balance is achieved when Rexford reestablishes the rivalry and recognizes the necessity of allowing Stoker to function without Rexford's openly affirming their relationship lest Stoker gain dangerous prominence. In effect, he becomes a whole man who has struck the proper balance between his own good and evil proclivities. This balance becomes Rexford's political philosophy as well. In his moderate idealism tempered by a thorough grasp of realities and by his cognizance of the power of the life force and of its inclination to excess in all, even himself, Rexford can operate effectively as a consummate politician and as a consummate human being. This striking of the proper balance in Rexford is, of course, a variant on the major theme of the Hero Myth—Giles's achievement of wholeness and completeness as a fully integrated human being. And this theme emerges as the idea underlying Barth's portrayal of nearly every other character in the novel.

One not-so-subtle manifestation of the theme appears in the pairing of Croaker and Eblis Eierkopf. They form a very apt complementarity of under- and overdeveloped mentality, of animality and rationality. The two are portrayed as a pair in an imperfect partnership that makes up a crude approximation of a human being. Croaker is reasonless animality in which love is an instinctual drive to tup, tup, tup. Lustless, emotionless Eierkopf, the former Bonifacist eugenicist who experimented with human subjects in the concentration camps, is an embodiment of heartless rationality, of the inhumanity of the disengaged intelligence and dispassionate scientific curiosity. Both are incomplete human beings; each needs the other to subsist.

A much more subtle and thorough exploration of the theme of consummate humanity is to be found in Barth's portrayal of Dr. Kennard Sear. Like the portrayal of Giles himself, the development of Sear traces the progress of an individual from ignorance of self to self-awareness; and, as is typical of Barth's utilization of mythology, Sear's character and plight are defined through comparison to a prominent mythological figure, Gynander (Tiresias).

The surname *Sear* is a play on at least two words: the adjective *sere,* suggestive of Sear's physical appearance of desiccation and of his sexual and spiritual sterility; and the noun *seer,* prophet or soothsayer, referring to his self-drawn comparison to Gynander. Like Gynander (from the Greek for "woman and man") Sear is a hermaphroditic figure and, so too is his wife, Hedwig. Both are bisexual, and their behavior gives the impression that her lesbianism and his homosexuality have been deliberately pursued as perversions to relieve the boredom that normal heterosexuality has long brought them. Both are connoisseurs, effete and sophisticated, who are driven in pursuit of hedonism to taste every perversion known to carnal man. Worst of all, they have perverted the principle of marriage: each uses the other as a means to gratify his sensuality.

Sear thinks his knowledge of the world comparable to Gynander's; but, as Giles makes clear, Sear mistakes extensive experience for comprehensive understanding. Unlike Gynander, who understood the whole man and his plight, Sear is surfeited with experience and loathes himself as he loathes all men because he attributes to them only the depravity he finds in himself. Yet, with the help of Giles's tutoring, Sear does become like Gynander. Finally, in blindness, Sear sees his failing clearly and comprehends the whole truth of human nature. He has learned that to come to his wife in simple love to beget a child would not be the "consummate perversion" for a man of his tastes but the consummate humanization. Though it is Croaker who impregnates Hedwig, Sear has recognized his love for her and their need to be together; he gladly accepts Croaker's child as his own in token of what should have been. Realizing that "spiritedness" or impassioned attachment to another human being makes life meaningful and worthwhile, he, at the point of death, is reborn as a whole man.

III

In the Founder's Hill Myth the rivalry between Rexford and Stoker is a parodic version of the ancient mythological conflict between two poles of the psyche that are integral components of the whole man. Similarly, the international rivalry between East and West is given mythical delineation as a competition for ascendancy between two dimensions of the mind. Man has always externalized his interior life by projecting upon the external world or macrocosm his own emotional stresses or psychic conflicts, as he has in representing the contrary moral duality of his own nature as a cosmic opposition between forces of good and evil. And often this kind of projection of the psyche's opposing components takes mythic form in images of opposition between nations.

Barth's mythopoeic imagination has conceived of the West-East rivalry as a conflict between man's inherent proclivities to selfishness and selflessness; or, to put it another way, this natural competition within the psyche is projected on a large scale as a competition between nations committed in principle to selfishness (capitalistic America) and selflessness (communistic Russia). That these nations represent poles of the psyche is suggested by the fact that one Control Room, located in Founder's Hill, channels Stoker's power to both East and West and operates EASCAC and WESCAC. As Stoker says, "Me they have to put up with, like it or not. . . . They've got to have power if they're going to be enemies" (p. 176/ 217). The natural psychic conflict animated by Stoker's life force is that between a concern for the personal self (greed for material acquisition and insistence upon the inviolability of the individual will) and a concern for the group self (submission to the will of the group, whose welfare takes precedence over the individual's). Selfishness is caricatured in "greedy and grasping" Ira Hector, and selflessness in Classmate X, who eradicated his self and replaced his "personal, fallible will with the Will of the Student Body, impersonal and infallible" (p. 547/600).

Within this pattern of gross caricatures, two other characters, the American Peter Greene and the Russian Leonid Alexandrov, function as vehicles of a far more penetrating and subtle analysis of American selfishness and Russian selflessness than the caricatures allow. In his portrayal of these two exuberant and optimistic *naïfs,* Barth seems to be exploring the effect of human love upon the dehumanizing pressures exerted by their respective societies.

In the trio of figures who serve as vehicles of Barth's satire on capitalism and the American way of life—Reginald and Ira Hector are the others—Greene represents the active, aggressive class of business executives and industrialists as distinguished from the financiers and speculators. He is a doer; he embodies the spirit of rugged individualism. His life history (pp. 228–46/271–92), an encapsulated allegorical history of American capitalism, is Barth's sharply satirical commentary on the system of free enterprise, on the Protestant ethic, and on the spiritual wasteland of American social and domestic life.

As a man and a thinker, Greene well earns his name; he is indeed a kindergartner. Full of Goodwill ("I never met a man I didn't like," p. 426/473), an almost unlimited capacity for love, and an unquestioned self-satisfaction reeking of insecurity ("I'm okay, and what the heck anyhow," p. 240/285), Greene represents in particular American optimism and innocence (both largely matters of ignorance) and in general that naiveté which is the condition of all who have no insight into their own moral nature. That Greene is able finally to overcome that naiveté, to start again to build a sound and lasting relationship with his wife, and to devote his life to selfless service to others suggests that Greene's capability for love and self-understanding may be the saving grace of the essentially selfish American character.

So too may Leonid's need of love be the saving flaw in the Russian ideal of selflessness and impersonality. Aspiring to uphold the Nikolayan ideal of self-effacement and to emulate his stepfather, Classmate X, the epitome of selflessness, Leonid deplores the selfishness he sees in himself and castigates himself for failing to be a good Nikolayan. To his own Nikolayan dismay, he craves the love of his stepfather and feels love for nearly everyone he meets. Because of his uncontrollable impulsiveness in the expression of his boundless love, Leonid can be shackled by no ideology. Anl this is the reason why, for Leonid, all locks are open: for him there are no mind-forged manacles; he is a free and natural spirit.

In spite of these depictions of the force love exerts to defeat the dehumanizing pressure of ideology, Barth is by no means giving us an optimistic interpretation of the rivalry between East and West. On the contrary, it is a soberly grim interpretation, for it is based squarely on the recognition that the tendencies to assert and to eradicate the self are equally powerful psychic forces striving for supremacy in the mind. As Giles remarks upon learning for the first time about the Boundary Dispute, the competition between East and West is "essentially a selfish competition"; each is "guilty of seeking advantage over the other in every sphere . . . " (p. 456/505).

What Giles fails to realize at this time is that the Boundary Dispute spoken of by Chancellor Rexford as "now virtually an institution" (p. 447/496), is a ritualization of the conflict, a peaceable institutionalization that allows intercourse between the opposing nations and keeps the rivalry from becoming catastrophic warfare. On the psychic level, such intercourse prevents a sort of schizophrenia. It is a perilous balance, nearly tipped toward disaster when Giles advocates first the absolute separation of East and West and later the eradication of distinction between them. But he finally comprehends that the competition maintained peaceably by the Boundary Dispute is really a balance between two forces of the psyche as manifested in nations. This paradox of separate yet inseparable forces he must and does accept as another of the fundamental contradictions of human nature. The danger resides in those who cannot accept or even see the paradox, those who cannot see things whole and thus perceive not balance but outright opposition. Labeling one side "light" or "good" (their side, of course) and the other "darkness" or "evil," they are eager for the victory of light over darkness, of good over evil. It is they who will push the EAT button and bring chaos.

In the "Posttape," Giles remarks that, during the twelve years since his illumination, "the Boundary Dispute alternated (as indeed it does yet) between crisis and stalemate—each crisis a little more critical, each stalemate a quantum uneasier, than the last" (p. 701/757). Neither East nor West has pushed the EAT button, but chaos still impends. Nothing has basically changed. For all of his wisdom Giles has been unable to teach anyone anything: "I go this final time to teach the unteachable, and shall fail" (p. 707/763); and he envisions himself driven from the campus to his death.

As J. B. of the "Postscript to the Posttape" observes, the view that Giles has expressed in the "Posttape" is indeed "what can be most kindly called a tragic view of His life and of campus history" (p. 710/766). That J. B. rejects as spurious this tragic view of Giles's and of campus history, preferring instead to believe in the gloriously transcendental power of Giles's Answer to remake the world, is evidence enough that J. B. is an object of Barth's satire. Precisely how J. B. functions in Barth's satire is of considerable interest, for through the creation of the *persona* J. B. in the "Cover-Letter to the Editors and Publisher" who speaks volumes in the passionate intensity of the less-than-two-page-long "Postscript," Barth has encapsulated the satiric and thematic implications of the whole novel.

IV

We have seen that numerous structural and thematic interrelations bind together the three basic myths of the novel into a coherent interpretation of the condition of man, each myth in its particular way exploring the components of the psyche as manifested in human affairs; that Barth's central concern is to illuminate mythopoeically the plight of man divided against himself and man divided against man; and that through a wide range of mythology—ancient and modern, pagan and Christian, Oriental and Occidental—Barth interprets the plight of man as a universal condition, universal because it arises from a fragmentation of the psyche witnessed in the myths of all ages and countries. We can now see that in J. B. Barth sums up, as it were, gives us a character of the present moment, outside the world of the novel proper, who epitomizes the condition and plight of a contemporary Everyman. And in so doing, Barth projects the past and present into the future, implying that what has been and is universal will continue to be so.

To what degree we are to assume that in J. B. John Barth has portrayed his own realistic awareness that he shares J. B.'s condition and plight, we cannot tell. Certainly Barth identifies himself with J. B. by having him say, "like most of our authors these days I support myself by preaching what I practice" (p. xviii/*xxii*), and it takes no great stretch of the imagination to expand this autobiographical note to hear the voice of Barth in J. B. 's lament:

> My every purchase on reality—as artist, teacher, lover, citizen, husband, friend—all were bizarre and wrong, a procession of hoaxes perhaps impressive for a time but ultimately ruinous. (P. xxiii/*xxviii*)

We all at times sense that our hold on reality is "bizarre and wrong" and like J. B. "yearn to shrug off the Dream and awake to an order of things—quite new and other!" (p. xxiv/*xxix*). And in that yearning do we not admit to "the ineluctable shortcomings of mortal studenthood"? Has not Barth admitted that J. B. is a reflection of his—and our—own desperate search for an "order of things," no matter how illusory that order may be?

At any rate, in J. B. Barth has epitomized the precariousness of the human purchase on reality and those weaknesses in man that militate against a true perception of reality, against self-awareness, and thus against fulfillment as integrated human beings. His attitude is the reason why man cannot, unlike the extraordinary hero Giles, assimilate the wisdom of the ages and profit from experience to come to know himself. His spirit, while superficially exuberant and optimistic, creates the continuous tragedy that history records; and it blinds him to the tragic implications of his own unrealized life.

As an "aspirant professor of Gilesianism," J. B. is linked, almost equated, with Peter Greene and Anastasia, those disciples of the New Christ who in their desperate search for the Answer, for the comforting assurance of doctrine, effectually create a new religion and thus perpetuate the powerful urge in man to locate in suprahuman authority the reason for and explanation of his existence. Without awareness of what he is doing, J. B., like Anastasia and Greene, is invoking another Bray and confirming Giles's belief that Bray in one form or another will never die. Ironically, Bray will now be re-created in the form of Giles. In terms of the Hero Myth, J. B. is creating another dragon, who will maintain the status quo of self-blindness by encouraging man's inherent tendency to hide from the truth about himself, to refuse to accept his fate. In short, Barth represents in J. B. an abbreviated etiological myth accounting for the existence of religion and its institutionlization. Man is too weak to live without the comfort of religion.

J. B.'s attribution to Giles of "joy, hope, knowledge, and confident strength" is symptomatic of an attitude that almost guarantees that man will never harmonize the polarities of his psyche, never integrate the Evil One, never know himself as a whole embracing good and evil. J. B.'s elevation of Giles to godhood as an embodiment of the good, taken along with his inability to see, let alone accept, the tragic implications of Giles's Grand Tutorhood, is representative of the powerful human tendency to leap to any judgment that will put the most favorable interpretation on the nature of man. Anthropomorphically, J. B. has created a god in his own mistaken and shallow image of himself. The difference between the real Giles and J. B.'s creation is the measure of J. B.'s refusal to face the truth about himself. The inevitable consequence of this attitude will be the propagation of that consistent error that Barth made clear in his portrayal of Stoker: refusing to locate the source of evil either in Giles or himself, J. B. will re-create the devil as an embodiment of the evil he knows to exist; and the resulting moral duality will be the projection of his own failure to harmonize the poles of his own psyche. That this age-old psychic split is at work in J. B. is evidenced in the "Postscript" by his identification of the enemy, as yet undefined but powerful in potential, an "antigiles" to whom he attributes the concoction of the "Posttape" as an attempt "to gainsay and weaken faith in Giles's Way" (p. 710/766).

In J. B. Barth has created an all-too-typical human being who, finding the truth unbearable, refuses to see it and erects potent illusions that will comfortably serve as substitutes for the truth. J. B. is a *persona* created to speak for those whose happiness consists in the *"perpetual Possession of being well Deceived."* Barth's insight into the condition of man is very much like Jonathan Swift's, from whose *A Tale of a Tub* I have just quoted. *Giles Goat-Boy* offers at its core a satirical view that is Swiftian in its intensity and profundity, a moral realism that begs man to see himself as he truly is, a satirical view that is given tragic depth, as it is in the *Tale,* by the pervasive implication that man has so thoroughly accustomed himself to live by illusion that the satirist has little hope of ever seeing that illusion stripped away. This is the tragic burden of Barth's comic novel.

Solid Ground in John Hawkes's *Second Skin*

CAREY WALL

San Diego State University

John Hawkes has said, "As a writer I'm concerned with innovation in the novel and obviously I'm committed to nightmare, violence, meaningful distortion, to the whole panorama of dislocation and desolation in human experience."[1] And also, "my aim has always been . . . never to let the reader (or myself) off the hook."[2] Out of these aims come the structures of his novels. His structures violate our expectation of a plot that will designate relationships, identities, causes, and the like; a plot that will, in short, settle the fictional material into a comfortable set of recognizable and comprehensible categories. It is, above all, this very sense that human experiences are fairly easily classifiable that Hawkes wants to destroy. He has a vision not just of great complexity but of characteristic ambivalence in human experience, of fluid indentities of people and realities of events in which there is a tendency for opposites to meet—sexual opposites, moral opposites, opposites of power and impotence and vitality and death. With this vision he wants to overpower his readers, so he uses the system of correspondences that dominates his books to bring strange, unlike things into continuity and to break up or dcny our beliefs in the separability of good and evil, as well as the pairs of opposites we tend to accept for the sake of convenience and comfort. Hawkes's correspondences stretch our sense of reality; they test our assumptions and even our faiths.

For this reason, Hawkes has been said to tear down and to dispense with much more than he actually does. His fiction has frequently been described as obscure,

This is the first publication of the essay.

1. John Enck, "John Hawkes: An Interview," *Wisconsin Studies in Contemporary Literature* 6 (1965): 142.

2. *Ibid.*, p. 145.

exciting, but essentially loose. Hawkes himself contributed to that idea, no doubt, by stating that "I began to write fiction on the assumption that the enemies of the novel were plot, character, setting, and theme" and by speaking of his increasing need to parody the conventional novel."[3] Nevertheless, the first of these statements is hyperbole (at least as the assumption is reflected in the novels), and Hawkes criticism has been made more obscure than the novels when we take it too literally. In fact, Hawkes uses the conventional plot to give us solid ground in the otherwise spinning worlds of his novels. Plot identifies the basic nature of his characters' experience. It does only that; correspondences infiltrate and play with its assurances, never demolishing them but limiting them if only by elaborating so fantastically on their diminished truths, as is the case in *Second Skin.* The importance of all this is that Hawkes is a much more lucid, significant, and comprehensible writer than has as yet been generally recognized.

The first wave of Hawkes criticism, just past, was so entranced by what Leslie Fiedler has called the elements of decomposition in Hawkes's fiction that it gave little attention to those structures of the conventional novel which, once clearly seen, show us how much order and lucidity there is in Hawkes's infiltrating system of correspondences, through which the dimensions of reality open so much wider. Speaking of *The Lime Twig,* Fiedler grants it order and lucidity of only the most tenuous sort: "Yet he does not abandon all form in his quest for the illusion of formlessness; in the random conjunction of reason and madness, blur and focus, he finds occasions for wit and grace. . . . Hawkes gives us . . . reason's last desperate attempt to know what unreason is; and in such knowledge there are possibilities not only for poetry and power but for pleasure as well."[4] How misleading this comment is: Hawkes does intentionally take us into realms of perception where there is no easy explanation for connections or disconnections, but he deals not with formlessness but always with identifiable experiences. There is nothing so vague as Fiedler's statement suggests: nothing random at all.

Fiedler's piece has been reprinted[5] and its vein of commentary seems to have produced one of the first of the essays on *Second Skin,* Donald Greiner's argument that the book's structure consists chiefly of a thematic use of color.[6] But other discussions happily reveal that Hawkes's readers have got over the initial impact of the dislocations he administers to conventional structure and now find in his work structures both firm and traditional. Richard Pearce talks about Skipper as a "harlequin" figure.[7] Tony Tanner argues that "the patterning of alternating kinds of landscape is what makes up the patchwork fabric of the book, providing a more than narrative meaning for the story we can reconstruct from Skipper's recalled episodes," and examines those landscapes in

---

3. *Ibid.,* p. 149.

4. Leslie Fiedler, "The Pleasures of John Hawkes," in *The Lime Twig* by John Hawkes (New York: New Directions, 1961), p. xiv.

5. Leslie Fiedler, *The Collected Essays of Leslie Fiedler* (New York: Stein & Day, 1971), 2: 319–24.

6. Donald Greiner, "The Thematic Use of Color in John Hawkes's *Second Skin,*" *Contemporary Literature* 11 (1970) : 389–400.

7. Richard Pearce, "Harlequin," in *Stages of the Clown* (Carbondale, Ill.: Southern Illinois University Press, 1970), pp. 102–16.

some detail.[8] Norman Lavers points out the romance structures in *Second Skin*.[9] My own approach to the solid ground of definition in Hawkes's visionary world[10] takes a different perspective on Skipper but complements these discussions by Pearce, Tanner, and Lavers. I argue that the "psychological coherence" to which Hawkes says he is dedicated[11] is here that of the journey within, out of the darkness of misunderstanding and into the light of vision and peace. This perspective on Skipper's narrative does produce some different readings of causation in his personal drama and in life's operations and this psychological structure is the backbone of Skipper's "serpentine tale."

Skipper, the first-person narrator and central figure of *Second Skin* who tells his story from a paradise island, is living a life of love as the artificial inseminator of cows and the impregnator (if it was not Sonny, his alter ego, who did it) of a glorious native girl named Catalina Kate. He tells his story of "the terrible seasons of this life when unlikely accidents, tabloid adventures, shocking episodes, surrounded a solitary and wistful heart"[12] simply to arrive at a necessary final understanding of a brutal past that he has survived.[13] Proof of that survival is all about him in the lyrical (and comic) idyll of his present life, and he periodically summons this evidence to bolster his courage in going on with his investigation of the past. But he talks mostly of that black world of violence and the lifelong conviction of guilt that, unexorcized, keeps him from final submersion in his new life of bliss.

This black world is the U.S.A. in its death-ridden dead-ends: a hot lavatory in the living quarters of a mortuary; the U-Drive-Inn where anonymous unmarried couples furtively make love; the honeymoon hideaway, a trap on a mountainside in a decayed mining town; an American naval boat at sea during World War II, its sick bay full of terrified men and its chaplain desperate, "on the skids" (here is the desolate U.S.A. afloat); a crumbling bedroom in a flophouse on Second Avenue in New York; and a black Atlantic island, the cruel realm of a "black widow"— all backwaters into which the motion of life barely reaches and where in the desperation of their failure to move into the currents that would bear their lives onwards, people turn compulsively to violent acts of revenge and self-torture or self-destruction. These are the locales of the brutalities that are Skipper's history: the suicides of his father, wife, and daughter; the murder of his son-in-law; and the series of cruel attacks Skipper himself has suffered from family, the widow Miranda and her friends, and from that ringleader of a sea mutiny, Tremlow.

In talking of these places and their inhabitants, Skipper focuses his narrative on his attempt to prevent his daughter Cassandra's suicide, but this is a diversionary

---

8. Tony Tanner, "Necessary Landscapes and Luminous Deteriorations," in *City of Words* (New York: Harper & Row, 1971), p. 220.

9. Norman Lavers, "The Structure of *Second Skin*," *Novel* 5 (1972): 208–14.

10. Hawkes attests to "that absolute need to create from the imagination a totally new and necessary fictional landscape or visionary world." See Enck, p. 141.

11. Enck, p. 149.

12. John Hawkes, *Second Skin* (New York: New Directions, 1963), p. 5. All further page references are incorporated in the text.

13. Hawkes says about Skipper, "by the end of the novel, I think we do have, in effect, a survivor." See John Graham, "John Hawkes on His Novels," *The Massachusetts Review* 7 (1966): 459.

approach to the real effort—the exorcism of his guilt, a means of initially circumventing the most painful territory he must finally traverse. It allows him to make Cassandra the overt object of concern: Cassandra, the daughter whom he loves with more than a father's love; Cassandra, whom, in fact, he unconsciously sees from the beginning as an extension of himself and whose life he tries to save finally as his own.[14] It allows him, too, to make Miranda his antagonist—Miranda, antagonist enough for any man, to be sure, but not the real "devil" of his past. The crucial core of Skipper's problem is not Cassandra's death but his own homosexual rape by Tremlow at the height of the mutiny on the *Starfish,* and the real issue, identified especially with this rape, is Skipper's very moral identity, his innocence or guilt. Tremlow's rape and his own moral identity are things that Skipper cannot at first directly face, and so he plunges into his cathartic effort through the subsidiary and surrogate affair of Cassandra and Miranda. And inevitably these things lead him, as it is his protectively half-unconscious intention that they should, to the ultimate confrontation. From the beginning, when Skipper says "there is no place here for Tremlow—my devil, Tremlow—or for Mac, the Catholic chaplain who saved my life. No place for them. Not yet" (p. 5), his narrative winds its way from brutality to brutality, each of them evoking Tremlow in Skipper's mind and on his lips, to those moments on the *Starfish* more shocking than any others.

When Skipper is finally brought to allow himself to present the mutiny and the rape, that episode of his life comes immediately attended, and succeeded, by the stories of Fernandez's murder and of Skipper's father's suicide. He has given a brief account of this suicide in the opening chapter and thus identified it as another of the most troublesome parts of his past, but now, after confronting Tremlow's rape, he returns to it and gives a fuller account, considers this, too, more openly. The conjoining of these three episodes under the title "The Brutal Act" helps to reveal the unifying issue (theme, if you will) of the entire fabric of Skipper's tale: the complex problem of victims and bullies.

Ever since he had as a child witnessed his father's suicide, Skipper has been afraid of himself, afraid that he may have contributed, however unwittingly, to his father's decision, or ability, to take his life. Refusing to be "intimidated" (he sees himself as "the aggressive personification of serenity" [p. 3]), and convinced that his is the role of the sacrificial victim, he nonetheless cannot be rid of the feeling, dominating like all irrational convictions, that he is somehow to blame. His "own large breast," he says in his opening introduction of himself, is "the swarming place of the hummingbirds terrified and treacherous at once" (p. 2). The real horror of the rape he has suffered from Tremlow is not that, like all the other brutalities he has suffered, it attacked his masculinity and his dignity, but that Skipper somehow sees himself in Tremlow—"the phantom bully, the ringleader of my distant past" (p. 88). And although Skipper strives always for peace, although there is nothing he desires to be so much as like the sunny, sweet but effectual Sonny, his faithful companion, there is indeed reason for his doubt and fear, support for them in the events of his life.

Skipper's problem, in short, is the guilt of being alive when almost everyone

---

14. "And it was in the month of May that I raced down the beach for *my* life in Miranda's hot rod, in May, the month of my daughter's death" (p. 175; italics mine).

close to him has died violently, and *Second Skin* explores the problem by pursuing the impenetrable mysteries of the life force and the death force. In this book, some people are death-driven and others are life-driven and no more capable of suicide than the suicides are capable of staying their self-destructive violence. The suggestion is that there is no explanation for the drive of anyone toward either life or death; that lies beyond our vision. Skipper himself is life-driven; that is why he survives. Those about him who meet violent deaths are death-driven; that is why they do not survive. Skipper is not guilty of the deaths of any of them, but he is involved as a vehicle of the mystery of their courses toward death and this involvement, combined with the false psychology he shapes as a response to his feelings of guilt, only intensifies his conviction that he is to blame.

Skipper's response to his father's suicide has been a stance of withdrawal, avoidance, and self-sacrifice. He divides the world into bullies and victims and makes sure that he is a victim. But to get into this position, he has to be aggressive. He adopts a manner of sweetness that is half specious. Those around him detect the speciousness and are infuriated; they correctly recognize the manner as a masked mode of bullying. So they attack him and in his victimization Skipper seeks to allay his fear that he is a bully. But the retaliation in the attack he receives is so pronounced and undeniable that Skipper's system of self-exculpation does not work. While one part of his mind is congratulating itself on his self-sacrifice, another part persists in observing his aggression and reading it as evidence of guilt. In fact, Skipper has no more responsibility for the suicides than the settings in which they take place; like those settings, he serves as a means, not a cause. But as long as he clings to the distinction between bully and victim, everything that happens around him feeds his guilt.

The process is illustrated succinctly in the brief story of his wife, Gertrude. Whether throughout their marriage or only during the last few years of her life, she feels that Skipper has virtually ignored her. Seeing her decline into drunkenness, confusion, and despair, he has, out of his old fear that any action may produce the wrong result, refused to participate in her life. Lacking love, she has tried for hate by means of "motorcycle orgies with members of my own crew, half a season on a nearby burlesque stage, the strange disappearances, insinuating notes to Washington, and bills, bruises, infidelity here at the U-Drive-Inn, and even a play for faithful Sonny" (pp. 130–31). But Skipper, fearing even more, has responded with that specious sweetness: "the further she went down-hill the more I cared. And Gertrude was no match for my increasing tolerance" (p. 131). He knows that she was "a flower already pressed between the leaves of darkness before we met" (p. 2), but he also knows that in the relationship be-tween them he has aggressively demanded to be the victim. So her suicide augments the earlier horror of his father's. His effort fails, and he comes out not the victim but the bully.

The dynamics of his involvement with Gertrude are the same as those of his encounters with all the others who do violence to themselves or to him. This psychology is perhaps most shocking when Cassandra has Skipper tattooed, and is most strikingly wrong-headed in the episode of Tremlow's mutiny. Then after Sonny, who is never wrong, has informed Skipper of the mutinous activities afoot, Skipper retires to his cabin and his bunk and spends the day reading the

Bible and sleeping. The story of the mutiny, like all the other episodes, is not detailed in the way it would be in "the conventional novel"; the characters' motivations are not so knowingly defined because Hawkes has a vision of ultimate forces of motivation too little fathomed to be crisply (and superficially) identified. But the contours of motivation are lucid, and whatever the deepest source, it is evident that the immediate means lies in Skipper. Tremlow, like Gertrude, like Cassandra, like Miranda, finds Skipper's suffering sweetness, his bullying refusal to hit back, a violently annoying goad. And so they oblige him, and he is ensnared in their destruction.

This is the confusion, the tangled and snarled interrelationship of victims with bullies (and thus death with life) that in his black world Skipper can never see his way out of. The fear that he acted the part of the bully in those days keeps Skipper, even seven years later, from fully accepting the evidence of the "virtue" of life all about him; it necessitates this "courageous" exploration of the past. Then, as he tells his story, he gradually sees the interrelationship of bullies and victims in another light. He discovers that the distinction between the two, which he has always made in order to list himself as a victim and so absolve himself of guilt, is a false classification. There are no bullies, no victims; instead, in everyone there is a combination of the two, the manifestations of those drives toward life and toward death in their entanglement. Individual fates, deaths, and survivals, lie in the mystery of the duality of life and death and there is no reality in the guilt that has crabbed his life until now. While Skipper arrives only gradually at this insight in the course of telling his story, the beginnings of his discovery lie further back in the past he talks about. In that black world, too much weighed against those flickerings of understanding and quashed them; but with the contrasting reality of the golden world all about him, Skipper is now able to put the story together in the sequence that will luminously deliver the saving truth to full consciousness.

As he presents his evidence, the insight begins to come almost subliminally. He first presents the chief characters of his drama as either bullies—Tremlow and Miranda, or victims—Cassandra and Fernandez. But as he searches out the fullness of each episode, as he attempts to get what he calls in talking of Fernandez's murder "the true tonality of the thing" (p. 149), he builds the evidence that in everyone bully and victim coexist.

The bullies, Tremlow and his female counterpart, Miranda, are physically large and powerful, almost colossal: Tremlow is "a true Triton," Miranda an Amazon. (Skipper, too, is a large man.) The victims, Fernandez and Cassandra, are contrastingly frail, doll-like. But both Miranda and Cassandra are young widows, tormented by the violent loss of their husbands, self-mocking and brutal in their sexuality. Skipper observes that "Cassandra was Miranda's shadow" and that the yarn of Miranda's knitting joins them like a "black umbilicus" (pp. 69, 70). Miranda the bully (she slashes baby-bottle nipples, dresses up a dressmaker's dummy in Skipper's naval uniform with a pillow pregnancy and catsup for the blood of a murderous attack, and aids and abets her cohorts, lecherous Captain Red and his sons, to assist Cassandra to the lighthouse from which she leaps to her death) is periodically racked by asthma attacks; Cassandra the victim has the name of the homosexual husband (whom Skipper has found for her and who has abandoned her) burned into the skin over her father's heart. Actually, then, they are psychological twins. Miranda appears as the bully because she is life-driven, suffering but unkillable; Cassandra appears as the victim because she is death-driven, unable in any circumstances to live.

In the same manner, Tremlow and Fernandez are counterparts. Note, for instance, Tremlow's mutiny-rousing grass-skirted hula and Fernandez's rebellious bare-legged "cheesecake." The victim Fernandez, the cruelly murdered "helpless Peruvian orphan," holds his pants up with a rattlesnake-skin belt and carries next to his Bible a "little hook shaped razor blade" and on his honeymoon undergoes "a triumphant and rebellious change of character" (p. 4). The bully Tremlow, sadistic rapist, may have died in his rebellious attempt at freedom or in his generous attempt to save Fernandez. As Skipper presents these men, his subliminal insight into this psychological and moral reality, which enables him to produce this counterpart characterization, has brought him to face the issue of guilt and innocence in its most crucial episodes, and they, in turn, bring the recognition into consciousness in "The Brutal Act."

First the mutiny: Skipper recalls his own withdrawal and his brutal victimization by the man in the grass skirt. But, although the bully's cooperative violation of Skipper is the major strand of this story, Tremlow's case is not unconditional. Skipper sees his tiny boats in the vast sea sailing off to probable death and indeed reports that the boats have been lost. In the middle section of this chapter he then presents Fernandez's murder by sailors out to brutalize homosexuals. On his last shore patrol Skipper has come suddenly on the scene of the violence. There are two bodies, Fernandez's, face up, and that of a sailor of large build, face down. The prostitute who tells Skipper what has happened explains that this sailor is Fernandez's buddy, who tried to save him. Fernandez left Cassandra "for the love of another person. . . . A gunner's mate named Harry" (p. 23); now here is this dead sailor with him, named Harry. Having just confronted the most painful of his memories, the brutalization by Tremlow that haunts his mind, Skipper now juxtaposes with it the event that puts Tremlow in a different light: "Was Tremlow's first name Harry? Was it Tremlow lying now at the bare feet of the streetwalker sitting in the shiny, partially chopped-up straw chair? Tremlow killed at least while defending my little lost son-in-law? Or was it Tremlow who had swung the sacrificial hatchet, destroyed the hideaway, lopped off the fingers? This, I thought, was more like Tremlow, but I could not be sure and was careful that I would never know" (pp. 157–58). Skipper refuses to see the sailor's face because the possibility that here Tremlow may have been the victim, not the bully, is of tremendous value to him. It is too important to be lost by his seeing the sailor's face and knowing he is not Tremlow. If Tremlow was not wholly a bully, then perhaps Skipper is not either. He now confronts once more the memory of his father's suicide and his own part in it, his being implicated by playing the cello to dissuade his father and his horrible fear that his music instead broke the spell of the dripping faucet and enabled his father to pull the trigger. Now that this event is in the context, clearly focused, of Tremlow's ambiguity, Skipper exorcises the animus of this first suicide, which began his fear of himself.

With this climactic effort and deliverance, Skipper has in a sense got ahead of himself, so ready has he been at last to come to this understanding. For it has been especially in the outcome of his attempt to keep Cassandra alive that he has begun to see how inexplicable her suicide is and thus how little his own behavior can be held to account. This is the next part of his story and the last of the black world events to be reported before he concludes with the remaining evidence of his "triumph." The explanation of Cassandra's suicide, insofar as one is possible, comes in the single extended speech she makes: "My life has been a long blind date . . . nothing comes of a blind date, Skipper. Nothing at all" (p. 31). It has been in recognition of her desperation that Skipper has found a husband for her, and once the husband has abandoned her, that Skipper has taken her off to what he has thought would be a soothing place—that Atlantic island. Genuinely loving her, and also making a last effort to prove his innocence, he has to try to save her and overcomes the fear of action that has kept him from responding to Gertrude's need. But from the time, at least, of Fernandez's departure, he has known full well that she will die: in the Chinatown café he dances with her "wondering how to restore this poor girl who would soon be gone" and "regretting my sensitivity but regretting more the waste, the impossibility of bringing her to life again" (pp. 10, 11). And on his first morning at Miranda's he comes upon that lighthouse, that place for leaping to death, and has a vision of a woman's frail, nude body on the beach "triangulated by the hard cold point of the day." Not only Gertrude's fate but also Fernandez's goes into his understanding; this image repeats that of Fernandez's frail, nude, mutilated body on the floor of his room.

Refusing to accept the inevitable end, maintaining the attempt at self-sacrifice to the end, Skipper tries to prevent Cassandra's suicide by surrounding her, giving her no opportunity for self-destruction. But in doing so, as in finding her the wrong husband and in bringing her to this ungentle island, he is a pawn in the inexorable logic of her fate. His omnipresence and hovering anxiety help to madden her and she retaliates against him, joining Miranda and Red and the others in their attacks on him. He recognizes the old retaliation and feels the old guilt, so that when on the fatal evening of her death he follows her to the lighthouse (tall, in the wind, like the mast on which Tremlow stood on the morning of the day of the mutiny), Skipper undergoes the agony, while making the climb, of fearing that this action, like his playing the cello to his father, will set off the very action it is intended to prevent. When he gets to the top, he finds she has already jumped, of course. But despite his feelings of guilt, and even before Miranda gives him the grotesque gift that she says is a two-month-old human fetus, Cassandra's, and the cause of her leap, Skipper already knows that while he does not really understand her reasons, his own actions have not produced her suicide. At the end of his drag race with Bub, he is at last able to strike a blow where it is due. He speaks of his climb as "this caterpillar action up the winding stairway to the unknown" (p. 197). And when at the top of the lighthouse he finds Cassandra gone, he says, "I won't ask why, Cassandra. Something must have spoken to you, something must have happened. But I don't want to know, Cassandra. So I won't ask" (p. 199).

Cassandra kills herself because her attempts to swim into the current of life are unsuccessful. Her marriage ends in denunciation, not even of the wife herself but of her father who arranged the marriage. As they are dressing to go to Gertrude's funeral, Fernandez says, "That's all you are, Papa Cue Ball. The father of a woman who produces a premature child. The husband of a woman who kills herself. I renounce it, Papa Cue Ball. I renounce this family, I renounce this kind of a man. Can you explain? Can you defend? Can you speak to me with honor of your own Papa? No. So I renounce, Papa Cue Ball, I will escape one of these days" (p. 129). He does escape, and Cassandra thus comes to the blind-date description of her life. The second act of her story combines another attempt— this one cynical and self-punishing where the first was hopeful—with the violent conclusion implicit but delayed at the end of her first attempt, her marriage. On Miranda's island she gives herself to Red and perhaps to Jomo, too, and she has the miscarriage that, despite the frail contradictory evidence of little Pixie, is the final unbearable proof that life turns to death all around her.

In Skipper's "I don't want to know, Cassandra," there is something of the old avoidance, but also something of that same positive insight that kept him from looking at the face of the dead sailor in Fernandez's room. These are the beginnings of his understanding and acceptance, the first dark glimmers of his realization of the mysteries of the relationship between life and death. It is on the strength of this dawning recognition that he has been able to terminate his life in the black world by leaving Pixie with Gertrude's cousin and to travel to the golden island of his new life and enter into its creative rhythms. In turn, his seven years of "the virtue of life itself" have brought him to this point of telling his story in order to discover how the black world of his past fits into the golden reality of his present.

The brutality of the black world is not wholly eradicable—Skipper says he will aways remember his daughter and that other island—but it can be redeemed: "And the work itself? Artificial insemination. . . . Yes, my triumph now. And how different from my morbid father's. And haven't I redeemed his profession, his occupation, with my own?" (p. 47). In view of the total reality, which Skipper now knows, the black world and Skipper himself can be forgiven. That total reality is the mystery of the duality of violence and of love. This passage comes early in his narrative and is a major force guiding his recognition: "I can afford to recount even the smallest buried detail of my life with Miranda. Because I know and have stated here, that behind every frozen episode of that other island— and I am convinced that in its way it too was enchanted, no matter the rocks and salt and fixed position in the cold black waters of the Atlantic—there lies the golden wheel of my hot sun; behind every black rock a tropical rose and behind every cruel wind-driven snow storm a filmy sheet, a transparency, of golden fleas" (p. 48). Even in his childhood in the black world, Skipper's mother's death, or his vision of it, has indicated another reality than that of his father's suicide: "my father had begun my knowledge of death as a lurid truth but . . . my mother had extended it toward the promise of mystery" (p. 8). Now on this island he has discovered that mystery.

Skipper's black world is a realm of confusion (particularly in sexual identities), of bizarre violations and unexpected traps, of arrested journeys, ineffectual rituals, and time misshapen or stopped; it is a world of abortion. In contrast, his golden world is one of the continuous, mysterious meetings of life and death: dry waterwheel and lush plants; scummy swamp and "green transparent tint of the endless sea"; iguana and hammock of flowers. Here death (everything is moldering—flesh, clothes, barn) is a part of life, rituals acknowledge that connection and the reign of love, and the virtue of life is as deep and mysterious as the compulsive violence and death of the black world. In accordance with this duality, Skipper's act of exorcising his guilt is also a continuing act of redemption. He does not simply face his past and discover the forces at work in it; he also parallels all those brutalities with the graces of the golden world, and it is in this ability to redeem all of the past with the present that he is satisfied and arrives at his final peace.

The high school dance, for instance, has its counterpart in the procession of Skipper's new family to the pasture where Sweet Phyllis calls; Skipper's belly-bumping with Uncle Billy, that "obscene tournament," is redeemed by the belly-bumping that produces Kate's child; the *Starfish* mutiny is exorcised by Kate's willing submission to the iguana—the manifestation of evil in this realm of peace—for the good of her baby's, and Skipper's, souls; the honeymoon fete of Fernandez and Cassandra—and Skipper—with all its abortive results, is countered by the All Saints Night feast at the cemetery—another "fete with the dead"—in which, with the new baby, Skipper and Sonny and Catalina Kate solemnize again the continuity of life, the community of the living and the dead. By the end of the book Skipper, who has been the son, husband, and father of three suicides, is now merged not only with his alter ego, Sonny, in their joint fathering of Kate's child, but even beyond that, with people he has never known, with all the people who have lived. That is what Kate is telling him when she says that the baby looks neither like him nor like Sonny but rather "like the fella in the grave."

From black U.S.A. to golden South Pacific-like island: an impossible or non-sensical leap? Not at all. T. A. Hanzo made a comment that reveals the connection between these two worlds in his unusually fine review of *Second Skin*. Commenting on Skipper's golden island and his "time of no time" there, he states that they are "in fact the sacral place and time, as described by Mircéa Éliade."[15] In *Cosmos and History* Éliade talks of prehistorical man's division of places into those belonging to chaos and to cosmos.[16] In the beginning the gods created cosmos out of chaos by means of certain acts, and it is the primary concern of prehistorical men to repeat those original acts of the gods and so to "cosmize" any place they conquer or live in. By repeating those acts of the gods, they assimilate the temporal place to the "center," which is the gateway or axis of heaven, earth, and hell. In achieving that assimilation, they coalesce any place with the center of the universe, and any time with the time before there was time, with the timelessness of the eternal reality of life. The center is, in fact, exactly the zone of the most intense reality. Correspondingly, just as any place can be made to share in the reality of the center, so any place that is not so assimilated to it remains chaos, unformed as was everything before the gods' act of creation; those regions of chaos are "desert places inhabited by monsters."

As Hanzo says, we must recognize in Skipper's golden world—"It *is* a wandering island, of course, unlocated in space and quite out of time" (p. 46)—the reality of cosmos. His black world is correspondingly well summarized as "desert

15. T. A. Hanzo, "The Two Faces of Matt Donelson," *Sewanee Review* 73 (1965) : 112.

16. Mircéa Éliade, *Cosmos and History,* 2nd ed. (1954; rpt. New York: Harper & Row, 1959), pp. 3–48.

places inhabited by monsters";[17] it is chaos. Éliade speaks not only of the two regions but also of the journey between them:

> The center, then, is pre-eminently the zone of the sacred, the zone of absolute reality. Similarly, all the other symbols of absolute reality (trees of life and immortality, Fountain of Youth, etc.) are also situated at a center. The road leading to the center is a "difficult road" . . . and this is verified at every level of reality: difficult convolutions of a temple . . . pilgrimage to sacred places . . . danger-ridden voyages of the heroic expeditions in search of the Golden Fleece, the Golden Apples, the Herb of Life; wanderings in labyrinths; difficulties of the seeker for the road to the self, to the "center" of his being, and so on. The road is arduous, fraught with perils, because it is, in fact, a rite of passage from the profane to the sacred, from the ephemeral and illusory to reality and eternity, from death to life, from man to divinity. Attaining the center is equivalent to consecration, an initiation; yesterday's profane and illusory existence gives place to a new, to a life that is real, enduring, effective.[18]

Skipper's Golden Fleece appears in the comically diminutive—and realistic—guise of golden fleas, his attainment of divinity in the comic diminutive of the creative power of the artificial inseminator; but his journey first through life and then, as he writes his story, through his past, is exactly the soul's journey that is defined by the locales of chaos and cosmos.

There it is, tight and clear, events laid into the patterns that show us that whatever its novelties and peculiarities, this is at bottom the old tale of the soul's journey—old and endlessly new, and *Second Skin* is wonderful in its renewal. The problem of victims and bullies, of the soul's journey: these are the solid ground between the swamp and the sea (pp. 104–5), the almost fully graspable experience between what can be called the black and the golden acts of the mind. Hawkes also gives us the swamp of the nightmare of fears into which Skipper's anxiety transforms the events of his life so that they become a compulsive series of rapes, and we are made to know the rape in the grotesque practical joke (Miranda's joke with the dummy and Skipper's uniform) and the castration in the slashing of baby-bottle nipples despite the gap between the vehicle and the act. He gives us as well the sea of sea changes, rich and strange, by means of which, through a free-wheeling but persistent allusion to *The Tempest,* we are made to know those fluidities of relationship between chaos and cosmos and that nearly magical appearance of cosmos out of chaos that makes Skipper's final triumph possible. But these are inner landscapes and patterns of correspondences that require their own space and time. They vastly expand the story I have been talking about here by adding to this objective reality those dimensions of vision which turn reality into experience—the mind's compulsions and sudden openings Richard Wilbur speaks of in an analogy between mind and bat in "Mind," its entrapments in darkness and its discoveries of grace.

---

17. " . . . there she was—my monster, my Miranda, final challenge of our sad society" (p. 5).

18. Éliade, pp. 17–18.

Notes on Contributors

MAURICE BEEBE: Teaches at Temple University. Author of numerous works on literature of the nineteenth and twentieth centuries. He was the founder and editor of *Modern Fiction Studies* and is now the editor of *Journal of Modern Literature*. Currently at work on a history of the Age of Modernism.

JOHN Z. BENNETT (1923–1972): His special interests included American literary magazines, Southern writers, Joyce. He taught at Colorado State University.

BERNARD BENSTOCK: Teaches at University of Illinois. He has written extensively on Irish writers.

GERMAINE BRÉE: Teaches at University of Wisconsin. Published books on Proust, Gide, Camus, Sartre and is at present working on the last volume of a new history of French literature, the series under the direction of Claude Pichois.

CLINTON S. BURHANS, JR.: Teaches at Michigan State University. Published articles on nineteenth- and twentieth-century novelists: Hawthorne, Twain, Crane, Hemingway, Vonnegut, Heller.

MARGARET CHURCH: Teaches at Purdue University. Published books on *Don Quixote* and on contemporary and earlier authors of the twentieth century. Present project is a book-length study of relationships between structure and theme in the novel (from Cervantes to Kafka).

THOMAS CORDLE: Teaches at Duke University. Published works on Gide, Malraux, Proust.

HORST S. DAEMMRICH: Teaches at Wayne State University. He has written extensively on German literature and aesthetic theory.

MOTLEY F. DEAKIN: Teaches at University of Florida. Special interest in American and comparative literature. Publications on James, Rebecca West, Gothic fiction.

HARRY R. GARVIN: Teaches at Bucknell University. Publications on literature of nineteenth and twentieth century and on theory of the novel. Currently at work on a book-length study of literature and the arts.

JOHN HAGAN: Teaches at State University of New York, Binghamton. Special interests and publications in nineteenth-century fiction. At present he is working on a study of the nineteenth-century *Bildungsroman* and its intellectual background.

FREDERICK J. HOFFMAN (1909–1967): Among his major publications are *Freudianism and the Literary Mind; The Little Magazine; The Twenties.*

STANTON DE VOREN HOFFMAN: Teaches at Sir George Williams University. Published on medieval literature (*The Pearl* and Chrétien's *Conte del graal*), Borges, American literature of homosexuality, contemporary Canadian poetry, as well as a book, *Comedy and Form in the Fiction of Joseph Conrad.*

DAVID L. KUBAL: Teaches at California State University. Published a book on Orwell, as well as a number of essays on James, Conrad, Trilling, Graham Greene, contemporary literature. Now at work on a book-length study of Jane Austen and the politics of comedy.

DANIEL MAJDIAK: Teaches at University of Illinois. Published on John Barth, Iris Murdoch, Bellow, William Blake. Currently at work on projects involving Byron and Stendhal, Emily Brontë and Dickens, and contemporary French literary criticism.

HERBERT MARDER: Teaches at University of Illinois. Special interests in British fiction, Woolf, improvisation in the writing of poetry. At present he is doing a study of Doris Lessing's fiction.

FRANK D. McCONNELL: Teaches at Northwestern University. Has published numerous articles on Romantic poetry, modern literature, film, the novel, and politics.

JAMES M. MELLARD: Teaches at Northern Illinois University. Published works on twentieth-century authors (including the contemporaries) and on rhetoric and fiction. At present he is finishing a book-length study of Faulkner's *The Sound and the Fury* and beginning a thematic study of contemporary fiction.

J. MITCHELL MORSE: Teaches at Temple University. Author of *The Sympathetic Alien: James Joyce and Catholicism* (1959), *Matters of Style* (1968), *The Irrelevant English Teacher* (1972), and *Race, Class, and Metaphor* (1975). He has written many articles for literary, scholarly, and professional journals.

LESLIE A. SHEPARD: Teaches at Washington State University. Special interests include twentieth-century French literature.

ROBERT M. SLABEY: Teaches at University of Notre Dame. In addition to essays on Faulkner, he has published on Hemingway, James, Salinger, Cheever, Ellison. Currently he is working on "Poets of the Earth: the Ecological Sensibility in America."

DABNEY STUART: Teaches at Washington and Lee University. Published a great many poems; a critic of fiction and poetry.

JOHN W. TILTON: Teaches at Bucknell University. Primarily interested in the theory and practice of satire, especially in neoclassical literature and increasingly in the contemporary novel. Has published articles on Browning, Kafka, and

Swift. A book, *Cosmic Satire in the Contemporary Novel,* is scheduled for publication.

ELISEO VIVAS: An emeritus professor at Northwestern University. Published many books in philosophy and in theoretical and practical criticism. Has just completed a book tentatively entitled *Two Roads to Ignorance: The Biography of Alonzo Quijada as Told to Eliseo Vivas.* Projected is a short book on Dostoevski.

CAREY WALL: Teaches at San Diego State University. Has written essays on Faulkner and Dreiser and is currently working on a book-length study of Henry Green's symbolism.

MADELEINE WRIGHT: Teaches at University of Wisconsin Center System—Madison. Special interests in twentieth-century novel, and particularly the French. Has also published on comparative linguistics and on semantics.

HAROLD A. WYLIE: Teaches at The University of Texas. Special interests in psychology and literature, surrealism, schizophrenia and modern French literature, black writers in the French language.